EASY~TO~MAKE
TOYS

EASY~TO~MAKE
TOYS

BOOK CLUB ASSOCIATES
London

This edition published 1982 by
Book Club Associates
by arrangement with
Marshall Cavendish Books
58 Old Compton Street
London W1V 5PA
© Marshall Cavendish 1982

ISBN 086307 001 9

Consultant Editor: Sarah Jones
House Editor: Yvonne Deutch
Designer: Caroline Dewing

Introduction

Making toys for your children is part of the fun of being a parent; they are also perfect gifts from a loving aunt, uncle or grandparent. *Easy-To-Make Toys* is a fairy-tale collection of some fifty wonderful projects – including soft toys to sew, knit and crochet, imaginative toys to make from wood, and a mixed media group that you put together from odds and ends of everyday materials.

Any child whose parents or relatives are blessed with nimble fingers is fortunate indeed. For the not-so-expert grown-ups (and that includes most of us), we've provided comprehensive know-how sections so beginners can tackle the techniques involved in any project in the collection.

With a well-stocked bag of fabric scraps, some bits of yarn and leftover decorative trimmings, you can create some marvellous characters. With the easy-to-follow step-by-step instructions you get clear, detailed diagrams and inspiring full-colour illustrations, so you can't go wrong. Most of the wooden toys, too, are made with scraps – in this case odd pieces of timber. For guidance, there are simple-to-use trace patterns.

Easy-To-Make Toys is a truly varied collection, with something to delight any child in your life. There are all sorts of dolls and doll clothes; crocheted bunnies, lambs; a knitted lion, and a most unusual doctor and nurse team to knit for budding young doctors. There are glove puppets for every kind of playacting, plus a revival of a good, old-fashioned idea – a teach-me rag book to help a child learn to manage buttons all by himself.

As for cost, these toys are anything but expensive to make. For example, with a few empty cotton reels and some fabric scraps, you can create the most exquisite tiny Victorian four-poster bed literally for just a few pence.

You'll never regret a minute of the time spent on these delightful toys. You may even enjoy the project as much as the child does the toy – and that is saying a great deal.

Contents

SOFT TOYS

Basic know-how 10

Sewn toys

Letter shapes 21
Finger puppets 22
Dog and cat 26
Animal glove puppets 28
Pipe-cleaner dolls 32
Poupard dolls 37
Rag doll 42
Rag doll wardrobe 47
Topsy turvy doll 51
Jenny and Joey 57
Wool doll 62
Patterns for dolls' clothes 63
Doll's wardrobe 65
Traditional teddy bear 70
Patchwork animals 74
Owl and pussycat 78
Fabric book 86
Hobby horse 91
Tepee 95
Play house 99

Knitted toys

Doll 104
Rabbit 107
Pirate 110
Doctor and nurse 112

Crochet toys

Aeroplanes 116
Snail and alligator 118
Clown 120

Lion 122
Lamb 124
Rabbits 126
Dutch doll 128
Glove puppets 131

WOODEN TOYS

Basic know-how 136
Toys from scrapwood 150
Noughts and crosses 153
Submarines 155
Truck 159
Railway engine 164
Toy-box house 169
Sailing boat 176
Doll's house 183
Chessboard 188
Laying hen 192

MIXED MEDIA TOYS

Basic know-how 200
Papier mâché puppets 202
Kite making 206
Oriental kites 210
Doll's house furniture 216
Four poster bed 220

Toy Tidies

Toy bag 222
Wall hanging 226
Hanging shelves 230

Glossary 233
Index 237

SOFT TOYS

In the following pages you'll find a colourful selection of delightful soft toys to sew, knit and crochet. Children regard these cuddly playmates as very special friends – they are taken to bed, hugged, squeezed and kept close by as constant companions. Any one of these adorable characters will make a perfect gift for your child.

Basic know-how

Sewing techniques
Basic sewing tools

pins

tailor's chalk (for marking around
   patterns)

needles in a range of sizes for plain
   sewing and embroidery

tape measure with metric/imperial
   markings

scissors, small for clipping seams
   and threads and large for cutting
   out

iron and ironing board

sewing machine (useful but not
   essential)

pinking shears (useful for making
   decorative edges on felt toys) and
   neatening seams

Basic sewing
Layouts

Some of the projects in this book
have a layout diagram included.
This shows how to arrange the pattern pieces on the fabric most economically. Study this and arrange
your pattern pieces in the same way.
Mark round all pattern pieces with
tailor's chalk.

Making a graph pattern

Graphs are a way of giving readers a
full-sized pattern that is scaled down
to fit on to the pages of a book. A
graph is simply a plan, drawn to
scale, from which you can draw up
the pattern. You will need to work
on a flat surface such as a table,
using a pencil, ruler, and sheets of
either graph paper or dressmaker's
pattern paper which is already
drawn up into squares. You can rule

the squares yourself but this needs
accuracy and is rather tedious.

To draw up the pattern, first check
the scale given with it, which could
read 'each square equals 1cm ($\frac{3}{8}$in)',
but the scale will vary with the
project. To copy a pattern, say for the
bodice of a doll's dress, start from
the top left-hand corner of the diagram. Count the squares to the lower
point of the neckline and mark on
paper. Now measure distance of
upper point of neck from side and top
of paper, mark and connect the two
points to copy the neck curve. Draw
the remainder of the pattern to scale
similarly. Copy all pattern pieces in
the same way. Always check that
pieces fit together well before cutting out in fabric. You might have to
make small adjustments. Identify
every pattern piece—back, front and
so on. Also mark in any details such
as centre back or front.

Changing the size of a pattern

It is a simple matter to make a graph
pattern larger or smaller than the
patterns given.

If you want to make the patterns
twice as large, simply interpret the
1cm ($\frac{3}{8}$in) grid as being a 2cm ($\frac{3}{4}$in)
grid and plot the graph on to 2cm
($\frac{3}{4}$in) squares. Similarly you can
make it $1\frac{1}{2}$ times larger by using a
1.5cm ($\frac{5}{8}$in) grid or smaller by reduc-
ing the size of the squares. One word
of warning, however, the seam allowance gets enlarged or reduced in
the same proportion and if you do
not take the new seam allowance the
toy will be out of proportion. A way
of overcoming this is to draw in the

stitching line on the original graph,
then follow it when drawing out the
new pattern size. Add the required
seam allowance.

Cutting out

If the fabric is creased, press carefully before cutting.

Note if any of the pattern pieces
have a left and a right side. If you are
cutting out on a single layer of
fabric, you will need to place the
pattern first with the right side of
the pattern facing upwards, then
turn the pattern over and cut a
second piece with the wrong side of
the pattern facing upwards.

Seams

Seams are used to join pieces of fabric
and can be either hand- or machine-
stitched.

To sew a plain seam place the
pieces of fabric to be joined with
right sides facing each other, unless
otherwise directed, and with edges
level. Pin at the ends, at any notches, at the centre and then at regular intervals in between. Make
tacking stitches (like large running
stitches) along the line that will be
the seam. This is a given distance
from the edge of the fabric usually
from 6mm–1.5cm ($\frac{1}{4}$in to $\frac{5}{8}$in) for toys.
Place the fabric under the machine
foot with the edges to the right and
stitch along the seam line. A stretch
machine stitch is useful for toys. If
sewing the seam by hand, use small
back stitches.

French seam

1. With WS facing, pin, tack and

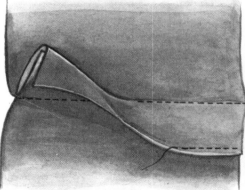

Plain seam

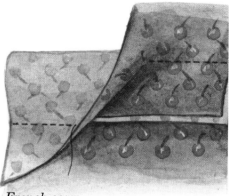

French seam

Flat fell seam

1. *Glass safety eyes positioned correctly onto fabric.*

2. *Eye made from plastic button.*

3. *Eye made from felt pieces.*

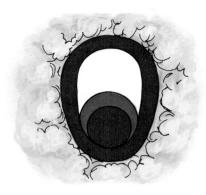

machine-stitch the edges together about 6mm ($\frac{1}{4}$in) from the fitting line. Press as stitched.

2. Trim the seam allowances to 3mm ($\frac{1}{8}$in) of the stitching and press the seam open.

3. Turn the RS of the fabric together, fold on the stitched line and press.

4. Tack, then machine-stitch along the fitting line.
Press as stitched.

Flat fell seam

1. Start by forming a plain seam.

2. Press the seam open and trim one of the allowances to half the original width.

3. Press the other allowance over the trimmed one and fold under the edge 3mm ($\frac{1}{8}$in). On curved seams clip into the turning just short of the fold at even intervals.

4. Pin, tack and then machine-stitch near the fold through all thicknesses.

Cutting and sewing felt

Felt does not fray, so no seam allowances are needed, nor is there a right and a wrong side, so it is very easy to use. But, felt is not hard-wearing.

Cutting and sewing fur fabric

Fur fabrics have woven or knitted backings. In either case, lay the fabric pile side down checking that the pile is running in the same direction on all pieces. Cut one layer at a time, using sharp scissors and taking care not to cut the pile.

Stitch with a strong needle and use synthetic thread that has some elasticity. Separate hairs of pile before stitching. When stitched, use a pin to ease out pile along the seams.

Fillings

There are several alternatives for filling soft toys. Kapok gives a very firm filling but is not washable. So do be sure before you use it that you will not want to wash the toy. Synthetic wadding filling on the other hand, are washable but do not pack as firmly as kapok.

An alternative to the above is foam pieces. These are washable but they can provide quite a lumpy finish unless the fabric is very firm. Foam pieces are best used on large toys which would take vast quantities of a synthetic wadding filling.

A large knitting needle is useful for pushing the filling into place. Fill the narrowest parts first and also the parts farthest away from the opening. Ensure that the toy is evenly filled, especially if made in a stretch fabric. When the filling is completed, slip stitch the opening together with the seam allowances turned in. Fasten off securely.

Safe toys

For young children make sure that the toys you make are free from anything that could cause injury. Substitute embroidered eyes for buttons and do not include anything with wire in it.

Features

Special glass safety eyes can be bought at most toy-making suppliers. The eyes have an extension at the back of the eye and are supplied with a metal ring. These eyes must be attached before the toy is made up. Make a hole where the eye is to be placed, push the extension through the hole from the right of the wrong side. Place the metal ring over the extension on the wrong side and push against back of eye (fig. 1).

Felt eyes can be made from buttons (fig. 2) or by cutting a series of shapes in felt of different size, colour and tone. Place them on top of each other in graduation of size and move the pieces around until the required expression is obtained (fig. 3).

Animal noses are often attached after the toy has been filled and sewn up. Noses can be round, oval or triangular shaped. If a round shape needs filling, cut it double the size and work a row of oversewing around the outside edge. Place the filling in the middle and pull up the thread tightly. Fasten off securely. Slipstitch to the face so that the drawn-up edge is not showing (fig. 4). For a flat nose draw the shape required on a piece of thin card. Cut out and place on to the felt. Cut around the shape leaving at least 12mm ($\frac{1}{2}$in) extra all round. Oversew the edges and pull up evenly and tightly all round the card. Fasten off securely. Slipstitch on to face from the wrong side (fig.5).

Whiskers can be bought or made with transparent synthetic thread. The simplest way of attaching them is to cut a whisker double the length required, fold in half and stitch to the face across the centre crease of whisker (fig. 6). However, these can be pulled out easily and it is safer to attach them in the following way, before the toy is filled. Cut a long piece of synthetic thread and tie two knots in it at the distance apart required between the whiskers. From the wrong side of the face thread the two ends of the synthetic thread through to the right side with a needle, leaving the knots on the

4. *Making a stuffed nose.*
5. *Making a flat nose.*
6. *Attaching folded whiskers to face.*
7. *Attaching whiskers with knots.*
8. *Small felt dots placed on whiskers.*
9. *How to make a tongue.*

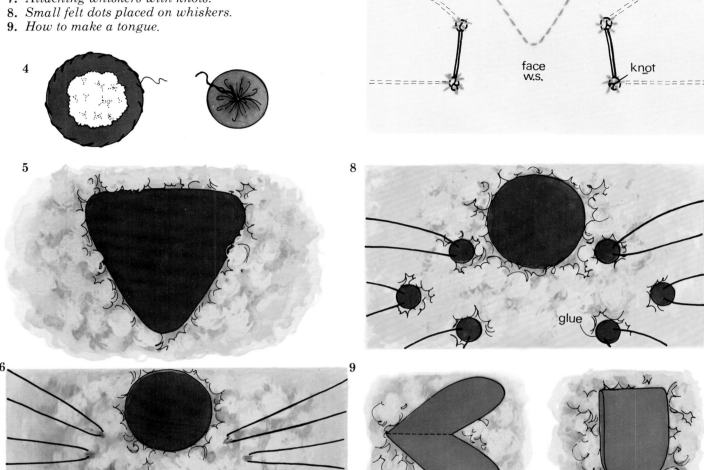

wrong side of the face. Work a few stitches on the wrong side of the face to hold the whiskers in place (fig. 7). To add character, the whiskers can be threaded through small black felt dots which can have fabric adhesive applied to the wrong side and pushed down on to the face (fig. 8).

To make a toy animal's tongue, use colour-fast felt or leather. Cut double the length required and fold in half. Open the tongue out and with right sides together, back stitch into place along the fold on to the right side of the face. Apply fabric adhesive to the ends of the tongue and press them together (fig. 9).

Rag dolls' faces
Faces tend to be flat, so it is best to aim for stylized features rather than realism. Felt circles make effective eyes and embroidery can be added.

Hair is usually made from wool and can be 'styled' in various ways. If you use unravelled wool you will get a frizzy effect.

Machine-stitched patchwork
Decide on the size of the squares or rectangles to be used, allowing 1cm ($\frac{3}{8}$in) seam allowances on all sides of the patch. Patchwork is used for the toys on pages 74–77.

Choose the fabric pieces to be used in the design – they should be the same weight, thickness and washability. Press fabrics.

Working along the straight grain of the fabric, draw each patch accurately on to the wrong side of fabric using a ruler and pencil, or sharp white crayon for dark fabrics. When cutting a large number of patches of equal size it is helpful to make a template from stiff card or

plastic. Include seam allowances and mark and cut out accurately.

When you have cut the required number of patches, you can begin to plan the exact design of the patchwork and building up the required pattern.

With right sides facing and taking 1cm ($\frac{3}{8}$in) seam allowance, machine stitch the patches together into a strip the required length (fig. 1). When you have enough strips to make the required width of fabric, press all the seams open.

With right sides facing, machine stitch the strips together, taking 1cm ($\frac{3}{8}$in) seam allowance. When you have finished, press seams open and tie off and cut the ends of thread.

To give extra strength to the fabric, you can carefully stitch the patchwork on the right side, working close to seams as shown (fig. 2).

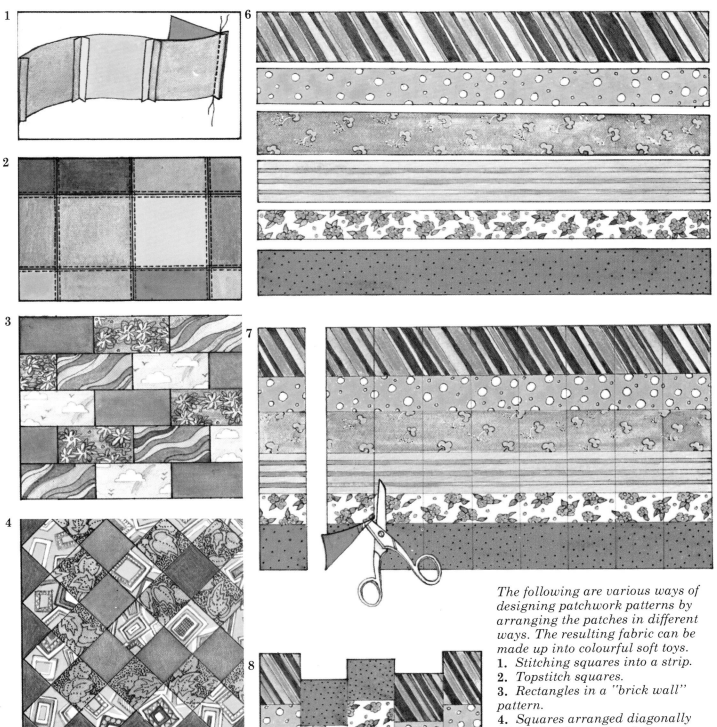

The following are various ways of designing patchwork patterns by arranging the patches in different ways. The resulting fabric can be made up into colourful soft toys.

1. Stitching squares into a strip.

2. Topstitch squares.

3. Rectangles in a "brick wall" pattern.

4. Squares arranged diagonally with triangles at the edges.

5. Border of diagonal squares.

6. First stage in arranging strips of fabric in a "cut and stagger" technique. Strips are cut and arranged horizontally.

7. Strips are sewn together, then cut vertically.

8. Rearranging the squares to make a "staggered" patchwork pattern.

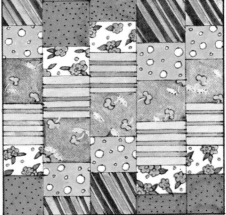

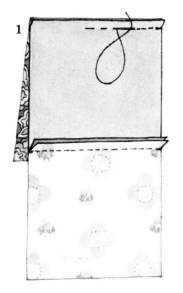

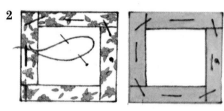

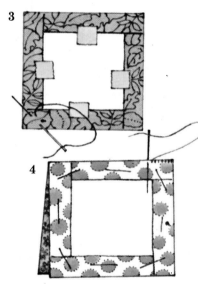

1. *Sewing patches together by hand with a running stitch.*
2. *Many people like to use paper patches to provide support when they are doing hand-sewn patchwork. Here the patch is shown basted to the paper.*
3. *If using fine fabrics, stick edges of paper with masking tape and baste corners through the seam allowances.*
4. *Overcasting the patches together.*

Hand-sewn patchwork

This method is suitable for squares or rectangles.

Patches are joined in a similar way to machine worked patchwork. Cut out number of patches required, then take two and with right sides facing, join them carefully with a small running stitch (fig 1). Join the patches into strips, press seam allowances to one side and join the strips together. Do not press seams open as this will put too much strain on the running stitch.

Hand and embroidery stitches

Back stitch
Bring the thread through on the stitching line, then take a small backward stitch through the fabric. Bring the needle through again a little in front of the first stitch. Then take another stitch, inserting the needle at the point where the first stitch came through.

Blanket stitch
The thread loops underneath the needle which lies vertically in the fabric.

Buttonhole stitch
Work from right to left forming a tiny loop at the top of each stitch. Do not pull stitches too tightly or the edge will pucker.

Chain stitch
Work from right to left, making a chain of loops on the right side of the fabric. The needle returns to the place where it came out, the thread looping under it.

Lazy daisy (detached chain)
Each stitch is held down separately with the working thread.

Finish a row of chain stitch in this manner.

French knots
Bring the thread through the fabric, hold down with the left thumb, and wind the needle around it (a). Insert the needle beside the point where it emerged and pull through (b).

Overcasting (oversewing)
Used on raw edges to prevent fraying. Working from either direction make diagonal, evenly spaced stitches over edge of fabric.

Running stitch
Weave needle in and out of fabric before pulling through. Several stitches can be made on needle at the same time. Draw up stitches if gathers are required. Large running stitches are used for tacking.

Satin stitch
Work straight stitches closely together across the required shape. Stitches should be of even tension and not too long.

Slipstitch
Working from right to left, take a stitch through fabric and then pass along the turned-in edge.

Stab stitch
Worked from right to left. Working from one side, push needle down vertically, pull needle through from other side. Then push needle up vertically and pull through from top side. Stitches should be very small.

Stem stitch
Work from right to left, taking regular slightly slanting stitches along the line of the design. The needle always emerges on the left side of previous stitch.

Cross stitch
For an even appearance, work one row below another. Make sure that all stitches have the top thread slanting in the same direction throughout. Work the first diagonal stitch all along a row, then work back along adding the second stitch. Stitches should form a square.

Catch stitch (herringbone stitch)
Work from left to right, taking a small horizontal stitch in the upper layer and then a small horizontal stitch in the lower layer diagonally. Do not pull stitches too tightly.

Split stitch
This stitch looks rather like chain stitch and is ideal for outlining. It can also be stitched in curving and spiral lines in close fillings as well as in straight lines.

Make a new stitch as diagram shows, and bring the needle through again half way along the stitch just made, splitting each thread into equal halves. The stitches can be gradually increased or decreased in

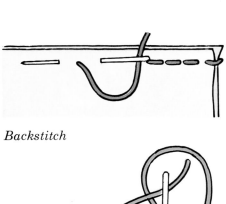

Backstitch

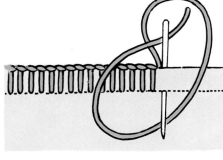

Blanket stitch

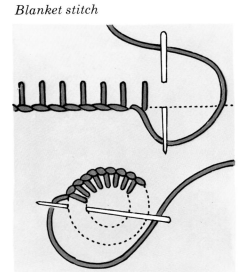

Buttonhole stitch

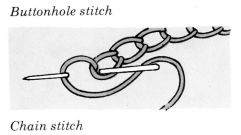

Chain stitch

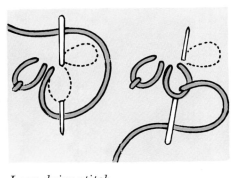

Lazy daisy stitch

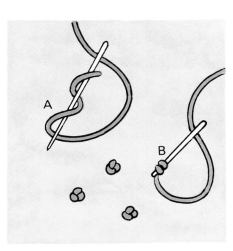

French knots

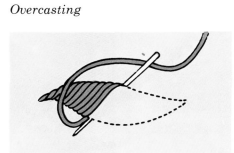

Overcasting

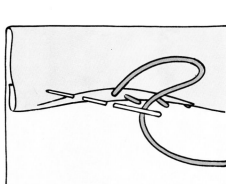

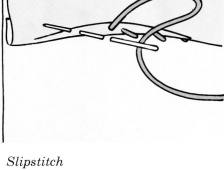

Satin stitch

Slipstitch

Stab stitch

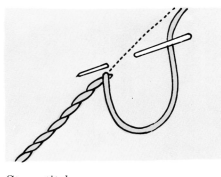

Stem stitch

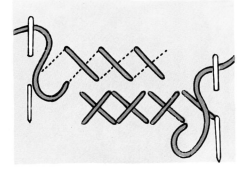

Cross stitch

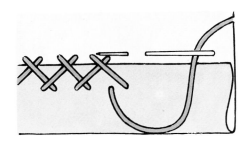

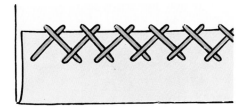

Catch stitch

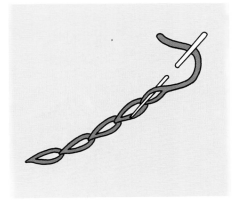

Split stitch

length to fill the shape, but each should be brought up close to the centre of the one before. When you are working curves use shorter stitches.

Knitting techniques

Following patterns

Apart from the knitting instructions themselves, patterns usually contain basic information under a number of different headings so that you can see at a glance such details as size, and materials needed. Read through the instructions before you actually begin, to check that you have everything you need and to help you get an idea of the way the pattern is worked.

Tension

The tension of a knitted fabric describes its elasticity and the tightness of its stitches. It is expressed in terms of the number of rows and stitches that are worked over a given measurement. Work a test piece of knitting to check your tension; it can be adjusted by using a different needle size.

It is important to work the instructions in the order in which they are given. Asterisks (*) are often used to save repetition; in a pattern row an asterisk denotes that you should repeat the sequence of stitches from that point as instructed. A single or double asterisk at the beginning and end of a complete section of the pattern shows that a whole set of instructions is later repeated.

Making up instructions tell you the order in which pieces should be sewn together and how to work any final edgings or trimmings.

Abbreviations

alt	alternate(ly)
approx	approximately
beg	begin(ning)
cont	continue(ing)
dc	double crochet
dec	decrease
foll	follow(ing)
g st	garter stitch
inc	increase
K	knit
K-up	pick up and knit
K-wise	knitwise
M1	pick up strand between needles and knit into back of it. (Called "make 1" or M1)
No.	number
psso	pass slipped stitch over
P	purl
P-up	pick and purl
P-wise	purlwise
rem	remain(ing)
rep	repeat
RS	right side
sl	slip
sl st	slip stitch
st(s)	stitch(es)
st st	stocking stitch
tbl	through back of loop
tog	together
tr	treble
WS	wrong side
yrn	yarn round needle

Yarns

The word "yarn" was once synonymous with wool; now there are a wide range of synthetic yarns which imitate wool but have other qualities.

Casting on and off

All knitting begins with a row of loops being cast on to one needle and subsequent rows are worked into these loops. At the end of a piece of work the knitted stitches are secured by casting off so that they do not unravel.

Casting on

Two-needle method for a firm edge.

1. Make a slip loop on the left-hand needle. Holding the yarn in your right hand, take up the second needle and insert it into the slip loop from front to back. Wind the yarn under and over the point of the right-hand needle.

2. Draw a new loop through the slip stitch: transfer this new loop to the left-hand needle and withdraw the right-hand needle.

3. Insert the right-hand needle from front to back between the two loops on the left-hand needle. Wind the yarn under and over the point of the right-hand needle and draw a loop through. Transfer the new loop to the left-hand needle. Always inserting the right-hand needle between the last two loops on the left-hand needle, continue in the same way until you have the number of stitches that you want cast on.

Casting off

1. With the yarn and needles in the usual working position, work the first two stitches so that they are transferred to the right-hand needle. Use the point of the left-hand needle to lift the first stitch worked over the second one and off the needle. This leaves one stitch on the right-hand needle.

2. Work the next stitch on the left-hand needle and repeat the process of lifting one stitch over another. Continue in this way until you have one stitch remaining on the right-hand needle. Secure this last stitch by breaking off the yarn about 10cm (4in) from the knitting, drawing this through the stitch on the needle and tightening. Darn in the end when making up. Casting off is usually done on a knit row (figs 1 & 2), but

Slip loop

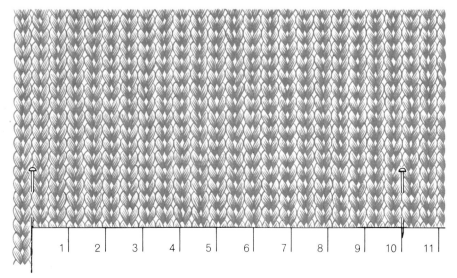

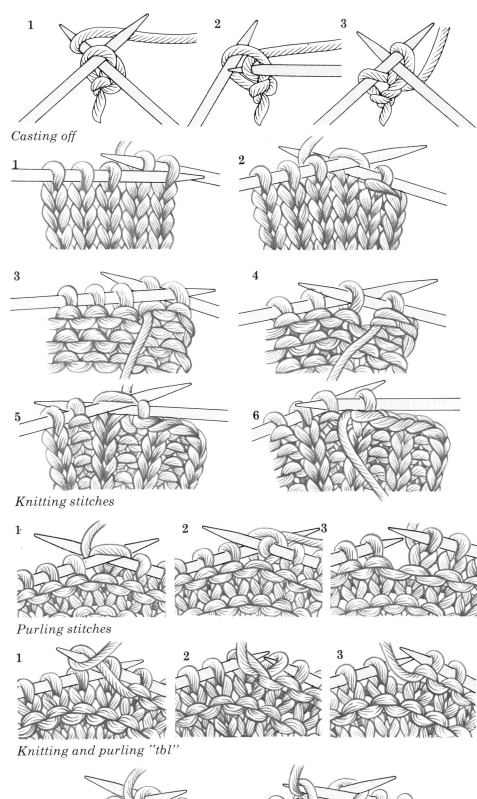

Casting on
2-needle method for a firm edge

1 2 3

Casting off

1 2

3 4

5 6

Knitting stitches

1 2 3

Purling stitches

1 2 3

Knitting and purling "tbl"

the same principle applies when purling (figs 3 & 4) and when knitting in rib (figs 5 & 6).

Basic stitches

Two simple stitches—knit and purl—are the basis of innumerable stitch patterns. The projects included use very easy stitches.

Knitting stitches

1. Hold needle with cast-on stitches in left hand and insert free right-hand needle from front to back into first stitch on left-hand needle. Keeping yarn at back of work, wind it under and then over right-hand needle point.
2. Draw new loop through stitch on left-hand needle.
3. The new stitch remains on the right-hand needle and the one worked into falls from left-hand needle. Work into each stitch in same way until you have transferred them all to right-hand needle.

Garter stitch

This is simply knitting every stitch in every row, producing a horizontally ridged effect

Purling stitches

1. Hold needle with cast-on stitches in left hand and insert free right-hand needle from back to front into first stitch on left-hand needle. Keeping yarn at front of work, wind it over and round right-hand needle point.
2. Draw new loop through stitch on left-hand needle.
3. The new stitch remains on right-hand needle and the one worked into falls from left-hand needle. Work into each stitch in same way until you have transferred them all to right-hand needle.

Knitting and purling "tbl"

To give a stitch a twisted appearance and make it firmer, you can knit "through the back of the loop". Insert right-hand needle into back of stitch of left-hand needle, then knit, in usual way.

To purl through the back of the loop insert right-hand needle through back of stitch on left-hand needle and purl in usual way.

Stocking stitch

Knit and purl rows are worked

17

alternately to produce a smooth fabric on the right side and a looped texture on wrong side.

Reverse stocking stitch
The purl or "wrong" side of stocking stitch is used as the right side.

Single rib
Knit one stitch and purl one stitch alternately across the first row. Keep the yarn at the back of the work when you knit a stitch, bring it between the stitches to the front when you purl a stitch and take it to the back of the work for the next stitch. On the next and every subsequent row each stitch knitted in the previous row must be purled and each one purled must be knitted. To vary the pattern you can work a different number of stitches for the knit and purl 'ribs'; for example double rib you knit two stitches and purl two stitches alternately.

Another variation is to knit into knit stitches and purl into purl stitches on subsequent rows; thus producing a textured effect called moss stitch.

Increasing and decreasing
This is used to shape the fabric as it is created. Doing this at the edge of a fabric alters the shape of the outline; doing it within a row will alter the flat shape.

Increasing one stitch
This can be worked anywhere in a row. Knit or purl into the stitch as usual, but do not let the loop fall from the left-hand needle. Insert the right-hand needle into the back of this loop and knit or purl the same stitch again.

Making one stitch (M1)
This is worked within the body of the knitting rather than at the side edges. Use the right-hand needle to pick up the horizontal strand of yarn between the stitch just worked and the next stitch on the left-hand needle (fig. 1). Place the strand on the left-hand needle to form a loop (fig. 2).

Knit into the back of the loop in the usual way so that the new stitch is twisted and does not leave a hole in the fabric (fig. 3). If the increase is on a purl row, pick up the strand of yarn in the same way and purl into it from the back.

Increasing 1 stitch (inc 1)

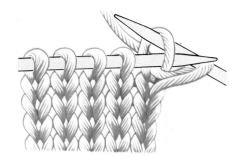

Making 1 stitch (M1)

1

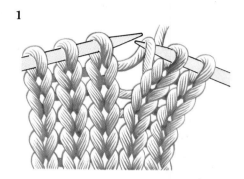

2

3

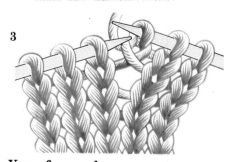

Yarn forward
Increase a stitch between two knit stitches by bringing the yarn forward between the two needles to the front of the work and keeping it there while you knit the next stitch.

Yarn over needle
When you want to make a stitch between a purl and a knit stitch, you will see that the yarn is already at the front of the work. Take it over the top of the right-hand needle to

Yarn forward (yfwd)

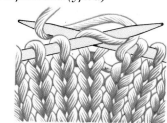

Yarn over (yo)

Yarn round needle (yrn)

Knit 2 together (K2 tog)

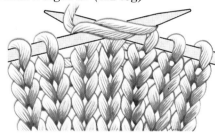

Slipped stitch decreasing (sl 1, K1, psso)

knit the next stitch in the usual way.

Yarn round needle
To make a stitch between two purl stitches, or a knit and a purl stitch, wind the yarn over the top of the right-hand needle and round between the needles to the front of the work again. The next stitch is purled as usual.

Knitting two stitches together
This decrease can be worked at

Grafting

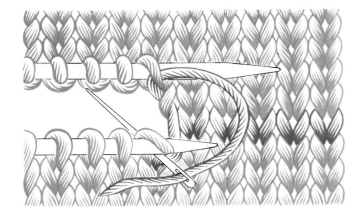

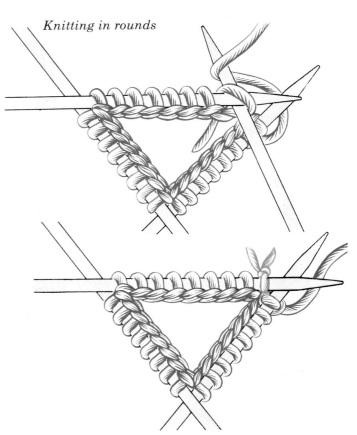

either end of a row or at any given point. Simply insert the right-hand needle through two stitches instead of one and knit them both together in the usual way. The same procedure can be followed for purling two stitches together.

Slipped-stitch decreasing

When you are ready to work a decrease, slip the next stitch from the left-hand needle on to the right-hand needle without knitting it, then knit the following stitch. Using the point of the left-hand needle, lift the slipped stitch over the knit stitch and right off the right-hand needle.

Seams

When seaming knitting use a blunt-ended yarn needle. Work back stitch between knitted stitches and avoid splitting the yarn. Sew firmly, but not too tightly, without stretching.

Place right sides together and work along the wrong side of the fabric about one stitch in from the edge. To secure the sewing yarn at the end, work one or two oversewing stitches.

Knitting in rounds

There are usually four double-

pointed needles of uniform size in a set. This method is used to produce tubular knitting.

Casting on

Either cast on all the stitches required on to one needle and then divide them equally among three needles, or cast them on to each of the other three needles separately; leave the fourth needle free for working.

Cast on required number of stitches on to first, second and third needles. Form the three needles into a triangle making sure the stitches are not twisted round the needles or between the needles and work with the fourth needle.

Working method

Use the spare needle to work all the stitches on the first needle, then the first needle to work the stitches on the second and so on. Always pull the yarn tightly across the first stitch of each needle to avoid making a loose stitch. One round is complete when you have worked the stitches on all three needles.

Marker loops in a contrasting colour are useful to mark the beginning of each new round.

Grafting

This is a method of joining two sets of stitches invisibly without first casting them off.

1. Do not cast off the stitches of the two pieces to be joined. Leave them on two needles, one behind the other, with both points facing to the right and with wrong sides of fabric together. Check that there are an equal number of stitches on both needles.

2. Break off yarn from one section leaving approximately three times the length of the edge to be grafted. Thread yarn into a blunt-ended sewing needle.

3. Insert sewing needle K-wise through first stitch on back needle and pull yarn through; leave the stitch on the knitting needle. Repeat this action through the first stitch on the front needle, but slip this stitch off the knitting needle.

4. Insert sewing needle P-wise through next stitch on the front needle and pull yarn through. Leave this stitch on the knitting needle. Repeat this action through next stitch on the back needle, but let this stitch slip off the needle.

5. Follow these steps until you use up all the stitches from both needles.

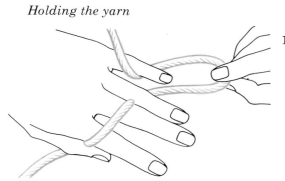

Holding the yarn

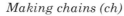

Making chains (ch)

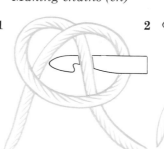

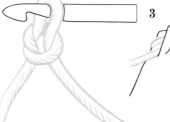

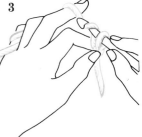

Crochet techniques

Chains

1. Begin with a slip loop on the hook: make a loop about 10cm (4in) from the end of yarn. Insert hook behind vertical strand as shown, then pull the ends of yarn to tighten the loop.
2. Hold the hook with the slip loop in your right hand and control the yarn with your left. Bringing the hook towards you, take it under and then over the top of the yarn in your left hand, so catching it in the curve of the hook—this is called "yarn round hook" (yrh).
3. Holding the knot of the slip loop firmly between thumb and forefinger of your left hand, draw the yarn from back to front through the slip loop, so completing one chain. One working loop remains on the hook.
4. Repeat the actions in steps 2 and 3 until you have the length of chain needed.

Slip stitch (sl st)

This is a way of getting from one point in a row to another.
1. Insert the hook in the usual way into the next chain or stitch.
2. Wind the yarn round the hook from the back as shown.
3. Draw the yarn through the chain or stitch and loop on the hook; a single loop remains on the hook and one slip stitch is complete.

Double crochet (dc)

Make the required number of chains, plus one extra (the turning chain).
1. Insert the hook from front to back into the third chain from the hook; wind the yarn round the hook from the back as shown and draw a loop through the chain, so making two loops on the hook.
2. Wind the yarn round the hook

again and draw it through both loops on the hook; a single loop remains on the hook and one double crochet is complete.
3. Repeat steps 1 and 2 into each chain until you reach the end. Still holding hook in your right hand, turn the work from right to left so that the last stitch of this row becomes the first stitch of the next row.
4. For second and subsequent rows, make one turning chain to count as the first dc; work one stitch into each stitch in the previous row by inserting the hook under the two horizontal loops at top of stitch.

Half treble (htr)

Make the required number of chains plus one extra (turning chains).
1. To work the first row, wind the yarn completely round the hook as in the diagram; insert the hook into the third chain from the hook and draw a loop through the chain, so making three loops on the hook.
2. Wind the yarn round the hook again and draw it through all three loops. A single loop remains on the hook, and 1htr is complete.
3. Repeat 1 and 2 into each chain until you reach the end. Turn the work so that the last stitch of this row becomes the first stitch of the next row.
4. To work the second and subsequent rows, make two turning chains to count as the first htr; insert the hook under the two horizontal loops at the top of each stitch in the previous row.

Treble

Make the required number of chains plus two extra (turning chains).
1. Wind the yarn round the hook; insert the hook into the fourth chain from the hook and draw a loop through, so making three loops on the hook.

Slip stitch (sl st)

Treble stitch

Double crochet (dc)

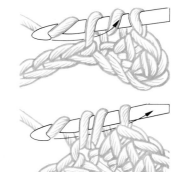

2. Wind the yarn round the hook and draw it through the first two loops on the hook, so leaving two loops on the hook.
3. Wind the yarn round the hook again and draw it through the remaining two loops; a single loop remains on the hook and one treble is complete.
4. Follow steps 3 and 4 of instructions for double crochet, but work three turning chains at the beginning of each new row.

Letter shapes

Finished height
Varies according to individual letter.

Tools required
Basic sewing tools.

Techniques involved
Basic sewing; drawing patterns on to graph paper; filling soft toys.

Materials
squared paper for patterns, with 2.5cm (1in) squares
felt or other non-fraying fabric scraps
kapok or synthetic stuffing
matching thread

Copy simple letter shapes, perhaps from a book on calligraphy, on to graph paper.

Cut out two shapes for each letter.

Now cut out gusset strips the same width as the letter (fig. 1). It is easier to cut longer strips than necessary and trim them to fit as you sew. Some letters, such as B, D and O, have inner as well as outer gussets. Others, like M, C and H, have only outer gussets.

You will also need to cut small squares the same width as the letter to close the ends of letters such as E, L, I and T (fig. 2).

To make up the letters
First attach a gusset edge to the outer curve of one letter piece. Begin sewing at any corner and work all round using a neat stab stitch or glove stitch (fig. 3).

With a letter which has sharp corners, like M, N or T, it is best to piece the gusset strip from corner to corner as the stitching of these joins will give better definition to the shape of the letter (fig. 4).

Overlap the ends slightly where edges meet and then stitch together.

Next, sew inner curves in the same way.

Join the second letter piece to the remaining edge of the gusset strip. If the letter has no square ends, leave an opening for the stuffing.

Fill the shape firmly with stuffing material, pushing down the filling with a pencil or knitting needle if necessary, then stitch the squares to

the ends and close up other openings.

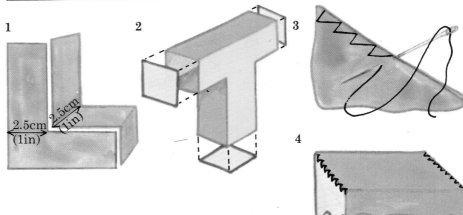

1. *Gusset and letter shape are equal in width.*
2. *The ends of certain letters must be closed with square shapes.*

3, 4. *For glove stitch bring the needle through the same hole twice to make neat corners.*

21

Finger puppets

Finished height
Varies according to puppet.
Tools required
Basic sewing tools.
Techniques involved
Basic sewing; embroidery stitches.

Materials
For each finger puppet:
tracing paper and dressmaker's
  carbon paper for patterns
10cm (4in) square of white felt (grey
  for dog)

scraps of pink and other coloured
  felt
scraps of fabric
matching and contrasting threads
fabric adhesive
felt-tipped pens or crayons

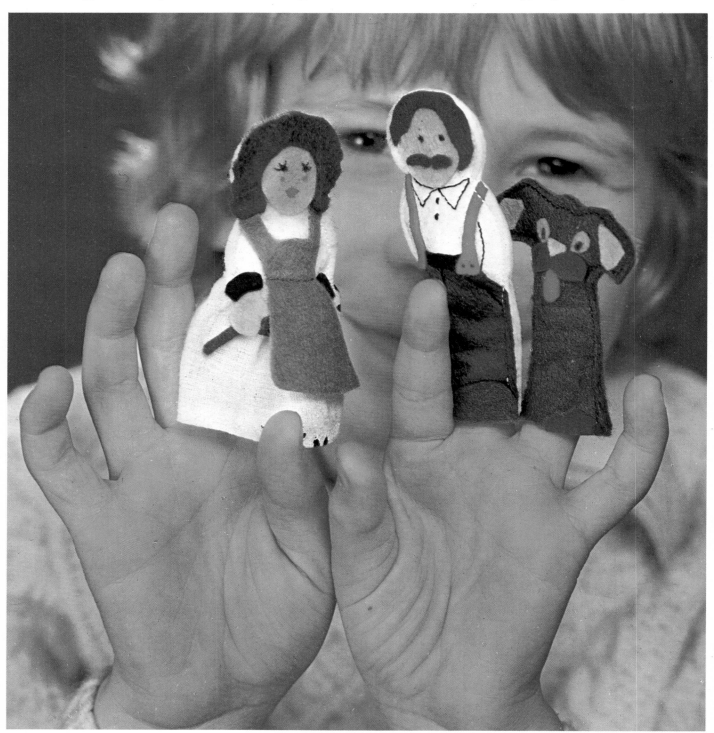

scraps of 1.5cm ($\frac{5}{8}$in) and 6.5cm (2$\frac{1}{2}$in) wide lace for baby and granny

fuse wire for granny's glasses

To make the father

Trace off all the pattern pieces for the father plus a body shape and face, transferring markings with dressmaker's carbon paper.

Cut out two body shapes from white felt, a face from pink felt, and all other pieces from felt scraps.

Place the trouser piece on top of one body piece and stitch down the centre stitching line marked on the pattern and along the top of the pockets. Stick the belt at the top of the trousers with fabric adhesive, and sew on the braces to cover the ends of the belt, using French knots.

With contrasting coloured thread, embroider the outlines of arms and shirt collar in back stitch and the buttons in satin stitch.

Sew the body shapes together leaving the bottom end open. Glue on the shoes to cover the lower edge of the trousers.

Draw the features on to the face with felt-tipped pens or crayons, and stick the face to the head. Glue the hair and moustache pieces into place.

To make the mother

Trace off the pattern pieces given for the mother plus a body shape and face, transferring markings.

Cut out two body shapes from white felt, and two hands and one face from pink felt. Cut out all the other pieces from scraps of felt.

Sew the body shapes together, leaving the bottom end open.

For the skirt cut a piece of fabric 15cm × 6.5cm (6in × 2$\frac{1}{2}$in). Stitch the short ends together, then hem the lower edge. Run a line of gathering stitches 3mm ($\frac{1}{8}$in) from the edge round the waist, turn in the raw edge.

Position the skirt on the puppet so that the hem of the skirt is level with the open end, and pull up the gathering thread so that the skirt fits round the waist. Stitch the skirt to the body at the waist, taking care not to sew the back and the front of the puppet together.

Sew the apron to the front of the body across the waistline and stick the strips to the shoulders with fabric adhesive. Stick the spoon to one hand. Stitch the wrist edges of

Trace patterns

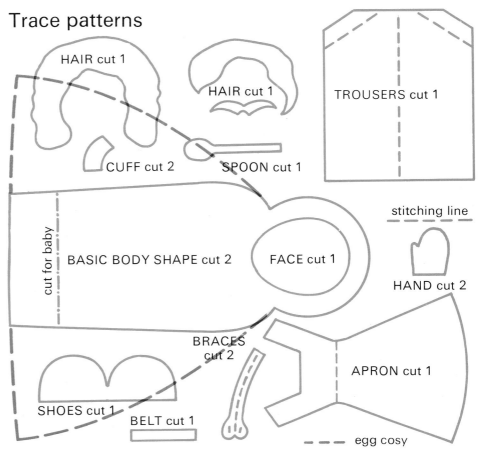

HAIR cut 1

HAIR cut 1

TROUSERS cut 1

CUFF cut 2

SPOON cut 1

cut for baby

BASIC BODY SHAPE cut 2

FACE cut 1

stitching line

HAND cut 2

BRACES cut 2

APRON cut 1

SHOES cut 1

BELT cut 1

- - - egg cosy

the hands to the front of the body at the waist of the skirt, then stick cuffs over the stitches on the hands.

Draw the features on the face with felt-tipped pens or crayons and stick the face piece to the head. Stick the hair in place as illustrated.

To make the granny

Trace off all the pattern pieces given for the granny, plus a body shape, face and hands. Cut two body shapes from white felt, and two hands and one face from pink felt. Cut the hair from grey felt.

Sew the body pieces together, leaving the bottom end open. For the skirt, cut a piece of fabric 11.5cm × 6.5cm (4$\frac{1}{2}$in × 2$\frac{1}{2}$in) and make up and attach as for the mother.

Cut out the shawl triangle from felt, then arrange around the puppet's shoulders and, overlapping the ends at the front, catch stitch to the front of the body.

For the jabot, cut a 4cm (1$\frac{1}{2}$in) length of 1.5cm ($\frac{5}{8}$in) wide lace. Run a line of gathering stitches along the straight edge, draw up the gathers, then fold and stitch the jabot to the front of the body in the neck of the

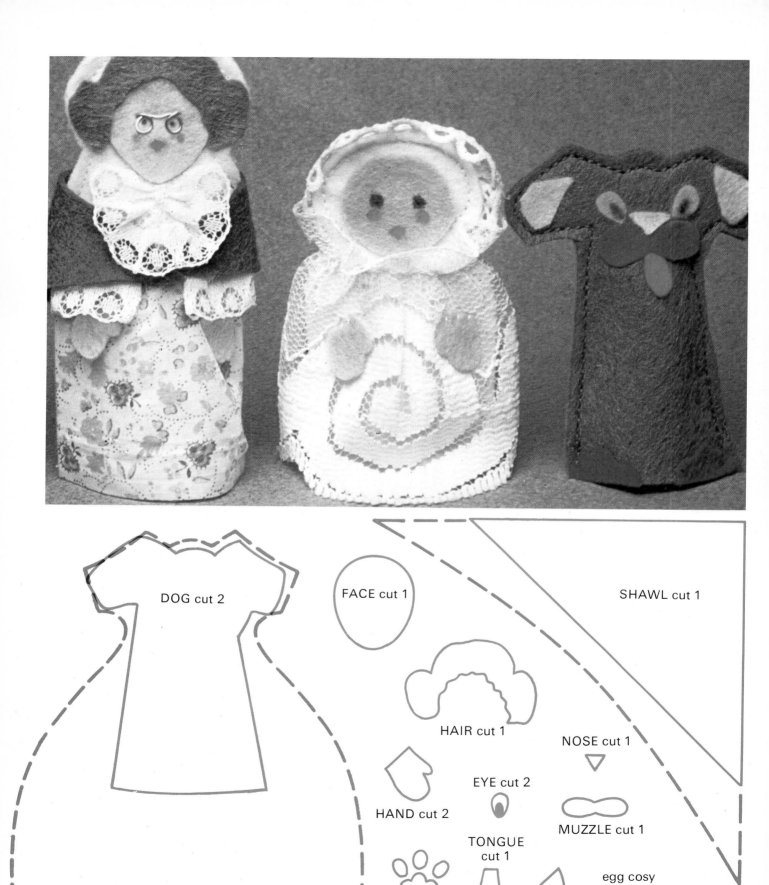

DOG cut 2

FACE cut 1

SHAWL cut 1

HAIR cut 1

NOSE cut 1

HAND cut 2

EYE cut 2

MUZZLE cut 1

TONGUE cut 1

FOOT cut 2 (egg cosy)

INNER EAR cut 2

egg cosy

FOOT Cut 2 (puppet)

Trace patterns

shawl (fig. 1). Turn in raw edges at top and sew in place.

For cuffs, cut two pieces of the same lace each 4.5cm (1½in) long. Join the short ends of one piece, then make up the other cuff in the same way. Attach these to the body front at the waist beneath the edge of the shawl. Slip a hand into each cuff and stitch into position.

To make the glasses, shape a length of fuse wire around two match sticks (fig. 2a). Push the ends through the felt face and flatten at the back (fig. 2b).

Draw in the features and stick the face piece to the head. Stick the hair in place as illustrated.

To make the baby

Trace off the pattern pieces for the body shape, face and hands from the patterns given, but rounding off the face as illustrated.

Cut out two body shapes from white felt, and two hands and one face from pink felt.

For the bonnet, cut a 7.5cm (3in) length of 1.5cm (⅝in) wide lace and gather along the plain edge. Draw up the gathers to fit round the head, and tack on to the wrong side of one body piece.

Sew the two body pieces together, enclosing the gathered edge of the lace and leaving the bottom edge open.

For the dress, cut a 14cm (5½in) length of 6.5cm (2½in) wide lace and join the short edges to form the back seam. Run a line of gathering stitches 1.5cm (⅝in) from one of the long edges, then put the dress on the puppet with the gathered edge at the neck. Pull up the gathers to fit round the neck and stitch the dress to the puppet on the gathering line, taking care not to sew the back and the front of the puppet together.

Draw in the features and stick the face piece to the head with fabric adhesive. Stitch the wrist edge of the hands to the front of the body through the dress.

To make the dog

Trace off the pattern pieces for the dog. Cut out two body shapes, two feet and all the features from appropriately coloured felt.

Stitch the two body shapes together, leaving the bottom end open.

Using a felt-tipped pen or crayon,

draw a pupil on to each eye, then stick the feet and features on to the front of the body.

Matching egg cosies

These puppet designs can be adapted very simply to make them into egg cosies. Each body will need a 22cm (8¾in) square of felt. Use the alternative (red dotted) cutting line on the trace pattern for each body and for the granny's shawl, and make the following alterations when making up the various characters.

Father

Place the trouser piece on the centre of one body piece and stitch down the outer edge of the trousers. When embroidering the figure, outline the outer edge of the arms (cutting line for puppet) as well as the inner edge (fig. 3).

Mother

Work a line of back stitch to outline the outer edge of the arms, as for the father, before assembling the body.

Granny and mother

Cut the pieces of fabric 24cm × 5cm (9½in × 2in) for each skirt.

Baby

Cut a 24cm (9½in) length of 9cm (3½in) wide lace for the dress.

Complete each of the cosies as for the puppets.

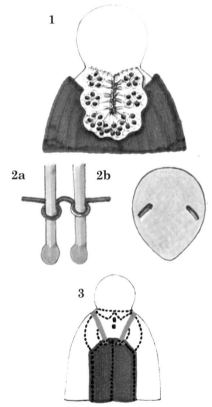

1. Lace sewn in the neck of shawl.
2a. Shaping copper wire around matches.
2b. Wire flattened at back of face.
3. Trousers positioned on egg cosy.

Dog and cat

Finished heights
10cm (4in).
Tools required
Basic sewing tools.

Techniques involved
Basic sewing
filling soft toys
embroidery stitches.

Materials
For the dog:
tracing paper for patterns
30cm (12in) square of brown felt

single strand embroidery thread in matching colour
scraps of white and black felt
27cm × 1cm (11in × ⅜in) strip of cerise felt
kapok or synthetic stuffing
fabric adhesive

For the cat:
tracing paper for patterns
20cm (8in) square of orange felt
15cm (6in) square of white felt
single strand embroidery thread in matching colours and black
scraps of green and black felt
27cm × 1cm (11in × ⅜in) strip of green felt
bristles cut from soft broom for whiskers
stuffing and glue as for dog.

To make dog

Trace pieces for the dog from the patterns given. Using the brown felt, cut out two side body sections, one tail, and ear section and an underbody on the fold of the material.

Mark the darts on each side of the body section. Stitch in the darts on the wrong side.

With wrong sides together, tack the two body sections together along the top from A to B. Sew, using a small blanket stitch.

Tack and blanket stitch the underbody to the sides, matching points A and C. Leave the back of the dog open between B and C.

Fold the tail in half lengthways, wrong sides together. Tack and blanket stitch along the long edge. Stuff the tail, pushing the filling down with a knitting needle or a pencil.

Now stuff the body firmly, pushing the filling in with a pencil or knitting needle.

Slipstitch the tail into the back opening, matching the tail seam to point B. If necessary, push more stuffing into the body. Close the opening by tacking then blanket stitching together.

Using small coins as templates, cut out circles of white and black felt for the eyes and nose—the black circles should be a little smaller than the white. Now cut half circles from brown felt, slightly larger than the white circles, for eyelids. Glue on the nose, eyes and eyelids.

Back stitch the centre of the ears in place on the head, over the centre seam. Bend each ear forward and secure the fold with a dab of glue.

Trace patterns

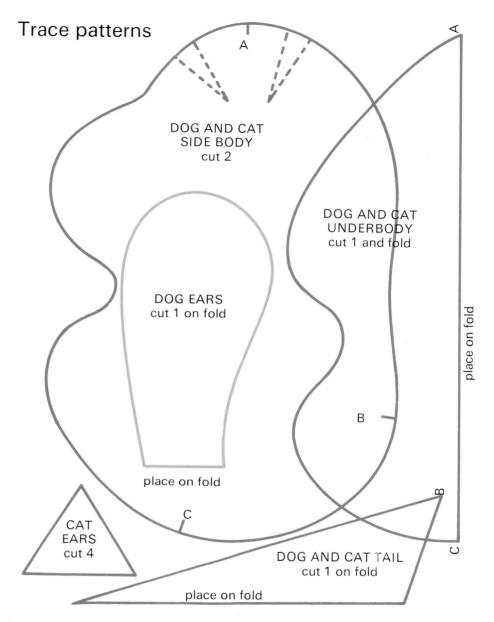

Take the strip of cerise felt and tie round the base of the tail in a bow. Glue in position if desired.

To make the cat

Trace pieces for the cat from the patterns given. In orange felt, cut out two side body sections, two ears, and then one tail piece on the fold. Cut two more ears, and one underbody on the fold, from white felt.

Stitch and stuff the body and tail following the instructions given for the dog

Using a small coin as a template, cut green felt circles for the eyes. Make one long stitch down the centre of each circle with black embroidery thread, then glue in position. Cut half circles for the eyelids in orange felt, with a diameter slightly larger than the eyes. Glue.

Sew or glue the centre of the bristle whiskers to the middle of the cat's face, over the stitching. Make three long straight stitches in black embroidery thread for the mouth.

Cut out a small heart-shaped nose in black felt and glue in position over the whiskers.

Take one orange ear piece and one white one, and blanket stitch them together on two of the sides. Sew the other two pieces together in the same way. Oversew the ears to the head, above the eyes, along the third side.

Finally, take the strip of green felt and tie it round the base of the tail in a bow, gluing in place if desired.

Animal glove puppets

Finished size
Patterns given for a medium-sized adult hand.

Tools required
Basic sewing tools; large-eyed needle.

Techniques involved
Basic sewing; embroidery stitches; filling soft toys.

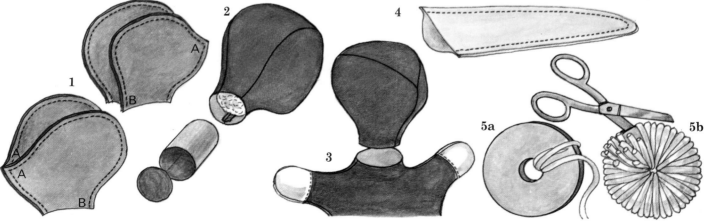

Materials

Cat:

tracing paper for patterns

dressmaker's carbon paper

60cm (24in) square of black felt or patterned cotton fabric for head and body

scraps of white and coloured felt for the muzzle, nose and eyes

matching threads

white button thread

small amount of black wool for mouth

kapok or synthetic filling

4cm (1½in) cardboard tube 2.5cm (1in) in diameter

fabric adhesive

beeswax or candlewax.

Rabbit:

tracing paper for patterns

dressmaker's carbon paper

60cm (24in) square of white felt for head and body

15cm (6in) square of pink felt for inner ears and paw pads

18cm (7in) square of blue felt for waistcoat;

scraps of grey and black felt for eyes

12cm (4¾in) of 2cm (¾in) wide red ribbon for bow tie

matching threads

small amount of white wool for tail

small amount of black wool for paws and nose

kapok or synthetic fillings

2 card circles 5cm (2in) in diameter

fabric adhesive.

Trace off the pattern pieces given and mark in the stitching lines, using dressmaker's carbon paper. A 6mm (¼in) allowance is included on all seams. Label each piece with its name and the number to be cut out, and mark the straight grain line.

For a black cat, cut out all the body pieces including the tail, outer ears and irises for the eyes in black felt. Use white felt for the eye whites, inner ears, paws and muzzle, and pink felt for the nose.

For a cat in cotton fabric, cut out the body, head and tail in printed cotton. Use coloured felt for the paws, muzzle, eyes, outer and inner

1. *Head pieces sewn together.*
2. *Insert tube; add felt to seal in stuffing.*
3. *Inserting stiffened neck into body.*
4. *Inner ear stitched to outer ear.*
5. *a, b. Making a yarn tail pompon.*

ears, and black felt for the nose.

To make the body, sew the two back body pieces together, right sides facing, along centre back seam.

For the paws, stitch each felt paw piece to the corresponding front or back body, overlapping by about 6mm (¼in) and topstitching in place.

Pin the front body piece to the back, matching the paws and side seams, with right sides facing. Stitch all round, leaving the bottom and neck open. Trim seams neatly, clipping at curves, turn right side out.

To make the tail, fold the tail piece in half lengthwise, with right sides facing. Stitch along the long edges and around the curved end, leaving the short straight end open. Trim the seam and turn right side out. Stuff the tail lightly, then turn in the raw edges of the open end and stitch to close. Sew the tail firmly to the body across the back seam and level with the back legs.

For the head, pin the centre gusset piece to the side head pieces with right sides together, matching points A and B. Tack and stitch the gusset and chin seams, leaving the neck edge open (fig. 1). Trim the seams and turn right side out. Stuff the head firmly, pushing down the filling with a pencil if necessary, but do not stuff the neck.

Insert the cardboard tube into the neck and add more filling so as to make the head firm. To prevent the filling getting into the tube, cut a circle of felt slightly bigger than the diameter of the tube. Stick this to filling above upper end of tube (fig. 2).

Slip the stiffened neck into the body opening, overlapping by about 2cm (¾in) as shown in fig. 3 and slipstitch together. Note that if you are using cotton fabric you must first turn in the neck edge of the body all round and tack with double thread.

For the ears, stick the inner to the outer ears with fabric adhesive. Fold a dart in the centre of each ear, then pin both ears to the head.

Now pin the white felt muzzle and the eyes in position on the head, using the illustration on page 28 as a guide and adjusting them as necessary to produce an effective cat-like expression. Sew on the ears and the muzzle using contrasting coloured thread and large stitches to achieve a furry look.

Stick the black felt irises on to the eye whites, then stick the completed eyes to the head. Stick on the pink nose piece, then embroider the mouth with black wool, using the illustration on page 28 as a guide.

Make whiskers by threading three 15cm (6in) lengths of white button thread to either side of the muzzle and making a small stitch. Secure the six whiskers by knotting close to the muzzle, and stiffen the whiskers with beeswax or candlewax. To make claws, sew three large stitches in black thread through each paw.

Note: if you are using cotton fabric, you will need to turn under and sew a small hem at the base edge of the puppet. Narrow elastic may be inserted into the hem so that the puppet fits neatly over the wrist.

Make the rabbit's body following the instructions given for the cat. Cut out the same basic pattern pieces as for the cat, but use the rabbit trace patterns for the ears, paws, pads and eyes. Use white felt for the main body pieces, pink felt for the inner ears and paw pads, grey felt for eyes and black felt for irises.

Stitch pink inner ears to the outer white outer ears so that the pink felt is taut while the white felt is loose and curved (fig. 4). This leaves a hollow centre, and will help to keep the ears upright.

After making and attaching the white paws, stick a pink paw on the front of each paw. Sew black claws as for the cat. Stick the irises to the eye pieces, then stick the assembled eyes to the head. Embroider the nose and mouth in black wool, using the illustration on page 28 as a guide.

For the tail, make a pompon by winding white wool round the two card circles which have had their centres cut out (fig. 5a). Snip the wool all round the outer edge as in fig. 5b, and secure firmly round the middle. Remove the card and stitch the pompon in place on the puppet.

For the simple felt waistcoat, cut along the green lines marked on the body pattern and cut out a piece in blue felt. Stitch the shoulder and side seams. Put the waistcoat on the rabbit, then turn back the corners at the neck and stitch down to form revers.

Make a bow tie out of the length of red ribbon and sew this in position under the chin to complete the rabbit.

cut for other fabric
cut for felt only

RABBIT
OUTER EAR
cut 2 in felt

RABBIT
INNER EAR
cut 2 in felt

BACK BODY
cut 2

fold

FRONT BODY
cut 1 on fold

back B

fold

HEAD GUSSET
cut 1 on fold

WAISTCOAT

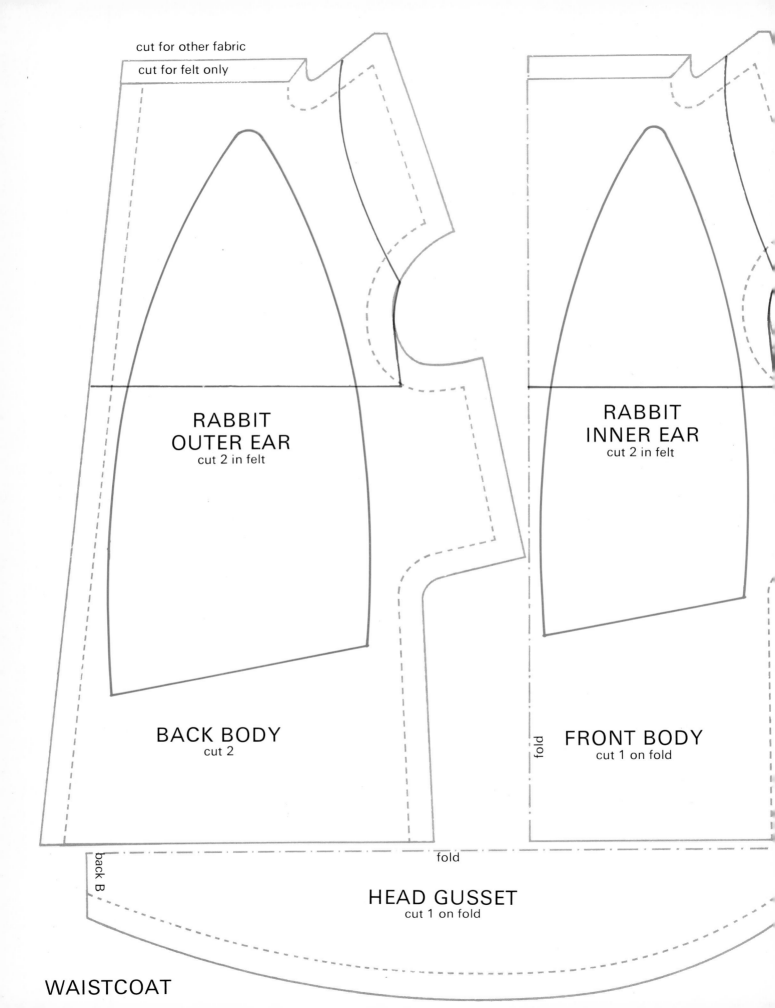

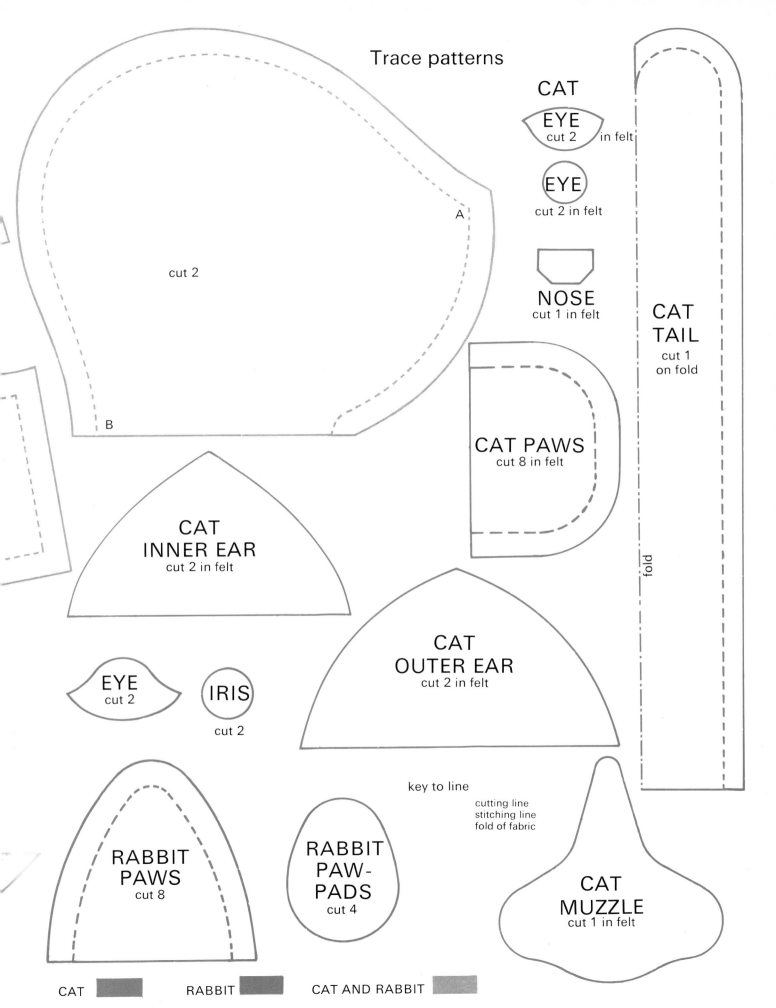

Trace patterns

cut 2

A

B

CAT

EYE
cut 2 in felt

EYE
cut 2 in felt

NOSE
cut 1 in felt

CAT
TAIL
cut 1
on fold

fold

CAT PAWS
cut 8 in felt

CAT
INNER EAR
cut 2 in felt

EYE
cut 2

IRIS
cut 2

CAT
OUTER EAR
cut 2 in felt

key to line

cutting line
stitching line
fold of fabric

RABBIT
PAWS
cut 8

RABBIT
PAW-
PADS
cut 4

CAT
MUZZLE
cut 1 in felt

CAT   RABBIT   CAT AND RABBIT

Pipecleaner dolls

Finished height
The dolls vary from 15cm (6in) for the children to 18cm (7in) for the father.

Tools required
Basic sewing tools.

Techniques involved
Basic sewing; embroidery stitches.

Materials
for the basic body:
3 pipecleaners
cotton wool

pink bias binding
small piece of pink felt or cotton
    fabric for head
matching thread
4 ply wool for hair

For the clothes:
tracing paper for patterns
scraps of felt, cotton fabric, lace
   and ribbon as appropriate.

Trace patterns are given for clothes for a family of dolls—mother, father, girl, boy and governess. They are dressed in clothes which were fashionable during the early 1900s. The clothes patterns should only be regarded as a basic guide.

The patterns for these pipecleaner dolls do not include seam allowances, and 6mm ($\frac{1}{4}$in) must be added all round, except where felt is being used.

To make the basic body

Join the pipecleaners together (fig. 1a). You can adjust the arm and leg lengths by making an extra twist or two round the body.

Following fig 1b, pad the pipecleaner 'skeleton' with cotton wool and wind sewing thread round it to keep it in place.

Wind pink bias binding round the legs, arms and body in overlapping layers (fig. 1b) and slipstitch in several places to hold the layers in position, especially at the ends of the arms.

Using the trace pattern given, make a pattern for the head and cut out the two head pieces in pink felt or cotton fabric.

With right sides facing, sew round the edges of the head, leaving the neck edge open. Trim the seams and turn right side out.

Stuff the head with a little cotton wool, place over the top of the pipecleaner ends, and continue to stuff (pushing down the cotton wool with a pencil or knitting needle if necessary) until you have obtained a proper head shape as in fig. 1b. Slipstitch the neck edge neatly to the body all round.

To make the mother

Make the body as described. To emphasize the S-line of the Edwardian dress, pad the bust with extra cotton wool.

For the dress, cut out the skirt, bodice and sleeve patterns from the trace patterns given. Check the length and width against the doll. Lay all the patterns on a double thickness of fabric and cut out. With right sides facing, sew the front

bodice pieces to the back bodice at the shoulders and sides. Turn right side out.

Form a high collar by wrapping a short piece of broderie anglaise around the neck of the doll. This can be trimmed to 1.3cm ($\frac{1}{2}$in) at the sides and back of the neck, but it should be wide enough at the front to make a blouse front under the V-neck. If the trimming is already too narrow for this, sew a piece of white ribbon to the front of the doll's body before putting on the collar. Place the bodice on the doll. Turn in the neck and front edges and sew to the body along the fold line.

Pull the sleeves on to the arms, turn under the armhole edges and stitch to the bodice. Sew one or two layers of narrow lace trimming to cover this stitching line.

Take the skirt piece and sew the back seam, right sides facing. Turn right side out. Put the skirt on the doll, turn in at the waist and sew to the bodice, starting at the front and gathering at the back to obtain a bustle effect. Turn up and hem the bottom of the skirt and the sleeve edges (unless you have managed to cut these edges against a selvedge or have used non-fraying fabric).

For the train, use a piece of ribbon or lace about 10cm (4in) square. Taper this to 5cm (2in) at the top and 10cm (4in) at the bottom by folding in the sides the required amount. Sew to the back of the skirt at the waist and sew down with a couple of stitches on either side of the train. A waist petticoat could also be made using the skirt pattern. Add lace trimming to the bottom edge for a dainty effect.

To make the hair, sew wool onto the head, starting at the top and working from the centre parting to the sides. Loop more wool loosely at the sides and finish with a bun on top of the head. Embroider features on the face of the doll.

For the hat, make a frame out of pipecleaners with a 2.5cm (1in) crown and approximately 5.5cm ($2\frac{1}{4}$in) brim (fig. 2). Cover the frame by winding brown tape or ribbon round and round the frame in layers lengthwise and slipstitch in position at intervals. Cut out two or three different sizes of coloured felt circles, preferably with pinking shears. Arrange them around the hat in layers and sew in place. If young children will be playing with the doll, the hat should be sewn on to the

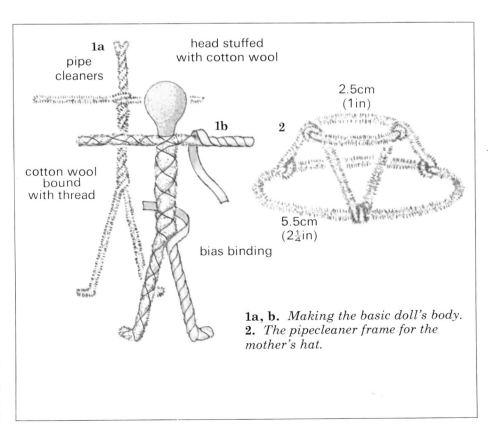

1a, b. *Making the basic doll's body.*
2. *The pipecleaner frame for the mother's hat.*

Trace patterns

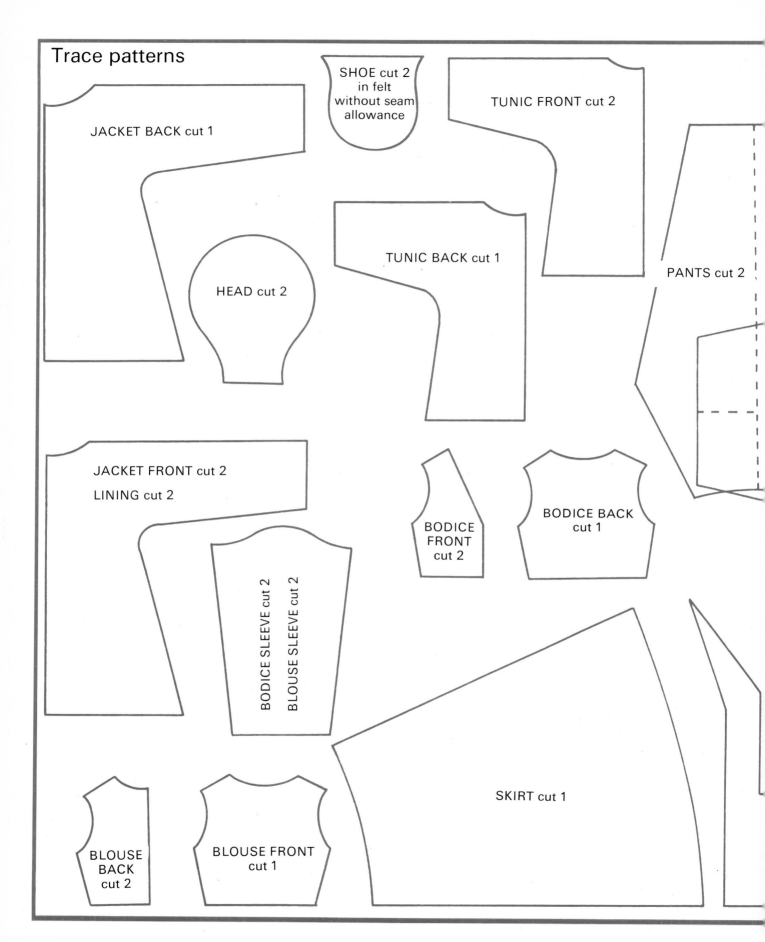

JACKET BACK cut 1

SHOE cut 2
in felt
without seam
allowance

TUNIC FRONT cut 2

HEAD cut 2

TUNIC BACK cut 1

PANTS cut 2

JACKET FRONT cut 2

LINING cut 2

BODICE
FRONT
cut 2

BODICE BACK
cut 1

BODICE SLEEVE cut 2

BLOUSE SLEEVE cut 2

SKIRT cut 1

BLOUSE
BACK
cut 2

BLOUSE FRONT
cut 1

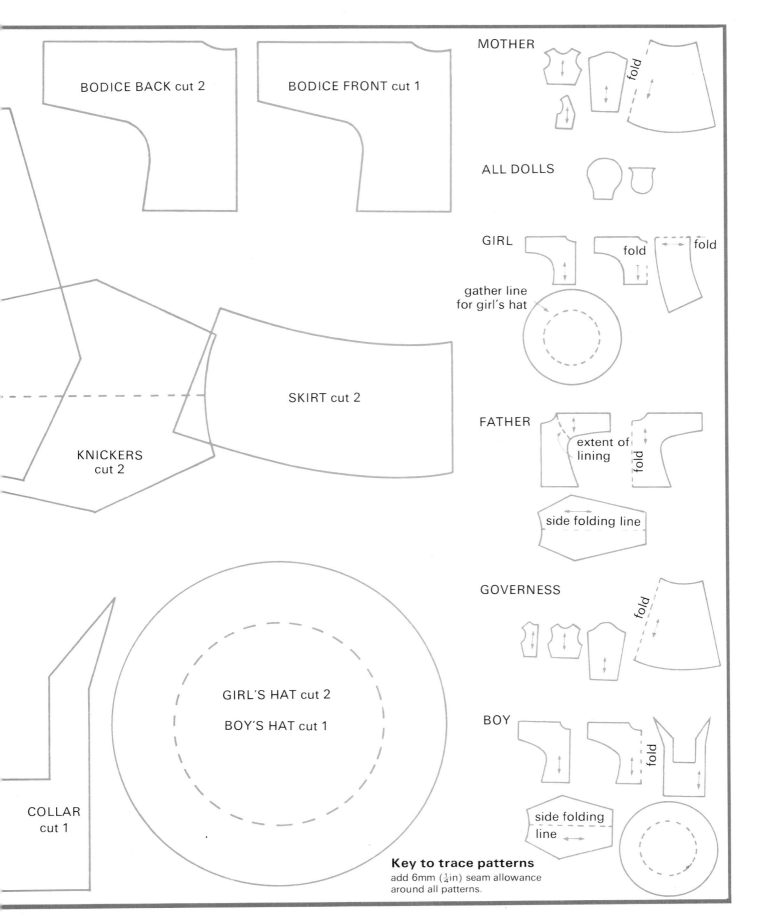

BODICE BACK cut 2

BODICE FRONT cut 1

MOTHER

fold

ALL DOLLS

GIRL

fold

fold

gather line
for girl's hat

SKIRT cut 2

KNICKERS
cut 2

FATHER

extent of
lining

fold

side folding line

GOVERNESS

fold

GIRL'S HAT cut 2

BOY'S HAT cut 1

BOY

fold

COLLAR
cut 1

side folding
line

Key to trace patterns
add 6mm ($\frac{1}{4}$in) seam allowance
around all patterns.

35

head, but if not, it may be simply pinned in position.

To make the governess

Following the instructions for the mother, make the body, skirt and blouse, but omit the V-neck and make an opening at the back.

Put the skirt and blouse on the doll, sew up the back overlap of the blouse, turn in the sleeve edges and hem. Trim the sleeve edges with ribbon to indicate cuffs. Make a belt by sewing on a strip of felt at the waist and embroidering a buckle.

Form a collar by wrapping a piece of white ribbon or binding round the doll's neck and sewing down at the back. Cut out a small felt bow and sew this to the collar front.

For the hair, sew wool on to the head, working from front to back, and finishing with a neat bun at the centre back. Embroider features on the face.

The pince-nez are made from fuse wire bent to the required shape and sewn in position between the eyes. Attach one side of the frame to a piece of black wool or very fine cord and tuck the other end into the belt.

To make the father

Make the body as before but slightly taller than that of the mother.

Using the trace patterns given, make patterns for the trousers, jacket and sleeveless lining for the front of the jacket. Check for size against the doll's body. Lay all the patterns on a double thickness of fabric and cut out. Cut a sleeveless lining for the front of the jacket, using the jacket pattern up to the dashed line.

For the trousers, put right sides together and join the centre front and back seams. Lay the trousers so that the front and back seams lie on top of each other, and join inner leg seams. Trim the seams and turn right side out. Put the trousers on the doll and sew to the body at the waist, gathering in any surplus width. Turn in trouser hems and sew.

To make the jacket, stitch the front pieces to the back piece at the sides and shoulders, right sides facing. Turn right side out. Pin the lining to the front of the jacket on each side, with right sides together, and sew along the shoulders and front edges. Trim seams and turn the lining to the inside of the jacket. Make the back collar by binding the edge with matching ribbon or jacket fabric. Press flat.

The shirt collar is a small length of white ribbon or bias binding turned in at the edges. Sew this around the doll's neck, leaving a small gap at the front. Make a shirt front by sewing a piece of white ribbon to the front of the doll's body. For a cravat, tie a knot in a black ribbon and sew in position on the shirt neck.

Put the jacket on the doll. If the jacket is too wide at the back, it can be taken in by making a tuck at each shoulder. Turn in the sleeve hems and sew. Turn back the lapels and slipstitch in place. Details, such as felt or bead buttons, pockets and a breast pocket with handkerchief, may all be added if desired.

For the hair, sew wool to the head, beginning at the centre front and working to the sides and back. Start with long stitches and build up with shorter ones. Embroider features, whiskers and a moustache.

To make the girl

Make the doll's body as before, but about 2.5cm (1in) shorter than that of the mother.

Using the trace patterns given, make patterns for the bodice, skirt and hat, and check against the doll for size. Lay them on double thickness of fabric and cut out.

To make the dress, stitch the front bodice to the back sections at sides and shoulders, right sides facing. Turn right side out. Turn in and sew neck edge. Put the bodice on the doll, turn the edges of the back opening and join by overlapping and sewing down.

Sew the side seams of the skirt, right sides together. Turn right side out. Pin and sew the skirt to bodice, taking large pleats as you go. Turn up and sew sleeve edges and hem. If the pleats stick out, sew down each pleat.

Trim the sleeves and neck with narrow lace and trim the waist seam of the skirt with narrow ribbon.

For the hair, sew long lengths of wool from the centre parting to the sides and back, securing them at ear level. Embroider features.

To make the hat, join the edges of two circular hat pieces, right sides facing, leaving a small gap. Trim the seam and turn right side out through the gap. Turn in the edges of this gap and oversew them together. Gather at the line shown on the trace pattern to fit the head. Press the edge of brim. Trim gathering line with ribbon. Attach to head as for mother's hat by pinning or sewing.

To make the boy

Make the body as for the girl doll.

With the trace patterns given, make patterns for the sailor's outfit and check against doll for size. Lay patterns for tunic and trousers on double thickness of fabric (preferably white for tunic and navy blue for trousers) and cut out.

Lay the patterns for the hat and collar on a single thickness of navy blue fabric and cut out. It is a good idea to make the collar in felt, to avoid turning in the edges. In this case do not add the 6mm ($\frac{1}{4}$in) seam allowance to the pattern.

Make knickerbockers as the father's trousers. The only difference is that they end at the knees. Stitch the knickerbockers to the doll's legs, taking a tuck on the outside of each trouser leg, and trim with a strip of blue felt or ribbon.

The tunic is made as the girl's bodice, but with the opening at the front. Trim the collar with a thin strip of navy felt or narrow ribbon and trim the sleeve edges at the wrist with two strips of navy blue felt or narrow ribbon. Trim the collar piece at the back and sides with a strip of white felt stitched in place near the edge. Fasten the collar piece at the front by sewing to the blouse at the point where ties cross.

For the hat, gather the circle of fabric at the edge so that it fits the head, and flatten the crown. Sew a narrow band of felt around the edge of the opening, and stitch this band to the head. Add two small strips of felt at one side of the head. Stitch brim to head in one or two places to keep the crown flat.

To make shoes

The shoes for all the dolls are made from felt, using the trace pattern given (no seam allowance is necessary).

Poupard dolls

Finished height
28cm (11in).

Tools required
Basic sewing tools; hand drill with 6mm (¼in) bit.

Techniques involved
Basic sewing; simple woodworking; painting.

Materials
1 wooden ball for head, 4cm (1¼in) in diameter (you may prefer to use a polystyrene ball see separate instructions on page 41)
1 piece of 6mm (¼in) dowel rod 25.5cm (10in) long
fine paintbrush
enamel paints or felt pens
scraps of double knitting wool for hair
scraps of pink wool for hands

pipe cleaner about 25cm (9½in) long for arms
15cm × 11.5cm (6in × 4½in) of cotton calico material for body covering
small pill box about 4cm (1½in) deep and 2.5cm (1in) in diameter
small amount of rice
woodworking glue

For the clothes
tracing paper for patterns

- 25.5cm × 7.5cm (10in × 3in) of broderie anglaise or 7.5cm (3in) wide lace
- 15cm × 5cm (6in × 2in) of cotton calico material for first underskirt
- 36cm × 20cm (14in × 8in) of silky fabric for blouse and second underskirt
- 115cm (1¼yds) of 1cm (⅜in) wide lace for trimming blouse and bonnet or mob cap
- 30cm × 15cm (12in × 6in) of velvet or corduroy for skirt
- 90cm (1yd) of 6mm (¼in) wide velvet ribbon;
- 45cm (17¾in) of 6mm (¼in) wide nylon ribbon
- 90cm (1yd) of fine braid
- about 18cm × 15cm (7in × 6in) of muslin for bonnet or 13cm (5in) square of cotton fabric for mob cap
- 5 small bells (optional as these should not be used if the doll is to be handled by very young children).

To make the doll

Drill a 6mm (¼in) diameter hole in the wooden ball 1.3cm (½in) deep and glue the dowel rod in place (fig. 1).

Paint the features with enamel paint or felt pens, following the suggested features in fig. 2 or designing your own.

Spread glue on to the back of the head and coil the double knitting wool round the head, working from the centre. You can make the hair-style more elaborate by plaiting some extra lengths of wool, twisting them into a bun shape and gluing to the back of the head (fig. 3).

Cut a small slit in the centre of the piece of calico material just big enough to insert the dowel rod. Slip the fabric on to the rod with the short sides across the shoulders and the long ends to the front and back. Push the material up to the head.

For the arms, take the pipe cleaner and, starting from the centre, twist it round the dowel rod immediately below the material.

This will help to keep the fabric in position (fig. 4). Bend the arms into shape and bind the ends of the pipe cleaner with a little pink wool, the double back the ends of the bound pipe cleaner and bind them to the arms with more pink wool to form hands.

Glue the arms in place on the dowel rod.

Make a hole in the middle of the lid and also the base of the pill box which is just large enough to insert the dowel rod. Slide first the lid and then the box up the rod, put some rice into the box to make the rattle and glue on the lid. Now glue the box to the pipe cleaner arms at the top of the rod.

Fold the material down on either side of the box and sew first firmly in place (fig. 5).

Dressing the doll
To make the underskirts
and blouse

For the underskirt, work a row of

1. *The dowel glued in place.*
2. *Features can be painted or drawn with felt-tip markers.*
3. *The hair style can be as elaborate as you wish.*
4. *How to form the arms.*
5. *Unbleached muslin sewn over pill box.*

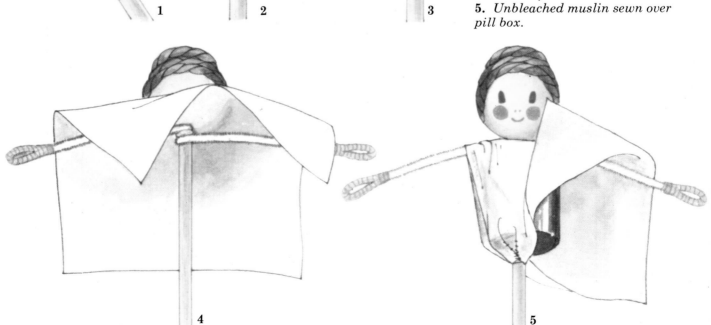

Trace patterns

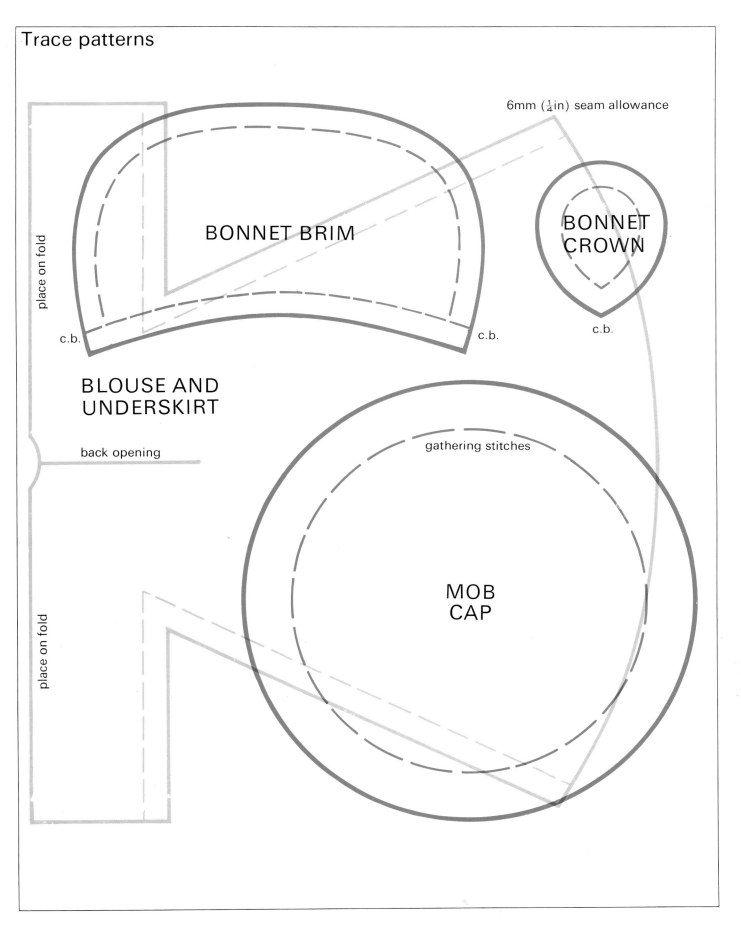

6mm ($\frac{1}{4}$in) seam allowance

BONNET BRIM

BONNET CROWN

place on fold

c.b.

c.b.

c.b.

BLOUSE AND UNDERSKIRT

back opening

gathering stitches

MOB CAP

place on fold

6a, b. *Construction of underskirt.*
7. *Underskirt sewn to doll.*
8. *Blouse/second underskirt completed.*
9. *The finished doll.*

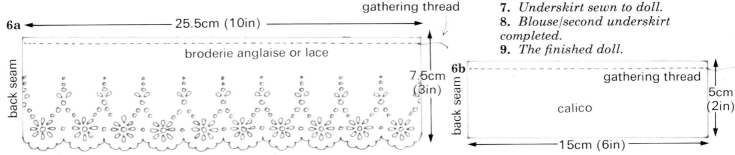

6a ← 25.5cm (10in) →

gathering thread

back seam

broderie anglaise or lace

7.5cm (3in)

6b gathering thread

back seam

calico

5cm (2in)

← 15cm (6in) →

gathering stitches (fig. 6a) along the top edge of the broderie anglaise or lace and gather up to match one long edge of the calico material. Pin and stitch the edging to the calico, with right sides facing.

Work a row of gathering stitches along the top of the calico material leaving a long thread for finishing (fig. 6b).

Stitch the centre backseam, with right sides facing.

Pull up the gathering at the waist and sew firmly to the body of the doll (fig. 7).

The blouse is cut full length to form a second underskirt.

First cut out a paper pattern using the trace pattern given.

Fold the silky material in half to measure 20cm × 18cm (8in × 7in).

Position the pattern with the shoulder edges on the fold and pin in place. Cut out. Now cut an opening in the back of the neck large enough to insert the doll's head.

Sew 6mm ($\frac{1}{4}$in) hems at the wrist and hem edges.

Tack and stitch the side and sleeve seams, with right sides together.

Turn to right side. Trim hem and sleeves with lace.

Slip the garment over the doll's head and slipstitch the back opening together, turning in the raw edges. Trim the neckedge with lace.

Work a row of gathering stitches around the wrists of the sleeves and draw up thread to fit (fig. 8).

Cut the nylon ribbon in half and tie one piece round each arm at the shoulders. Tie into bows at the top of the shoulders and sew in place with tiny invisible stitches.

To make the overskirt

With right sides facing, place the two short ends of the velvet together and stitch to form the centre back seam. (If you have chosen thick or stiff fabric, you will require less width in the skirt.)

Turn up the hem and stitch.

Turn the skirt to the right side and run a row of gathering stitches along the top, leaving a long thread for finishing. Put the skirt on the doll, draw up the gathering thread to fit and sew firmly in place at the doll's waist.

Cut five 13cm (5in) lengths of velvet ribbon and five 13cm (5in) lengths of braid. Sew a bell to the end of each piece of braid and stitch on to the overskirt at the waist, alternating with the pieces of velvet ribbon.

Using a strip of velvet, cover the ends of the velvet and braid so as to neaten and form a waistband. Pull the ribbon tightly to cover all the raw edges, and sew firmly in position (fig. 9).

10. *The finished bonnet.*

To make bonnet

Using the trace pattern given, cut out a paper pattern for the bonnet trim and crown.

Fold the muslin in half to make an oblong 18cm × 7.5cm (7in × 3in) of double material, place the brim and crown patterns on the muslin, pin and cut out.

Turn in a 6mm ($\frac{1}{4}$in) hem round the long curved edge of each brim piece. Pin together with wrong sides together. At the same time insert a 23cm

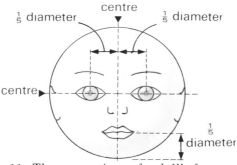

11. *The proportions of a doll's face.*

(9in) length of lace trimming sandwiched between the two brim pieces. Topstitch the layers together using small running stitches.

Sew the brim to the crown, starting at the back and easing any fullness. Cover the raw edges round the crown with a double row of lace.

Place the bonnet on the doll's head. Sew the last piece of braid over the bonnet to make ties (fig. 10).

To make mob cap

You may prefer to make a mob cap for the doll's head-dress.

Using the trace pattern given, make a pattern for the mob cap, place on the cotton fabric and cut out.

Sew a small hem around the outer edge and trim with narrow lace.

Run a gathering thread round the cap 1.3cm ($\frac{1}{2}$in) from the edge. Pull up to fit the doll's head and fasten off securely.

To substitute a polystyrene doll's head

You may find it easier to use a high-density polystyrene ball instead of a wooden ball for the doll's head.

Materials

1 high-density polystyrene ball, 4cm (1$\frac{1}{2}$in) in diameter
1 piece 6mm ($\frac{1}{4}$in) dowel rod 25.5cm (10in) long sharpened to a point.
water-based paints: emulsion paint in flesh tone and poster colours or gouache for features
fine paintbrush
PVA adhesive
scraps of wool for hair (optional)

Work out a design for the face, following fig. 11 for the proportions.

Pierce the base of the polystyrene ball with the sharpened point of the dowel rod, and push in till firmly secured.

Paint the ball with the flesh-coloured emulsion. When this base coat is thoroughly dry, lightly mark out the features in pencil, then paint them using appropriate colours of poster paint or gouache. Allow to dry completely before assembling the doll.

Warning: polystyrene is an inflammable material and must be kept away from naked flames.

A collection of alternative heads.

Ragdoll

Finished height
60cm (24ins).
Tools required
Basic sewing tools; sewing machine.

Techniques involved
Basic sewing; machine stitching; drawing patterns from a graph; filling soft toys; embroidery stitches.

Materials
squared paper for patterns
90cm × 70cm (35in × 27½in) of cotton calico material

25gm (1oz) ball of light brown
  double knitting wool for hair
15cm (6in) square of brown felt
15cm (6in) square of black felt
scraps of pink and white felt
pink and brown embroidery thread
matching thread
225gm (8oz) kapok or synthetic
  stuffing
2 tiny red buttons for shoe straps.

Draw up pattern pieces for the doll from the graph patterns given. A seam allowance of 1cm (⅜in) is included on the pattern.

Using the calico material, cut one head front, two head backs, two body sections, and cut two legs and two arms on the fold. Cut all pieces on the straight of the grain. Mark the point and top of the head dart with single tailor's tacks.

Cut out four shoe uppers in black felt, two soles and two eye centres in brown felt, two eye whites in white and a mouth in pink.

With right sides facing, tack and stitch the head back sections from A to B. Trim the seam, clip the curve and press open.

Tack and stitch the dart in the head front, with right sides facing. Press the dart to one side.

With right sides together and matching darts to the centre back seam, tack and stitch the head front to the head back, easing where necessary. Trim the seam and turn the head through to the right side.

Fill the head firmly, pushing down the stuffing with a pencil. Oversew the raw edges together.

To make the hair, loop the wool backwards and forwards across the head, back stitching the wool to the head along the line of the dart and down the centre back seam. Begin stitching on the face 2.5cm (1in) below the seam line (fig. 7) and continue to 4cm (1½in) above the neck edge at the back. Pull the strands evenly across the head at the back, and back stitch to the side seam on each side, beginning 2.5cm (1in) above the neck edge and finishing 4cm (1½in) from the centre line of back stitch (fig. 8). Tie the hair.

With right sides facing, tack and stitch one arm on the stitching line. Trim the seam, clip into the angle of the thumb and turn through to the right side. Lightly fill the hand and machine stitch lines for fingers. Fill

1

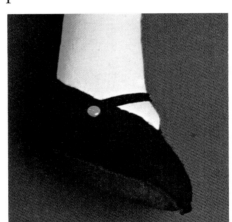

2

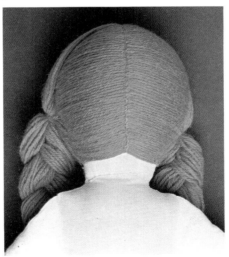

3

4

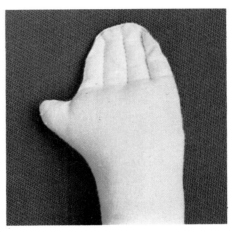

5

6

the arm firmly to with 2.5cm (1in) of the top, pushing down the stuffing with a pencil or knitting needle. Machine stitch across the tops 1cm (⅜in) from the raw edge. Make up the other arm in the same way.

Place two body sections with right sides together and place one arm between them. Match the raw edges

1. *Finished doll, undressed.*
2. *Doll's face (hair can be braided if you prefer).*
3. *Shoe with strap.*
4. *Lines of machine stitching for fingers.*
5. *Hair backstitched to centre back seam.*
6. *The dressed doll.*

43

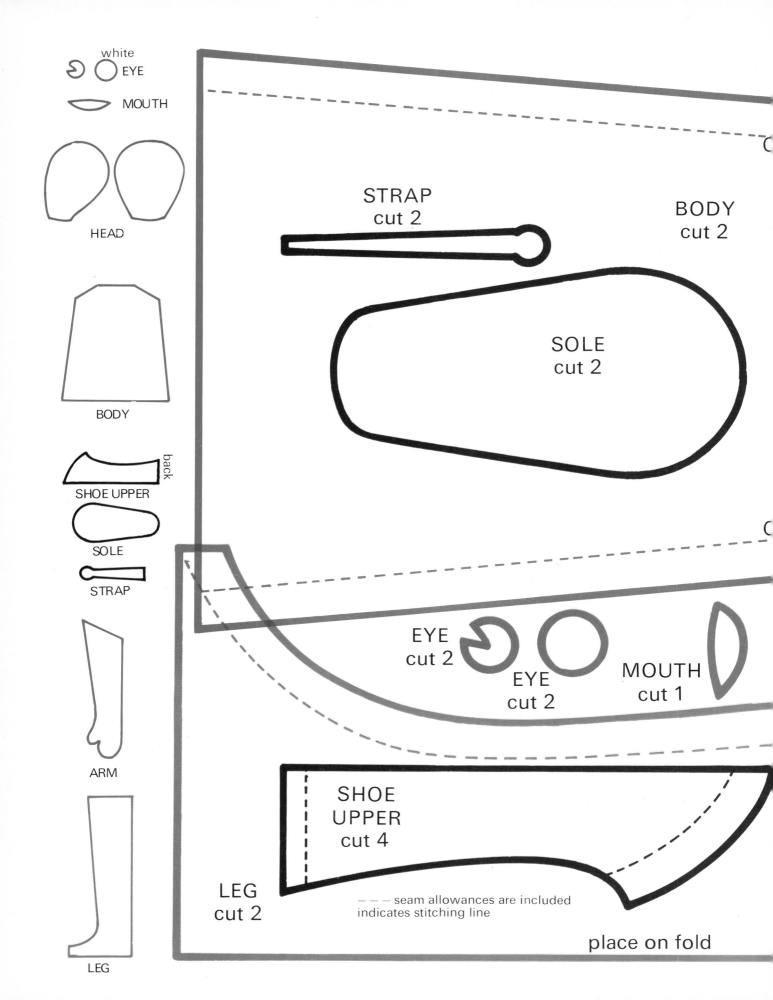

white
EYE

MOUTH

HEAD

BODY

SHOE UPPER

back

SOLE

STRAP

ARM

LEG

STRAP
cut 2

BODY
cut 2

SOLE
cut 2

EYE
cut 2

EYE
cut 2

MOUTH
cut 1

SHOE
UPPER
cut 4

LEG
cut 2

— — seam allowances are included
indicates stitching line

place on fold

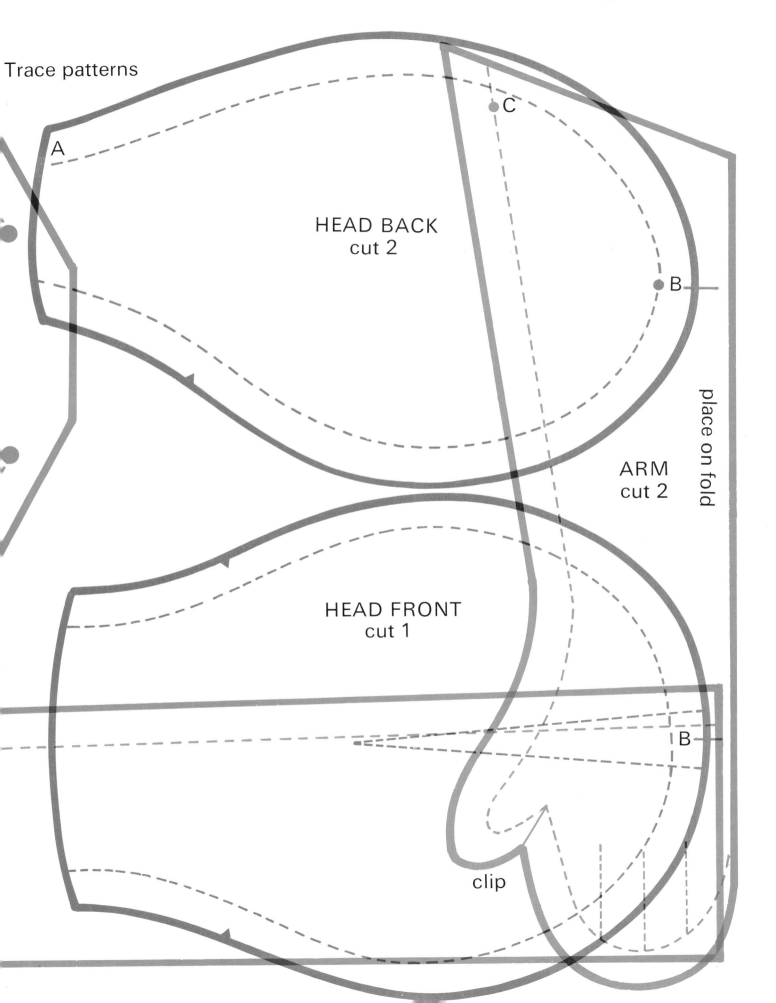

Trace patterns

A

HEAD BACK
cut 2

C

B

place on fold

ARM
cut 2

HEAD FRONT
cut 1

clip

B

and points C. Tack and stitch the side seam from C to the bottom (fig. 9). Repeat with the other arm.

Sew shoulder seams and turn through to the right side.

Turn in the raw edge on the body and insert the head about 1.3cm ($\frac{1}{2}$in) into the opening, matching side seams on the head to shoulder seams on the body. Tack, then oversew the body to the head (fig. 10). Fill the body firmly to within 4cm (1$\frac{1}{2}$in) of the lower edge, pushing down the stuffing with a pencil. Turn in 1cm ($\frac{3}{8}$in) along the lower raw edge and tack temporarily to close.

With right sides together, sew the back seam of one pair of shoe uppers 6mm ($\frac{1}{4}$in) from the edge. Press the seam open and trim.

Place the top edge of the upper over the bottom edge of one leg, right sides up, overlapping by 1.3cm ($\frac{1}{2}$in). Tack and topstitch by hand or machine 3mm ($\frac{1}{8}$in) from the edge of the upper (fig. 11). (You may have to stretch the felt slightly.)

With right sides together, stitch the leg and front seam of the shoe as one. Trim the seam, clip the curve on the leg and turn to the right side.

Back stitch the sole opening to the shoe upper 3mm ($\frac{1}{8}$in) from the edge, leaving one side open to enable the filling to be pushed into the leg from the foot as well as from the top of the leg. Fill the leg firmly to within 2.5cm (1in) of the top, pushing down from the top.

Back stitch sole opening and machine across the top of the leg with the seam at the centre front, stitching 1cm ($\frac{3}{8}$in) from the raw edge.

Work two rows of machine stitching along the length of one shoe strap and oversew to the shoe. Stitch a button at the outer end of the strap. Make up the other leg.

Remove the tacking from the lower edge of the body. Insert the legs into the body opening so that the raw edges are about 1.3cm ($\frac{1}{2}$in) inside the body. Tack and back stitch across the lower edge of the body with two rows of stitching, one close to the edge and the other about 1.3cm ($\frac{1}{2}$in) up from the edge (fig. 12).

Stitch the centre of one eye to one white (fig. 13). Repeat with the other eye. Arrange the eyes and mouth on the face and sew in position as illustrated. Embroider eyebrows and nostrils and then "stars" for cheeks.

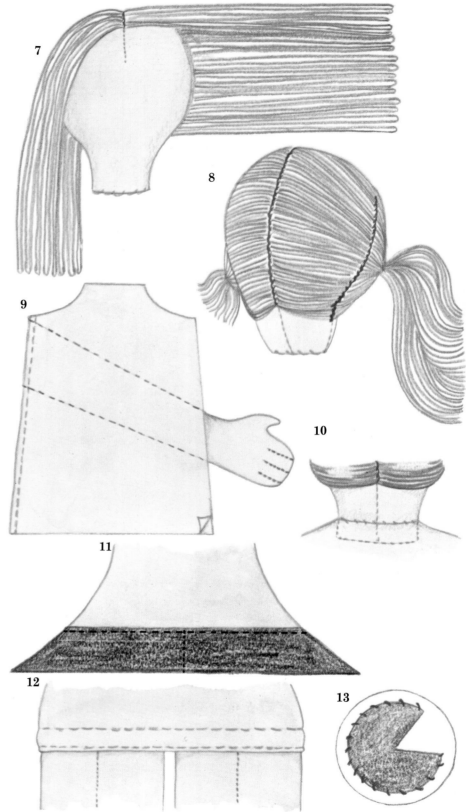

7. *Backstitching for hair starts 1in below seamline.*
8. *Backstitching on side seam.*
9. *Arm stitched in between two body pieces.*
10. *Body overcast firmly to head.*
11. *Shoe top stitched to leg 3mm ($\frac{1}{8}$in) from the edge.*
12. *Legs inserted into body.*
13. *Assembling the eye.*

Rag doll wardrobe

Tools needed
Basic sewing tools.
Techniques involved
Basic sewing; making doll's clothes.

Materials
tracing paper for patterns
90cm × 50cm (35in × 20in) of printed
cotton fabric for dress

50cm of 5cm (2in) wide lace for
sleeves
20cm (8in) of 1cm (⅜in) wide lace for
neck

3 small buttons or press studs
90cm (35in) of 6mm (¼in) wide
  elastic for sleeves and for waist of
  petticoat and panties
90cm × 40cm (35in × 15¾in) of white
  cotton lawn for petticoat and
  panties
1.15m (1¼yd) of 5cm (2in) wide
  broderie anglaise, insertion and
  edging combined (approximately
  1.5cm (⅝in) wide insertion and
  3.5cm (1⅜in) wide edging)
matching thread.

To make the dress

Trace off the patterns for the bodice and sleeves from the patterns given. Seam allowances of 6mm (¼in) are included.

Using printed cotton, cut a piece 74cm × 27cm (29in × 10½in) for the skirt, next cut out the two sleeves, two bodice back pieces and then one bodice front on the fold.

With right sides facing, tack and stitch the front and back bodice together at the shoulders.

Run a gathering thread along the top of each sleeve 6mm (¼in) from the raw edge. Pin the sleeves to the armholes and bodice, with right sides together and matching the shoulder seams to the centre top of each sleeve. Pull up the gathers to fit. Tack and stitch.

Turn in 3mm (⅛in) and then 1.5cm (⅝in) on the bottom of each sleeve to the wrong side. Tack and stitch close to the edge of the first fold.

Cut two pieces of 5cm (2in) wide lace to fit the bottom edges of the sleeves and topstitch in place along the extreme edge of each sleeve.

Cut two pieces of elastic 11.5cm (4½in) long and thread through the casings you have just made and secure the ends.

With right sides together and matching at all points, tack and stitch the raw edges of the lace, sleeve seam and bodice side seam in one operation (fig. 1). Trim the seams to 6mm (¼in) and neaten with pinking sheers. Repeat with the other side.

Stitch the two short edges of skirt piece together, right sides facing, to within 10cm (4in) of one long edge (waist edge). Mark the side and centre front of the top of the skirt with single tailor's tacks or pins.

Run a gathering thread along the top edge of the skirt 1cm (⅜in) from the edge. Pin the skirt to the bodice,

right sides facing, and pull up the gathers to fit. Tack and stitch.

Press the seam up on to the bodice. Turn in 3mm (⅛in) and then 6mm (¼in) on either side of the back opening to the wrong side. Tack and stitch close to the first fold.

Cut a 2.5cm (1in) wide bias strip in printed cotton to fit the neck, plus a little extra for seams.

With the right side of the binding to the wrong side of the bodice, tack and stitch the strip to the neck edge. Trim the seam allowance to 6mm (¼in).

Trim the raw ends to 6mm (¼in) and turn to the wrong side of the bias strip. Turn the bias on to the right side of the bodice. Turn under 6mm (¼in), tack and topstitch close to the lower edge of the bias. Slipstitch the ends.

Slipstitch the 1cm (⅜in) wide lace around the neck on the stitching line, turning in and neatening the ends.

Sew buttons to the left side of the bodice back and make buttonholes

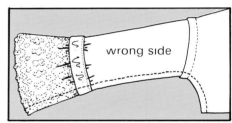

1. Lace, sleeve seam, and bodice side seam stitched in one operation.

in the other side to correspond. Alternatively, attach press studs.

Turn 3mm (⅛in) and then 1.5cm (⅝in) to the wrong side at the lower edge of the dress and slipstitch the hem.

To make the petticoat

Cut a strip of white lawn 74cm × 24cm (29in × 9½in).

For the bottom edge of the petticoat, turn 1cm (⅜in) on one long edge to the right side and press.

Cut a piece of broderie anglaise 74cm (29in) long, and pin it to the bottom of the petticoat on the right side. The lower edge of the insertion

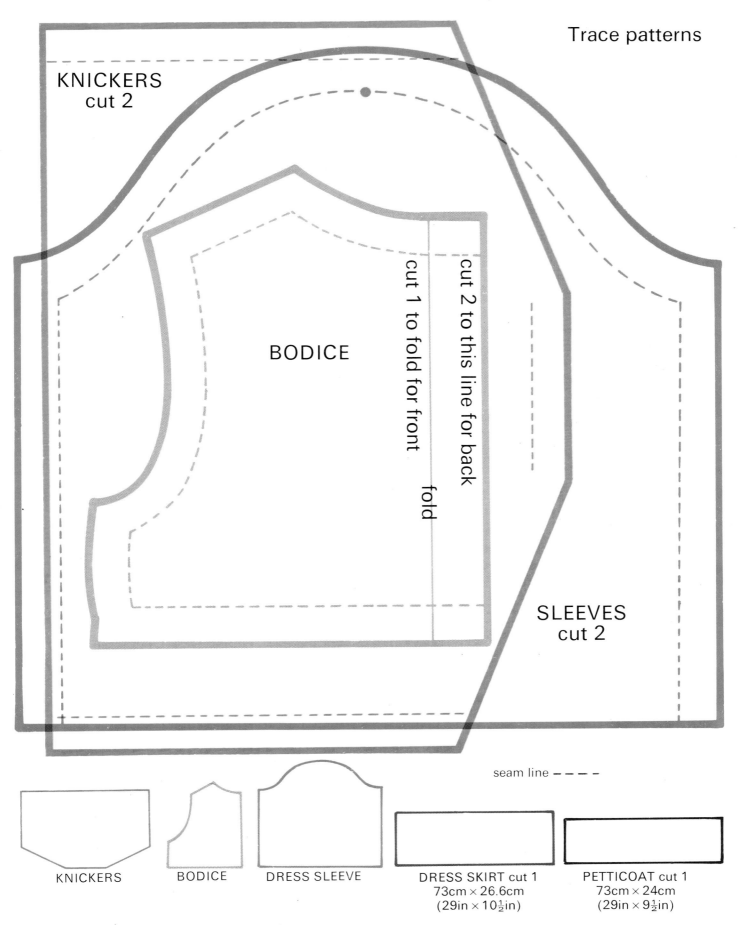

Trace patterns

KNICKERS
cut 2

BODICE

cut 1 to fold for front

cut 2 to this line for back

fold

SLEEVES
cut 2

seam line – – – –

KNICKERS

BODICE

DRESS SLEEVE

DRESS SKIRT cut 1
73cm × 26.6cm
(29in × 10½in)

PETTICOAT cut 1
73cm × 24cm
(29in × 9½in)

49

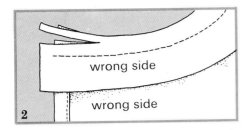

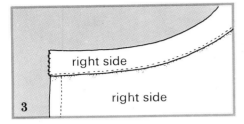

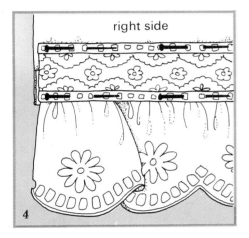

2. *Trimming bias strips and neck edge.*
3. *Bias turned to right side of bodice, ¼in turned under and lower edge topstitched.*
4. *Eyelet lace pinned to right side of petticoat bottom.*

For a crisp country look, make the outfit in gingham check and add a matching sash and ribbon.

should be just above the folded edge of the petticoat.

Tack and stitch along both edges of the insertion to enclose the raw edge of the petticoat.

With right sides facing, tack and stitch the seam and broderie anglaise in one operation. Neaten seams.

On the waist edge turn 3mm (⅛in) and then 1.3cm (½in) to the wrong side. Tack and stitch close to the first fold, leaving a 2.5cm (1in) opening for inserting the elastic.

Cut a length of elastic to fit the doll's waist, thread it through the casing and oversew the ends securely. Slipstitch the opening.

To make the panties

Using the pattern given, trace the pattern for the panties and cut two pieces in lawn on the straight grain of the fabric.

Cut a piece of broderie anglaise to fit each leg edge, including the seams (four pieces in all).

Turn 6mm (¼in) on one leg edge to the right side and press. Attach one of the pieces of broderie anglaise to cover the raw edge as for the bottom of the petticoat. Repeat with the three other leg edges.

With right sides facing, tack and stitch the side seams, stitching the short ends of the broderie anglaise in the same operation. Neaten seams.

With right sides together, tack and stitch the crotch seam and broderie anglaise. Trim seams to 6mm

(¼in) and neaten.

Following the instructions for the petticoat, make the casing and insert elastic at the top of the panties to fit the doll's waist. Turn the finished panties through to the right side.

Adapting the wardrobe

This rag doll wardrobe can supply you with quite a range of alternative doll's clothes if you adapt the patterns imaginatively. First, different fabrics can give a whole new look. We show a richly coloured Victorian type fabric, and a contrasting gingham.

Topsy turvy doll

Finished height
48cm (19in).
Tools required
Basic sewing tools; sewing machine.

Techniques involved
Basic sewing; machine stitching; filling soft toys; embroidery stitches; making doll's clothes.

Materials
Tracing paper for patterns dressmaker's carbon paper 90cm × 40cm (35in × 15¾in) of pale

pink cotton fabric for body
90cm × 50cm (35in × 19¾in) of floral printed cotton/wool mixture fabric for sad doll's dress
90cm × 50cm (35in × 19¾in) of plain cotton/wool mixture fabric for happy doll's dress
112cm × 35cm (44in × 13¾in) of cream cotton fabric for petticoat and apron
1m (1yd) of 1cm (⅜in) wide pale pink and pale green velvet ribbons
1m (1yd) of 1cm (⅜in) wide cream satin ribbon
1m (1yd) of 1cm wide lace edging
2m (2¼yd) of 3cm (1⅛in) wide lace edging
1 ball of red-brown bouclé wool
1 ball of pale brown mohair wool
30cm (12in) of 1cm (⅜in) white tape
matching threads
stranded embroidery thread in white, black, dusky pink, dark pink, red-brown and moss green
kapok or synthetic filling
3 small pearl buttons
small bunch of pink fabric flowers.

The body and heads

Using the patterns given, trace off the pattern pieces for the body and hands, and mark these patterns on the wrong side of the appropriate fabrics, with dressmaker's carbon paper. Seam allowances of 1cm (⅜in) are included throughout. Cut out all the pieces.

Trace off the features given for the sad face and for the happy face.

Take one body piece and matching the features marked on the body pattern, mark the features for the sad face at one end and the features for happy face at opposite end.

Using three strands of embroidery thread, embroider both the faces. Work the lips, tear drops, pupils and irises in satin stitch. Work the lines of the cheeks, the nostrils, eye outlines and lashes in back stitch, and the eyebrows in split stitch. Use French knots for the base of the nostrils and eye sparkles. Follow the feature patterns for the colours. Press both faces on the wrong side.

Match the body piece with features to the plain body piece, right sides facing. Pin, tack and stitch round the body, leaving an opening in one side. Clip into the seam allowance all round (fig. 1). Turn the body right side out and stuff firmly, pushing the filling down with a pencil if

1. *Doll body stitched at sides.*
2. *Hand sewn together at wrist.*
3. *Bouclé yarn stitched to tape.*
4. *Hair in position on doll's head.*
5. *Hair tied into bunches.*
6. *Lace stitched to hem of petticoat.*
7. *Petticoat gathered to fit waist.*

necessary. Turn in the edges of the opening. Slipstitch together.

Place hands with right sides together in pairs. Pin, tack and stitch around each pair, leaving the wrist edges open. Clip into the curves all round. Turn each of the four hands right side out, and stuff each firmly, pushing down the filling with a pencil or knitting needle if necessary. Pin, tack and stitch across each hand at the wrist (fig. 2).

For the hair for both heads, make up using the following instructions: sad doll, red-brown wool bouclé; happy doll, brown mohair-type.

Cut the length of white tape in half, then cut the wool you are using into pieces 45cm (17¾in) long. Lay these pieces side by side and at their centre point across the tape, leaving 6mm (¼in) of the tape free at each end. Pin, tack and stitch the wool to the tape, using a zigzag stitch. Make the wool thick enough to form a solid covering on the head (fig. 3).

Place the hair in position on the appropriate head, with the zigzag stitching forming the centre parting. Tuck under the raw ends of the tape to neaten. Back stitch the hair to the head by hand, sewing down the centre parting (fig. 4).

Cut the satin ribbon into four equal pieces, using two for each head. Form a bunch of hair at each side. Tie one of the lengths of ribbon round each bunch in a neat bow. Sew the bunches to the sides of the head and stitch a few of the flowers to each bow (fig. 5).

Both sets of doll's clothes

Petticoat
Cut a piece of the cream cotton fabric 80cm × 32cm (31½in × 12½in). Turn under a tiny hem along one long edge, and pin, tack and stitch in place by hand.

Cut a piece of 3cm (1⅛in) wide lace edging 130cm (51¼in) long, and run a line of gathering stitches along its straight edge. Pull up the gathers to fit the hemmed edge of the petticoat. Pin and tack the lace to the wrong side of the petticoat over the hem edge. Sew in place using a zigzag stitch (fig. 6).

Fold the petticoat in half widthways, matching edges. Pin, tack and stitch the side edges together with a French seam.

Run a line of gathering stitches

around the top edge of the petticoat. Fit the petticoat round the waist edge of the doll with the wrong side over the happy face and the seam to the centre back. Pull up the gathering stitches to fit the waist and fasten off securely (fig. 7).

Apron
Trace off the pattern piece for the apron from the pattern given and cut out in cream cotton fabric. Trace the flower motif from the pattern given and using dressmaker's carbon paper, mark the motif on the right-

53

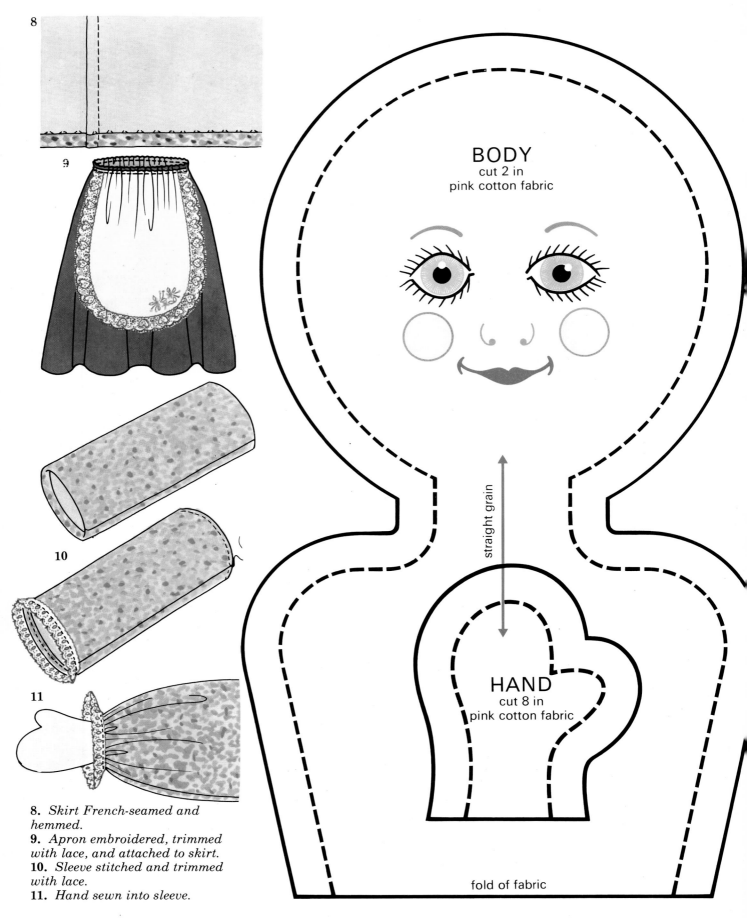

8. Skirt French-seamed and hemmed.
9. Apron embroidered, trimmed with lace, and attached to skirt.
10. Sleeve stitched and trimmed with lace.
11. Hand sewn into sleeve.

BODY
cut 2 in
pink cotton fabric

straight grain

HAND
cut 8 in
pink cotton fabric

fold of fabric

Trace patterns

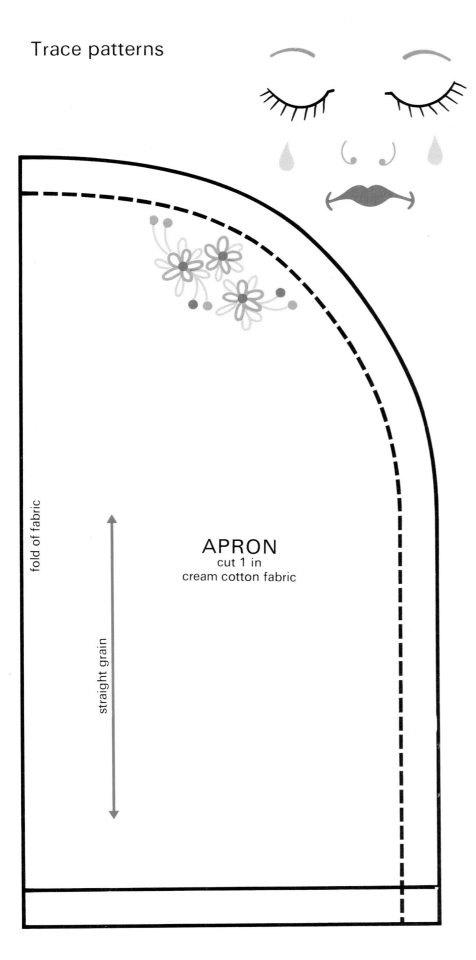

APRON
cut 1 in
cream cotton fabric

fold of fabric

straight grain

hand side of the apron.

Using three strands of pink and green embroidery thread, work flowers and leaves in chain stitch, back stitch and French knots.

Skirts

From the following instructions make two skirts in the same way, using patterned fabric for the sad half of the doll and plain fabric for the happy half of the doll. Start with the patterned skirt for the sad doll.

Cut one piece of fabric 80cm × 30cm (31½in × 11¾in). Turn under a tiny hem along one long edge and pin, tack and stitch in place by hand.

Fold the skirt in half widthwise, wrong sides facing and matching the edges. Pin, tack and stitch together with a French seam (fig. 8).

Run a line of gathering stitches along the top edge. Place the skirt over the doll with the right side up on the sad doll over the petticoat and with the seam to the centre back. Draw up the gathering stitches to fit the waist and fasten off.

Now make up the skirt in plain fabric for the happy doll, then place the apron on the centre of the skirt, matching the top edges. Work a line of gathering stitches round the top edge of the skirt, catching in the top edge of the apron (fig. 9). Place the skirt and apron over the doll with the right side upon the happy side. Draw up the gathering stitches to fit.

Bodices

Cut out two pieces of fabric, each 15cm (6in) square, for sleeves. Fold each sleeve in half, right sides facing, and pin, tack and stitch the side seams. Turn the sleeves right side out (fig. 10).

Turn under 1cm (⅜in) at one end of each sleeve and pin, tack and stitch in place. Cut two pieces of narrow lace edging each 15cm (6in) long. With right sides facing, pin, tack and stitch each piece of lace into a ring. Pin, tack and stitch the lace edging round the hem edge of each sleeve with a gathering thread (fig. 11).

Slip a hand inside the lace-edged end of each sleeve. Pull up the gathering stitches tight and fasten.

Cut a piece of the dress fabric 25cm × 20cm (9⅞in × 7⅞in) and fold in half lengthwise, right sides together and edges matching. Cut a narrow

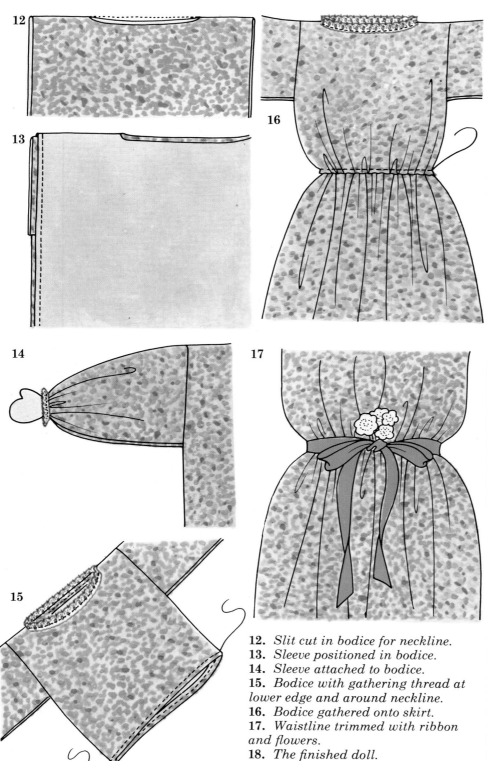

12. *Slit cut in bodice for neckline.*
13. *Sleeve positioned in bodice.*
14. *Sleeve attached to bodice.*
15. *Bodice with gathering thread at lower edge and around neckline.*
16. *Bodice gathered onto skirt.*
17. *Waistline trimmed with ribbon and flowers.*
18. *The finished doll.*

slit along the fold edge for the neck opening, large enough to push the head through (fig. 12).

Place the sleeves inside the bodice, with the tops of the sleeves matching the top of the bodice at the sides. Pin, tack and stitch the side seams, catching in the sleeves (fig. 13). Trim the seams and turn right side out (fig. 14).

Turn under 1cm (⅜in) at the neck edge of the bodice. Cut a length of narrow lace edging to fit the neck edge, plus seam allowance. With right sides facing, pin, tack and stitch the short edges of the lace. Place the lace edging to the right side of the neck hem, and pin, tack

and stitch round the neck edge with a gathering thread (fig. 15).

Place the bodice on the sad end of the doll, pull up the gathering thread to fit the doll's waist so that it covers the raw upper edge of the skirt. Fasten off the thread securely, (fig. 16). Draw up the gathering threads round the neck to fit, and fasten off. Repeat for happy doll.

Finishing touches

For the sad doll pin, tack and stitch the green velvet ribbon around the waist of the dress and tie into a bow in the front at the centre. Tuck some flowers into the ribbon at the waist and secure with a few stitches. Sew a few flowers to the right hand.

For the happy doll, sew three buttons down the centre front of the bodice, spacing them at equal intervals with the first button 2cm (⅞in) down from the neck edge. Pin, tack and stitch the pink velvet ribbon around the waist of the plain bodice and tie into a bow at centre front.

Jenny and Joey

Finished height
24cm (9½in).
Tools required
Basic sewing tools; sewing machine;
pinking shears; large-eyed needle.

Techniques involved
Basic sewing;
machine stitching;
making doll's clothes.

Materials
For Jenny:
tracing paper for patterns
dressmaker's carbon paper
1 man's white cotton sock size 9–11

26cm × 16cm (10¼in × 6¼in) of white
cotton fabric
40cm × 29cm (15¾in × 11½in) of
blue/white spotted cotton fabric
22cm (8¾in) of 5mm (¼in) wide lace
22cm (8¾in) of 7.5cm (3in) wide
scalloped broderie anglaise
36cm (14¼in) of 8mm (⅜in) wide
white tape
11cm × 2cm (4⅜in × ¾in) of white felt
14cm × 5cm (5½in × 2in) of red felt
25cm (9¾in) of 5mm (¼in) wide red
ribbon
1 red button 8mm (⅜in) in diameter
gold coloured bouclé wool for hair
matching threads
kapok or synthetic filling
felt-tipped pens and lipstick

For Joey:
tracing paper for patterns
dressmaker's carbon paper
1 man's white cotton sock size 9–11
21cm × 15cm (8¼in × 6in) of
blue/white gingham fabric
36cm × 15cm (14¼in × 6in) of denim
fabric
14cm × 5cm (5½in × 2in) of yellow felt
14cm (5½in) square of red/white
spotted cotton fabric
20.5cm (8in) long green plan stick
3mm (⅛in) in diameter
4 yellow buttons 8mm (⅜in) in
diameter
brown bouclé wool for hair
13cm × 2cm (5⅛in × ¾in) of iron-on
interfacing
matching and contrasting threads
kapok or synthetic filling
felt-tipped pens and lipstick

To make Jenny's body

Seam allowances of 6mm (¼in) are
included throughout.

Cut the toe off the sock across the
instep (fig. 1) and fold the sock so
that the back of the heel is on the top
– this will be the face.

Cut up through the middle of the
sock from the ankle for about 10cm
(4in) to make the legs. Turn the sock
wrong side out. Pin, tack and stitch
round the slit to form the legs (fig. 2).
Trim near to the stitching line and
turn the body right side out.

Stuff the legs, being careful not to
overfill as the fabric is easily stret-
ched out of shape. Pin, tack and
stitch across the tops of the legs.

Fill the rest of the body up to the
neck and wind a length of thread
around the neck and fasten off
securely (fig. 3).

Fill the head, again being careful

not to pack in too much stuffing, so
that the head will be the correct
shape. Turn in the open edges of the
head and slipstitch together.

For the arms, use the toe part of
the sock, Cut this in half lengthwise,
turning each part wrong side out
(fig. 4). Pin, tack and stitch round
each part to form an arm, leaving an
opening. Turn the arms right side
out.

Fill each arm, using the same
procedure as for the legs, and leave
the top of each arm flat. Turn in the
opening edges and slipstitch together to close (fig. 5). Stitch an arm to
each side of the body.

To make Jenny's clothes

Trace off the pattern pieces for the
clothes from the patterns given, positioning the centre of the dress on
the fold of the paper. Mark the
pattern pieces of the wrong side of
the appropriate fabrics the number
of times stated. Seam allowances of
6mm (¼in) have been included
throughout. Cut out all the fabric
pieces, then cut out the shoe soles
and uppers in felt.

Turn back a tiny hem on the base
edges of each pantaloon leg, then
pin, tack and stitch a length of
narrow lace to fit these edges on
each leg, matching the right side of
lace to right side of fabric (fig. 6).

Place the two pantaloon pieces
with right sides together, and pin,
tack and stitch the side and leg
seams, catching in the lace. Turn the
pantaloons right side out.

Make a 3mm (⅛in) double hem at
the waist edge of the pantaloons,
then pin, tack and stitch a row of
gathering stitches round this hem
(fig. 7). Slip the pantaloons over the
doll, pull up the gathering thread to
fit the waist and fasten off securely.

Run a line of gathering stitches
round the base edge of each pantaloon leg. Draw up the gathering
stitches to fit each leg and fasten off.

For the dress, fold the dress piece
in half, right sides facing, at the
shoulder. Pin, tack and stitch the
side and underarm seams (fig. 8).

Make a double 3mm (⅛in) hem at
each wrist, then pin, tack and stitch
around each of these hems. Repeat
procedure for hem at neck edge.

Make a double 6mm (¼in) hem
round the lower edge of the dress
and pin, tack and sew in place using

a zigzag stitch (fig. 9).

Put the dress on the doll. Pull up
the gathering thread around the
neck and fasten off securely. Pull up
the gathering stitches round each
wrist and fasten off securely.

Place the collar round the neck
over the dress with the collar ends
meeting at the front. Sew in position.
Stitch the button at the neck (fig. 10).

For the apron, run a line of gathering stitches along the straight long
edge of the broderie anglaise. Pull
up the gathering to measure 10.5cm
(4⅛in) and fasten off. Turn in a 6mm
(¼in) double hem at each side, then
pin, tack and sew the hem (fig 11).

Fold the apron waistband in half
lengthwise, with the edges matching
and the wrong side inside. Position
over the gathered edge of the apron
with the long edges of the band
turned in, so that all the raw edges
are hidden inside the waistband.
Pin, tack and stitch in place (fig. 12).

Cut the length of white tape in
half and tuck the ends of the tape
into each end of the waistband as
apron strings (fig. 12). Pin, tack and
stitch in place. Tie the apron round
the doll.

To make the shoes, fold one shoe
upper in half and pin, tack and
stitch the back seam (fig. 13). Match
the shoe sole to the lower edge of
the shoe upper and blanket stitch
the seam. Repeat for second shoe.

Push the feet into the shoes,
adding a little more filling in the
toes of the shoes. Stitch the shoes in
place on the feet.

For the hair, cut enough 22cm
(8¾in) lengths of wool to cover the
head. Lay the wool pieces side by
side and stitch a line down the
centre to form a parting (fig. 14).
Place the hair across the head,
slightly in front of the sides, and
hand sew to the head along the
centre parting. Cut the red ribbon in
half and tie the hair in bunches at
each side of the head with neat bows
(fig. 15).

For the features, draw the nose,
eyes and mouth with felt-tipped pens
and colour the cheeks with lipstick.

To make Joey

Follow the instructions for Jenny's
body for the basic shape.

Trace off the pattern pieces for
the clothes from the patterns given.
Mark the pattern pieces on the

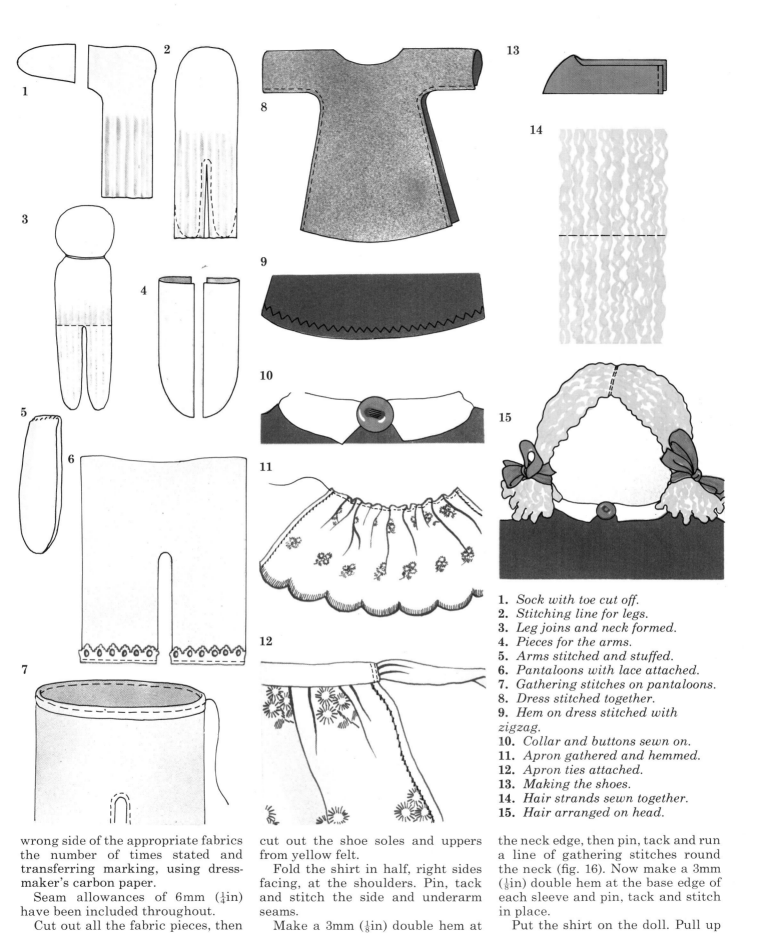

1. Sock with toe cut off.
2. Stitching line for legs.
3. Leg joins and neck formed.
4. Pieces for the arms.
5. Arms stitched and stuffed.
6. Pantaloons with lace attached.
7. Gathering stitches on pantaloons.
8. Dress stitched together.
9. Hem on dress stitched with zigzag.
10. Collar and buttons sewn on.
11. Apron gathered and hemmed.
12. Apron ties attached.
13. Making the shoes.
14. Hair strands sewn together.
15. Hair arranged on head.

wrong side of the appropriate fabrics the number of times stated and transferring marking, using dressmaker's carbon paper.

Seam allowances of 6mm ($\frac{1}{4}$in) have been included throughout.

Cut out all the fabric pieces, then cut out the shoe soles and uppers from yellow felt.

Fold the shirt in half, right sides facing, at the shoulders. Pin, tack and stitch the side and underarm seams.

Make a 3mm ($\frac{1}{8}$in) double hem at the neck edge, then pin, tack and run a line of gathering stitches round the neck (fig. 16). Now make a 3mm ($\frac{1}{8}$in) double hem at the base edge of each sleeve and pin, tack and stitch in place.

Put the shirt on the doll. Pull up

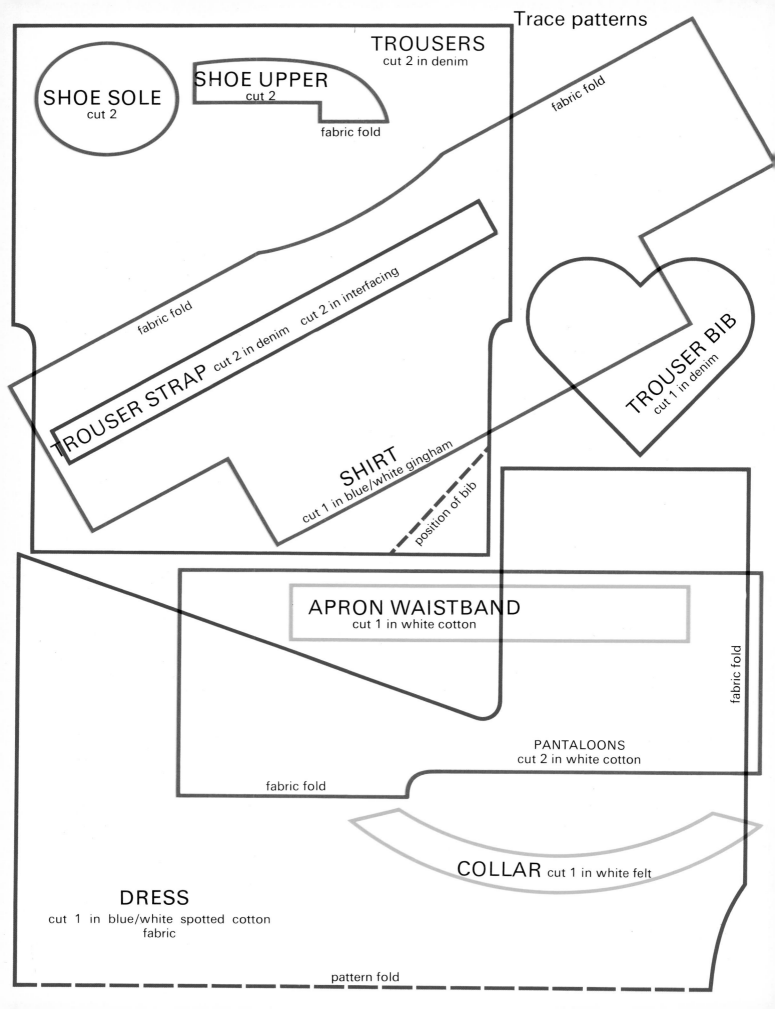

Trace patterns

TROUSERS
cut 2 in denim

SHOE UPPER
cut 2

SHOE SOLE
cut 2

fabric fold

fabric fold

fabric fold

TROUSER STRAP cut 2 in denim cut 2 in interfacing

TROUSER BIB
cut 1 in denim

SHIRT
cut 1 in blue/white gingham

position of bib

APRON WAISTBAND
cut 1 in white cotton

fabric fold

PANTALOONS
cut 2 in white cotton

fabric fold

COLLAR cut 1 in white felt

DRESS
cut 1 in blue/white spotted cotton
fabric

pattern fold

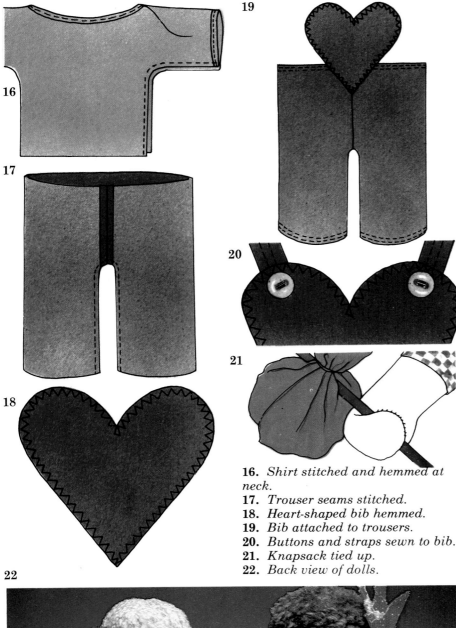

16. *Shirt stitched and hemmed at neck.*
17. *Trouser seams stitched.*
18. *Heart-shaped bib hemmed.*
19. *Bib attached to trousers.*
20. *Buttons and straps sewn to bib.*
21. *Knapsack tied up.*
22. *Back view of dolls.*

the gathering thread around the neck and fasten off securely.

For the trousers, place the trouser pieces with right sides together. Pin, tack and stitch the back and front seams. Fold the trousers with seams matching at the centre. Pin, tack and stitch the inner leg seams (fig. 17).

Make a 3mm ($\frac{1}{8}$in) double hem at the top edge of the trousers, then pin, tack and topstitch in place using contrasting coloured thread.

Using contrasting thread, sew all round the edge of the heart-shaped bib with zigzag stitch (fig. 18). Pin, tack and stitch the bib over the top edge of trousers.

Make a 3mm ($\frac{1}{8}$in) double hem at the lower edge of each trouser leg. Pin, tack and topstitch in place with two rows of stitching, using contrasting coloured thread (fig. 19).

Position the interfacing with the shiny side to the wrong side of each trouser strap, then iron in place. Topstitch lengthwise down centre of straps with contrasting thread.

Tuck one end of each strap under the top edge of the heart-shaped bib. Sew the two buttons to the bib where the straps meet, so as to hold the straps in position (fig. 20). Put the trousers on the doll. Take the straps over the shoulders, cross over at the back and fasten behind the trousers with two buttons, as before.

For the shoes, follow the sewing and fitting instructions given for Jenny on page 58.

To make the hair, sew small loops of the single-thickness wool all over the head, using a sharp, large-eyed needle and knotting the wool at every stitch so that the hair will not come undone. Once the head is covered, cut through all the loops and trim if necessary. For the features, follow the instructions given for Jenny's features on page 58.

To make the bundle, pink round the edge of the spotted fabric with pinking shears. Place some filling on the wrong side of the fabric in the centre. Take up the four corners and bunch them together, then wind a length of matching thread round the bunch and fasten off securely.

Cut a small hole through the bundle, just under the binding thread. Push the green stick through the hole. Sew the bundle firmly to one hand, turning the 'fingers' round the stick (fig. 21).

Wool doll

Finished height
35.5cm (14in).
Techniques involved
Basic sewing.
Tools required
Basic sewing tools.
Materials
2 × 50gm (2oz) balls of double
  knitting yarn in a natural shade
1 × 50gm (2oz) ball mohair-type
  brown yarn for hair
hollow plastic ball, about 18cm (7in)
  in circumference
scraps of red felt
scraps of non-woven interfacing
fabric adhesive
25.5cm (10in) of 12mm (½in) wide
  ribbon
felt-tip pens in brown and black.

To make the doll

Cut two 25.5cm (10in) lengths of
main colour yarn for binding the
arms.

Make a skein, 40.5cm (16in) long
and 100 strands thick. Cut the skein
at each end and bind it with one of
the lengths of yarn, about 2.5cm
(1in) from one end.

Plait the skein to make arms and
bind the other end.

Cut five 25.5cm (10in) lengths of
yarn for binding the body and legs.
Make a skein 101.5cm (40in) long
and 150 strands thick, cut the skein
at each end and bind it firmly in
the middle. Lay the arms across
the middle of the skein, fold the
skein over them and then bind it
firmly just below the arms to hold
them in place.

Bind the skein again about 5cm
(2in) further down to make the hips.
From this point, divide the skein in
half and plait each half to make the
legs. Bind each leg firmly at each
end. Trim the ends of the arms and
legs into a neat shape.

Cover the plastic ball with fabric
adhesive, leaving a small space at
the top and bottom so you can hold it
between your thumb and forefinger.

Wind the yarn round and round
the ball taking care that all the
strands go in the same direction and
cross each other at the top and
bottom. When the ball is completely
covered, darn in the loose end of the

yarn to neaten it. Leave the head to
dry.

Thread a darning needle with yarn
and sew head to body.

Using non-woven interfacing, cut
two eye shapes and colour them
carefully as shown using felt-tip
pens.

Cut the mouth shape from red felt.
Stick this and the eyes on to the
head.

Use felt-tip pens to make the eyebrows, two dots for the nose and
eyelashes.

For hair, cut 80 35.5cm (14in)
lengths of mohair-type yarn and 20
7.5cm (3in) lengths for the fringe.

Stitch the fringe first. Taking four
strands at a time, fold in half and
sew on to the head. For the remainder of the hair, once again

taking four strands at a time, stitch
them down centre of head to make
centre parting. Sew the grouped
strands closely together so that the
head does not show through.

When all the hair has been sewn,
tie into bunches as shown. The back
strands will be too long when the
bunches are tied. Trim them evenly.

Cut ribbon into two lengths and
tie the bunches with bows.

Patterns for dolls' clothes

Drawing patterns

Pattern shapes are based on the doll's torso, so it is necessary to draw a template as a guide for making the pattern pieces. Divide the torso pattern piece in half lengthways and trace around it on to a piece of cardboard. Do not add seam allowances. Fig. 1 shows the measurements of depth and width to be taken (half the width of the torso pattern).

If you are making patterns for a purchased doll, trace round the doll's torso and then take the measurements as before. Many dolls have plumper figures than the shape shown, in this case it is better to make dresses without fitted waists, taking a measurement just below the arm holes for a dress with a yoke. With the template completed you can begin pattern designing.

Pin a piece of tracing paper over the template and on it sketch the shape of the desired garment. Keep in mind where the pattern can be placed on a fabric fold and where seams and facings will be. Remember to add seam allowances to the pattern pieces. Also allow a little room for ease when dressing the doll. Most dolls have fairly large heads, so when shaping neck openings allow for this.

A petticoat pattern is shown in fig. 2. This has been drawn over the template. Underwear such as panties and petticoats fit more closely than outerwear and therefore follow the shape of the body more distinctly. Note that the neckline of the petticoat falls roughly half-way between the bottom of the shoulder and the base of the armhole.

The diagrams on this page show how to measure and cut a cardboard template as a base for drawing up patterns for individual dolls.
1. How to work out the proportions of the template for your doll.
2. Making a slip pattern to fit over the completed template.
3. Making a basic bodice pattern over the completed template.

Patterns for smock-type dresses, pinafores and dresses with a fitted bodice and gathered or pleated skirt are made on the same principle. Figs. 3 and 4 show respectively a bodice pattern and ways of varying the basic shape. Necklines can be round, square or V-shaped.

To determine fabric requirements for a dress with gathers at either the waistline or on to a yoke, double the width measurement to allow for enough fullness. For a pleated skirt the width will be three times the measurement you are fitting.

A gathered skirt can be made,

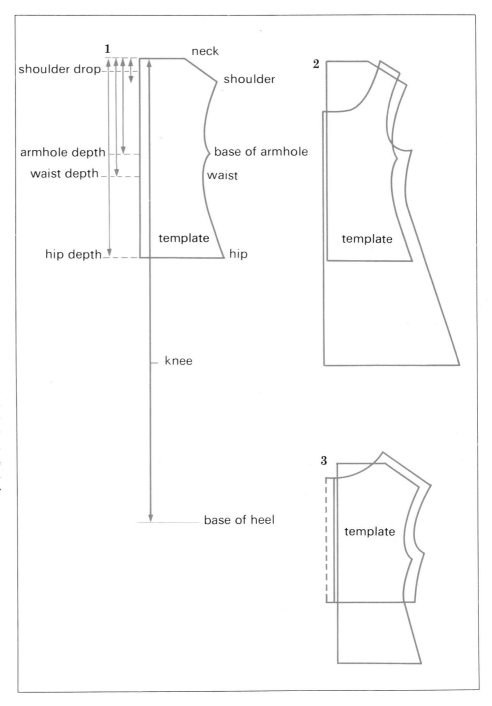

using two rectangles of fabric; their size determined by the desired finished length plus hem allowance, and double the waist measurement plus seam allowances. Gather the skirt on to a waistband or stitch a casing for elastic to be threaded through, in which case you must allow for a turning at the waist edge as well as at the hem. Elastic is probably the easiest way to finish a waist as it is simpler than buttons for a small child to manipulate.

Circular skirts are made by drawing a circle with a radius larger than the required finished length of the skirt. Cut out the circle, fold it evenly into four and trim off a quarter of the total waist measurement at the apex (fig. 5a). Unfold the circle and use as a pattern. Cut the waist opening on the straight grain, finishing with bias binding and a hook and eye fastening.

The pattern for a gored skirt is made in a similar way, but seam allowances are added to each gore (fig. 5b).

For shoes, use the doll's foot or foot pattern for drawing a template. Remember that shoes will fit over the foot, so allow an extra 6mm ($\frac{1}{4}$in) all round the sole pattern piece. If you wish to make boots, the width and length of the leg from the knee down must also be taken into consideration. It is best to use felt or soft leather scraps for footwear as these do not fray and you will not have to worry about hiding seams.

Although it is possible to make a blouse with set-in sleeves, you will probably find this a chore. Therefore try to incorporate the sleeves in the body of the blouse. Fig. 6 gives a shape for a blouse with full sleeves gathered at the wrist.

Don't throw pattern pieces away. Keep them stored with suitable scraps of leftover fabrics.

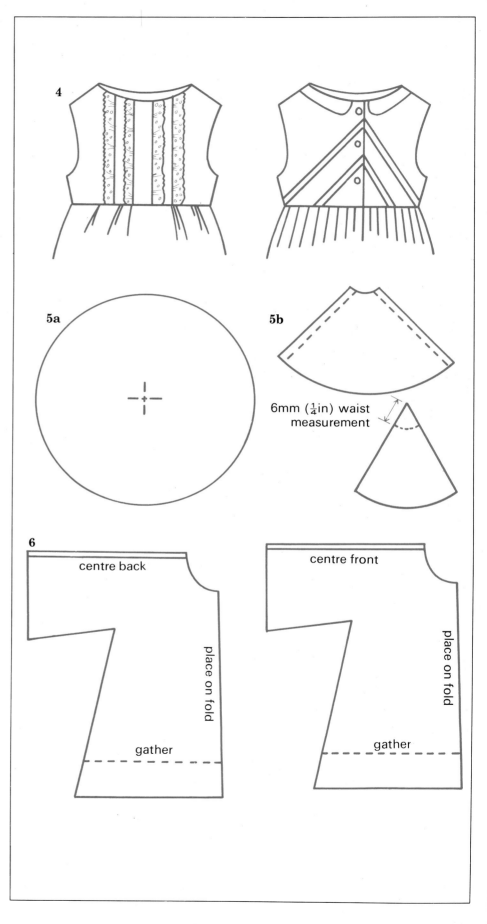

4. *Variations on the basic bodice.*
5a, b. *Making circular and gored skirts.*
6. *Pattern shape for a blouse with full sleeves gathered at the wrist.*

Doll's wardrobe

Finished size
The wardrobe is designed for a 35.5cm (14in) doll.

Tools required
Basic sewing tools.

Techniques involved
Drawing patterns from a graph; changing the size of a pattern; making doll's clothes.

Materials
For the petticoat and panties:
Squared paper for pattern
51cm × 30.5cm (20in × 12in) white cotton fabric
51cm (20in) of 4.5cm (1¾in) wide broderie anglaise frilling
scrap of narrower broderie anglaise frilling
30.5cm (12in) of 1cm (⅜in) wide lace white bias binding
10cm (4in) of 1cm (⅜in) wide ribbon sewing thread

For the skirt and blouse:
Squared paper for pattern
50cm (½yd) of 90cm (36in) wide cotton fabric
bias binding
round elastic
sewing thread

For the duffle coat:
Squared paper for pattern
90cm × 30.5cm (36in × 12in) of felt
4 tiny toggle buttons
sewing thread.

For the Wellington boots:
Squared paper for pattern
30.5cm × 20.5cm (12in × 8in) wet-look vinyl
10cm (4in) square black felt
cardboard
fabric adhesive
sewing thread

For the dressing gown:
Squared paper for pattern
50cm (½yd) of 90cm (36in) wide quilted fabric
3 tiny buttons
3 press fasteners
sewing thread

For the nightdress:
Squared paper for pattern
50cm (½yd) of 90cm (36in) wide seersucker fabric
51cm (20in) of 2.5cm (1in) wide trimming
2 rosebud trims
1 press fastener
sewing thread

Changing sizes
Before cutting out any of these doll's clothes, check that each pattern piece fits the doll and make any alterations necessary.

If a different size is needed, re-draw the graph patterns and adjust fabric quantities.

To make the petticoat and panties

Using squared paper, draw each pattern piece to scale and cut out.

Stitch all seams with right sides facing unless otherwise stated. 6mm (¼in) seam allowances are included.

Using white cotton fabric, cut out petticoat front and back, placing pattern on fold of fabric. Cut out panties, placing pattern on fold of fabric as indicated.

Turn under 6mm (¼in) along top edge of each petticoat piece and trim with narrow broderie anglaise frilling. Join side seams and bind armholes with bias binding. Turn under 6mm (¼in) hem and stitch on wider broderie anglaise frilling. Cut ribbon into two pieces and sew to front and back to form shoulder straps.

Bind legs of panties with bias binding. Join side seams. Make a 1cm (⅜in) casing along top edge, leaving one end open for elastic. Insert elastic, pull up to fit doll's waist and fasten. Stitch lace around each leg.

1. *A slip and matching panties can be made from fabric scraps with very little effort.*

To make the skirt and blouse

Using squared paper, draw each pattern piece to scale and cut out.

Stitch all seams with right sides facing unless otherwise stated. 6mm ($\frac{1}{4}$in) seam allowances are included.

For skirt frill, cut a 4cm ($1\frac{1}{2}$in) wide strip from each selvedge edge of fabric (using the selvedge in this way dispenses with a hem). For skirt cut a rectangle, 31.5cm × 12cm ($12\frac{1}{2}$in × $4\frac{3}{4}$in). Cut out two blouse fronts and one blouse back, placing pattern on fold. Cut out two blouse sleeves.

Join short edges of skirt piece for centre back seam. Press. Turn under 6mm ($\frac{1}{4}$in) along top edge to form casing for elastic, leaving opening to insert elastic. Join the two frill pieces to make a circle. Run a gathering thread around one long edge of frill. Pull up the gathers until the frill fits the skirt hem. Distribute the gathers evenly, pin and stitch frill to skirt. Trim join with bias binding. Insert elastic in waist casing and pull up to fit doll's waist, fasten off securely.

Join the centre front seam of blouse as far as notch marked on pattern. Turn in and hem edges above notch for front neck opening. Stitch sleeves between armhole seams of front and back. Clip seam allowances and press.

Run a line of gathering stitches all round neckline. Pull up gathers until neck measures about 16.5cm ($6\frac{3}{4}$in) or to fit neck of doll. Distribute gathers evenly and bind neck with bias binding, leaving 15cm (6in) at each end for ties. Stitch sleeve and side seams. Turn up and stitch hem of blouse and on either wrist edge, making casing for elastic at wrists. Insert elastic and fasten.

To make the duffle coat

Using squared paper, draw each pattern piece to scale and cut out.

Stitch all seams with right sides facing unless otherwise stated. 6mm ($\frac{1}{4}$in) seam allowances are included but no hems are needed.

Using felt, cut out two fronts, one back (placing pattern on fold), one

2. *Smart separates in printed cotton with contrasting trimming.*
3. *Snug duffle coat and boots.*

hood (placing pattern on fold), two sleeves, two pockets and two toggle flaps.

Stitch pockets to fronts in positions shown on pattern.

Stitch sleeves to armholes between front and back pieces. Stitch sleeve and underarm seams. Stitch seam line on top of hood, then, matching centres, stitch hood to neck line of coat. Stitch toggle flaps to right front so that half the flap overlaps the coat opening. Make a small slit in the overlap to form buttonhole. Sew on toggle buttons.

To make the Wellington boots

Using squared paper, draw pattern pieces to scale and cut out.

Cut out two boot uppers, placing pattern on fold of vinyl. Cut two soles from black felt. Cut two smaller soles from cardboard.

With right sides together, taking 6mm ($\frac{1}{4}$in) seam, stitch the seam in each upper. If you have a spear-point machine needle, use this, otherwise sew by hand with a darning needle.

Using fabric adhesive, stick each cardboard sole on to felt sole, leaving seam allowance all round. Leave to dry.

With right sides together, stitch soles to uppers. Turn to right side.

To make the dressing gown

Using squared paper, draw each pattern piece to scale and cut out.

Stitch all seams with right sides facing unless otherwise stated. 6mm ($\frac{1}{4}$in) seam allowances are included.

Using quilted fabric, cut out two fronts, one back, placing pattern on fold of fabric, two sleeves and one collar.

Join shoulder seams. Pin and stitch tops of sleeves into arm holes.

Turn under and stitch 6mm ($\frac{1}{4}$in) hem on curved edge of collar. Pin and stitch collar to neck opening, matching centre backs and ends of collar to notches on fronts. Overcast seam allowances together so that collar stands up.

Stitch side and sleeve seams.

Turn under front facings and hem in position. Turn up and stitch hems on sleeves and lower edge.

Sew buttons on to right side of dressing gown and stitch press fasteners underneath.

To make the nightdress

Using squared paper, draw each pattern piece to scale and cut out.

Stitch all seams with right sides facing, 6mm ($\frac{1}{4}$in) seam allowances are included. Note that the nightdress is made up of two layers.

Using seersucker, cut out four front and back pieces. Cut four yoke pieces.

Stitch side seams of two front and back pieces. Repeat to make second layer.

Join one shoulder seam of yoke. Repeat for second layer.

Slip one layer of nightie inside the other, wrong sides facing. Repeat for yoke.

Run a line of gathering stitches along top neck edge of front and back of nightdress. Pull up gathers until they fit between notches on front and back yoke.

Turn in seam allowances all round front and back yoke edges and tack. Sandwich back and front of nightdress in between layers of yoke and slipstitch in place. Slipstitch remaining yoke edges together. Turn in seam allowances on front and back

4. Luxurious quilted dressing gown and a pretty nightgown to go with it.

armhole edges and slipstitch together in the same way.

Make separate 1cm ($\frac{3}{8}$in) hems on both layers of nightdress and stitch. Stitch trimming to upper layer around hemline. Sew rosebud trims to yoke and fasten shoulders with press fastener.

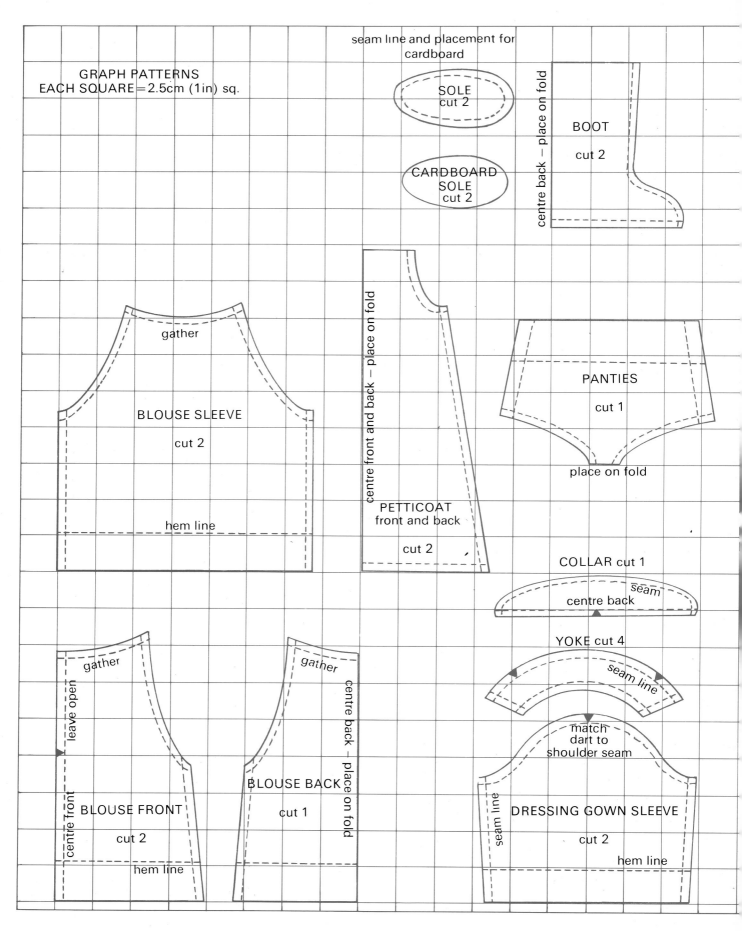

GRAPH PATTERNS
EACH SQUARE = 2.5cm (1in) sq.

seam line and placement for cardboard

SOLE
cut 2

CARDBOARD
SOLE
cut 2

centre back – place on fold

BOOT
cut 2

BLOUSE SLEEVE
cut 2

gather

hem line

centre front and back – place on fold

PETTICOAT
front and back
cut 2

PANTIES
cut 1

place on fold

COLLAR cut 1

seam
centre back

YOKE cut 4

seam line

leave open

gather

centre front

BLOUSE FRONT
cut 2

hem line

gather

centre back – place on fold

BLOUSE BACK
cut 1

match
dart to
shoulder seam

seam line

DRESSING GOWN SLEEVE
cut 2

hem line

68

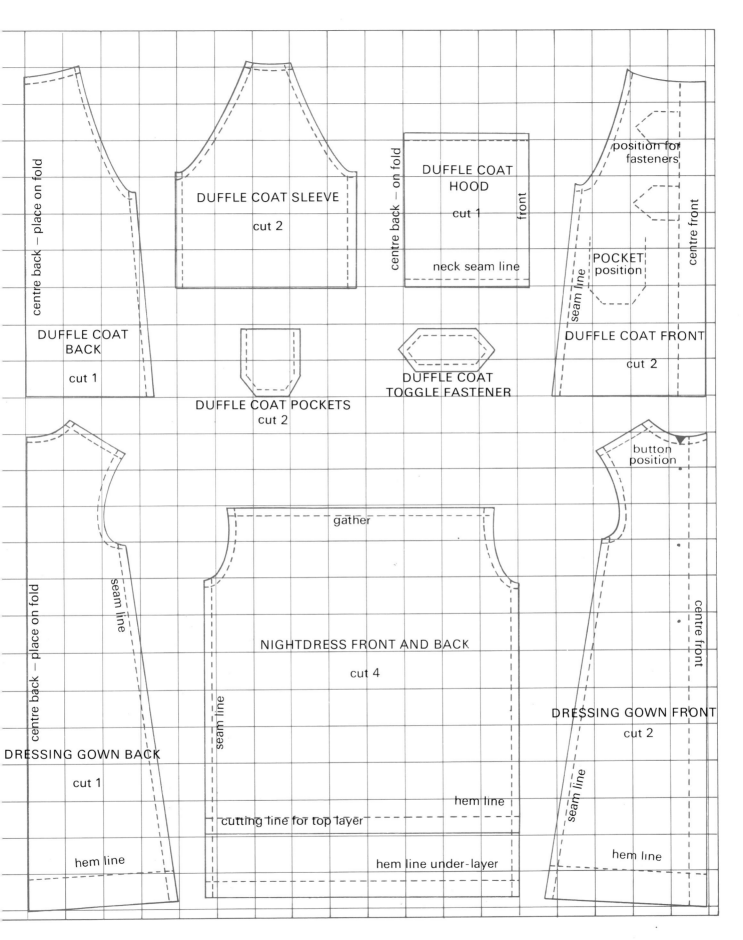

DUFFLE COAT SLEEVE

cut 2

DUFFLE COAT
HOOD

cut 1

front

neck seam line

centre back – on fold

position for
fasteners

centre front

POCKET
position

seam line

DUFFLE COAT FRONT

cut 2

centre back – place on fold

DUFFLE COAT
BACK

cut 1

DUFFLE COAT POCKETS
cut 2

DUFFLE COAT
TOGGLE FASTENER

seam line

button
position

gather

NIGHTDRESS FRONT AND BACK

cut 4

centre back – place on fold

DRESSING GOWN BACK

cut 1

hem line

seam line

seam line

cutting line for top layer

hem line

hem line under-layer

DRESSING GOWN FRONT

cut 2

seam line

centre front

hem line

Traditional teddy bear

Finished height
60cm (23½in).
Tools required
Basic sewing tools; round-nosed
pliers; darning needle.
Techniques involved
Basic sewing; filling soft toys; cutting and sewing fur fabric; inserting
safety eyes, 'growler' and joints;
embroidery stitches.
Materials
tracing paper for patterns

dressmaker's carbon paper for
   patterns
100cm × 122cm (39½in × 48in) of
   medium-brown fur fabric
34cm × 11cm (13¼in × 4⅜in) of leather
15cm (6in) square of this fabric
kapok or synthetic filling
matching threads
black stranded embroidery thread
4 × 3cm (1⅛in) joints
1 × 3.5cm (1⅜in) joint
A pair of 1.6cm (⅝in) diameter
   brown safety eyes
A 'growler' (these last four items
   are available from large stores).

To make bear

Trace off the pattern pieces given
and cut out. From fur fabric, cut out
two body pieces, four ears, four legs,
two inner arms, two outer arms, two
head pieces, and one head gusset on
the fold of the fabric. Make sure you
place the patterns in the right direction on the fur, and that you reverse
the fabric for reverse pieces.
Transfer markings from patterns.

From the leather, cut out two
paws and two foot soles.

Seam allowances of 1cm (⅜in) have
been included throughout.

Head

Place the head gusset between the
two head pieces, right sides facing,
positioning it between the nose and
the back of the neck and matching
points A and B. Pin, tack and stitch
in place, along both seams (fig. 1).
From point of nose (A) to neck edge,
pin, tack and stitch head together
(fig. 2). Run a gathering thread
around the neck edge, leaving
thread to be pulled up later (fig. 3).
Turn the head right side out.

Insert the safety eyes into the
head. Find the position where they
look most appealing, and fix in
place. Stuff the head firmly.

For the neck joint, take the largest joint and insert one disc with
cotter pin and washer inside the
neck opening of the filled head (fig.
4). Put the second washer of the joint
to one side. Pack filling all round the
disc, so that the disc cannot be felt
from outside. Pull up the gathering
thread round the neck and secure
firmly in place.

Using all six strands of the black
embroidery thread, embroider the
nose in satin stitch and the mouth in
back stitch, with the V-shaped nose
positioned at point A (fig. 5).

For each ear, place two ear pieces
right sides together, and pin, tack
and stitch around the curved edge,
leaving the bottom edge open (fig. 6).
Turn the ear right side out.

Turn in the lower edges of the ear.

Pin, tack and sew a line of gathering
stitches round the lower edge. Pull
the gathering thread up tight and
fasten off securely. Repeat the
procedure for the second ear.

Tack and stitch the ears firmly in
position.

Body and limbs

Place two body pieces together,
right sides facing. Pin, tack and
stitch round the body from one side
of the neck to the other, leaving a
6cm (2⅜in) opening in the bottom
(fig. 7). Turn the body right side out.

Turn in the neck edge and pin,
tack and run a gathering thread
around the neck. Pull up the gathering thread and fasten off securely.

Insert the cotter pin of the head
joint through the hole formed by the
gathering at the top of the body.
Push on the second disc and washer
from the inside of the body. Turn the
body upside down and place on head.
Using round-nosed pliers, bend the
cotter pin so that the head is held
securely.

Match the straight edge of one
leather paw to the straight edge of
one inner arm, right sides facing.
Pin, tack and stitch in place (fig. 8).

Match one inner arm to one outer
arm, right sides facing. Pin, tack and
stitch all round, leaving a 6cm (2⅜in)

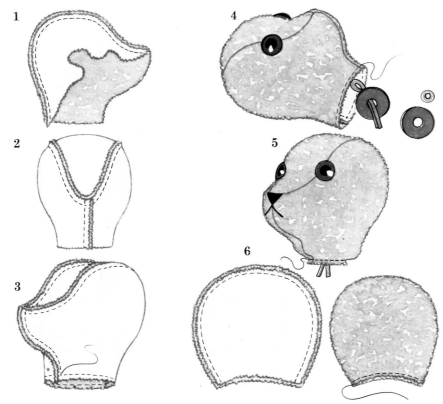
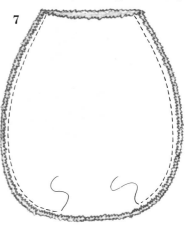

1. *Head gusset stitched to one side of head.*
2. *All head pieces stitched together.*
3. *Gathering stitches around neck.*
4. *Inserting disc and cotter pin in neck.*
5. *Features attached and embroidered on face.*
6. *Ear pieces stitched together.*
7. *Body pieces stitched together.*

71

opening at the top back (fig. 9).

Turn the arm right side out and fill to within 3.5cm (1⅜in) of the top, pushing down the stuffing.

To fix the arm joint in place, use one of the smaller joints and push one disc and cotter pin through the inner arm at the position marked by a cross on the pattern. Finish filling the arm firmly, keeping the top part fairly flat. Turn in the open edges and slipstitch together to close. Repeat for second arm.

For the legs, place two leg pieces right sides together. Pin, tack and stitch round the leg from the heel to the front of the toe, leaving an 8cm (3⅛in) opening in the top and leaving the base of the foot open (fig. 10).

Place a leather sole in the base opening of the leg and pin, tack and stitch in position (fig. 11). Turn the leg right side out.

Fill the leg to within 3.5cm (1⅜in) of the top. Position half of the third small joint; fill with more stuffing and close as for the arm. Repeat for second leg.

Push the cotter pins of both arms through the marked positions on the body. Attach the second discs and washers and secure as for the head.

Fill the upper body firmly, particularly around the neck, so that the joint disc in the neck cannot be felt from the outside.

For the "growler", first make the small bag which will hold it in place inside the body. Fold the square of lightweight material in half, then pin, tack and stitch the short edges (fig. 12). turn right side out. Put the growler inside the bag, turn in the edges and slipstitch together.

Place the bag inside the body, with the holes of the growler against the centre back seam. Sew the fabric surrounding the growler to the centre back seam of the bear to anchor the growler. Pack filling firmly around the growler.

Attach the legs to the body, following the same method as for the arms. Finish stuffing the bear's body firmly.

Turn in the opening edges in the base of the body and slipstitch together.

Using all six strands of the black embroidery thread, embroider four claw marks on each paw, stitching the marks at the ends, half over the edges of the leather pads.

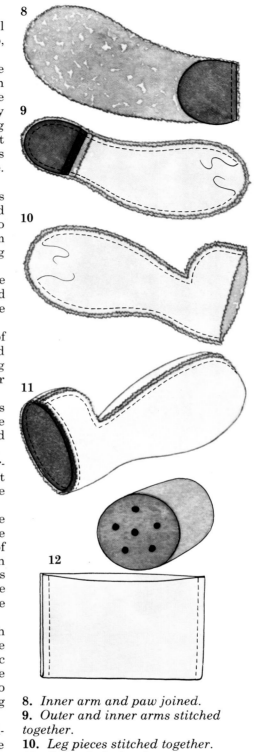

8. *Inner arm and paw joined.*
9. *Outer and inner arms stitched together.*
10. *Leg pieces stitched together.*
11. *Sole stitched to leg.*
12. *Bag for growler.*

Finishing touches
With the blunt end of the darning needle, pull out any fur pile that has been caught when stitching the seams, to cover the seam line. Give the teddy a brushing to raise pile, and tie a ribbon around his neck.

INNER ARM
cut 2 in fur fabric
(cut 1 in reverse)

B

FOOT SOL
cut 2 in leather

B

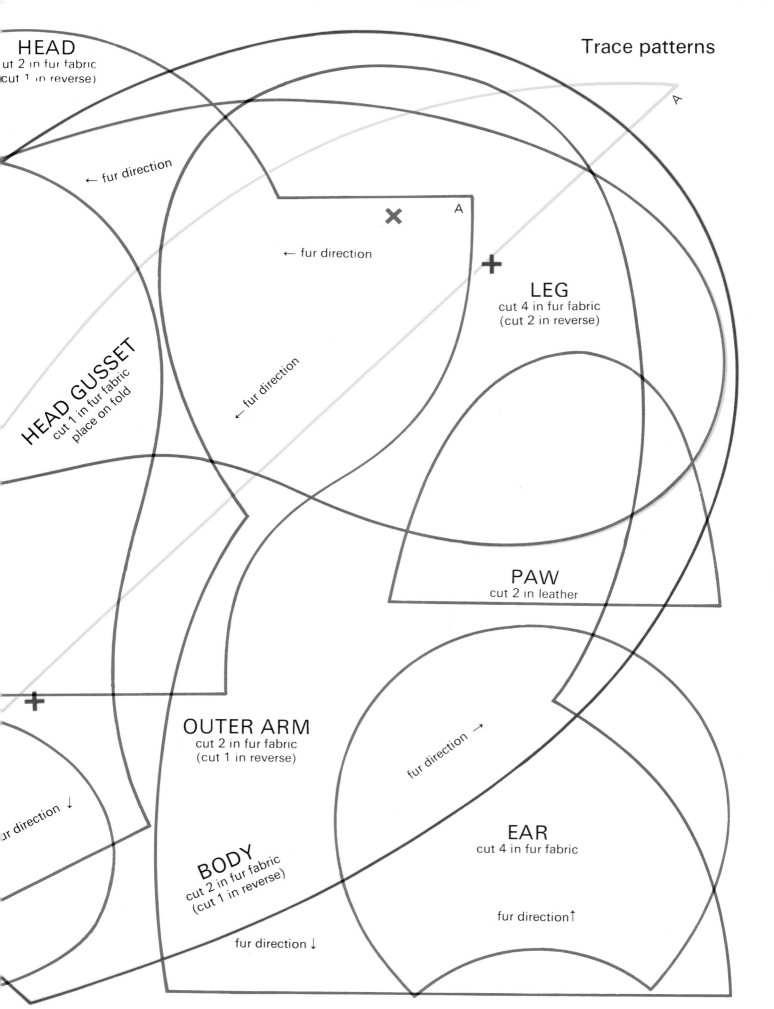

Trace patterns

HEAD
cut 2 in fur fabric
(cut 1 in reverse)

← fur direction

← fur direction

← fur direction

A

LEG
cut 4 in fur fabric
(cut 2 in reverse)

HEAD GUSSET
cut 1 in fur fabric
place on fold

PAW
cut 2 in leather

OUTER ARM
cut 2 in fur fabric
(cut 1 in reverse)

fur direction →

fur direction ↓

BODY
cut 2 in fur fabric
(cut 1 in reverse)

EAR
cut 4 in fur fabric

fur direction ↑

fur direction ↓

Patchwork animals

Finished sizes
Dog: 100cm (39½in)long. Cat: 90cm (36in) high. Horse: 112cm (44in) long. Doll: 112cm (44in) high.

Tools required
Basic sewing tools.
Techniques involved
Basic sewing; drawing patterns from

a graph; hand- or machine-sewn patchwork; embroidery stitches.
Materials
Scraps of assorted plain and

patterned, brightly-coloured fabrics of equal weight and thickness
kapok or synthetic filling
sewing thread
embroidery cottons
knitting yarn for horse's mane and doll's hair
scraps of coloured felt for doll's hands and boots
scraps of coloured felt for features
fabric adhesive

Making the patterns

Draw up paper patterns for the toys from the graph patterns given. A seam allowance of 1cm ($\frac{3}{8}$in) is included.

To make the dog

Using the paper patterns and following the graph pattern given, cut two head pieces from plain fabric. Cut two pieces each for cheeks, eyes, irises and tail using patterned fabric.

Cut eight foot pieces and four ear pieces from patterned fabric.

For the body, make up two pieces of patchwork in squares and rectangles to measure 70cm × 27cm (27$\frac{1}{2}$in × 10$\frac{3}{4}$in), plus 1cm ($\frac{3}{8}$in) seam allowance all round.

Place each head piece to the short end of each patchwork body piece, right sides facing, and sew along the edge to join.

Place one completed head and body section over the other, right sides facing, and stitch round the edges, leaving the tail end open for filling.

Turn right side out and fill head and body firmly.

Turn in seam allowance of opening and slipstitch edges together.

With right sides facing, stitch the two tail pieces together, leaving the body end of the tail open. Turn right side out and fill.

With right sides facing, stitch the foot pieces together in pairs, leaving the top ends open. Turn each foot piece to right side and fill.

Turning in the seam allowance as you work oversew tail and feet to body in positions shown in fig. 1.

With right sides facing, stitch

each pair of ears together, leaving an opening to turn through.

Turn to right side and folding in the raw edges stitch around the edges on the outside and sew ears to body (fig. 1).

Sew or stick eye pieces and cheeks to face.

Embroider mouth and eyelashes.

To make the cat

Using the paper patterns and following the graph pattern given, cut two head pieces from plain fabric.

Cut four leg pieces on fold of fabric and two eyes, two irises, two cheeks, two tail pieces and four ears from patterned fabrics.

For the body pieces, make up two pieces of patchwork measuring 40cm × 32cm (16in × 12$\frac{3}{4}$in) plus seam allowances all round.

With right sides facing, stitch the two body pieces together, leaving an opening to turn through.

Turn body right side out and fill.

Turn in raw edges and slipstitch opening.

With right sides facing stitch tail

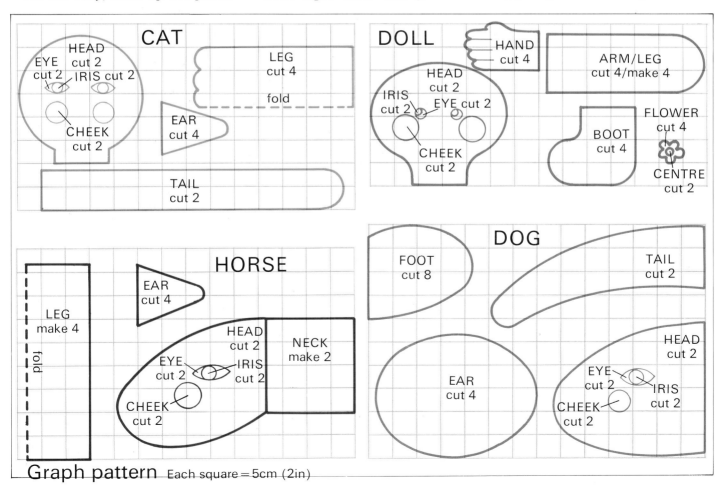

Graph pattern Each square = 5cm (2in)

70cm (28in)

27cm (11in)

1

65cm (26in)

36cm (14½in)

3

2

40cm (16in)

32cm (12½in)

39cm (15½in)

29cm (11½in)

4

pieces together, leaving an opening to turn through.

Turn right side out and fill.

Folding in raw edges as you work, sew tail to back body piece in position shown in fig. 2.

With right sides facing, stitch the two head pieces together, leaving the neck edge open.

Turn right side out and fill.

Stitch each pair of ears together, right sides facing and leaving the base edges open.

Turn to right side.

Stitch around outside edges as for dog and oversew each of the ears to the body (see fig. 2).

With right sides facing, fold leg pieces in half along fold line and stitch round edges, leaving the top edges open.

Turn to right side and fill.

Work a row of running stitches across the middle of each leg section, taking the needle through all the layers, to indicate a joint (see fig. 2).

Folding in raw edges as you work,

oversew legs to body in positions shown in fig. 2.

Sew or stick the eye pieces and cheeks to the face.

Embroider nose and mouth.

Sew or stick narrow strips of fabric to the face to suggest whiskers.

To make the horse

Using the paper patterns and following the graph pattern given cut two head pieces from plain fabric. Cut four ear pieces from patterned fabric.

Cut two eyes, two irises and two cheeks from coloured felt.

For the body, make up two pieces of patchwork, each one 66cm × 37cm (26in × 14½in), plus seam allowance.

Following the appropriate pattern pieces, make up for leg pieces and two neck pieces from patchwork.

With right sides facing, join each head piece to one neck piece and then the base of each neck piece to one body piece.

1. *Assembly of dog.*
2. *Assembly of cat.*
3. *Assembly of horse.*
4. *Assembly of doll.*

With right sides facing, sew the two complete head and body sections together, leaving an opening to turn through.

Turn to right side, fill and slip-

Delight your children with these appealing patchwork toys. Colours and patterns can be as bright and fantastic as you like.

stitch opening, folding in raw edges.

With right sides facing and each leg piece folded in half along fold line, stitch round the edges, leaving top edges open.

Turn legs to right side and fill.

Work a row of running stitches across middle of legs as for cat.

Turning in the seam allowance, oversew each leg to body in position shown in fig. 3.

With right sides facing, sew each pair of ears together, leaving base edges open.

Turn to right side and folding in the raw edges as you work, stitch around edges and oversew to body.

Make six bundles of 25cm (9¾in) lengths of wool for mane and knot each one in the middle.

Sew to horse's head and neck along seam in positions shown in fig. 3.

Make another bundle of wool, using 71cm (28in) lengths for the tail. Knot in the centre and sew to body.

Sew or stick the felt eye pieces and cheeks to the face.

Embroider mouth, nostrils and eyelashes.

To make the doll

Using the paper patterns and following the graph pattern, cut two head pieces and four arm pieces from plain fabric. Cut four hand pieces, four boot pieces, two eyes, two irises and two cheeks, four flowers and two flower centres from coloured felt.

For the body, make up two patchwork rectangles, 39cm × 29cm (15¼in × 11½in), plus seam allowance. Scraps of fabric can be used ingeniously to represent buttons and braces as illustrated.

Following the appropriate pattern pieces, make up four leg pieces in patchwork.

With right sides facing, sew the two body pieces together, leaving an opening to turn through.

Turn to right side and fill.

Fold in seam allowance and slipstitch the opening.

Sew or stick on features to one head piece and decorate the cheeks with two felt flowers.

Embroider mouth and nose. Make a happy expression by following the design shown (fig. 4).

With right sides facing, stitch the two head pieces together, leaving

the neck edge open.

Turn to right side and fill.

Folding in seam allowance, oversew head to body.

With right sides facing, sew the arm pieces together in pairs, leaving the hand edges open.

Turn to right side and work a row of gathering stitches round each hand edge. Fill the arms.

With right sides facing, sew the hand sections together.

Turn to right side and fill lightly.

Draw up gathering stitches on arms and sew the hands over them.

Make joints in arm pieces as for cat.

Make up the legs as for arms, using patchwork leg pieces and felt boots.

Decorate the boots with felt flowers and flower centres.

Sew the arms and legs to the body as shown in fig. 4.

Cut lengths of wool 90cm (36in) long for the hair and make into a bundle. Sew the centre of the bundle of wool to the centre back of head. Plait and tie with ribbons.

Make fringe, using 10 small bundles of wool as for horse's mane.

Owl and pussycat

Finished height
65cm (13in).

Tools required
Basic sewing tools; sewing machine; large-eyed needle.

Techniques involved
Basic sewing; machine stitching; filling soft toys.

Materials

For owl:
tracing paper for patterns
dressmaker's carbon paper
90cm × 70cm (35in × 27½in) of brown corduroy velvet for body
40cm × 30cm (15¾in × 12in) of brown felt for wings and eyes
30cm × 25cm (12in × 9¾in) of white felt for bib and eyes, orange felt for feet and beak
10cm (4in) sq of black felt for eyes
matching threads
70cm (27½in) of 4cm (1½in) wide blue gingham ribbon
kapok or synthetic filling

For pussycat:
tracing paper for patterns
dressmaker's carbon paper
90cm × 70cm (35in × 27½in) of black corduroy velvet for body ears and paws
30cm × 25cm (12in × 9¾in) of white felt for cheeks, eyes, bib and tail tip
30cm × 25cm (12in × 9¾in) of pink felt for nose, ears and tongue
10cm (4in) square of green felt
scraps of black felt for eyes
matching threads
white stranded embroidery thread
70cm (27½in) of 4cm (1½in) wide green gingham ribbon
160cm (63in) length of fine string for whiskers
starch or fabric stiffener
kapok or synthetic filling

To make the owl

Trace off all the pieces from the patterns given, and mark on the appropriate fabric using dressmaker's carbon paper. Cut out all the pieces.

Position the body feathers on one body piece, then place the white bib and eye rim pieces on top of this. Pin, tack and machine stitch around the bib and eye rims, keeping close to the edge and securing the feathering pieces at the same time (fig. 1).

For the eyes, pin and stitch the black circles on the centre of the brown circles. Sew the white crosses in place (fig. 2a). Pin eyes on to the rim section and topstitch close to the edge of the eyes (fig. 2b). While stitching this, put a little filling behind the eyes to give a slightly raised effect.

To make the beak, pin and stitch the two darts on the beak pieces, tapering the stitching towards the points to form a ridge on the outside

of the beak (fig. 3a). Pin the two beak pieces together and stitch along the sides close to the edge, leaving the base edge open (fig. 3b). Pin on the face and hand stitch securely.

For the wings, place the wing feathers along the lower curved edge of each wing piece on the right side of the fabric. Pin and tack in position before placing the wing pieces together in pairs, right sides together. Machine along the curved edges close to the seam line (fig. 4a). Turn to the right side and topstitch close to the seam line (fig. 4b). Stuff and stitch across the open end.

To make the feet, fold two claw pieces in half, wrong sides facing (fig. 6). Sew a narrow line of stitching along the fold, tapering towards the point of the centre claw (fig. 5a). With wrong sides facing, pin these upper claw pieces to the lower pieces. Stitch close to the edge around the claws, leaving the straight edge open. Stuff (fig. 5b) and stitch along the open edge.

For the body, pin the wings in position on the seam lines on front of the body, as indicated by the pattern (fig. 6). With right sides facing, pin, tack and stitch the body seam lines together, making sure that they meet exactly at the top of the body. Pin and tack the feet in the same way on the base seam line of the front body piece. With right sides facing and matching the corners of the base with the body seam lines, pin, tack and stitch the base, leaving an opening (fig. 7). Turn right side out and stuff firmly, pushing down the filling. Ensure that all the curves are well packed and shaped. Sew up the opening.

Tie the gingham ribbon into a bow and stitch it firmly in place on the bib. If the corduroy has become flattened, brush up the pile.

To make the cat

Transfer the patterns on to the

1. *Bib and eye rims stitched in place.*
2a. *White cross stitched to black circle.*
2b. *Eyes stitched to eye rims.*
3a. *Darts stitched on beak.*
3b. *Beak pieces stitched together.*
4a. *Feathers basted to wing and wing pieces stitched together.*
4b. *Topstitching around wing.*

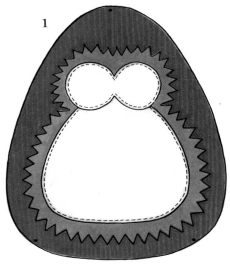

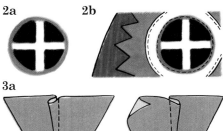

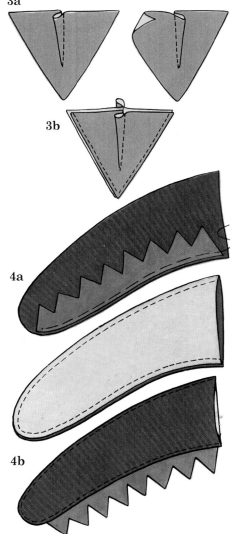

Trace patterns (Owl)

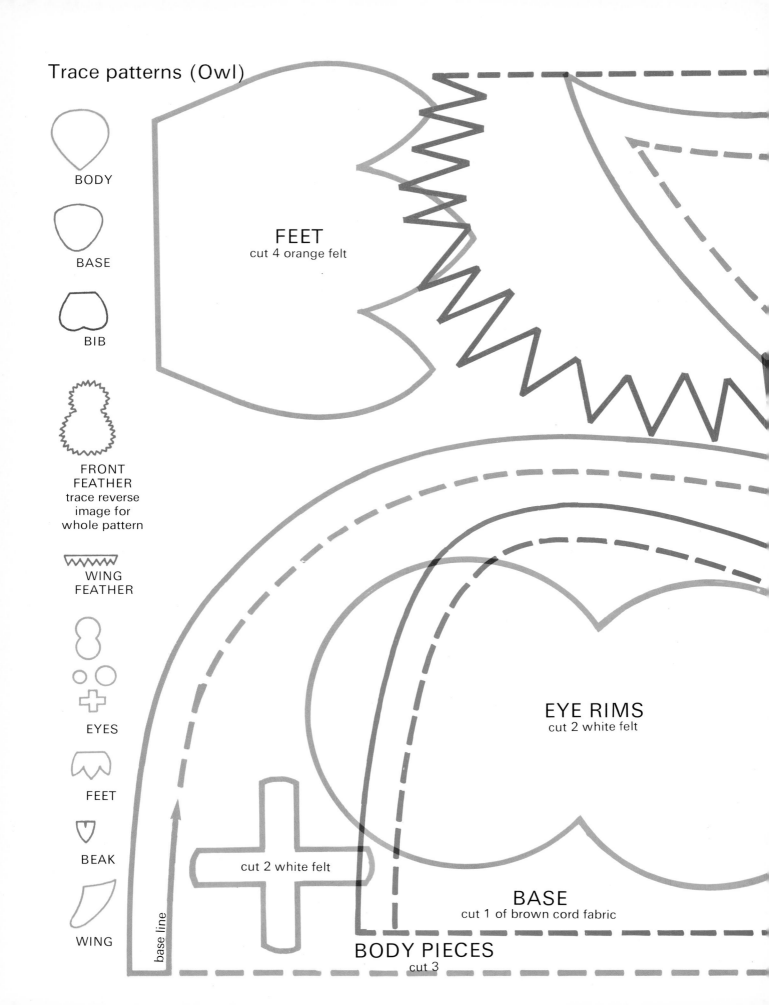

BODY

BASE

BIB

FRONT
FEATHER
trace reverse
image for
whole pattern

WING
FEATHER

EYES

FEET

BEAK

WING

base line

FEET
cut 4 orange felt

EYE RIMS
cut 2 white felt

cut 2 white felt

BASE
cut 1 of brown cord fabric

BODY PIECES
cut 3

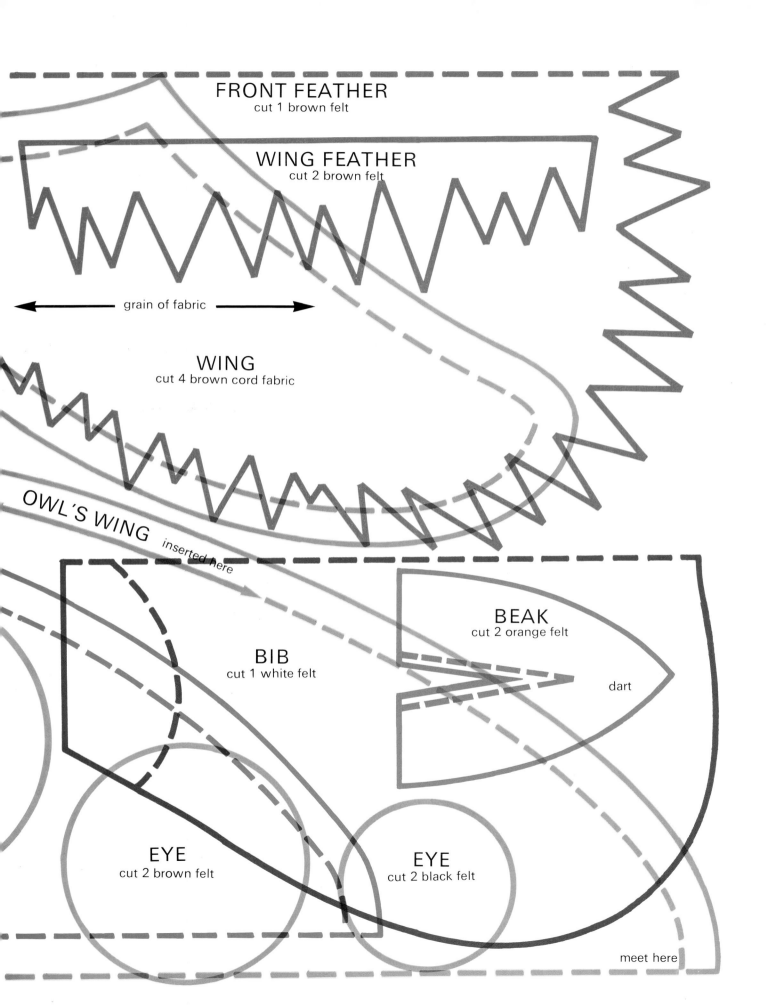

FRONT FEATHER
cut 1 brown felt

WING FEATHER
cut 2 brown felt

grain of fabric

WING
cut 4 brown cord fabric

OWL'S WING   inserted here

BIB
cut 1 white felt

BEAK
cut 2 orange felt

dart

EYE
cut 2 brown felt

EYE
cut 2 black felt

meet here

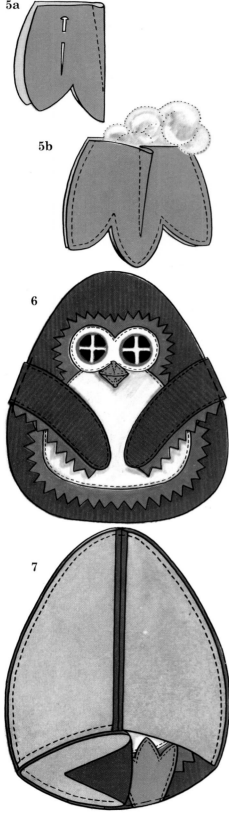

5a. *Dart stitched on claw.*
5b. *Stuffing the joined claw pieces.*
6. *Wings basted to front body piece.*
7. *Base being stitched to body sections.*

appropriate fabrics as for the owl, and cut out all the pieces.

For the face, tack, pin and top-stitch the white bib in place on the body piece. Topstitch the two tongue pieces together, keeping close to the edge. Pin this in position on the body, then place the cheeks over the upper edge of the tongue. Stitch these pieces in place, padding with a little filling as for the owl's eyes on page 79 (fig. 8).

To make the eyes, pin, tack then topstitch the green pieces on to the white, and the black pupils on the centre of the green pieces. Using white stranded thread, embroider about four straight stitches together in a block to give a "sparkle" to each eye (fig. 9). Pin, then stitch the eyes on to the body piece.

For the ears, pin and tack one felt and one corduroy piece together,

remembering to make a left and a right. Stitch along the seam lines, leaving the straight edge open (fig. 10). Turn right side out and topstitch along the edge with matching thread. Fold over one edge of each ear and tack along the seam line to give shape to the ear.

For the feet, pin, tack and stitch the feet pieces together, right sides facing, along the seam lines and leaving the straight edge open. Turn right side out and stuff each foot (fig. 11a). Sew along the opening to hold the filling in place. Using white stranded thread, embroider four straight stitches for claws on each foot (fig. 11b).

To make the tail, pin, tack and stitch the straight edge of the white tail tip to the black corduroy strip, right sides facing. Press the seam open. Fold the tail in half lengthwise and stitch along the seam line, leav-

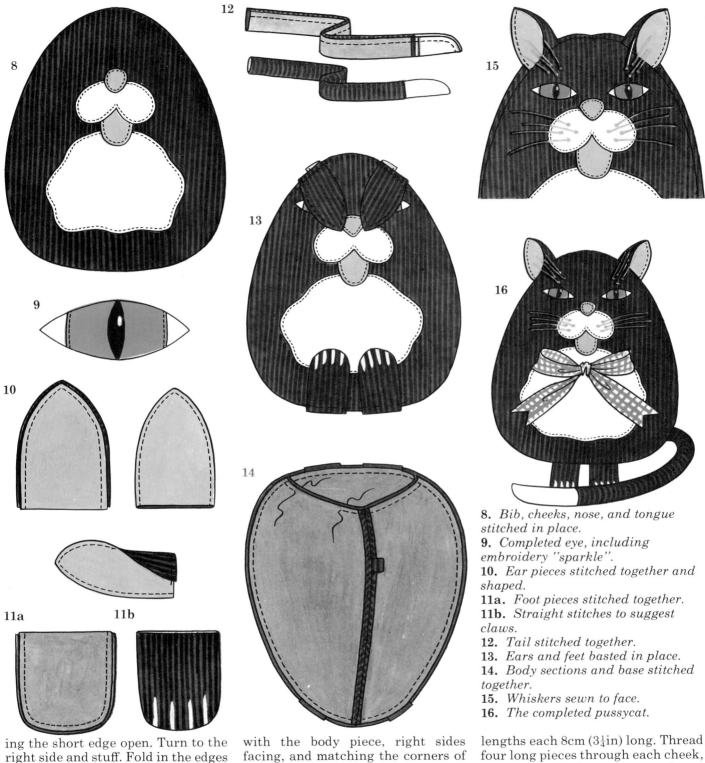

8. Bib, cheeks, nose, and tongue stitched in place.

9. Completed eye, including embroidery "sparkle".

10. Ear pieces stitched together and shaped.

11a. Foot pieces stitched together.

11b. Straight stitches to suggest claws.

12. Tail stitched together.

13. Ears and feet basted in place.

14. Body sections and base stitched together.

15. Whiskers sewn to face.

16. The completed pussycat.

ing the short edge open. Turn to the right side and stuff. Fold in the edges of opening and sew up (fig. 12).

For the body, pin and tack the ears into position on the body front. Now pin and tack the feet in place along (fig. 13) the base seam line of the body front. With right sides facing, join the side seams and the back seam, inserting the tail at the base of the back seam. Place the base together

with the body piece, right sides facing, and matching the corners of the base with the body seam lines. Pin, tack and stitch the base in position, remembering to leave an opening (fig. 14). Turn right side out.

To make the whiskers, coat the length of string several times with starch or fabric stiffener until it is fairly rigid. Cut eight lengths each about 10cm (4in) long and eight

lengths each 8cm (3¼in) long. Thread four long pieces through each cheek, and four short pieces above each eye, using a large-eyed needle. Tie a knot on each side of the fabric to hold the whiskers firmly in place (fig. 15).

Now stuff the body firmly and turn in the edges of the opening, then stitch by hand to close. Make a bow out of the gingham ribbon and sew firmly in place on the bib (fig. 16).

Trace patterns (Cat)

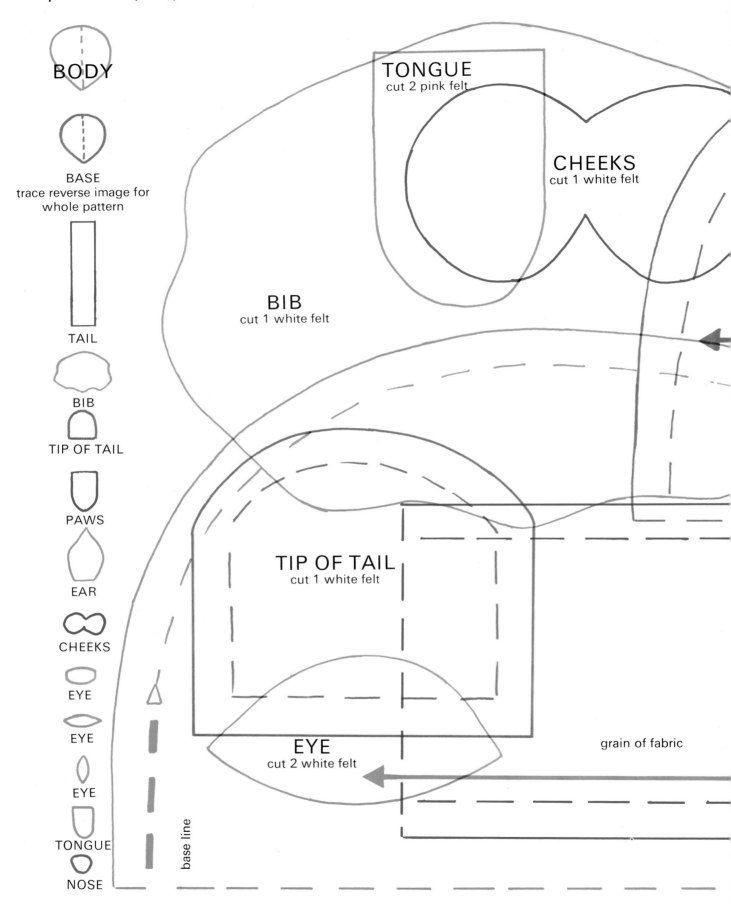

BODY

BASE
trace reverse image for
whole pattern

TAIL

BIB

TIP OF TAIL

PAWS

EAR

CHEEKS

EYE

EYE

EYE

TONGUE

NOSE

base line

TONGUE
cut 2 pink felt

CHEEKS
cut 1 white felt

BIB
cut 1 white felt

TIP OF TAIL
cut 1 white felt

EYE
cut 2 white felt

grain of fabric

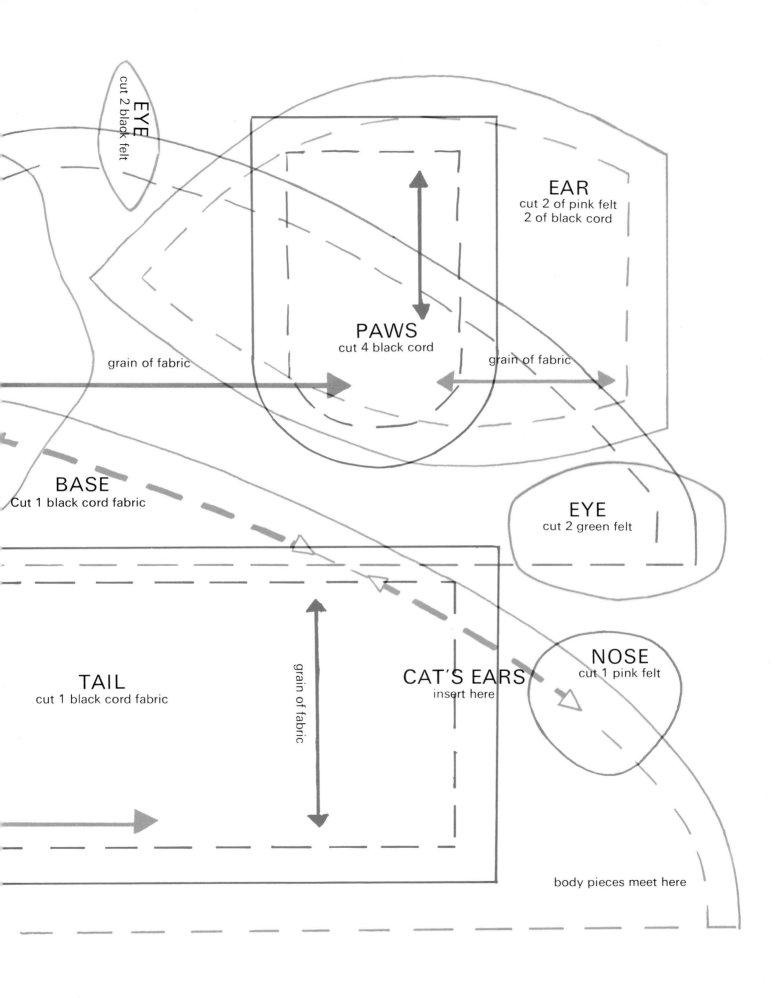

EYE
cut 2 black felt

EAR
cut 2 of pink felt
2 of black cord

PAWS
cut 4 black cord

grain of fabric

grain of fabric

BASE
Cut 1 black cord fabric

EYE
cut 2 green felt

NOSE
cut 1 pink felt

TAIL
cut 1 black cord fabric

grain of fabric

CAT'S EARS
insert here

body pieces meet here

Fabric book

Finished size
Approximately 35cm × 29cm (13¾in × 11¼in).
Tools required
Basic sewing equipment.
Techniques involved
Basic sewing; machine stitching.
Materials
70cm (27in) medium weight calico

90–100cm (36–40in) wide
10cm (4in) each of 4 contrasting printed cotton fabrics 90cm (39in) wide
felt—orange, turquoise, pink, red, dark green—each 10cm (4in) square; light grass green—30cm (11¾in) square; small scraps of white and black felt

white sewing thread
black and white stranded cotton embroidery thread
15cm (6in) white zip
3 medium-sized press studs
1 green button, 2.5cm (1in) in diameter
1 white shoe lace, 45cm (17¾in) long
8 white eyelets and punch

86

tracing paper
dressmaker's carbon paper

To make the book
First wash the calico, as this fabric will probably shrink quite a lot. Iron it while it is still damp to remove any creases.

Trace up all pattern pieces on the tracing paper. Cut out each piece on the appropriate fabric. Large, simple shapes can be pinned to the fabric and cut around. Smaller pieces and those with intricate shapes should be traced on to the fabric using dressmaker's carbon paper. Place the carbon between the fabric and the tracing paper and firmly trace the outline with a pencil or ball point pen. Cut out the shapes.

Cut the calico into 6 pieces, each measuring approximately 35cm × 30cm (13¾in × 11¾in).

In the centre of each piece of calico, measure and draw a rectangle 30cm × 22cm (11¾in × 8½in), which represents the finished size of each page (fig. 1). Tack along this outline.

Cover page
Place the letters, flower pieces and leaf stem in position within the tacked lines on one of the calico pages. When you are satisfied the lettering is well spaced and straight, pin and tack all the pieces in place (fig. 2). Set your sewing machine to a narrow zigzag stitch, and—using white thread—work around all the letters and leaves. Alternatively, hand stitch the shapes to the page, using blanket stitch. Make sure the raw edges are covered by the line of stitching, as this not only attaches the pieces to the calico but also prevents the appliquéed pieces from fraying.

Draw all loose ends through to the wrong side and tie securely. Remove all tacking threads. Do not, however, remove the tacking lines around the pages at this stage.

Page 1—Frog and zipper
Pin, tack, and zigzag stitch the grass in position on a calico page. Pin and tack the zipper in position under the frog's mouth slit (fig. 3). Using the zipper foot of the machine and a straight stitch, carefully machine all round mouth, close to edges, to secure the zip in place.

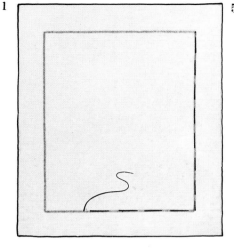

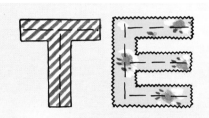

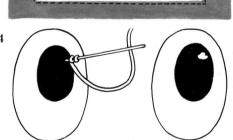

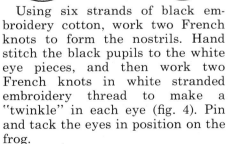

Using six strands of black embroidery cotton, work two French knots to form the nostrils. Hand stitch the black pupils to the white eye pieces, and then work two French knots in white stranded embroidery thread to make a "twinkle" in each eye (fig. 4). Pin and tack the eyes in position on the frog.

Pin and tack the frog in position on the calico page and zigzag stitch around all raw edges. Also stitch around the eyes and around the body shape, using the dashed line on the pattern as a guide. Remove tacking threads and tie loose ends (fig. 5).

Page 2—Flowers and press studs
Pin and tack the centres of the flowers in place on the felt shapes. Zigzag stitch around the raw edges

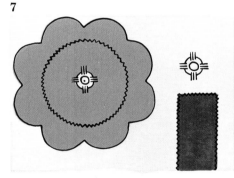

1. *Baste around rectangle.*
2. *Baste letters in place.*
3. *Baste zipper in position.*
4. *Work French knots in eyes.*
5. *Frog positioned on page.*
6. *Stitching centres on flowers.*
7. *Sew on ball part of snap.*

of centres and cast ends off neatly (fig. 6).

In the centre of the wrong side of each flower, hand sew one part of a press stud (fig. 7); make sure you do not stitch through to the right side of the flower centres. Arrange the flower heads above each stalk, and lightly mark on the calico the position of the press studs. Sew the other parts of the studs in place. Remove tacking threads and tie off loose ends.

Place the leaf stems in position on

LETTERS

FLOWER CENTRE PETALS

FLOWER CENTRE

LEAF STEM

EYE

PUPIL

GRASS

FROG

Trace patterns

PUPIL
cut 2 black felt

EYE
cut 2 white felt

FROG
cut 1 light green felt

cut 1 printed cotton

cut 2 printed cotton

cut slit for zipper mouth

cut 1 light green felt

cut 1 printed cotton

line of stitching

FLOWER PETALS
cut 1 cotton

cut 1 printed cotton

cut 1 printed cotton

FLOWER CENTRE
cut 1 cotton

GRASS
cut 1 dark green felt

LEAF STEM
cut 1 dark green felt

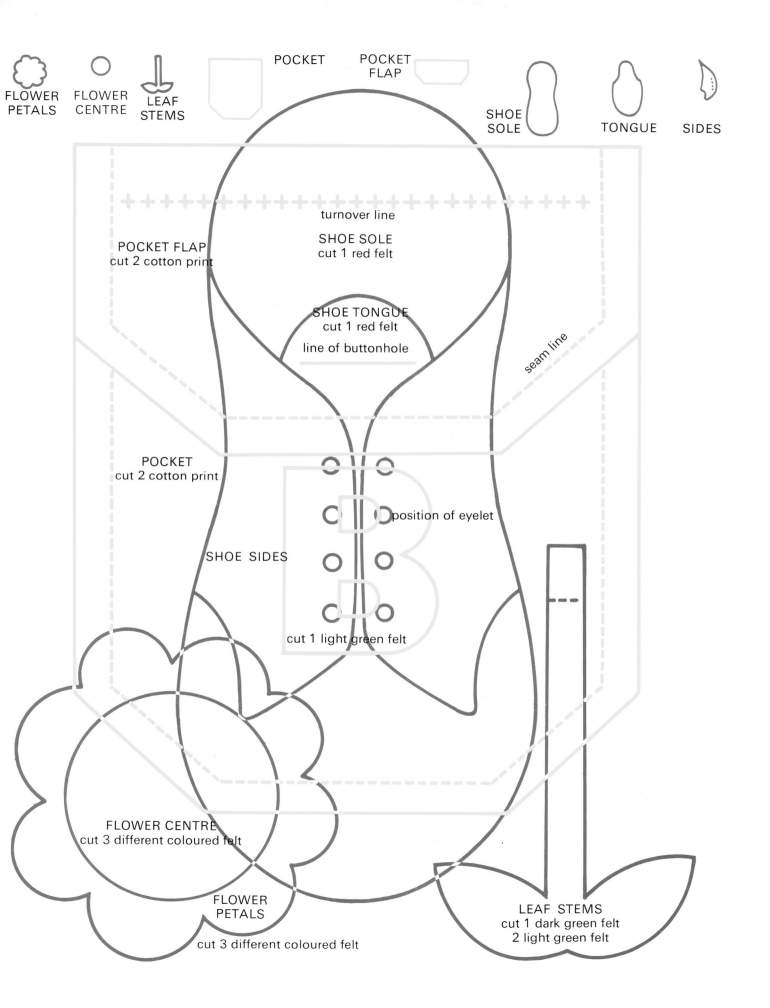

FLOWER PETALS

FLOWER CENTRE

LEAF STEMS

POCKET

POCKET FLAP

SHOE SOLE

TONGUE

SIDES

turnover line

POCKET FLAP
cut 2 cotton print

SHOE SOLE
cut 1 red felt

SHOE TONGUE
cut 1 red felt

line of buttonhole

seam line

POCKET
cut 2 cotton print

position of eyelet

SHOE SIDES

cut 1 light green felt

FLOWER CENTRE
cut 3 different coloured felt

FLOWER
PETALS

cut 3 different coloured felt

LEAF STEMS
cut 1 dark green felt
2 light green felt

a calico page as shown on (fig. 8). Pin and tack. Zigzag stitch in place.

Page 3—Pocket and button

Pin and tack the two pocket pieces together, right sides facing (fig. 9), repeat for pocket flap pieces. Machine stitch along seamlines of pocket and flap, leaving gaps of 5cm (2in) along edges. Turn both sections right side out.

Tack around all the edges, including the 5cm (2in) gap which was left unstitched. Press both sections of the pocket with a hot iron.

On the pocket piece pin and tack the letter "B"; zigzag stitch along edges. On the flap, work a buttonhole—either by machine or by hand—to fit the green button (fig. 10). Top stitch around lower and side edges of flap, close to the edge. Add a second line of stitching about 6mm ($\frac{1}{4}$in) inside the first line. Repeat on upper edge of pocket.

Centre the pocket on a calico page, pin and tack. Using straight stitch, machine the pocket in place with two lines of stitching along the sides and base. Place the pocket flap slightly above the pocket and straight stitch along top of flap with two lines of stitching. Hand sew the button on to pocket, positioning it directly underneath the buttonhole on the flap (fig. 11).

Page 4—Shoe and laces

Straight stitch around edge of shoe side pieces, except for outer edges. Also stitch around the upper edge of the tongue, working two lines of stitching close to each other (fig. 12).

If you've got an eyelet punch, use it to make four eyelets on each of the side pieces. Alternatively, make eyelets by hand, using two strands of white embroidery cotton and close blanket stitch (fig. 12).

Pin pieces of shoe on sole, then position shoe on calico page; pin, tack and straight stitch a double line around the shoe edge. Thread shoe lace in eyelets (fig. 13).

Press each page on the wrong side. Pin and tack the cover page and page 1 together. Similarly, join page 2 and 3, page 4 and the blank page. Remember to match up the original tacked lines which represent the page edges. Straight stitch inside the new tacking lines,

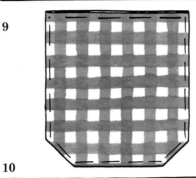

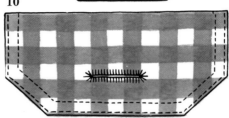

8. *Leaf stems in position.*
9. *Pin and baste pocket pieces together, right sides facing.*
10. *Work a buttonhole on the flap by hand or machine.*

6mm ($\frac{1}{4}$in) from the original tacking line around each page. Trim away excess calico using pinking shears (fig. 14).

Put the pages on top of one another in the correct order. Pin along left side and then straight stitch close to the edge several times in the same place to hold the pages together securely. Remove all remaining tacking threads.

11. *Sew the button onto the pocket directly under the buttonhole.*
12. *Stitching lines and eyelet positions on the shoe.*
13. *Thread the shoelace through the eyelets and tie a bow.*
14. *When pages are assembled trim the completed book with pinking shears.*

Hobby horse

Finished height
Approximately 1¼m (4ft 2in).

Tools required
Basic sewing tools; sewing machine
if wished.

Techniques involved
Basic sewing; drawing patterns from
a graph; machine stitching.

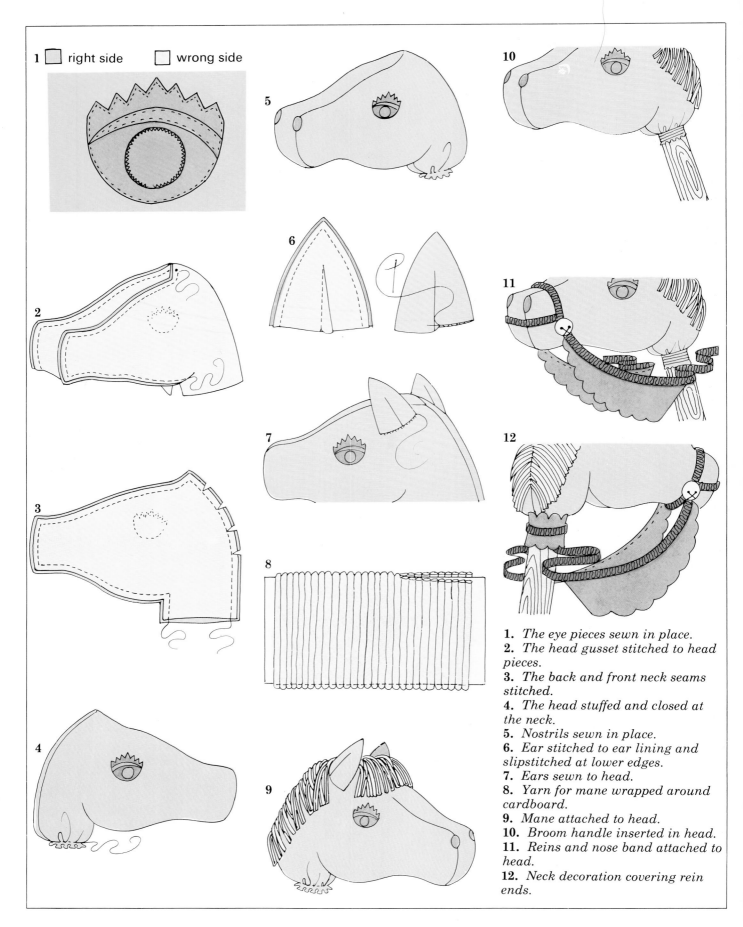

1. right side ▢ wrong side ▢

1. The eye pieces sewn in place.
2. The head gusset stitched to head pieces.
3. The back and front neck seams stitched.
4. The head stuffed and closed at the neck.
5. Nostrils sewn in place.
6. Ear stitched to ear lining and slipstitched at lower edges.
7. Ears sewn to head.
8. Yarn for mane wrapped around cardboard.
9. Mane attached to head.
10. Broom handle inserted in head.
11. Reins and nose band attached to head.
12. Neck decoration covering rein ends.

Materials

squared paper for patterns, with squares of 2.5cm (1in)

tracing paper for patterns

90cm × 70cm (35in × 27½in) of plain or patterned cotton fabric for head

matching thread

1 × 25g (1oz) of double knitting wool for mane

15cm (6in) square of yellow felt

2 × 25cm (10in) squares of brown felt

matching threads

1.85m (2yd) of decorative braid for the reins

2 small bells

kapok or synthetic filling

2 pieces of cardboard, 20.5cm × 10cm (8in × 4in) and 10cm × 7.5cm (4in × 3in)

1 broom handle, 2.5cm (1in) in diameter

woodworking adhesive

Using the squared paper, draw the ear, head and gusset pieces to scale. An allowance of 1.5cm (⅝in) has been included on seams for the head, gusset and ears. Mark dots, lines and positions for eyes. Trace the pattern for the eye and the nostril from the eye pupil piece. Cut out the pattern pieces.

Fold the cotton fabric in half with the selvedges together. Place the three main pattern pieces on the fabric, with the gusset on the fold and making sure that the grain line of the pattern lies on the straight grain of the fabric. Pin into place and cut out.

From yellow felt, cut out the ear piece twice and each of the eye pieces twice. From brown felt, cut out the neck decoration once, the rein decoration twice, the nostril piece twice and the eye piece twice. Transfer all markings from pattern pieces to fabric.

Tack and topstitch the yellow pupil to the brown eye piece. Using a small zigzag stitch (if you are working with a machine) or a close buttonhole stitch, sew the yellow eyelid to the brown eye piece. Stitch the eyes to the head pieces in the positions indicated on the pattern (fig. 1).

With right sides facing and matching dots, tack and stitch the gusset to the head pieces, easing on the curves (fig. 2). Tack and stitch the back neck seam and the front neck seam from the point of the gusset to the neck edge. Fasten off securely, trim the seams and clip the curves (fig. 3). Turn the head piece right side out, and run a line of gathering stitches 6mm (¼in) from the neck edge, leaving the thread loose.

Stuff the head with filling, pushing down with a pencil if necessary to ensure that it is evenly packed. Pull up gathers round the neck and secure to prevent the filling from escaping (fig. 4). Using tiny stitches, sew toe nostrils to the front of the nose, positioning them on top of the curve (fig. 5).

With right sides facing, tack and stitch darts on outer ears and yellow felt ears. Press to one side. With right sides together, tack and stitch the ears on the seam line. Make a small hem on the bottom edge of each ear and slipstitch to close (fig. 6).

Place the ears on either side of the head, close to the gusset seam. Stitch firmly into position, making sure that the ears are upright (fig. 7).

Wind the wool evenly round the larger piece of cardboard. Using matching thread, work a line of back stitches through the wool at one edge of the cardboard to hold the wool together. Cut through the loops on the other edge (fig. 8).

Position the mane down the back neck seam, starting from behind the ears. Using wool, stitch into position covering the back stitches.

Make a front fringe in the same way, using the smaller piece of cardboard, to measure 7.5cm (3in), and attach to the head with stitching running from one ear to the other ear. Make sure that the fringe and mane meet. Fold the fringe forward between the ears (fig. 9).

Carefully open neck gathers and push broom handle as far as possible into the head. Pack more filling round the broom handle and pull up the gathers, securing firmly.

Stick the seam turnings on the neck to the broom handle with strong adhesive and bind the head on to the handle with several strands of strong thread (fig. 10). Cut the braid into three lengths: one piece for the neck decoration 10cm (4in) long; one piece for the nose-band 42cm (16½in) long; remainder for the reins.

Tack and stitch the braid to the neck decoration. Find the centre of the reins and stitch the rein decoration on to the braid 14cm (5½in) either side of this point.

Pin the nose-band on to the horse's nose and join the ends under the chin. Pin the reins on to the head with the centre of the reins in the centre of the mouth. Stitch the reins to the nose, and attach bells where they cross (fig. 11). Glue the ends of the reins to the neck and cover these by sticking the neck decoration over all the raw edges. Neatly stitch the two ends together (fig. 12).

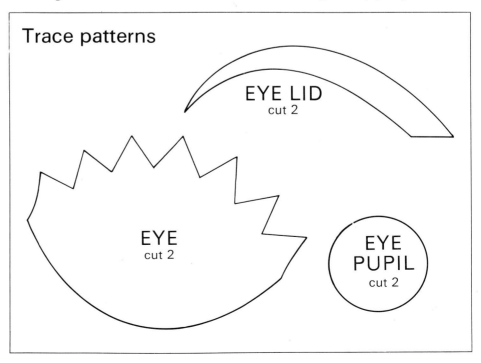

Trace patterns

EYE LID
cut 2

EYE
cut 2

EYE PUPIL
cut 2

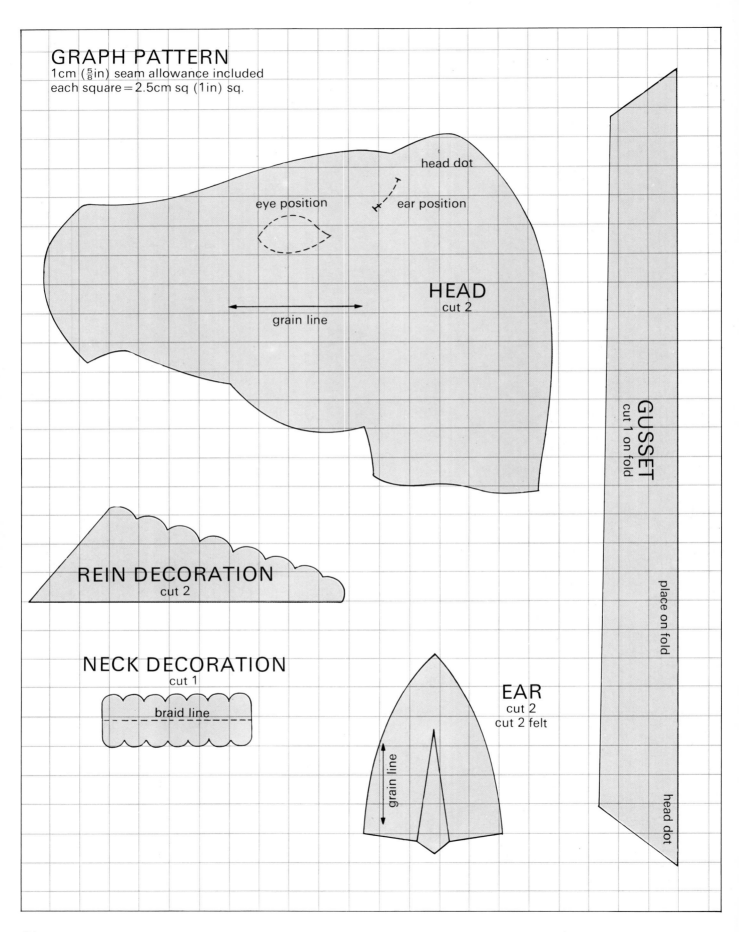

GRAPH PATTERN

1cm (⅝in) seam allowance included
each square = 2.5cm sq (1in) sq.

head dot

eye position

ear position

HEAD
cut 2

grain line

GUSSET
cut 1 on fold

place on fold

head dot

REIN DECORATION
cut 2

NECK DECORATION
cut 1

braid line

EAR
cut 2
cut 2 felt

grain line

Tepee

Finished size
Approximately 152cm (5ft).

Tools required
Sewing machine; basic sewing tools.

Techniques involved
Basic sewing; machine stitching; pattern shapes from diagrams.

Materials
4.26m × 2.60m (14ft × 8½ft) of strong cotton fabric for tepee
102cm × 90cm (40in × 35in) of cotton fabric for door flap
6.5m (7yd) of binding tape
4.6m (5yd) of 2.5cm (1in) wide

strong adhesive tape
matching machine cotton thread
embroidery thread (optional)
33 large eyelets as used for tents (optional)
strong string
2 stakes

11 × 3m (10ft) long bamboo poles
1 × 76cm (2½ft) bamboo pole
7 × 30cm (12in) long wooden pins
   made from 6mm (¼in) diameter
   dowelling
25 tent pegs
step ladder
waterproofing liquid (optional)

Suitable fabrics

Any strong cotton fabric is suitable for making a tepee—sailcloth, calico, cotton curtain lining or lightweight canvas. It does not matter where the seams lie, but it is important to use flat fell seams in order to make them both stronger and neater. A 1.5cm (⅝in) seam allowance is included in the total size.

To make the tepee cover

Divide the length of fabric into three 142cm (56in) sections and mark them off on the material using chalk or a felt-tipped pen.

Cut a 40cm (16in) slit at one end of both dividing lines (fig. 1) and bind the raw edges on the two outer edges of the slits (fig. 2).

Turn up a double fold on to the right side of the fabric to form a 20cm (8in) hem. Machine along both edges close to the folds.

Lay the material on a flat surface, wrong side upwards. Fix a pin at A—the centre point of the fabric level with the bottom edge of the two outer panels (fig. 3).

Draw a semicircle beginning and ending at the hemmed corners of the outer sections. You can do this with a piece of chalk tied to a piece of string, the length of the required radius, which is pinned to the centre of the material. This acts like a compass. Fix the pin 50cm (20in) from the outside edge in line with A, adjust the length of your string to 30cm (12in) and draw another semicircle.

Repeat this process on the other side. These two semicircles will form the front opening.

Turn up a 2cm (¾in) double hem all round the bottom curved edge of the tepee and machine stitch. Machine 8cm (3in) long loops of strong tape around this edge at about 30cm (11in) intervals (fig. 4a). If you are using scraps of material to make your tepee, you may have enough to make the loops from the same fabric,

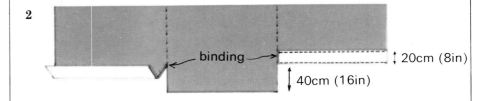

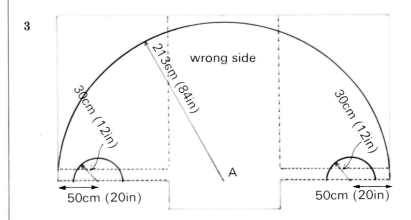

1. *Fabric divided into three sections and cut partway along dividing lines.*
2. *Outer edges of slits bound and* panels hemmed on right side.
3. *Drawing semicircles for lower edge and front opening using a tack, string and marking chalk.*

but make sure you turn in the edges to prevent them from fraying.

Mark two parallel rows of holes for the wooden pins that will close the tepee at approximately 10cm (4in) intervals along the front hem. Be careful to match up holes on either side and to keep them within the line of stitching.

To make the "wings" at the top of the tepee, follow the measurements and draw a freehand shape on the wrong side of the material as shown

in fig. 4. It is easier to obtain a symmetrical shape for the wings if you fold the fabric in half, right sides facing, with the centre point A lying along the fold, and cut through both layers of fabric. The wings let in light, but can be closed to keep out rain. (Traditionally, they also let out smoke.)

Now mark the holes for the tent cords and rear poles on the middle panel, following measurements given in fig. 4. Having marked all the

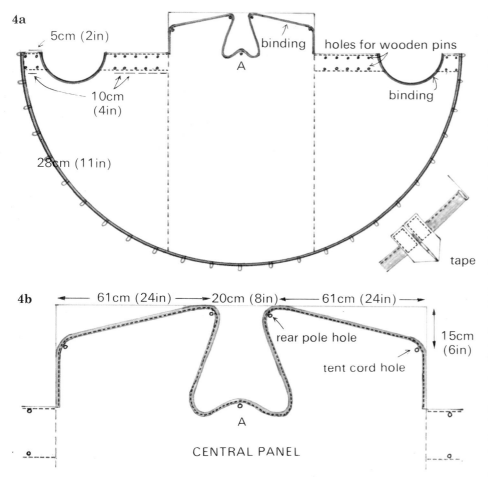

4a

5cm (2in)

binding

holes for wooden pins

A

10cm
(4in)

binding

28cm (11in)

tape

4b

61cm (24in) — 20cm (8in) — 61cm (24in)

15cm
(6in)

rear pole hole

tent cord hole

A

CENTRAL PANEL

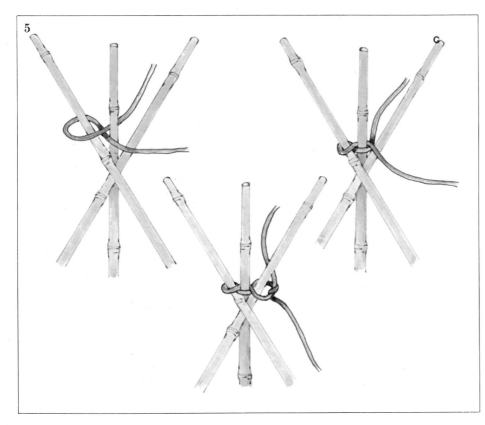

5

holes, cut out small diamond shapes with sharp scissors. If you are using eyelets, make sure the holes are smaller than the eyelets so that they can be pushed through firmly. Eyelets are available from most good camping shops, and are sold with instructions for fitting. However, if you are unable to find eyelets, or wish to avoid this extra expense, you can simply round off the holes and oversew the edges with strong thread.

Bind the edges of the front opening and wings. If you have any spare fabric, you can use it instead of binding tape. It is advisable to cut it on the cross, so that it eases round the curved edges. As before, you will need to turn in the edges to prevent fraying.

To construct the frame

Put up the frame by tying three bamboo poles together to form a tripod, making sure that you loop the string firmly in a chain around all three poles (fig. 5). Set up the tripod on the ground and tie in six more poles securely to form a circular frame.

To assemble the tepee

To attach the tepee to the frame, draw a string through the centre hole of the wings and tie it to the top of the poles underneath their intersection, so that the bottom edge of the tepee is level with the ground.

Drape the tent around all the poles, and close the front opening with wooden pins so that the double rows of holes overlap and each pin goes through four holes as illustrated in the photograph.

Peg down the bottom edge with tent pegs through the loops. Tie the top of the wings to two poles and prop them up behind the tepee so that they cross diagonally (fig. 6). Tie a string to each of the bottom holes of the wings and attach each string to a stake hammered into the ground at the front of the tepee. These strings should be taut, and the combination of the two rear poles

4a. *Finished tepee cover, raw edges bound or hemmed.*
4b. *Detail of wing shapes.*
5. *Tying three poles together to form a tripod.*

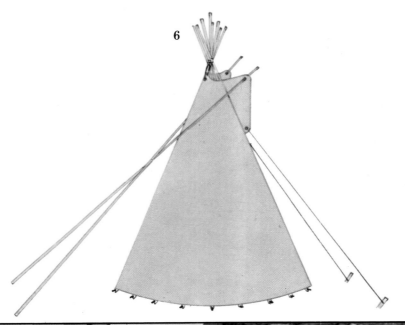

6

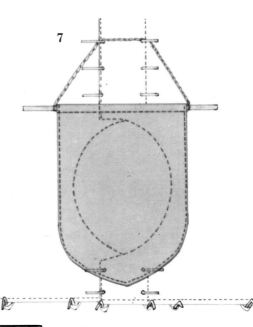

7

8

6. *Wings held open by combination of rear poles and front cords.*
7. *Positioning of door flap over front opening.*
8. *The front of the tepee is easily closed by inserting 30cm (12in) long wooden pins into the holes.*

and the front strings will open out the wings (fig. 6).

To make the door flap

You will find it easier to measure and make the flap after the tepee cover has been positioned over the frame. Measure the width and length of the door opening. Mark out a shield-shaped piece of material for the flap about 30cm (12in) wider and 27.5cm (11in) longer than this opening. Draw this shape freehand, fold in half and cut double to obtain a symmetrical shape. Hem the edge of the door flap.

Turn the straight edge of the top over and machine stitch down, leaving enough room to pull through the small bamboo pole.

Tie each end of a piece of string to either end of the hole and hang from one of the wooden pins (fig. 7). You can add finishing touches to the door flap with embroidery or macramé if you wish.

It is a good idea to waterproof your finished tepee with waterproofing liquid which can be bought in camping shops. If the tepee gets wet, make sure it is dry before storing away, as the damp will rot the fabric.

Play house

Finished height
Varies according to table size, but

approximately 127cm × 76cm × 76cm
(50in × 30in × 30in).

Tools required
Sewing machine; basic sewing tools.

Techniques involved

Basic sewing; machine stitching; drawing patterns from a graph; machine-sewn appliqué work.

Materials

To fit a table approximately
122cm × 73.5cm × 79cm (48in × 29in × 31in):

unbleached cotton calico material for walls, quantity to be calculated as follows: **side walls**: height of table + 5cm (2in) × width of table + 5cm (2in); **back wall**: height of table + 5cm (2in) × length of table + 28cm (11in) for underwrap at door; **front wall**: height of table + 15cm (6in)

red sailcloth for door: height of table + 5cm (2in) × width of table + 20cm (8in)

38cm × 36cm (15in × 14½in) of lace curtain net

1.5m (1¼yd) of 15mm (⅝in) wide black petersham ribbon

2 pieces, 36cm × 19cm (14in × 7½in), of red sailcloth for shutters

2 pieces, 42cm × 24cm (16½in × 9½in), of gingham for curtains

blue cotton fabric for roof: width of table + 5cm (2in) × length of table + 5cm (2in)

sewing thread in matching colours and tan thread

postcard for bricks template.

Materials for appliqué

squared paper for patterns

2 pieces, 50cm × 23cm (20in × 9in) and 30cm × 18cm (12in × 7in) of green felt for shrubs

2 pieces, 17cm × 13cm (7in × 5½in) and 9cm × 4cm (3½in × 2in) of brown felt for shrubs

18cm (7in) square of navy felt for bird house

50cm (18in) of 2cm (¾in) wide black petersham ribbon for bird house

scraps of red and mauve felt for birds and ladybirds

2.75m (3yd) of 2.5cm (1in) wide brown petersham ribbon for apple tree

1.5m (1¼yd) of 15mm (⅝in) wide brown petersham ribbon for apple tree

large quantity of scrap felt in two shades of green for leaves

30.5cm (12in) square of red felt for apples

sewing thread in matching colours

Choosing a suitable table

The play house will require a table

Front, back, and sides of the play house with decorations.

of the simplest kind—a rectangle of wood with a leg at each corner. Tables with crosspieces near the floor would not be suitable.

It does not matter how big the table is, so long as it is large enough to accommodate at least two children. If your table has different proportions from the table illustrated, you will need to change the shapes of the door and window to fit, and perhaps alter the position of the decorations. It may be helpful to make a scale drawing of the house before you begin, showing the proportions of each feature and also the colour scheme you have chosen.

To make the play house

Calculate the measurements of the walls, door and roof according to the size of the table. Cut out the pieces from the calico fabric allowing 1.5cm (⅝in) for seams.

Using the graph patterns given, cut out the appliqué decorations in the appropriate coloured materials.

Make a line of tacking stitches in the long back and front walls to indicate the corner folds.

Now pin, tack and machine stitch the side wall to the back and front wall, making flat fell seams for a neat finish. Stitch one side edge of the door to the front wall, leaving

door overlap

corner fold

BACK WALL

SIDE WALL

FRONT WALL

corner fold

DOOR

Above: *This diagram shows how to assemble the play house.*

the other edge of the door free.

Turn under a 2.5cm (1in) hem on the side edge of the door, on the side edge of the back wall and all round the bottom of the house.

Stitch the roof to the walls and door, overlapping the open side of the door with the back wall for about 12.5cm (5in). Machine stitch the black felt knocker, letter box and door knob in place as illustrated.

To make the bricks

Using a postcard as a template, draw round the four sides on to the calico material with a sharp pencil, rounding off the corners. Place bricks at random on the walls. Machine stitch three times round the shapes, using slightly irregular lines to create a more natural effect.

To make a window

Draw the shape of the window 36cm tall × 38cm wide (14in × 15in) in pencil on the right side of the fabric. Stay stitch the corners in order to strengthen them by sewing a line of small running stitches inside the machine seam line before doing the final seam.

Cut out the centre area of the window to within 1cm ($\frac{3}{8}$in) of the pencil line. Slash the corner as far as the stay stitching. Fold the seam allowance to the right side along the pencil line. Lay the house flat on a large table with the right side facing upwards. Place the curtain net over the window hole, pin and tack firmly in position.

For the window frame, make a centre cross over the hole, using petersham ribbon. Then finish off the top and bottom edges, covering the raw edges of the curtain net with petersham ribbon.

Now make the shutters by turning under the edges of the red sailcloth; then pinning, tacking and stitching in place.

Finally, hem all round the curtain pieces. Machine stitch these inside the house at the top of the window.

Now sew on the appliqué decorations, using the graph patterns given to cut pieces.

Apple tree

Lay the back wall on a flat surface, facing upwards, so that the whole area can be seen at once. Pin on the main branches, making neat folds at the corners and folding under the ends of the branches.

Fill in the spaces with the smaller branches, tucking the lower ends under the large branches.

Now machine the branches, beginning with those with ends which will be hidden under other branches.

The ribbon which forms the trunk should be sewn down last. Make about 17 apple shapes, pin and machine stitch.

Flowers

Using different coloured felt fabric, cut circles about 14cm (5$\frac{1}{2}$in) in diameter for the heads, or flower shapes. Now cut smaller felt circles for the centres.

Machine stitch the leaves and stems in place around the walls and position a flower head on top of each stem. Machine the flowers in place and decorate with simple embroidery stitches such as blanket stitch, herringbone, French knots and stem stitch.

Bird house and birds

Cut the bird house from the navy felt and machine in position. Use a length of petersham ribbon for the post. Attach the birds to the top of the bird house and decorate as for the flowers. Work blanket stitch around the bodies, stem stitch round the heads and lazy daisy stitch round the wings and necks.

Shrubs and ladybirds

Cut out one large and one small shrub and machine in place.

For the ladybird, cut a black felt circle as the body, pin then stitch to the wall. Sew red felt wings over this and decorate with black spots made of tiny circles of felt.

101

Graph pattern
Each square = 2.5cm (1 in)

Knitted doll

Finished size
Height: 68cm (26in).

Tools required
3.25mm (No. 10) knitting needles; medium-sized crochet hook; basic sewing tools.

Techniques involved

Basic knitting; filling soft toys, making doll's clothes; embroidery stitches, double crochet stitch.

Tension

24sts and 32 rows to 10cm (4in) over stocking st worked on to 3.25mm needles.

Materials

10 × 25g (1oz) balls of double knitting yarn in green
5 balls in flesh
4 balls in white
1 ball in black
1 ball in rust
1 × 400g (15oz) bag of kapok or synthetic filling
1m (1⅓yd) of 2.5cm (1in) wide ribbon
felt for features
3 buttons
1.5m (1⅔yd) of round elastic
1 pair 3.25mm (No. 10) knitting needles
medium-sized crochet hook

Body and head

Using 3.25mm (No. 10) needles and flesh, cast on 33sts. Beg with a K row, cont in st st inc one st at beg of next 4 rows. 37sts.

Work 58 rows without shaping. Cast off 6sts at beg of next 2 rows. 25sts.

Dec one st at each end of next row. 23sts. Inc one st at each end of next 3 rows. 29sts. Inc one st at beg of next 8 rows. 37sts. Work 38 rows without shaping. Dec one st at each end of next 9 rows. 19sts. Cast off.

Make another piece in the same way.

Arms (make two)

Using 3.25mm (No. 10) needles and flesh, cast on 11sts. Beg with a K row, cont in st st inc one st at beg of next 6 rows. 17 sts.

Work 6 rows without shaping. Dec one st at beg of next 4 rows. 13sts. Work 1 row, so ending with a K row. Cut off yarn and leave sts on a spare needle.

Make another piece in the same way, but do not cut off yarn.
Next row P to end, then on to same needle P the sts of first piece. 26sts. Work 8 rows.
Next row K1, M1, K to last st, M1, K1. 28sts.
Work 9 rows.
Next row K1, M1, K to last st, M1, K1. 30sts.
Work 40 rows without shaping.

Dec one st at each end of next 14 rows. Cut off yarn, leaving a long end. Thread end through rem sts, draw up tightly and secure.

Legs (make two)

Using 3.25 mm (No. 10) needles and flesh, cast on 18sts. Beg with a K row, cont in st st inc one st at beg of next 4 rows. 22sts.

Work 4 rows. Dec one st at beg of next row and at this same edge on foll 7 rows. 14sts. Work 1 row, so ending with a K row. Cut off yarn and leave sts on a holder.

Using 3.25mm (No. 10) needles and flesh, cast on 18sts. Beg with a K row, cont in st st inc one st at beg of next 4 rows. 22sts. Work 4 rows. Dec one st at end of next row and at this same edge on foll 7 rows. 14sts. Work 1 row, so ending with a K row.
Next row P to end, then on to same needle P the sts of first piece. 28sts.
Work 8 rows.
Next row K1, M1, K to last st, M1, K1. 30sts.
Work 9 rows.
Next row K1, M1, K to last st, M1, K1. 32sts.
Work 60 rows. Cast off.

To make up

With RS of both pieces of body tog, sew round outer edge, leaving an opening for stuffing. Turn through to RS. Stuff body, then slipstitch the opening. Join seams of arms and legs, leaving top edge open.

Stuff arms and legs, then slipstitch the opening. Work 4 lines of back stitch along each hand to indicate fingers. Sew arms and legs in position.

Cut features from felt, then stitch or sew to face. Make plaits in rust following photograph opposite. Tie ribbon into a bow round each end of plait.

Dress

Using 3.25mm (No. 10) needles and green cast on 149sts. K 3 rows. With green K 1 row and P 1 row. Join on white.

Commence patt.
1st row K2 green, 1 white, (3 green, 1 white) to last 2sts, 2 green.
2nd row P with green.
3rd row K with green.
4th row P1 white, (3 green, 1 white) to end.
5th row K with green.

6th row P with green.

These 6 rows form patt. Rep them 8 times more, then work the 1st row again.
Dec row P2, (P2 tog, P1) 49 times. 100sts.
Cut off yarn.

Divide for yoke

Work RS of work facing, place first 25sts on a holder, rejoin yarn to next st, K49 for front, turn and leave rem 25sts on a holder.

Beg with a 4th row, patt 17 rows. Cast on 22sts at beg of next 2 rows for sleeves. 93sts. Working 22sts of each sleeve in green only, cont in patt on centre 49sts work 30 rows. Cast off. With RS of work facing, rejoin yarn to first set of 25sts and K to end of row.

Cont in green only, work 18 rows.

Cast on 22sts at beg of next row for sleeve. 47sts. Work 30 rows. Cast off.

With RS of work facing, rejoin yarn to rem sts and work as first side, but work 17 rows before casting on sts for sleeve.

Pocket

Using 3.25mm (No. 10) needles and white, cast on 8sts.

Work 1 row, then inc one st at beg of next 4 rows. 12sts. Work 8 rows. Cast off.

To make up

Join back seam of skirt to beg of yoke. Join underarm seams and yoke and shoulder seams to fit neck of doll. Using crochet hook and green work a row of double crochet evenly along back opening and edge of each sleeve. Work three button loops on right side of back opening.

Collar

Using 3.25mm (No. 10) needles and white, cast on 30sts. K8 rows. Cast off.

Make another piece in the same way. Sew on buttons. Sew on collar and pocket as shown.

Bloomers

Using 3.25mm (No. 10) needles and white, cast on 58sts. K2 rows.

Cut off white, join on green.

Beg with a P row, work 48 rows st st, so ending with a K row. Cut off yarn and leave sts on a spare needle.

Work another piece in the same way, but do not cut off yarn.
Next row P to end, then on to same

needle P the sts of first piece. 116sts. Work 34 rows st st, then work 3 rows K1, P1 rib. Cast off in rib.

Join centre back seam and inner leg seam. Thread elastic through WS of knitting, 7 rows from cast-on edge to gather.

Mob cap

Using 3.25mm (No. 10) needles and green, cast on 150sts for brim. K 2 rows.

Cut off green. Join on white.

K 6 rows.

Dec row (K1, K2 tog) to end. 100sts.

Work 5 rows st st. Cut off yarn and leave sts on a spare needle.

Using 3.25mm needles and white, cast on 22sts for crown. Beg with a K row, cont in st st inc one st at each

end of next 14 rows. 50sts. Now inc one st at beg of next 22 rows. 72sts. Work 15 rows without shaping. Dec one st at beg of next 22 rows. 50sts. Now dec one st at each end of next 14 rows. Cast off.

With RS of work facing, using 3.25mm needles and white, K up 100sts evenly round outer edge of crown. With RS of brim and crown tog, K 1 row, working into sts on crown and corresponding sts on brim. Cast off.

Thread elastic through back of sts round join, draw up tightly to fit head. Join row ends of brim.

Shoes (make two)

Using 3.25mm (No. 10) needles and black, cast on 22sts. Beg with a K

The above illustration shows the back view of the completed doll with detail of the dress fastening.

row, cont in st st inc one st at beg of next 4 rows. 26sts. Work 6 rows. Dec one st at beg of next row and at this same edge on foll 7 rows. 18sts. Cast off.

Make another piece, reversing shaping. Join back and toe seam.

Make a button loop to simulate fastening.

Knitted rabbit

Finished height:
76cm (30in).

Tools required
3.25mm (No. 10) knitting needles

medium size crochet hook
basic sewing tools.

Techniques involved

Basic knitting; grafting; embroidery stitches; chain stitch (crochet); filling soft toys.

Tension

24 sts and 32 rows to 10cm (4in) over stocking stitch on No. 10 needles.

Materials

8 × 25g (1oz) balls of double knitting yarn in white
5 balls in blue
1 ball in red
46cm × 31cm (18in × 12¼in) of grey felt
31cm × 23cm (12¼in × 9in) of pink felt
scraps of black, blue, white and brown felt for features
matching thread
2 blue buttons
2 × 400g (15oz) bags kapok or synthetic filling

Back

1st leg

Using 3.25mm (No. 10) needles and white, cast on 36sts for sole of foot.

Working in st st throughout, inc one st at beg of next 8 rows. 44sts.

Work 11 rows without shaping. Dec one st at beg of next row and at this same edge on foll 9 rows. 34sts. Now dec two sts at beg of next row and at this same edge on foll 3 rows. 26sts.

Work 1 row.
Cut off white.
Join on blue.

Inc one st at end of every alt row until there are 38sts, ending with a P row.

Cut off yarn and leave sts on a spare needle.

2nd leg

As 1st leg, reversing shaping and do not cut off yarn.

Next row K to end, then onto same needle K the sts of 1st leg. 76sts.

Work 3 rows. Inc one st at each end of next and foll 4th rows. 80sts.

Work 24 rows without shaping. Now dec one st at each end of next and every foll 6th row until 72sts rem. Work 5 rows. Cut off blue. Join on white.

Work 4 rows. Dec one st at each end of next and foll 4th row. 68sts. Work 4 rows.

Cast on 20sts at beg of next 2 rows for arms. 108sts. Inc one st at beg of next 8 rows. 116sts. Work 14 rows without shaping. Dec one st at beg of next 8 rows. 108sts. Cast off 28sts at beg of next 2 rows. 52sts.

This completes the arms.

Dec one st at each end of next 4 rows. 44sts. Work 1 row. Inc one st at each end of next 12 rows. 68sts. Work 15 rows without shaping. Dec one st at each end of next and every foll 3rd row until 50sts rem, then at beg of every row until 40sts rem. Work 8 rows. Dec one st at each end of next 9 rows. 22sts.

Cast off.

Front

Work as given for back.

Braces (make two)

Using 3.25mm (No. 10) needles and blue, cast on 12sts.

Work in st st for 47cm (18½in). Cast off.

Bow tie

Using 3.25mm (No. 10) needles and red, cast on 12sts. Work in st st for 22cm (8¾in). Cast off. Using crochet hook and red, make a ch 55cm (21¾in) long.

Fasten off.

To make up

With RS of both pieces facing, sew round outer edge, leaving an opening for stuffing. Turn to RS. Stuff firmly, then slipstitch the opening. Sew braces in position on back, cross them at back, then fasten at front with buttons. Join short ends of bow tie, then fold in half. Tie crochet chain round centre of tie to gather, then tie chain round neck.

Using trace pattern cut cheeks and outer ears from grey felt. Cut inner ears from pink felt. Cut eyelids and nose from black felt. Cut pupils from blue felt. Stitch pupils, eyelids and nose on to cheeks. Embroider features on face as indicated, working French knots, back stitch and long stitch.

Position felt on face, then using matching thread sew all round outer edge, stuffing cheeks with kapok. Sew inner ears to outer ears, then

The illustration above shows the back view of the finished rabbit, with his crossed braces and bob tail attached.

The diagrams opposite are the trace patterns for the rabbit's ears and features. These are cut and padded to produce the characteristic full-cheeked bunny expression.

Adults as well as children will take to this white rabbit.

sew ears in position. Using white, make a pompon for tail. Sew tail to back.

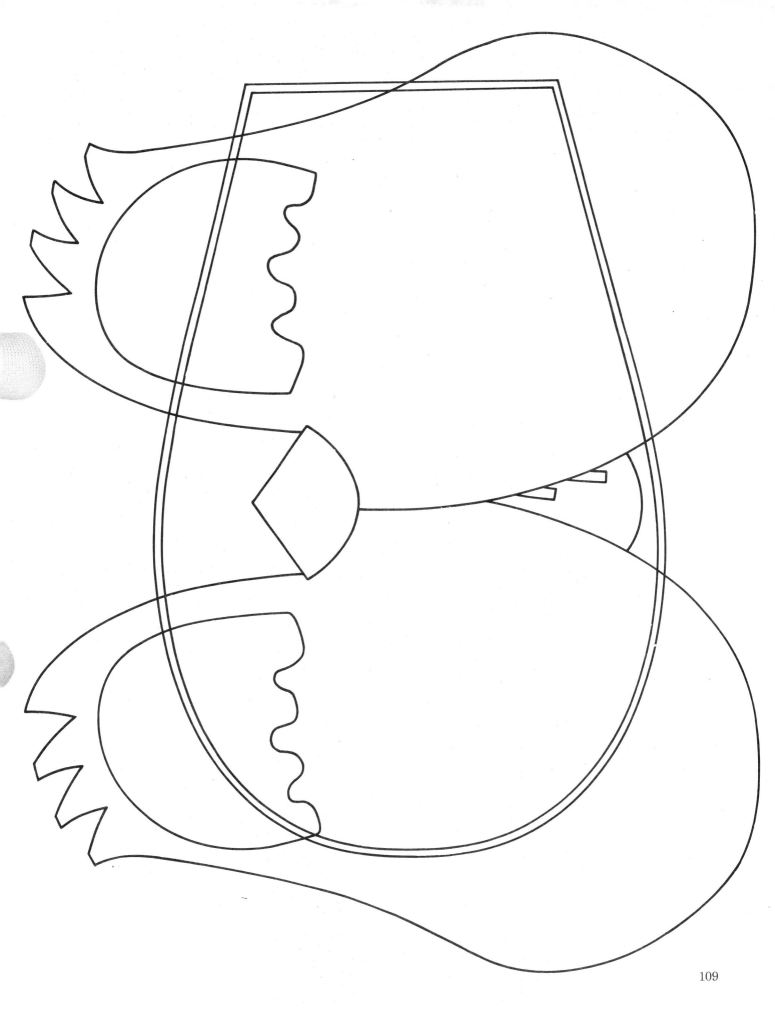

Knitted pirate

Finished height:
about 38cm (15in).

Tools required
Knitting needles; stitch holder; 2 large safety pins; basic sewing tools.

Techniques involved
Basic knitting; grafting; filling soft toys; embroidery stitches.

Tension
6sts and 8 rows to 2.5cm (1in) over st st worked on 3.25mm (No. 10) needles.

Materials
double knitting nylon yarn
2 × 25g (1oz) balls in main shade, A
1 ball each of contrast colours, (B), (C), (D) and (E)
one pair 3.25mm (No. 10) needles for body
one pair 3.75mm (No. 9) needles for clothes
one small brass buckle
two large brass rings
scraps of black felt
small piece of card and silver foil to cover it
20cm (8in) length of narrow elastic filling.

Doll

Shape feet
*Using 3.25 mm (No. 10) needles and A, cast on 48sts.
1st row K to end.
2nd row P to end.
3rd row K22, K2 tog, K2 tog tbl, K22.
4th row P21, P2 tog tbl, P2 tog, P21.
5th row K20, K2 tog, K2 tog tbl, K20
6th row P19, P2 tog tbl, P2 tog, P19.
Cont to dec in this way until 28sts rem.

Work legs
Beg with a K row work 30 rows in st st. *. Break off yarn and leave sts on st holder.
Make another foot and leg by working from * to * once more. Break off yarn.

Join legs
**With RS of leg facing, sl first 7 sts on to safety pin and fold to back of work, rejoin A to next st and inc by working twice into it, K12, inc in next 25, sl rem 7 sts on to another safety pin and fold to back of work. **. Cont across next leg on st holder

by working from ** to ** once more still using same needle, turn. 32sts.
Note The legs are seamed at back but remainder of doll is seamed at sides.

Body front
***Beg with a P row work 27 rows in st st on these 32sts.
Shape arms
Cast on 30sts at beg of next 2 rows. 92sts.
Next row Inc in first st, K28, inc in each of next 2sts, K30, inc in each of next 2sts, K28, inc in last st.
Next row P to end.
Next row Inc in first st, K30, inc in each of next 2sts, K32, inc in each of next 2sts, K30, inc in last st. 104sts.
Next row P to end.
Next row K to end.
Dec 1st at both ends of next row and foll alt row. 100sts.
Shape shoulders
Cast off 17sts at beg of next 4 rows. 32sts. Cast off 8sts at beg of next 2 rows. 16sts.
Shape neck
Beg with a K row, work 4 rows in st st.
Shape head
Inc 1 st at both ends of next row and every foll row until there are 32sts on needle.
Work 10 rows in st st. Break off A. Join in B.
Beg with a K row, work 2 rows in st st.
Dec 1 st at both ends of each of foll 8 rows, 16sts.
Cast off. ***.
Embroider features with scraps of wool.

Body back
Return to sts left on safety pins at top of legs. With WS of body facing but right side of folded back sts facing, place 4 lots of 7sts on to left hand needle so that the RS rows are facing and ready to form back body. 28sts.
Join in A.
Next row Inc first st, K12, inc in each of next 2sts, K12, inc in last st. 32sts.
Now work on these sts as given for front body from *** to ***.

Clothes
Jumper
Using 3.75mm (No. 9) needles and B, cast on 32sts. Beg with a K row work in st st in striped patt of 2 rows B, 2 rows C, until 22 rows completed.
Shape sleeves
Cast on 26sts at beg of next 2 rows. 84sts. Keeping striped patt correct, work 12 more rows in st st.
Next row K26, rib 32, turn, cast off 32sts in rib, turn, cast on 32sts, K26 to end.
Next row P26, rib 32, P26.
Beg with a K row, work 12 rows in striped st st.
Cast off 26sts at beg of next 2 rows. 32sts. Cont on these sts in striped st st for 22 rows. Cast off.

Headband
Using 3.75 (No. 9) needles and B, cast on 1st.
1st row P1, K1, P1 into same st. 3sts.
2nd row Inc in first st, K1, inc in last st. 5sts.
3rd row Inc in first st, K3, inc in last st. 7sts.
K 100 rows.
Dec 1st at both ends of next 2 rows. 3sts. K3 tog and fasten off.

Belt
Using 3.75mm (No. 9) needles and D, cast on 9sts and work in g st for 33cm (13in) then dec 1st at each end of every row until 3sts rem. K3 tog and fasten off.

Trousers
Using 3.75mm (No. 9) needles and E, cast on 40sts. Beg with a K row work in st st for 3 rows.
Next row K to mark hemline. Beg with a K row, work 18 rows in st st.
Shape leg
Work 10 rows in st st. (Note on other leg this should be 4 rows only.)
Next row K6, K2 tog, turn, P to end.
Cont in st st dec 1st at end of every K row until 2sts rem. P1 row. K2 tog and fasten off. Rejoin yarn to remaining 28sts, K2 tog, K8, K2 tog, turn, P to end.
Next row K2 tog, K6, K2 tog.
Next row P to end.
Cont to dec each end of every K row until 2sts rem.
P1 row.
K2 tog and fasten off.
Rejoin yarn to rem 16sts, K8, turn

and P back.

Next row K2 tog, K4, K2 tog.

Next row P to end.

Cont to dec both ends of each K row until 2sts rem.

P1 row.

K2 tog and fasten off.

Rejoin yarn to remaining 8sts, K2 tog, K6.

Next row P to end.

Cont in st st dec 1st at beg of every row until 2sts rem.

P1 row.

K2 tog and fasten off.

Work another piece in the same way noting that the number of rows worked for leg should be reduced as given in note to make trousers uneven length.

To finish

Join seams of doll, filling each section firmly as you work.

Stitch headband round head over colour change, crossing ends over and leaving approximately 2.5cm (1in) free at one side of head. Join side and sleeve seams of sweater and place on doll. Join centre front and back seams of trousers. Join leg seams. Stitch elastic tog to form circle. Turn waistband over circle of elastic to form hem and sl st to WS of trousers. Place trousers on doll. Sew ragged ends to legs. Stitch buckle to unshaped end of belt and fasten round waist of doll. Cut curved dagger out of cardboard. Wind thread or yarn round handle section and cover blade section with foil. Cut features and patch out of felt and glue or stitch to face.

This colourful sea dog comes complete with "silver" dagger made from cardboard and aluminium foil. Add glittering brass rings to his ears for an authentic "swashbuckling" look.

Knitted doctor and nurse

Finished height
52cm (20½in).
Tools required
2.75mm (No. 12) knitting needles;
2.75mm crochet hook; sewing tools.
Techniques involved
Basic knitting; grafting; filling soft
toys; chain and double crochet stitches; embroidery stitches.

Tension
32sts and 40 rows to 10cm (4in) over
st st worked on 2.75mm (No. 12)
needles.
Materials
medium-thick cotton yarn:
For doctor:
2 × 50g (2oz) balls in main colour (A)
pink

2 balls of contrast colour (B) white
2 balls of contrast colour (C) black
1 ball of contrast colour (D) ginger
3 buttons
3 press fasteners
waist length of elastic
kapok for filling
pair of safety eyes
oddment of fabric for cravat

toy medical accessories

For nurse:
2 × 50g (2oz) balls each of A and B
1 ball of C and D
2 balls of E, blue
oddment of F, red
8 press fasteners
length of narrow ribbon for dress
kapok for filling
pair of safety eyes, or felt
glasses and toy medical accessories

Doctor
Body
Using 2.75mm (No. 12) needles and A, cast on 112sts. Beg with a K row work in st st for 19cm (7½in). Cast off.

Head
Using 2.75mm (No. 12) needles and A, cast on 46sts.

Beg with a K row work 10 rows st st.
Shape head
Next row K1, (pick up loop lying between needles and K tbl—called inc 1—, K14, inc 1, K1) 3 times. 52sts.
Next row P to end.
Next row K1, (inc 1, K16, inc 1, K1) 3 times. 58 sts.

Cont inc 6sts in this way on every alt row until there are 88sts. Cont without shaping until work measures 11.5cm (4¼in) from beg, ending with a P row.
Shape crown
Next row K1, (K2 tog, K1) to end. 59sts.

Work 3 rows st st.
Next row K2 tog, (K1, K2 tog) to end. 39sts.

Work 3 rows st st.
Next row K1, (K2 tog) to end. 20sts.
Work 1 row st st.
Next row (K2 tog) to end. 10sts.
Break off yarn, thread through rem sts, draw up.
Fasten off.

Legs (make two)
Using 2.75mm (No. 12) needles and A, cast on 48sts.

Beg with a K row work, 14 rows st st.
Shape leg
Dec one st at each end of next and every foll 8th row until 32sts rem. Cont without shaping until work measure 20cm (7¾in) from beg, ending with a P row.

Break off A. Join in C and work 2 rows st st.

Shape shoe
1st row K20, turn.
2nd row P8, turn.

Cont on these 8sts in st st for 4cm (1½in), ending with a P row. Break off yarn.

With RS of work facing, rejoin yarn at inner edge of 12sts which were left, K up 10sts along side of foot, K across 8 instep sts, K up 10sts along other side of foot then K rem 12sts. K9 rows g st. Cast off 22sts at beg of next 2 rows. Cont on rem 8sts in g st until this piece is long enough to fit along bottom of shoe to heel.
Cast off.

Arms (make two)
Using 2.75mm (No. 12) needles and A, cast on 32sts. Beg with a K row work 11cm (4¼in) st st, ending with a P row.
Next row K1, (K2 tog, K2) to last 3 sts, K2 tog, K1. 24sts.
Work 3 rows st st.
Shape hand
1st row K11, inc 1, K2, inc 1 K11.
2nd row P11, pick up loop lying between sts and P tbl—called inc 1— P4, inc 1, P11.
3rd row K11, inc 1, K6, inc 1, K11.
4th row P11, inc 1, P8, inc 1, P11.
5th row K21, turn.
6th row P10, turn.
7th row K2 tog, (K2, K2 tog) twice. 7sts.
8th row P1, (P2 tog, P1) twice. 5sts.
Cast off rem 5sts and join thumb seam.

With RS of work facing, rejoin yarn to rem sts, K up 2sts from base of thumb, K to end. 24sts.
Beg with a P row work 7 rows st st.
Next row (K2 tog, K8, sl 1, K1, psso) twice.
Next row (P2 tog tbl, P6, P2 tog) twice.
Next row (K2 tog, K4, sl 1, K1, psso) twice.
Next row (P2 tog tbl, P2, P2 tog) twice.
Fold work in half and graft rem sts tog.

Nose
Using 2.75mm (No. 12) needles and A, cast on 2sts. Beg with a K row, cont in st st inc one st at each end of 2nd and every row until there are 12sts. Work 5 rows st st.

Dec one st at each end of every row until 2sts rem.
Cast off.

Trousers
Using 2.75mm (No. 12) needles and C, cast on 48sts. Beg with a K row cont in st st, inc one st at each end of 21st and every foll 20th row until there are 56sts. Cont without shaping until work measures 22cm (8¾in) from beg, ending with a P row. Cast on 3sts at beg of next 2 rows. 62sts. Mark each end of last row for crotch. Work 2 rows without shaping. Dec one st at each end of next and every foll 10th row until 56sts rem. Cont without shaping until work measures 13cm (5in) from markers. Cast off.

Make another leg in same way.

Coat back
Using 2.75mm (No. 12) needles and B, cast on 56sts. Beg with a K row work 20cm (7¾in) st st, ending with a P row.
Shape armholes
Cast off 2sts at beg of next 2 rows. Dec one st at each end of next and foll 3 alt rows. 44sts. Cont without shaping until armholes measure 7.5cm (3in) from beg, ending with a P row.
Shape shoulders
Cast off 5sts at beg of next 4 rows. Cast off rem 24sts.

Right front
Using 2.75mm (No. 12) needles and B, cast on 26sts. Beg with a K row work 7 rows st st. With separate length of contrast yarn cast on 13sts and leave.
Next row P to end then P across 13sts.
Next row K6, sl 1, K to end.
Next row P to end.
Rep last 2 rows until work measures same as back to underarm, ending with a P row.
Shape armhole and front edge
Next row Inc in first st, K3, K2 tog, sl 1, K2 tog, K to end.
Next row Cast off 2sts, P to end.
Next row Inc 1, K3, K2 tog, sl 1, K2 tog, K to last 2sts, K2 tog.
Cont dec at armhole edge on alt rows 3 times more, *at the same time* cont to shape front edge on every alt row until 17 sts rem.

Cont without shaping until armhole measures same as back to shoulder, ending at armhole edge.
Shape shoulder
Cast off at beg of next and foll alt row 5sts twice.

Cont on rem 7sts for 4cm (1½in). Cast off.

Left front
Work as given for right front, reversing all shaping.

Sleeves
Using 2.75mm (No. 12) needles and B, cast on 40sts. Beg with a K row cont in st st, inc one st at each end of 15th and every foll 10th row until there are 46sts. Cont without shaping until work measures 14.5cm (5¾in) from beg, ending with a P row.

Shape top
Cast off 2sts at beg of next 2 rows. Dec one st at each end of next and foll 4 alt rows. 32sts. Cast off at beg of next and every row 2sts 4 times, 3sts 4 times and 12sts once.

Large pockets (make two)
Using 2.75mm (No. 12) needles and B, cast on 14sts. K 24 rows g st.
Cast off.

Small pocket
Using 2.75mm (No. 12) needles and B, cast on 8sts. K 12 rows g st.
Cast off.

To make up
Press each piece under a damp cloth with a warm iron.
Body Join back and lower seam. Join top seam for 4.5cm (1¾in) from each side, leaving centre open for head. Join head seam. Fill body and head firmly and sew tog. Join arm seams, fill and sew to sides of body so that thumb comes to front of each arm. Join leg seams, fill and sew to bottom of body so that seams go to back. Run thread round outer edge of nose, draw up, fill and sew to face. Sew on eyes. Make cravat and tie round neck.
Hair Using 2.75mm hook and D, make 40ch.
1st row Into 3rd ch from hook work 1dc, 1dc into each ch to end. 39dc.
2nd row 1ch, *insert hook into next dc, take yarn round 2 fingers of left hand and draw a loop through, yrh and draw through one loop on hook, yrh and draw through 2 rem loops on hook, rep from * to last st. 1dc into turning ch.
Rep these 2 rows 6 times more. Fasten off and sew round head.
Moustache Cut D into 5cm (2in)

lengths. Using 3 strands tog, knot fringe under nose.
Trousers Join back and front seams to markers. Join leg seams. Turn 2cm (¾in) hems at waist and legs to WS and sl st down. Thread elastic through waist.
Coat Join shoulder, side and sleeve seams. Set in sleeves. Take out contrast yarn from fronts, fold in half at sl st line and graft sts. Turn in front edges to WS and sl st down. Join ends of neck facing and sew to back neck. Turn up 2cm (¾in) hems at lower edge and cuffs to WS and sl st down. Sew on pockets. Sew on 3 press fasteners and sew buttons on top.

Nurse

Make head, arms and nose as given for doctor. Using C throughout, make legs as given for doctor. Using A, cast on 100sts and make body as given for doctor.

Dress
**Using 2.75mm (No. 12) needles and E, cast on 157sts and work in one piece. Beg with a K row work 21cm (8¼in) st st, ending with a P row.
Next row K1, (K2 tog, K1) to end. 105sts. **.
Cast on 3sts at beg of next 2 rows, then cont in st st for a further 24 rows, ending with a row.

Divide for armholes
Next row P28, cast off 4 sts, P47, cast off 4sts, P28.
Complete left back first. Cont in st st, dec one st at armhole edge on next and foll 2 alt rows, then cont without shaping until 47 rows have been completed from beg of armhole shaping, ending with a K row.
Shape shoulder
Cast off at beg of next and every alt row 5sts twice and 15sts once.
With RS of work facing, rejoin yarn to 47 front sts. Cont in st st dec one st at each end of next and foll 2 alt rows, then cont without shaping until 43 rows have been completed from beg of armhole shaping.
Shape neck and shoulder
Next row P16, cast off 9sts, P16.
Complete this side first.
Next row K to end.
Next row Cast off 2sts, P to end.
Rep last 2 rows once more. Cast off at beg of next and every row 5sts

once, 2sts once and 5sts once.
With RS of work facing, rejoin yarn to rem sts and complete to match first side.
With RS of work facing, rejoin yarn to rem sts and complete right back to match left back, reversing shaping.

Sleeves
Using 2.75mm (No. 12) needles and E, cast on 40sts. Beg with a K row cont in st st, inc one st at each end of 5th and every foll 10th row until there are 46sts. Cont without shaping until work measures 11.5cm (4½in) from beg, ending with a P row.
Shape top
Work as given for doctor's jacket sleeve.

Apron
Using B, work as given for dress from ** to **, working 16cm (6½in) before dec row.
Next row K to end to form ridge.
Beg with a K row work 9 rows st st.
Next row Cast off 35sts K-wise to form ridge, K35, cast off 35st K-wise. Break off yarn.
With RS of work facing, rejoin yarn to centre 35sts.
Next row K to end.
Next row K5, P25, K5.
Rep last 2 rows 13 times more, then first row again. K4 rows g st.
Next row K5, cast off 25, K5. Cont on each set of 5sts in g st for approx 18cm (7in). Cast off.
Pockets (make two)
Using 2.75mm needles and B, cast on 10sts. K 17 rows g st. Cast off.

Cap
Using 2.75mm (No. 12) needles and B, cast on 101sts. P 1 row. Beg with a P row work 9 rows st st. P 1 row to reverse work. Beg with a K row work 10 rows st st.
Next row K2, *K twice into next st, K4, rep from * to last 4 sts, K twice into next st, K3. 121sts. Beg with a P row work 11 rows st st.
Shape top
Next row *K8, K2 tog, rep from * to last st, K1.
Next row P to end.
Next row *K7, K2 tog, rep from * to last st, K1.
Next row P to end.
Cont dec in this way on next and every alt row until 25sts rem, ending

with a P row.
Next row *K2 tog, rep from * to last st, K1.

Break off yarn, thread through rem sts, draw up and fasten off.

To make up
Body as given for doctor.

Hair Cut D into 76cm (30in) lengths. Lay across top of head evenly and st securely along centre. Catch ends tog at nape of neck. Plait ends tog then form into a bun and st in place.

Dress Join shoulder and sleeve seams. Set in sleeves. Join skirt seam to 3cm (1¼in) below waist. Turn in 3sts at both sides of centre back and sl st down. Make collar and cuffs from ribbon and st in place. Sew on 4 press fasteners to centre back. Turn 8 rows for hem at lower edge to WS and sl st down.

Apron Using F, embroider red cross on front as given in chart. Sew on pockets. Sew on 2 press studs to back waist and one to end of each strap to fasten at back. Turn up hem as given for dress.

Cap Using F, embroider red cross on band as given in chart. Join centre back seam. Turn headband to RS and catch in place.

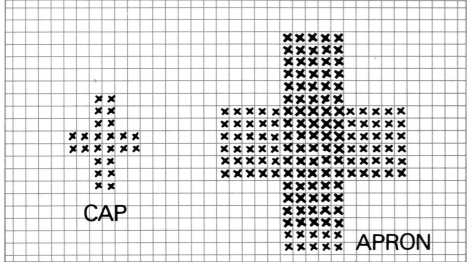

The nurse wears the traditional uniform of European nurses; the doctor wears the familiar white coat.

Aeroplanes

Finished length:
24cm (9½in).

Tools required
3.50mm crochet hook; sewing tools.

Techniques involved
Basic crochet; filling soft toys.

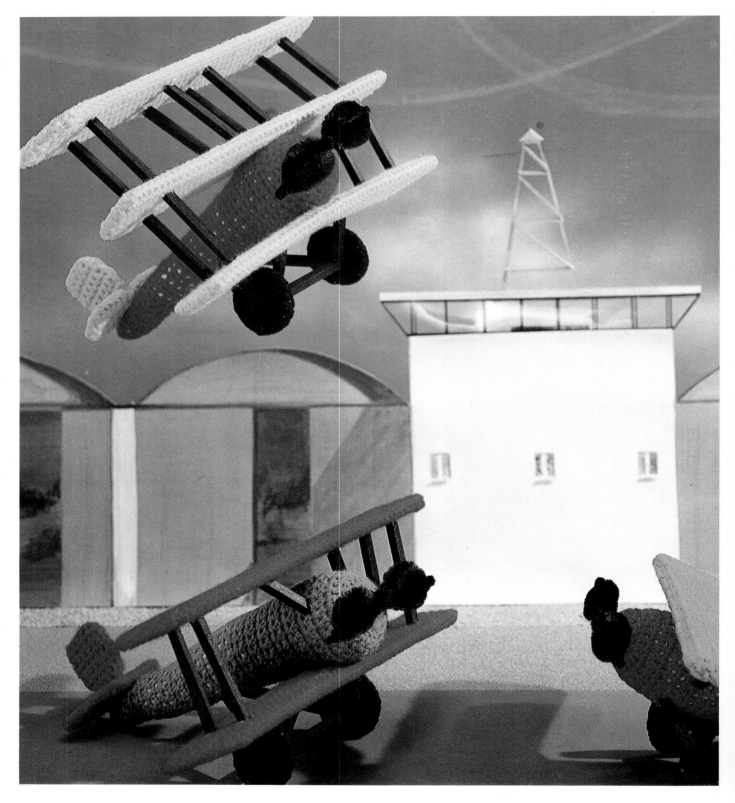

Tension
20dc and 24 rows to 10cm (4in) worked on 3.50mm crochet hook.

Materials
For each plane allow:
1 × 40g (1½oz) ball of double knitting yarn in main colour (A)
1 ball in contrast colour (B)
scrap in contrast colour (C)
kapok or synthetic stuffing
cardboard for wings
balsa wood
woodworking adhesive
chenille "bumps" for propeller

Monoplane
Body
Using 3.50mm hook and A, make 21ch.

Base row 2dc into 2nd ch from hook, 1dc into each of next 4dc, *2dc into next dc, 1dc into each of next 4dc, rep from * to end. Turn.

1st-5th rows 1ch, 1dc into each dc to end. Turn.

6th row 1ch, work next 2dc tog. 1dc into each dc to within last 2dc, work last 2dc tog. Turn.

7th-9th rows 1ch, 1dc into each dc to end. Turn.

Rep last 4 rows 6 times more. 10dc.

Next row 1ch, 1dc into each dc to end. Turn.

Next row 1ch, *work next 2dc tog, rep from * once more, 1dc into each of next 6dc. Turn. 8dc.

Next row 1ch, 1dc into each dc to end. Turn.

Next row 1ch, work next 2dc tog, 1dc into next dc, work next 2dc tog, 1dc into each of next 3dc. Fasten off.

Using 3.50mm hook and A, make 4ch, ss into first ch to form a circle.

1st round 1ch, work 7dc into circle, ss into first dc.

2nd round 1ch, 1dc into ss, *2dc into next dc, 1dc into next dc, rep from * twice more, 2dc into last dc, ss into first dc, 12dc.

3rd round As 2nd. 18dc. Fasten off.

Wing
Using 3.50mm hook and B, make 45ch.

Base row 1dc into 2nd ch from hook, 1dc into each ch to end. Turn.

1st row 1ch, 1dc into each dc to end. Turn.

2nd row 1ch, 2dc into next dc, 1dc into each dc to within last dc, 2dc into last dc. Turn. 46dc.

3rd and 4th rows As 1st.

5th row As 2nd. 48dc.

6th-9th rows As 1st.
Fasten off.

Make another piece in the same way.

Tail
Using 3.50mm hook and B, make 11ch.

Base row 1dc into 2nd ch from hook, 1dc into each ch to end. Turn.

1st row 1ch, 2dc into next d, 1dc into each dc to within last dc, 2dc into last dc. Turn.

2nd and 3rd rows 1ch, 1dc into each dc to end. Turn. 12dc.

4th row 1ch, 2dc into next dc, 1 dc into each of next 5dc. Turn.

5th row 1ch, work next 2dc tog, 1dc into each of next 5dc. Turn.

6th row 1ch, 1dc into each dc to within last 2dc, work last 2dc tog. Fasten off. Rejoin yarn to centre of rem 6dc and work 1dc into each dc to end. Turn. Work 4th-6th rows once. Fasten off.

Make another piece in the same way.

Rudder
Using 3.50mm hook and B, make 6ch.

Base row 1ch, 1dc into each dc to end. Turn.

1st row 1ch, 1dc into each of next 4dc, 2dc into last dc. Turn.

2nd–4th rows 1ch, 1dc into each dc to end. Turn.

5th row 1ch, 2dc into next dc, 1dc into each dc to end. Turn.

6th row 1ch, work next 2dc tog, 1dc into each of next 3dc, work next 2dc tog. Turn.

7th row 1ch, work next 2dc tog, 1dc into next dc, work next 2dc tog.

Fasten off.

Make another piece in the same way.

Wheels (make two)
Using 3.50mm hook and C, make 4ch, ss into first ch to form a circle.

1st round 1ch, work 7dc into circle, ss into first dc.

2nd round 1ch, 1dc into ss, *2dc into next dc, 1dc into next dc, rep from * to last dc, 2dc into last dc, ss into first dc. 12dc.

3rd round As 2nd. 18dc. Fasten off.

Make another piece in the same way.

To make up
Using wing, tail, rudder and wheel as pattern, cut cardboard to shape. Join long seam of body section, stuff firmly, then sew circle in place. Join wing, tail, rudder and wheel sections together over cardboard. Fold a length of four chenille "bumps" in half to form propellers. Sew to body. Attach wing to body, then using balsa wood form struts and under-carriage as shown in picture (we painted the wood to match the pro-pellers). Attach wheels to undercarriage. Sew rudder to tail, then sew tail to body.

Biplane
Work as given for monoplane, but make two wings and join wings together with balsa wood as shown in picture.

Triplane
Work as given for monoplane, but make three wings and join wings.

Crochet snail and alligator

Finished size
Snail: 46cm (18in) long by 30cm (12in) high.
Alligator: 73cm (29in).

Tools required
4.00mm crochet hook; sewing tools.

Techniques involved
Basic crochet; filling soft toys, inserting safety eyes.
Tension
19dc and 24 rows to 10cm (4in) worked on 4.00mm hook.
19htr and 16 rows to 10cm (4in) worked on 4.00mm hook.
Materials
For snail:
3 × 25g (1oz) balls of double knitting yarn in first colour (A) for body
2 balls in second colour (B) for shell
kapok or synthetic filling
2 long beads and 2 small round beads
Body
Using 4.00mm hook and A, make 41ch.
Base row 1dc into 3rd ch from hook, 1dc into each ch to end. Turn. 40dc.
Patt row 1dc into each dc to end. Turn.

Rep the patt row until work measures 46cm (18in) from beg. Fasten off.

Shell
Using 4.00mm hook and B, make 44ch.
Base row 1htr into 3rd ch from hook, 1htr into each ch to end. Turn. 43htr.
Patt row 2ch to count as first htr, 1htr into each htr to end. Turn. Rep the patt row until work measures 73cm (29in) from beg. Fasten off.

To make up
Join long seam of body. Gather one end, stuff firmly, then gather other end.

Join long seam of shell. Gather one end, stuff firmly, then roll and sew shell and sew to body as shown in picture.

Make antennae from beads and sew to body.

If making snail for a very small child, leave off antennae.

Alligator
Materials
For alligator:
2 × 25g (1oz) balls of double knitting yarn in first colour (A) for body
4 balls in second colour (B) for legs and eyes
scraps of white felt for eyes
2 glass safety eyes

Use fanciful colours for these droll creatures.

30cm (12in) of ricrac braid

Body
Using 4.00mm hook and A, make 41ch.
Base row 1htr into 3rd ch from hook, 1htr into each ch to end. Turn.
Patt row 2ch to count as first htr, 1htr into each htr to end. Turn.

Rep the patt row until work measures 35cm (13¾in) from beg.

Cut off A. Join on B.

Cont in dc for head, until work measures 46cm (18in) from beg. Fasten off.

Legs (make two)
Using 4.00mm hook and B, make 41ch.
Base row 1dc into 2nd ch from hook, 1dc into each ch to end. Turn.
Patt row 1dc into each dc to end. Turn.

Rep the patt row for 15cm (6in). Fasten off.

Eyes (make two)
Using 4.00mm hook and B, make 27ch. Work base row as given for legs, then rep the patt row until work measures 5cm (2in) from beg. Fasten off.

To make up
Join long seam of body. Fold body in half, placing seam at centre, and join one short end. Stuff firmly, then gather other end.

Join long seam of each leg. Gather one end, stuff firmly, then gather other end. Sew legs to body, sewing through centre to form two legs each side. Join short ends of eyes. Gather one end.

Cut two circles of felt each 3cm (1¼in) in diameter. Sew felt to eyes, then place glass eyes in position. Attach eyes, stuff firmly, then gather other end.

Sew ricrac braid round head section.

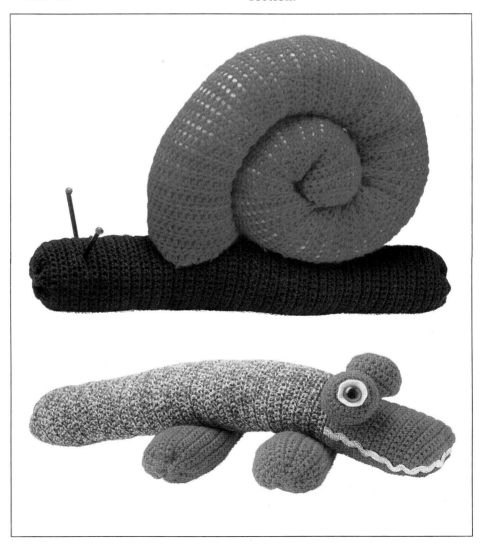

Crochet clown

Finished height
About 33cm (13in). Each circle

measures about 6.5cm (2½in) in
diameter.

Tools required
3.00mm and 4.00mm crochet hooks;

basic sewing tools.

Techniques involved

Basic crochet; embroidery stitches.

Materials

double knitting yarn:

3 × 25g (2 × 2oz) balls of main colour (A)

2 × 25g (1 × 2oz) balls of contrast colour (B)

2 × 25g (1 × 2oz) balls of contrast colours (C), (D), (E) and (F)

69 small beads to match colours of wool

4 larger orange beads

kapok or synthetic filling

5.5m (6yd) strong cotton thread

Tension

24sts and 26 rounds to 10cm (3.9in) over dc worked on 3.00mm crochet hook.

Circle

Using 4.00mm crochet hook and A, make 3ch and join with ss to form a ring.

1st round 1ch to count as first dc, 7dc into ring, ss into first ch. 8sts.

2nd round 1ch, *1dc into next dc, rep from * to end, ss into first 1ch.

3rd round 1ch, 1dc into same place, *2dc into next dc, rep from * to end, ss into first 1ch.

16sts.

4th round As 2nd.

5th round As 3rd.

32sts.

6th and 7th rounds As 2nd.

8th round Ss into each dc all round, ss into first ss.

Fasten off.

Make 12 circles in A, 12B, 13C, 12D, 12E, 14F.

Collar

Using D, work 6 rounds as given for circle.

7th round As 3rd.

64sts.

8th and 9th rounds As 2nd.

10th round *Ss into next dc, rep from * to end, ss into first ss.

Fasten off.

Using E, make a second piece in the same way.

Head

Using 3.00mm crochet hook and A, make 3ch and join with ss to form a ring.

1st round 5dc into ring, do not join end of round.

*1dc into each of next 2dc, 2dc into next dc, rep from * working in rounds without joining until there are 44dc in the round.

Mark this point.

Continue in rounds of dc without joining or further shaping until 10 more rounds have been worked from the marker.

****1dc into each of next 2dc, insert hook into next st and draw up a loop, insert hook into next st and draw up a loop, yrh and draw through all 3 loops on hook—called 2dc tog—, rep from ** until 24dc rem in the round.

Stuff head firmly, then continue with 1dc into next dc, 2dc tog, until only 3sts rem and stuff the remainder of head as work progresses.

Break off yarn, thread through rem sts, and draw up tight.

Fasten off.

Embroider eyes and nose in stem stitch as illustrated.

Hat

Using 3.00mm crochet hook and B, make 3ch.

1st round 6ch into first of 3ch, join with ss to form a ring.

2nd round 1ch, 1dc into same place, *2dc into next dc, rep from * to end, ss into 1ch.

12sts.

3rd round 1ch, *1dc into next dc, rep from * to end, ss into 1ch.

4th round As 2nd.

24sts.

5th round *Ss into next dc, rep from * to end, ss into first ss.

Break off B and join in F.

6th round 1ch, *1dc into next ss, rep from * to end, ss into 1ch.

7th and 8th rounds Work in dc without further shaping.

9th round 1ch, 1dc into same place, 1dc into each of next 3dc, *2dc into next dc, 1dc into each of next 3dc, rep from * to end, ss into 1ch. 30sts.

Break off F and join in E.

10th round 1ch, *1dc into next dc, rep from * to end, ss into 1ch.

11th and 12th rounds As 7th and 8th.

13th round 1ch, 1dc into same place, 1dc into each of next 4dc, *2dc into next dc, 1dc into each of next 4dc, rep from * to end, ss into 1ch. 36sts.

Break off E and join in D.

14th round As 10th.

15th and 16th rounds As 7th and 8th.

17th round 1ch, 1dc into same place, 1dc into each of next 5dc, *2dc into next dc, 1dc into each of next 5dc,

rep from * to end, ss into 1ch. 42sts.

Break off D and join in B.

Work 9 rounds without shaping.

Turn work inside out and continue in B for 5 rounds more.

Fasten off.

Turn work to RS, fold up brim at turning line.

To make up

Thread the cotton double into a fairly large tapestry needle.

Beginning with one arm, thread the yarn through one circle in F, leaving a tail of about 25.5cm (10in), thread on a small bead, then continue, placing one bead between the circles, with 3 circles in A, 3 in B, 3E, 3D, 3C, thread on one larger orange bead for hand then take the yarn back through all these circles and beads to the beginning.

Continue threading one circle in F without a bead, then 8 circles in F with one bead between, then one more without a bead for the body.

Continue with one leg, working as given for the arm with one larger orange bead for foot, then thread back through the leg.

Work the second leg in the same way, bringing the thread back to the top of the leg and then through the circles of the body.

Work a second arm in the same way as the first, then bring the thread back to the beginning of the arm as before.

Take the needle thread together with the thread which was left at the beginning of the first arm and thread all four thicknesses through one circle in C, the E collar circle and then the D collar circle (without beads), then thread on the last beads and tie the ends firmly but do not trim, continue with the same four threads through the head to the top and fasten off securely.

Catch stitch hat in place on head.

Crochet lion

Finished height
33cm (13in).

Tools required
4.00mm and 5.00mm crochet hooks.

Techniques involved
Basic crochet; filling soft toys.

Tension

8sts and 10 rows to 5cm (2in) over dc worked on 4.00mm crochet hook.

Materials

double knitting yarn:

4 × 25g (1oz) balls of main shade (A) gold

scraps of contrasts (B) orange, (C) black, (D) camel, (E) rust and (F) brown

kapok or synthetic filling

felt for eyes and tongue

cardboard for base

Body and head (make two)

Using 4.00mm hook and A, make 25ch.

Base row Into 2nd ch from hook work 1dc, 1dc into each ch to end. Turn. 24dc.

1st row (dc row) 2ch to count as first dc, miss first dc, 1dc into each dc to end, working last dc into turning ch. Cont in dc until work measures 10cm (4in) from beg, ending with a WS row.

Next row 2ch, (insert hook into next st, draw loop through) twice, yrh and draw through 3 loops on hook—called dec 1—, 1dc into each dc to last 3sts, dec 1, 1dc into turning ch.

Work 3 rows dc without shaping. Rep last 4 rows 3 times more. 16sts. Dec in same way at each end of next and every alt row until 10sts rem, ending with a WS row.

Shape head

Work 2 rows without shaping. Inc 1st by working 2dc into 1dc at each end of every row until there are 18sts. Work 8 rows without shaping. Dec 1st at each end of every row until 10sts rem. Work 2 rows without shaping. Fasten off.

Legs

**Using 4.00mm hook and A, make 6ch. Work base row as given for body. 5dc. Work 1 row dc. Inc 1st at each end of next row. Work 1 row without shaping. **. Inc 1st at beg of next row. Dec 1st at beg of next row, (7dc), work 2ch at end of row. Fasten off.

Work another piece in same way from ** to **. Inc 1st at end of next row. Dec 1st at end of next row, (7dc).

Next row 2ch, miss first dc, (insert hook into next dc, draw loop through) 3 times, yrh and draw through 4 loops on hook—called dec 2—, 1dc into each dc to end, work

1dc into each of 2ch of other foot, 1dc into each dc to last 4sts, dec 2, 1dc into turning ch. 12dc.

Shape legs

Work 11 rows without shaping. Inc 1st at each end of next and every foll 4th row 3 times. 18dc. Work 5 rows without shaping. Dec 1st at each end of next and every alt row until 12dc rem. Work 1 row.

Fasten off.

Base

Using 4.00mm hook and A, make 13ch. Work base row as given for body. 12dc. Work 1 row dc. Inc 1st at each end of every row until there are 24dc. Work 4 rows without shaping. Dec 1st at each end of every row until 12dc rem. Work 2 rows without shaping.

Fasten off.

Tail

Using 4.00mm hook and A, make 11ch. Work base row as given for body. 10dc. Cont in dc until work measures 30cm (12in) from beg, ending with a WS row.

Fasten off.

Using E, make a tassel and st to inside of one end of tail. Fold tail in half and join seam, padding out slightly as you sew. Leave end open.

Ears (make two)

Using 4.00mm hook and A, make 5ch. Work base row as given for body. 4dc. Work 1 row dc. ***Inc 1st at each end of next 2 rows. 8dc. Work 2 rows without shaping. Dec 1st at each end of next 2 rows. 4dc. ***. Work 4 rows without shaping. Rep from *** to ***. Work 2 rows without shaping. Fasten off.

Fold each ear in half and st shaped edges tog, leaving straight edge open. Pad out slightly.

Muzzle

Using 4.00mm hook and D, make 4ch. Work base row as given for body. 3dc. Inc 1st at end of next row, work 2ch at end. Fasten off.

Make another piece in same way, inc 1st at beg of next row.

Next row 2ch, inc 1, 1dc into each dc to end, 1dc into each of 2ch of other piece, 1dc into each dc to last 2dc, inc 1, 1dc into turning ch. 12dc. Work 3 rows without shaping. Dec 1st at each end of next 2 rows. 8dc. Work 1 row without shaping.

Fasten off.

Using C, work small knots or cross sts on each side of muzzle as shown.

Nose

Using 4.00mm hook and C, make 7ch. Work base row as given for body. 6dc. Work 2 rows without shaping. Dec 1st at each end of next row. Work 1 row.

Next row 2ch, miss first dc, dec 1, 1dc into turning ch. 3dc.

Work 1 row.

Fasten off.

Mane

Using 4.00mm hook and F, make 57ch loosely. Work base row as given for body. 56dc.

Next row (loop row) 2ch, miss first dc, *insert hook into next dc, wind yarn round two fingers of left hand and draw a loop through, yrh and draw through 1 loop on hook, yrh and draw through 2 loops on hook—called L1—, rep from * into each dc to last dc, 1dc into turning ch.

Change to 5.00mm hook. Cont working 1 row dc and 1 row L1 in each of E, B and A. Fasten off.

Work another piece in same way. Join short ends and A loop edges tog.

Press seam.

To make up

Press each piece lightly on WS under a damp cloth with a warm iron. Join back and front parts of body and head tog, leaving lower edge open. Stuff firmly with kapok. Cut piece of card to fit base, place inside and st base to lower edge of body.

Place legs on to front of body as shown and st into place, leaving one side of legs and foot open. Stuff top part and legs and foot firmly with kapok. Sew other side of legs and foot to body.

St muzzle on to head as shown, stuffing firmly with kapok. St nose into position, padding out slightly with kapok. St ears into position. Cut lengths of C for whiskers and sew into place as shown. Cut felt shapes for eyes and tongue and st in place. Pad out mane slightly and st into position round head as shown. St tail to lower edge of back.

Crochet lamb

Finished size
18cm (7in) long by 12.5cm (5in) high.

Tools required
4.00mm crochet hook; sewing tools.

Techniques involved
Basic crochet; embroidery stitches.

Tension

6sts and 5½ rows to 2.5cm (1in) over dc worked on 4.00mm crochet hook.

Materials

double knitting yarn:
3 × 20g (2¼ × 1oz) balls in main shade (A)
1 × 20g (¾oz) ball in contrast shade (B)
kapok or synthetic filling

Head

Using 4.00mm hook and B, make 4ch, join with ss to form ring.

1st round Work 6dc into ring.

2nd round *1dc into next dc, 2dc into next dc, rep from * all round.

3rd and 4th rounds *1dc into each of next 2dc, 2dc into next dc, rep from * all round.

5th round *1dc into each of next 3dc, 2dc into next dc, rep from * all round. 20dc. Continue inc 4sts evenly on each round in this way (working one more st between inc) until there are 40dc.

Continue without inc until work measures 8cm (3¼in) from beg.

Next round *1dc into each of next 6dc, keeping last loop of each st on hook work 1dc into each of next 2dc, yrh and pull through all loops—called dec 1—, rep from * all round. 35dc.

Next round *1dc into each of next 5dc, dec 1, rep from * all round. 30dc.

Continue dec 4sts evenly on each round (working one st less between dec) until 10dc rem.

Fasten off.

Body

Using 4.00mm hook and A, make 5ch, join with ss to form a ring.

1st round Work 10dc into ring.

2nd round Insert hook into first st, yrh and index finger of left hand twice, yrh and draw through 3 loops, yrh and draw through 2 loops—called loop st—, 1 loop st into same st, *2 loop sts into next dc, rep from * all round.

3rd round *1 loop st into next st, 2 loop sts into next st, rep from * all round. 30 loop sts.

4th-17th rounds *1 loop st in next st, rep from * all round.

18th round 1 loop st into each of the next 8sts, (2 loop sts into next st, 1 loop st into next st) 7 times, 1 loop st into each of next 8sts.

19th round As 4th.

20th round 1 loop st into each of next 11sts, (2 loop sts into next st, 1 loop st into each of next 2sts) 5 times, 1 loop st into each of next 11sts.

21st-26th rounds As 4th.

27th round 1 loop st into each of next 12sts, (miss next st, 1 loop st into each of next 2sts) 6 times, 1 loop st into each of next 12sts.

28th round As 4th.

29th round 1 loop st into each of next 9sts, (miss next st, 1 loop st into each of next 2sts) 6 times, 1 loop st into each of next 9sts.

30th round As 4th.

Continue dec in this way, working 3sts less at beg and end of each dec round until 18sts rem.

Next round (Miss next st, 1 loop st into each of next 2sts) 6 times.

Next round *Miss next st, 1 loop st into next st, rep from * all round.

Fasten off.

Topknot

Work as given for first 3 rounds of body. Fasten off.

Back head piece

Using 4.00mm hook and A, make 11ch.

1st row 1dc into 2nd ch from hook, 1dc into each of the next 8ch, 3dc into last ch, turn and work along other side of foundation ch, 1dc into each of 9ch, turn.

Next row 1 loop st into each of next 10sts, 3 loops sts into next st, 1 loop st into each st to end, 2ch, do not turn but continue round other side of work.

Next row 1 loop st into each of next 11sts, 3 loop sts into next st, 1 loop st into each st to end. Fasten off.

Ears

Using 4.00mm hook and A, make 7ch.

1st row 1dc into 2nd ch from hook, 1dc into each of next 4ch, 3dc into last ch, turn and work along other side of foundation ch, 1dc into each of 5ch, turn.

Next row 1ch, 1dc into each of next 6dc, 3dc into next dc, 1dc into each of next 6dc, turn.

Next row 1ch, 1dc into each of next 7dc, 3dc into next dc, 1dc into each of next 7dc. Fasten off.

Join in B, 1ch, 1dc into each of next 8dc, 3dc into next dc, 1dc into each of next 8dc. Fasten off. Make a second ear in the same way.

To make up

Stuff body and head and close openings.

Stitch ears to head and position top knot over them, and catch stitch ears to fold in half. Stitch head to body. Work back stitches in white down centre front of body to make a suggestion of a division.

Embroider white eyes and lashes and a black nose. Attach back head piece to back of head.

Crochet rabbits

Finished height
For **small bunny:** 24cm (9½in).

For **medium bunny:** 32cm (12½in).
For **large bunny:** 39.5cm (15½in)

Tools required
3.00mm crochet hook; sewing tools.

Techniques involved

Basic crochet; filling soft toys; embroidery stitches.

Tension

11sts and 13 rows to 5cm (2in) over dc worked on 3.00mm crochet hook

Materials

The figures in brackets [] refer to the medium and large sizes respectively.

double knitting or double crepe
  yarn:
4[4:5], 20g ($\frac{3}{4}$oz) balls in main shade
  (A)
scraps of contrast colours for ears
  and embroidery
kapok or synthetic filling

Back

Using 3.00mm hook and A, make 16[19:21]ch and beg at foot.

Base row Into 2nd ch from hook work 1dc, 1dc into each ch to end. Turn.

Work 3 rows dc. **.

Next row Dec 1, work in dc to end.

Dec 1st at same edge on next 2[3:3] rows. Work 7[8:12] rows without shaping. Inc 1st at straight inside edge on next and foll alt row. Work 1 row. Fasten off.

Make another piece in same way to **.

Next row Work in dc to last 2sts, dec 1.

Dec 1 at same edge on next 2[3:3] rows. Work 7[8:12] rows without shaping. Inc 1st at straight inside edge on next and foll alt row. Work 2 rows to end at inner edge.

Now cont working in dc across other piece to end.

30[34:38]dc.

Next row *** Dec 1, work in dc to last 2sts, dec 1.

Work 3 rows without shaping.

Rep last 4 rows until 26[28:30]dc rem. Cont without shaping until 11[13:17] rows have been worked from ***.

Next row Inc 1, work to last dc, inc 1. Fasten off. 28[30:32]sts.

Shape arms

Using 3.00mm hook and A, make 13[15:17]ch, now work in dc across main part, turn and work 14[16:18]ch.

Next row Into 3rd ch from hook, work 1dc, 1dc into each ch, work in dc across main part inc 1dc in first and last st, 1dc into each ch to end.

Next row Miss 1dc, work in dc to last dc, turn.

Work 1[1:3] rows dc.

Next row 1ch, work in dc across 5[5:6]dc, ss into next dc, turn, miss ss, work in dc to end. Fasten off.

Rejoin yarn to inner edge of other arm, 1ch, work in dc across 5[6:6]dc, ss into next dc, turn, miss ss, work in dc to end. Turn.

Work 4[6:6] rows across all dc. Fasten off.

Rejoin yarn to centre 30[32:34]dc for neck and head. Work 1 row dc.

Next row Ss across 4dc, work to last 4dc, turn.

Next row Ss across 3dc, work to last 3dc, turn.

Next row Inc 1, 1dc into each dc to last dc, inc 1.

Inc 1dc at each end of next 3 rows. Work 1 row dc.

Next row Inc 1, 1dc into each dc to last dc, inc 1.

2nd and 3rd sizes only

Rep last 2 rows 1[2] times more.

All sizes

Work 3 rows dc. Inc 1dc at each end of next row. Work 3 rows dc. Dec 1 at each end of next row. Rep last 4 rows once more. Work 1 row dc. Dec 1dc at each end of next and every alt row 2[3:4] times in all. Dec 1st at each end of next 3 rows. Fasten off.

Front

Work as given for back.

Ears (make two)

Using 3.00mm hook and A, make 14[16:18]ch. Work base row as given for back. Work 10[12:14] rows dc. Dec 1st at each end of next row. Work 3 rows dc. Dec 1st at each end of next and every alt row until 2sts rem. Fasten off.

Using 3.00mm hook and contrast yarn, work 2 inner ears in the same way.

Tail

Using 3.00mm hook and A, make 3ch. Join with a ss to first ch to form circle.

Next round Work 6dc into circle. Join with a ss to first dc.

Next round Work 2dc into each dc. 12dc. Join with a ss to first dc.

Next round *1dc into next dc, 2dc into next dc, rep from * to end. Join with a ss to first dc.

2nd and 3rd sizes only

Next round *1dc into each of next 2dc, 2dc into next dc, rep from * to end. Join with a ss to first dc.

3rd size only

Next round *1dc into each of next

3dc, 2dc into next dc, rep from * to end. Join with a ss to first dc.

All sizes

Work 5[6:6] rounds dc. Break off yarn, thread through last round of dc, fill with kapok, draw up tightly and fasten off.

To make up

Press all pieces under a dry cloth with a cool iron. With RS facing and leaving opening at top of head, join body pieces tog. Turn to RS and fill very firmly with kapok, joining rem part of head. With RS of ear and inner ear tog, join long sides. Turn to RS and press. Sew ears to head. Sew tail in place. Embroider face.

Crochet Dutch doll

Finished height
about 40cm (16in).
Tools required
3.00mm and 4.50mm crochet hooks; basic sewing tools.
Techniques involved
Basic crochet; embroidery stitches.
Tension
24sts and 26 rounds to 10cm (4in) over dc worked on 3.00mm crochet hook.
Materials
double knitting yarn:
3 × 25g (1oz) balls in each of main colour (A) and contrast colours (B) and (C)
1 × 25g (1oz) ball in each of contrast colours (D) and (E)
kapok or synthetic filling

Legs

Using 3.00mm crochet hook and A, make 3ch.
1st round 10dc into first of 8ch, do not join end of round.
2nd round *1dc into next dc, 2dc into next dc, rep from * to end.
15sts.
3rd round 2dc into first dc, *1dc into next dc, rep from * to end.
Rep 3rd round twice more.
18sts.
6th round 2dc into first dc, 1dc into each of next 8dc, miss 1dc, 1dc into each of next 8dc. 18sts.
7th round As 3rd.
19sts.
8th round 2dc into first dc, 1dc into each of next 8dc, miss 1dc, 1dc into each of next 9dc.
19sts.
Rep 3rd round 3 times more.
22sts.
Mark this point, then continue in rounds of dc without joining at ends for 10 rounds more.
Break off A and join in B. Continue in dc for 8 rounds more.
Fasten off.
Make a second leg in the same way.
Place the two legs together and mark the centre 3sts on the inside of each leg.

Gusset

Using 3.00mm crochet hook and B, make 6ch.

1st row 1dc into 3rd ch from hook, 1dc into each of next 3ch. 5sts.
2nd row 1ch, *1dc into next dc, rep from * to end.
Rep 2nd row 3 times more.

Join gusset to legs

Continue working with yarn from gusset and beg with left leg: miss 3 marked sts, 1dc into each of rem 19sts, 1dc into each of foundation ch of gusset (5sts), continue with right leg: miss 3 marked sts, 1dc into each of rem 19sts, ss to first st of gusset.
48sts.

Body

Continue in dc for 17 rounds in B, 15 rounds D, 2 rounds E.
Break off yarn.

Arms

Using 3.00mm crochet hook and A, make 3ch.
1st round 5dc into first of 3ch, do not join end of round.
2nd round *2dc into next dc, rep from * to end. 10sts.
3rd round *1dc into next dc, 2dc into next dc, rep from * to end. 15sts.
4th round *1dc into next dc, rep from * to end.
5th round *1dc into each of next 2dc, 2dc into next dc, rep from * to end. 20sts.
Mark this point.
Work 20 rounds more in dc. Break off A.

Join arms to body

Mark 4sts at each side of body for the underarms making them slightly to the front (ie 3sts to the front and one st to the back on each side of body).
Beg at back of body, miss first st after right underarm, join B to next st, 1ch to count as first dc, 1dc into each of next 18dc, insert hook into next dc and draw up a loop, insert hook into 1dc of left arm and draw up a loop, yrh and draw through all three loops on hook, 1dc into each of next 14dc round left arm, insert hook into next st and draw up a loop, miss the 4sts marked for left underarm on body, insert hook into next st and draw up a loop, yrh and draw

through all 3 loops on hook, 1dc into each of next 17dc across front of body, join next st to one st of right arm as before, 1dc into each of next 14dc round arm, join next st of arm to rem st beyond the 4 marked sts of right underarm.
68sts.
Next round *1dc into each of next 15dc, insert hook into next st and draw up a loop, insert hook into next st and draw up a loop, yrh and draw through all 3 loops on hook—called 2dc tog—, rep from * to end. 64sts.
Work 2 rounds dc without shaping.
Do not break off yarn. Stuff arms, legs and body, joining the openings at underarms and between legs and gusset.
Next round Continue with B, *1dc into each of next 6dc, 2dc tog, rep from * to end. 56sts.
Work 1 round without shaping.
Next round *1dc into each of next 5dc, 2dc tog, rep from * to end. 48sts.
Work 1 round without shaping.
Next round *1dc into each of next 2dc, 2dc tog, rep from * to end. 36sts.
Work 1 round without shaping.
Next round *1dc into next dc, 2dc tog, rep from * to end. 24sts.
Break off B and join in E.
Next round Ss into next dc, rep from * to end.
Next round *1dc into next ss, rep from * to end.
Next round *1dc into next dc, rep from * to end.
Next round *Ss into next dc, rep from * to end.
Break off E.
Stuff remainder of body firmly.

Head

Using 3.00mm crochet hook, join A to back of neck, *1dc into next ss, rep from * to end. 24sts.
Next round *1dc into each of next 2dc, 2dc into next dc, rep from * to end. 32sts.
Next round *1dc into next dc, 2dc into next dc, rep from * to end. 48sts.
Work 14 rounds without shaping.
Next round *1dc into each of next 4dc, 2dc tog, rep from * to end. 40sts.
Work 2 rounds without shaping.
Next round *1dc into each of next

3dc, 2dc tog, rep from * to end. 32sts.

Work 1 round without shaping.

Stuff shaping.

Stuff head to here.

Next round *1dc into each of next 2dc, 2dc tog, rep from * to end. 24sts.

Work 1 round.

Next round *1dc into next dc, 2dc tog, rep from * until only 5sts rem and stuff the remainder of head as work progresses.

Break off yarn, thread through rem sts and draw up tight.

Fasten off.

Embroider eyes and nose in stem stitch as illustrated.

Dress

Left sleeve

Using 4.50mm crochet hook and C, make 23ch.

1st row 1dc into 3rd ch from hook, *1dc into next ch, rep from * to end. 22sts.

2nd row Join in E, 1ch, *1dc into next dc, rep from * to end.

3rd row Using E, as 2nd.

Break off E.

Using C, work 9 rows more.

Left bodice

Using a separate length of C, make 6ch and join to beg of last row.

Next row 7ch, 1dc into 3rd ch from hook, 1dc into each of next 4ch, *1dc into next dc, rep from * to end, 1dc into each of 6ch.

34sts.

Continue for 8 rows more.

Next row 1ch, 1dc into each of next 14dc, turn and continue on these sts.

Back

Work 6 rows more. Break off yarn.

Right bodice

Using 4.50mm crochet hook and C, make 20ch.

Next row 1dc into 3rd ch from hook, 1dc into each of next 17ch, 1dc into each of 15dc which were left.

34sts.

Work 8 rows more.

Next row Ss over first 6sts, *1dc into next dc, rep from * to last 6sts, turn. 22sts.

Work 8 rows more in C, then 2 rows E, 1 row C.

Fasten off.

Using C and with RS facing, work 1 row dc up front edge round neck and down other front, then 1 row of crab st (dc worked from left to right).

Skirt back

Using 4.50mm crochet hook and C, with RS facing, work 23dc across lower edge of bodice back.

Next row 1ch, 1dc into same place, *1dc into next dc, 2dc into next dc, rep from * to end. 35sts.

Work 2 rows.

Next row 1ch, 1dc into next dc, *2dc into next dc, 1dc into each of next 2dc, rep from * to end. 46sts.

Work 22 rows more in C, then 6 rows E, 2 rows C.

Fasten off.

Skirt front

Using 4.50mm crochet hook and C, with RS facing work 8dc across right front bodice, hold the two sections of the bodice together and work 1dc into the double thickness of the two edges together, 8dc across left bodice front.

front.

17sts.

Next row 1ch, 1dc into same place, 2dc into each of next 5dc, 1dc into each of next 5dc, 2dc into each of next 6dc. 29sts.

Work 2 rows.

Next row 1ch, 1dc into next dc, *2dc into next dc, 1dc into each of next 2dc, rep from * to end. 38sts. Work 22 rows more in C, then 6 rows E, 2 rows C.

Fasten off.

Join side and underarm seams.

Apron

Using 4.50mm crochet hook and B, make 76ch.

1st row 1dc into 3rd ch from hook, *1dc into next ch, rep from * to end. 75sts.

2nd row 1ch, *1dc into next dc, rep from * to end.

Break off yarn and turn.

3rd row Miss 31dc, rejoin yarn to next dc, 1ch, 1dc into each of next 12dc, turn.

13sts.

4th row 1ch, *2dc into next dc, 1dc into next dc, rep from * to end.

19sts.

Work 2 rows.

7th row 1ch, 1dc into same place, *1dc into each of next 2dc, 2dc into next dc, rep from * to end.

26sts.

Work 19 rows without shaping.

Break off yarn.

With RS facing, work 1 row dc down right front edge, along bottom and up left front edge, then 1 row crab st.

Fasten off.

Hat

Using 4.50mm crochet hook and B, make 7ch and beg at back.

1st row 1dc into 3rd ch from hook, *1dc into next ch, rep from * to end. 6sts.

2nd row 1ch, *1dc into next dc, rep from * to end.

Continue in dc, inc one st at each end of next 2 rows.

Work 10 rows without shaping.

15th row Ss into first dc, 1dc into each of next 8dc, ss into last dc, turn.

16th row Ss into first dc, 1dc into each of next 6dc, ss into next dc.

Fasten off.

With RS facing, rejoin yarn to beg of work and work 14dc up side of back, 10dc across top, 14dc down other side. 38sts.

Continue in dc, inc one st at each end of next and every alt row until there are 52sts, ending with a RS row.

Continue in dc across bottom edge of hat.

Work 1 row crab st all round.

Roll the wings of the hat as illustrated and catch stitch in position.

Catch stitch hat to head of doll.

Glove puppets

Finished sizes:
to fit an average 6-10 year old child's hand. Length: 19cm (7½in). Width from tip to tip: 20cm (8in).

Tools required
4.00mm crochet hook; sewing tools.

131

Techniques involved
Basic crochet; embroidery stitches.
Tension
20dc and 22 rows to 10cm (4in) worked on 4.00mm hook.
Materials
double knitting yarn

For cat:
1 × 20g ($\frac{3}{4}$oz) ball each of blue, maroon, grey and white
scraps of black yarn for embroidery
2 buttons

For dog:
1 × 20g ($\frac{3}{4}$oz) ball each of yellow, green, beige and mid brown
scraps of black, pink and maroon yarn
2 buttons

For pig:
1 × 20g ($\frac{3}{4}$oz) ball each of yellow and pink
scraps of white, black and maroon yarn

For rabbit:
1 × 20g ($\frac{3}{4}$oz) ball each of black, maroon and white
scrap of blue yarn
4 buttons

Basic glove puppet
Make 16ch.

Base row 1dc into 2nd ch from hook, 1dc into each ch to end. Turn. 15dc.

Next row 1ch to count as first dc, 1dc into each dc to end. Turn. Rep last row 13 times more.

Next row 1ch, 2dc into first dc, work to last dc, 2dc into last dc. Turn.

Next row 1ch, 1dc into each dc to end. Turn.

Rep last 2 rows until there are 27sts, ending with an inc row.

First arm
Next row Work across first 6sts, turn.

Next row 1ch, (insert hook into next st and pull yarn through) twice, yrh and pull through all loops on hook—called dec 1—, 1dc into each dc to last dc, 2dc into last dc. Turn. 6sts.

Next row 1ch, 1dc into each dc to end. Turn.

Rep last 2 rows twice more.

Next row 1ch, (dec 1) 3 times.

Next row Dec 2. Fasten off.

Second arm
Miss centre 15sts, rejoin yarn to next st, 1dc into same st, 1dc into each of last 5sts. Turn.

Next row 1ch, 2dc into first dc, 1dc into each of next 3dc, dec 1 over last

2dc. Turn.

Next row 1ch, 1dc into each dc to end.

Rep last 2 rows twice more. Complete as given for first arm.

Head
Rejoin yarn to first of 15dc at centre.

Work 9 rows in dc. Dec one st at each end of next 5 rows. 5sts rem. Fasten off.

Make another section in the same way. Place sections tog and work in dc around outer edge in appropriate colour.

Cat
Using blue, work first 15 rows of lower body. Change to maroon and work 11 rows of increasing for arms.

Work first 5 rows of arms in maroon, then remainder in white. Rejoin maroon to upper body and work 2 rows, then change to grey to complete head.

Ears (make two)
Using grey, make 10ch.

Base row 1dc into 2nd ch from hook, 1dc into each dc to end. Turn. 9dc.

Work 5 more rows in dc. Fasten off. Fold corners over to make a point and sew to top of head.

Features
Using black, embroider eyes, eylashes, nose and mouth. Thread 5 short lengths of white behind nose to form whiskers.

Collar
Using white, sew around neck in blanket stitch. Return in opposite direction, working blanket stitch over top to form a link patt.

Straps (make two)
Using blue, make 30ch. Attach to top of blue "skirt" at front and back. Sew buttons to end of front straps.

Dog
Using green, make 16ch.

Base row 1dc into 2nd ch from hook, 1dc into each ch to end. Turn.

1st row 1ch, 1dc into each of first 3dc, changing to yellow on last st, (3dc in yellow, 3dc in green) to end. Turn.

2nd row (3dc in green, 3dc in yellow) to last 3sts, 3dc in green.

3rd-4th rows (3dc in yellow, 3dc in green) to last 3sts, 3dc in yellow.

5th-6th rows As 2nd.

7th-8th rows As 3rd and 4th.

Cut off green. Cont in yellow, working first 5 rows of arms in yellow, then remainder in beige.

7th-8th rows As 3rd and 4th.

Cut off green. Cont in yellow, working first 5 rows of arms in yellow, then remainder in beige.

Rejoin yellow to upper body and work 2 rows, then change to beige to complete head.

Ears (make two)
Using mid brown, make 10ch.

1st row 1dc into 2nd ch from hook, 1dc into each of next 7ch, 3dc into last ch, then working along other side of ch, work 1dc into each of rem 8ch. Turn.

Next row 1ch, 1dc into each of first 8dc, 2dc into next dc, 1dc into next dc, 2dc into next dc, 1dc into each dc to end. Turn.

Rep last row twice more. Fasten off.

Gather up flat end and attach ears to head.

Features
Using black, embroider eyes and nose. Using pink, embroider mouth.

Braces (make two)
Using maroon, make 30ch. Attach to top of patterned "trousers" at front and back. Sew buttons to end of front braces.

Pig
Using yellow, work up to last 12 rows except arms which have first 5 rows in yellow, then rest in pink. Work remainder of head in pink.

Ears (make two)
Using pink, make 3ch. Join with a ss into first ch to form a circle.

1st round Work 8dc into circle.

2nd round Work 2dc into each dc. 16dc.

3rd round (1dc into next dc, 2dc into next dc) all round. 24dc.

4th round (2dc into next dc, 1dc into each of next 2dc) all round. 32dc.

Fasten off.

Fold ears in half and attach to head.

Features
Using black, embroider eyes.
Snout Using needle length of double pink, place needle between and just

One basic pattern, with suitable variations, makes all four of these hand puppets.

below eyes. Wind yarn several times round needle, then secure at each end. Using black, embroider nostrils.

Collar
Using white, make 31ch.
Next row 1dc into 2nd ch from hook, 1dc into each of next 2dc, *3ch, ss into last dc worked, 1dc into each of next 3ch, rep from * to end. Fasten off.

Attach collar round neck.

Using an odd length of yarn make a bow at neck.

Rabbit
Using black, make 16ch.
Base row 1dc into 2nd ch from hook, 1dc into each ch to end. Turn.
1st row 1ch, 1dc into each of first 3dc, changing to white on last st, (3dc in white, 3dc in black) to end.
2nd row (3dc in black, 3dc in white) to last 3sts, 3dc in black.

Rep last row 4 times more.

Change to maroon for rest of body.
Work first 5 rows of arms in maroon, then complete arms in white.

Rejoin maroon to upper body and work 2 rows. Complete head in white.

Ears (make two)
Using white, make 11ch.
1st row Work 1dc into 2nd ch from hook, 1dc into each of next 8ch, 3dc into last ch, then working along other side of ch, work 1dc into each of 9ch. Turn.
2nd row 1ch, 1dc into each of first 9dc, 3dc into top dc, 1dc into each of rem 9dc. Turn.
3rd row 1ch, 1dc into each of first 10dc, 3dc into top dc, 1dc into each of rem 10dc.

Fasten off.

Fold base of each ear to centre, stitch down, then attach to head.

Features
Using blue, embroider eyes. Using black, embroider nose and mouth.

Work a row of blanket stitch in black up centre front for "jacket" opening. Sew buttons to "jacket".

Thread black yarn round neck for "tie". Make bow at centre front.

WOODEN TOYS

A few scraps of leftover timber are all you need to construct many of the wooden toys in this section. They are well-designed, simple to make, and sturdy enough to withstand the most energetic play. There are toys to suit boys and girls of all ages, including boats, a railway engine, a super truck, also a lovely doll's house. The cost of the materials is easy on your budget too.

Basic know-how

Tools

Tools for model and toy making are quite widely varied, and some of them have only one special purpose. Each technique section explains what tools are available and how they are used. In each case, the tools discussed are the best or most convenient for the job in hand.

This means that the total number of tools mentioned is very large indeed. Fortunately, it is unnecessary to have or use them all. Use them if they are to hand, as they will make the job quicker and easier.

Certain basic tools are almost indispensable, but these are relatively cheap, and will probably already form part of even a modest tool kit.

At least one saw is essential, and a tenon saw is probably the most suitable for general use. It is useful to have a coping or fretsaw as well for cutting curves.

A trimming knife is invaluable for all sorts of odd jobs and shaping.

You will need a drill of some kind and a selection of bits for drilling holes for screws and other fittings.

One or two screwdrivers will be needed to drive screws fixing parts together.

A hammer will also be needed to fix parts which are pinned and nailed together. A lightweight type is the most useful.

A steel rule and some type of square are essential for marking parts accurately.

Pliers can be used for holding all sorts of parts which are difficult to hold in your fingers, and can also be used for bending metal parts or cutting wire and rods.

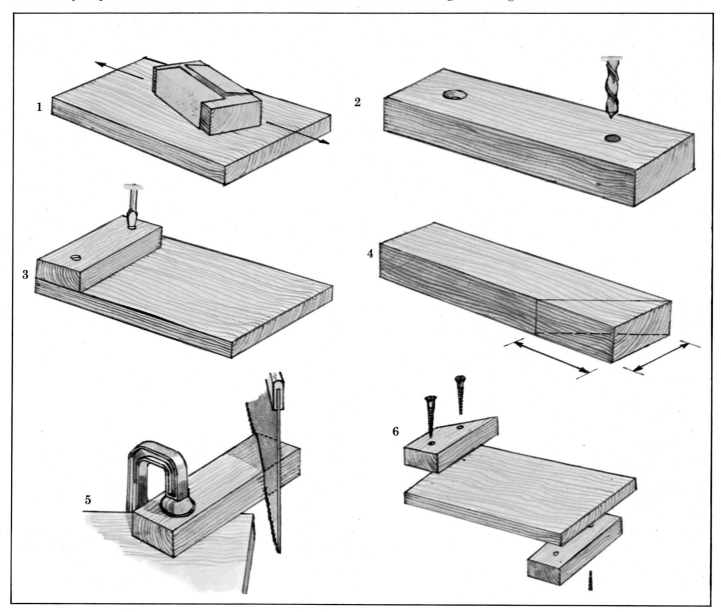

Right: *When scribing cutting lines around a piece of timber, it is important to work in the correct order, with the try square in the right place. After scribing a mark, turn the timber in the direction of the red arrow, and line your try square with the "nick" left by it to continue the line around.*

Left: *Making a bench hook. The instructions are as follows:*

Tools required
Pencil; rule; try square; 45° set square; sandpaper and block; saw; G-clamp; hand drill and bits (also countersink bit); screwdriver.

Materials
One piece pine 2cm ($\frac{3}{4}$in) × 17.5cm (7in) × 22.5cm (9in)
Two pieces pine 2.5cm (1in) × 5cm (2in) × 15cm (6in)
Four No. 10 3.1cm (1$\frac{1}{4}$in) flathead screws
PVA woodworking adhesive

1. *Smooth all wood surfaces with a sandpaper block.*
2. *Using a G-clamp, hold one of the short pieces in place on the larger piece (across the grain). Drill the pilot holes. Remove the short piece and drill out the pilot hole to make the shank hole. Countersink using the countersink bit.*
3. *Apply glue to both surfaces, and rub together to force out excess glue. Screw on the short piece.*
4. *Take the other short length of wood and check that the ends are square. Draw a diagonal line from one corner, and, using the try square, continue around the timber. Check the diagonals on both sides with the set square.*
5. *Clamp the piece to the bench and carefully saw off the triangular waste, then smooth the cut surface with the sandpaper block.*
6. *Turn the large work piece over and glue and screw the mitred short length in a similar way to the first. If you are left handed the short pieces will be attached to the opposite sides of the board.*

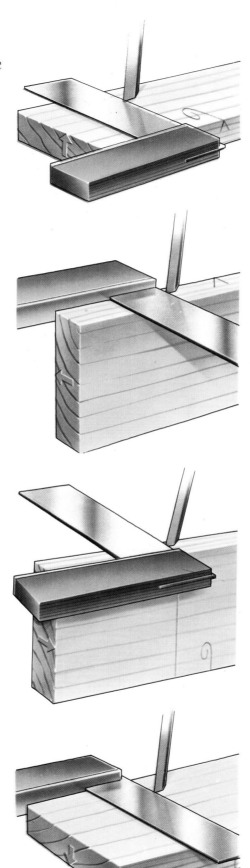

A junior hacksaw will be needed to cut parts which are made from sheet metal.

For shaping parts, a planer-file is the most versatile tool, but it is possible to manage with sandpaper and a sandpaper block alone. These will be needed in any case for finishing parts.

To apply the finish, you will need at least one paintbrush, and preferably a range of small to medium sizes.

Some kind of sturdy work surface will also be necessary, and a bench hook is invaluable for holding parts. This, however, is easy to make from offcuts and scrap timber.

Timber and boards
The majority of toys use three basic materials—softwood, plywood and dowels. Other materials occur less frequently.

Softwood covers most of the solid wood used. The term does not mean that the wood is particularly soft, although this is often the case. It is used to define the type of tree from which the boards were cut. Pine and deal are other generic names.

Softwood is sold in various lengths and can often be bought cut to order. It is sold in a variety of sections described as width and thickness, e.g. 50mm × 25mm (2in × 1in). It can be bought rough sawn to this size, but the normal way of buying it for these toys is to obtain timber which is planed all round (PAR), which leaves a smooth finish on all four faces and edges. It is important to remember that when buying timber in this form, it is measured when sawn, not when finished. This means that timber of the nominal size given above will actually be a few millimetres smaller than this in each dimension, because of the material removed in planing it smooth. If a part has to be, for example, exactly 50mm (2in) thick, do not buy 50mm (2in) timber as this will be appreciably less. Instead, buy timber of a larger size and cut it.

Because it is a natural material, the quality of softwood varies considerably and it is often graded for sale. Avoid poor quality timber which is split or badly warped, has a large number of knots or is watermarked or damp.

Veneers are very thin sheets of

wood—generally hardwood—used to give a decorative finish over cheaper woods. They are not often available except from craft shops or specialized timber merchants.

Plywoods are man-made boards made by gluing several cross-grained veneers together under heat and pressure. They are very stiff and strong, although the thinner varieties can often be bent to form curved shapes. They are sold in standard-sized large sheets, but the cheapest way to buy is usually to look out for offcuts large enough to cut the small parts needed.

Plywood is sold according to its thickness, and although it may vary very slightly, this is generally an exact figure. The thinnest plywoods are not easy to find at all timber merchants, but are often obtainable from model shops.

Special materials

Apart from wood, which forms the main part of these toys, some toys need parts made from other types of material. These are generally made from metal, and where other materials are used, they are detailed more fully in the individual instructions.

Metals are used in the form of sheet, tube and rods, and usually in quite small pieces. The best source for tubes and rods is usually model shops, although you may have to go to a metal stockholder for the sheet metal. Specify the kind of metal required (brass, mild steel, aluminium), and the dimensions. Thickness of sheet metal, and diameters of rod and tube may be given as a measurement in millimetres or inches, or as a gauge number. Check by direct measurement.

Marking out from measurements

Check the measurements from the diagram or the text, and note the material used. If the part is made from plywood or board, the size used is identified in terms of its thickness only, e.g. 6mm (¼in) plywood. You should select a piece of the appropriate material and make sure that it is big enough to fit in a panel of the size required.

If the part is made from softwood, the size required will be given in terms of two measurements—the width and thickness of the timber, e.g. 50mm × 25mm (2in × 1in) planed softwood. Note that the actual measurements of the timber will be slightly under these dimensions as the measurement is that of the wood before planing. Select a piece of timber of the appropriate size and make sure that it is long enough to fit in the part required. Take note also of any special requirements, such as that the timber has no knots.

Where parts are made from dowel, this will be identified in terms of its radius, e.g. 16mm (⅝in) hardwood dowel. Select a rod of this type, making sure that it is long enough.

Similar rules apply where the part is made from another material, such as metal sheet or tube, and detailed instructions are given where appropriate.

You should always try to use your materials as economically as possible. In the case of solid timber, this means cutting the parts from one end—with boards cutting them from an edge or corner. If several parts are to be cut from one piece you should fit them up against one another as far as possible. This also simplifies cutting, since one cut will do for two parts. However, bear in mind that any cut will remove a small amount of material, so mark out one part first, cut it, and then mark out the second. If you mark them out together and then cut, the second part will be undersize by the amount wasted in the saw cut.

Start your marking out from a true straight line. You should never assume that the edge of the board or the end of the timber is straight unless you have checked it. It may have been cut wrongly at first or damaged later.

To check the edge of a board, use the longest straightedge possible. Lay it along the edge and check that it touches at all points. If it does not, the edge is not true.

To check the end of a piece of timber, use a square. Hold the stock against the edge of the timber and try to align the blade with the cut end. Do this across the width and down the thickness of the material. If the blade does not align in either direction the end is not true. You should also inspect even a square end for any damage, such as dents or splits.

If the end or edge is true, proceed with the marking out. If not, move a short way on to the edge of the board or along the timber, far enough so that the new line will clear the old, and mark a new straight line.

Where a part is rounded, use compasses to mark it. Set the compasses against a ruler to the radius required. If a full circle is needed, mark this as close as possible to the corner of the board. If only the corner of a part is to be rounded, mark the radius distance along the two edges working down from the corner (you can use the compasses for this as they are already set to the correct distance). Square these two points into the board until they meet. Put the point of the compasses on this point and mark enough of a circle to meet the two edge lines.

In a few cases it is necessary to find the centre of an existing circle, such as on the end of a piece of dowel. To do this, use a simple jig. Fit the circle into the angle of the jig and mark a line across it along the edge of the guide rule. Turn the circle round through 90° and mark another line. The centre is where the two lines cross.

Measure materials other than

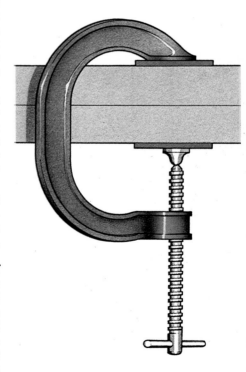

This G-clamp is ideal for holding smaller pieces of timber as the glue sets.

wood (e.g. metal or plastic) as for wood. To mark them, use a scriber, which has a hardened metal point, to scratch a line.

Where two parts are the same size, or have to fit accurately together, it is more accurate and often quicker to measure them against one another, rather than marking each individually. You can also fix the timber together and cut through them as one so that both parts are cut out together. Where a large number of parts have to be cut to the same size, use the first one only as a master pattern—do not cut out each and use it as a pattern for the next, since any errors will also be passed on, getting more severe each time.

Marking out from patterns
Parts which have a complex shape are very difficult to mark out from dimensions alone. Instead, they are shown in the form of scale drawings.

In a few cases these are full-size, and this is noted on the drawing. Use tracing paper to make an accurate copy of the outline, and the position of any holes. It is best to pin or tape the paper to the page to ensure it cannot move. Use a straightedge for any straight lines in the drawing.

Holding the work
For easy, accurate work it is essential to be able to hold the workpiece securely. The most important thing to have is a sturdy work surface. The ideal is a heavy fixed carpenter's workbench but this is expensive and not essential. A portable, collapsible bench is a very good substitute, and has the advantage of a built-in clamp. You can even use a sturdy kitchen table, but you should cover this with a piece of plywood or chipboard to protect the surface.

You must be able to hold the work in place. For sawing, the simplest solution is to make a bench hook, which can be done easily using offcuts and following the instructions on page 136. With this hooked over the edge of the bench, hold the workpiece into the angle formed by the short piece on top to lock it in position.

A vice is very useful for holding work in all kinds of situations. The clamp-on type is the cheapest, and quite adequate. G-clamps are a good alternative to a vice, and can be used

to hold two pieces together while they are being fixed. Very small modellers clamps are cheap and convenient for holding small pieces together, but you will need larger clamps to hold work down to the bench.

When you use clamps, you should always pack out the workpiece under the clamp with scraps of wood to prevent the clamp from marking the work. If you are using a Spanish windlass, pad the corners of the work with scraps of heavy card to prevent the cord from cutting into it.

Hold very small pieces of work with pliers. Use long-nosed pliers for the smallest parts. Self-locking pliers will avoid having to maintain pressure on the handles.

To hold small parts in place, particularly while gluing them rubber bands and adhesive tape make very useful clamps for light pressure. They can also be used where the parts are an awkward shape.

A temporary support, particularly where small parts require shaping, can often be provided by screwing them to a larger block or directly to the work surface. Insert the screws from below, making sure they do not protrude into the work area, and fill the remaining holes after shaping.

Sawing
Sawing is the most convenient way of cutting out parts from most materials. It can also be used to produce slots or grooves in some cases. There is a huge variety of different types of saw to cope with different materials and different types of cutting, but all work in much the same way. The blade has a series of sharpened teeth, each of which takes a small bite out of the material as the blade passes through it. Depending on the size of the teeth and how they are set (bent out from the blade, first to one side then the other), this means that any saw cut forms a groove (called the kerf) and wastes some of the material as sawdust. For this reason, it is essential that cuts are always made slightly to the outside of the marked line so that the kerf falls in the waste material and not on the part required. If it does, the part will be slightly undersized.

Also, depending on the type of saw used, the cut line will be rough to a greater or lesser extent. If a smooth

finish is important, cut oversize and finish to the marked line with glass-paper or a plane.

The finish achieved, and also the ease of sawing are governed by the sharpness of the teeth. If the blade is replaceable, change it when it becomes blunt. Fixed saw blades can be sharpened by a professional saw sharpener when they lose their edge.

In general, modelling work is done with hand saws. Although power saws are extremely useful for other types of woodwork and are much less effort to use, it is usually difficult to control them accurately enough for very fine work. Their use is largely confined to roughing pieces to an approximate size.

In all types of sawing it is impossible to do accurate work unless the material is adequately supported and firmly held on the work surface.

Making straight cuts
In wooden parts, straight cuts are required in two types of material—

1. *Handsaw (straight back blade).*
2. *Tenon or backsaw.*

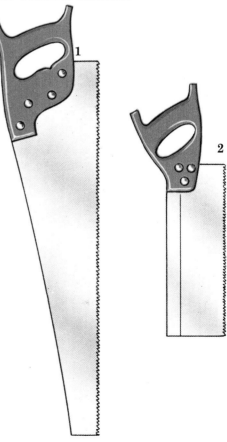

139

solid wood and boards. Two types of saw are needed to cover the different cuts required, a handsaw and a backsaw.

Handsaws have a long tapering blade. There are many types, classified by the type of teeth and their number in points per inch (ppi). The most generally useful is a panel saw which is suitable for cuts with or against the grain and with about 10ppi. Use the panel saw for making long cuts in board materials or for cutting larger pieces of softwood.

Support the work firmly so that the cutting line is just over the edge of the work surface with the waste to the outside. Start the cut by putting your free hand down on the workpiece with the back of the thumb aligned with the cut. Using your thumb as a guide, position the saw so that it is just to the outside of the cutting line. Hold it at an angle of about 45°. Draw it up towards you one or two times so that the teeth make a small notch in the edge of the board, just their width. Use your thumb to stop the saw running off line. This will start the cut accurately. Continue sawing by pushing and pulling the saw alternately, holding it at an angle of about 60°. Work smoothly and evenly, using the whole length of the saw and not trying to force it through the wood. Watch the marked line all the time to make sure that the cut is running true. Blow sawdust away from time to time as it accumulates. As you near the end of the cut, support the waste with your free hand to prevent it falling under its own weight, breaking free and tearing the wood. Slow down as you reach the very end.

When you are cutting very thin boards, there is a danger that the saw will tear rather than cut the board. You can cut thin boards by repeated scoring with a knife. Alternatively, clamp an off cut of scrap board (hardboard is ideal) on each side of the workpiece along the cut line. Then cut through the complete sandwich.

Backsaws are for more accurate cutting than panel saws. The blade is shorter and is stiffened by a solid metal back to keep it rigid. There are more, finer teeth. The heaviest backsaws are called tenon saws. One around 250 to 300mm (10 to 12in) and with about 16 to 18ppi is good for

most purposes. Backsaws for finer work are called in decreasing order of size—dovetail saws, bead saws and razor saws. All of these are useful but not essential.

Use a backsaw for cutting smaller sections of solid wood or short cuts in board. They are more accurate than handsaws but cannot be used on very large pieces, because the back limits the depth of cut. They also cut more slowly because of the finer teeth.

Start the cut in the same way as with a handsaw. If you are cutting right through a piece of wood, proceed as above. Backsaws are also used to cut horizontally when a cut has only to pass part of the way through the material.

Making curved cuts
Curved cuts in solid wood and board are made with saws which have very fine narrow blades that can follow the curve without binding in the cut. These are quite prone to damage and cannot be sharpened, so are replaceable. The rest of the saw consists of a frame and a handle. The frame curves right away from the blade so that it does not restrict it when working away from the edge of a board. The two most common types are the coping saw and the fretsaw.

Use the fretsaw when working on thin boards or on thicker boards a long way from the edge. It has a very thin blade for fine cuts and tight curves, and a large frame to work

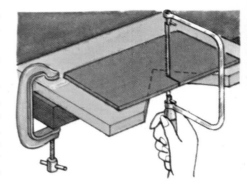

How to use a coping saw or fretsaw.

right into the panel. It is used from below the workpiece, cutting down, so fit the blade into the frame with the teeth angling towards the handle. You will need to compress the frame to do this—this also tensions the blade.

Support the workpiece over the edge of your work surface with the cutting line just unsupported. A fretsawing guide which has a V cut out of it to take the blade will make work easier. Hold the saw with the blade vertical and start it into the work with a downward stroke. Keeping it vertical continue with up and down strokes, working just outside the marked line. Turn the work and move it over the edge to keep the saw working in the same position while following the line. Continue in this way until the end of the cut.

If you have to start a cut in the middle of the board, drill a small hole in the waste near the cut line

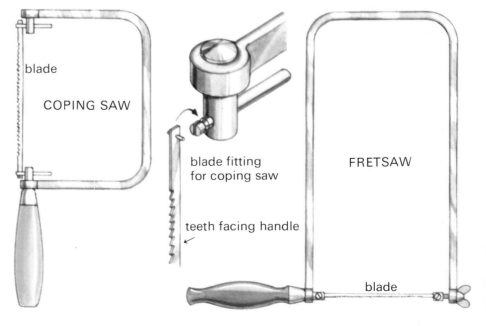

blade

COPING SAW

blade fitting
for coping saw

teeth facing handle

FRETSAW

blade

insert the blade through it before attaching it to the frame. Work over to the cut line then proceed as before. At the end of the cut, undo the blade and remove it from the hole (figs. 3 & 4).

If you have to cut a sharp point in the line, do not try to follow this. Instead of working around the point, start two cuts working into each side of the point. This will result in a sharp angle which is not possible in a single cut.

Coping saws are similar to fretsaws but have a heavier blade and smaller frame. The blade, which should be fitted facing the handle, is tensioned by a screw in the handle. Use it to cut softwood or thicker boards near to an edge. Unlike the fretsaw, the blade is mounted so that you can swivel it round. This means that you can work around a line which follows the edge of a board by turning the sawblade round and cutting sideways with the frame over the edge of the board.

You can use a coping saw with the work held vertically or horizontally, but it must be held securely.

Making slots

To make slots on the end or edge of a part, cut both sides with a backsaw. Work the blade of a coping saw or fretsaw into the cut and use it to cut across the bottom removing the waste. Wider slots can be cut across the bottom with a chisel narrower than the slot.

Slots in the middle of a part which go right through can be cut by drilling holes the width of the slot at each end and joining them with saw cuts using a coping saw or fretsaw.

Cutting special materials

Materials other than wood generally need a special purpose saw. Some types of plastic can be cut with wood cutting saws, but others, and all metals, need special blades. In general, these can all be treated in the same way and cut with a hacksaw.

Hacksaws have a metal frame and replaceable blades tensioned with a screw and fitted facing the handle. They are available in two basic sizes and with a range of blade lengths, but for most purposes, the smallest—called a junior hacksaw—is quite sufficient. They will cut straight lines or curves, and the smaller

blade of the junior type will follow a tighter curve. Clamp the work very securely and proceed as for the coping saw. Work slowly and smoothly. A little light oil on the blade will make cutting easier.

For cutting very tight curves in metal, use a piercing saw, which is similar to a coping saw for wood and takes fine blades, or work as close as possible with a hacksaw and finish with a file.

To cut thin, flexible metal sheet, use tinsnips if possible. You can cut it with a saw by supporting it on both sides with offcuts of hardboard and cutting through the complete sandwich.

Knives

At least one knife is essential for any modelling work, as they have literally hundreds of uses. The two most useful types are the trimming knife and the craft knife (figs. 1 & 2).

The trimming knife usually has a fat handle shaped to fit the palm of the hand. The blades can be sharpened to prolong their useful life, but are intended to be discarded and replaced when they become blunt. Some types have blades scored with a series of notches so the point can be snapped off, presenting a new cutting edge. The blade is quite short and stiff, so it can be used for heavy cutting. You can get different blades for various uses, including a hacksaw blade and a padsaw blade for light work and piercing in metals and wood.

Craft knives are similar, with replaceable blades fitted into a handle. The handle is smaller and lighter, so that it can be controlled even be-

tween finger and thumb for precise work. You can fit a wide variety of differently-shaped blades to suit different purposes—with straight edges, curves and points.

Using a knife

Knives can be used to cut parts out of very thin materials, such as plastics or thin plywood which a saw would damage. The cut edge is cleaner than a saw cut. Use them also to cut card and paper, as they will produce a better edge than using scissors. The trimming knife is more suitable for heavier materials than the craft knife.

Support the work on a sturdy working surface. You should cut onto a firm but resilient surface which will not blunt the blade if it should cut in, and which will protect

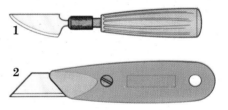

1. *A craft knife can be fitted with a variety of different blades.*
2. *Trimming knife. Some have retractable blades.*

3. *Drill access holes either on the line, or well into the waste area of timber.*
4. *One large hole, or two or more smaller ones, makes cutting awkward shapes easy.*

3

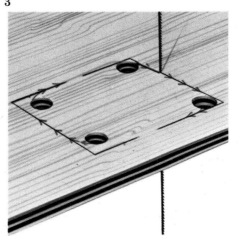

4

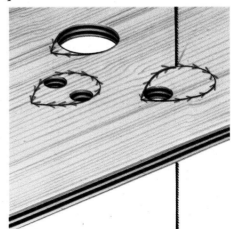

the worktop below. A piece of heavy-duty linoleum is ideal.

Straight cuts are much easier than curves. Use a straightedge as a guide to keep the knife on line. Hold it in place on the work with your free hand, pressing firmly to keep it in place. Do not let your fingers overhang the edge. Cut towards yourself, keeping the hand holding the straightedge behind the blade and standing out of the direct line of the cut. Keep the knife in line with the straightedge, and press the point up against the edge. Run the knife along the cut line, pressing down firmly, but not forcing the cut. If you are cutting hard or very thick material, do not try to cut right through in one attempt, but make several shallow cuts along the same line until you are through. You can score materials for bending by cutting through to only half their depth to form a fold line.

Curves must be cut freehand, unless you can make a suitable template with the right radius to act as a cutting guide. When you are cutting materials like plywood which have a grain, the knife will tend to follow the grain, so cut the curve along and across the grain in such a way that if the knife does get pulled off line by the grain, it will run outside the curve into waste material. Steady the work with your free hand, but never hold it in front of the blade.

Knives can also be very useful as carving tools, especially where you want to trim the corner or edge of a part. Use them to round off sharp points or edges, and for tapering dowels, with a whittling technique. Hold the part in a vice or with your free hand, use the knife to remove small flakes of the material as if sharpening a pencil. Always cut away from yourself. Do not try to remove too much material at one time, but work down gradually to the required shape. Always cut along or across the grain direction— never into it or it will pull the knife off line and may well split.

If you do not have a purpose-made marking knife, you can use an ordinary knife in place of one when scribing a line with a square or straightedge. This is better than using a pencil, as the line will be finer and more accurate, and because it scores the surface will make

it less prone to splitting or splintering.

Always change a blade whenever it becomes blunt during the course of work. A blunt blade will not cut cleanly, and because it will require more force, there will be a greater risk of it slipping off line.

Chisels

Chisels are one of the most important groups of tools in general woodworking, although they have less uses in model and toy making. They are available in a wide range of widths, and special shapes which include gouges.

They are really a special form of knife, in which the cutting edge is set square to the handle. This concentrates a cutting force on the edge, and makes it possible to reach points which are inaccessible to knives.

Their main use in toy making is as shaping and carving tools, and it is quite possible to use alternative tools for most toys in this book.

Planes

The plane is another tool which is invaluable in general woodwork, but have far fewer uses in toy making. A form of precision knife, its purpose is to remove accurate thin shavings of wood to produce a smooth surface or to shape it. The basic plane is available in a wide range of sizes, and there are many special-purpose planes for particular shaping work, including the spokeshave, which can be used to shape curved surfaces.

They are not essential for most of the toys in this book, although they, or a planer-file, are needed to finish wood blocks to thickness in a few cases. The spokeshave can also be used for shaping the boat hull, although it is not essential.

Using a plane

To cut efficiently, a plane blade must be very sharp. Sharpen it on an oilstone, sharpening it first to an angle of 25°, then finishing the very edge at an angle of 30°. Use the coarse side of the oilstone first, then finish on the smooth side. Use plenty of light machine oil as a lubricant. Fit the blade to the plane and adjust it so that only about 0.5mm ($\frac{1}{64}$in) is visible below the sole (base) of the plane.

Mark up the workpiece to show the finished line clearly on all sides. Support it firmly and clamp in position, but make sure that the plane will have an unobstructed run over it.

Study the grain direction before you start. You must always plane in the direction of the grain, and with it running upwards along the line of planing, otherwise the blade will dig in and not cut cleanly (figs. 3 & 4).

Plane smoothly and evenly along the whole length of the work. The blade should remove a thin, even shaving. If it does not, check that you are planing in the correct direction, and check that the blade is set correctly.

Continue in this way until you reach the finished thickness shown by your marked line.

If you have to plane end grain, use a block plane, which is adapted for

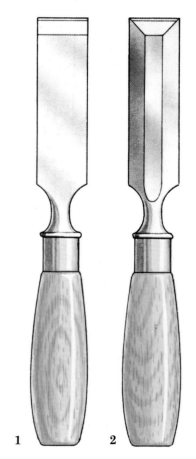

1. *This chisel is firm enough to hit with a mallet.*
2. *A bevel edged chisel for awkward corners.*

the purpose. Work in from both corners to the middle, not across the whole width as this will tear the grain at the corners (fig. 2).

You can use a plane to chamfer or round off an edge. Hold it at an angle to the face and edge of the wood (45° in the case of a chamfer) and plane along the edge until you have a chamfer of the desired width. To round the edge, vary the angle of the plane between strokes.

Use spokeshaves for curved surfaces. A flat-based spokeshave is for convex surfaces, a curved base for concave ones. Hold the spokeshave by both handles and draw it towards you along the grain, varying its angle to suit the curve. This is best judged by eye. Remove thin shavings until you have reached the desired shape.

Rasps, files and planer-files

This group of tools is generally useful for most shaping and finishing work. Although each type of tool works in a slightly different way, their method of use is virtually the same.

Each tool has a large number of very small teeth which cut or abrade the surface to remove material. Depending on the size, number and angle of the teeth, they can have a fine, medium or coarse cut. The classification of cut varies depending upon the type of tool. Each is made in a range of different flat and curved shapes to enable it to tackle different shaping tasks.

Rasps

These tools are normally half-round

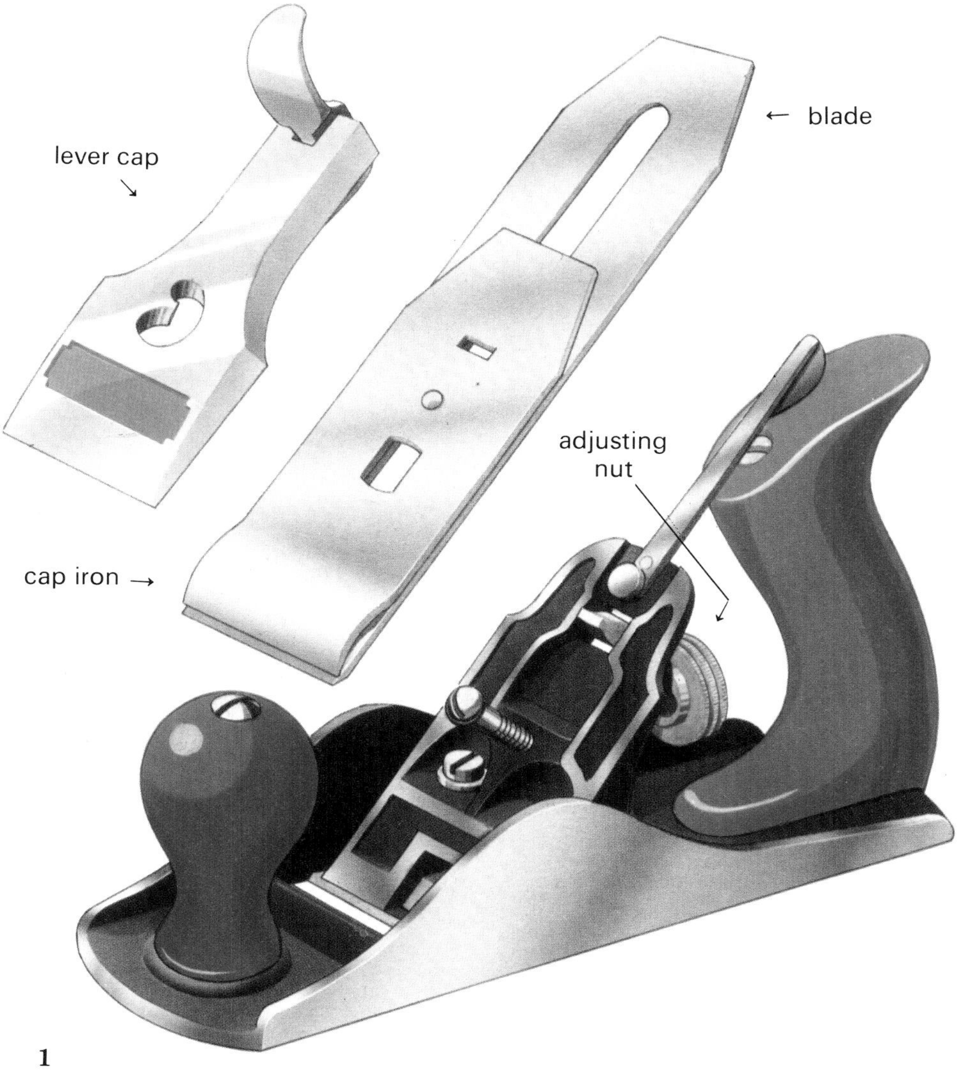

1

lever cap

← blade

cap iron →

adjusting nut

2

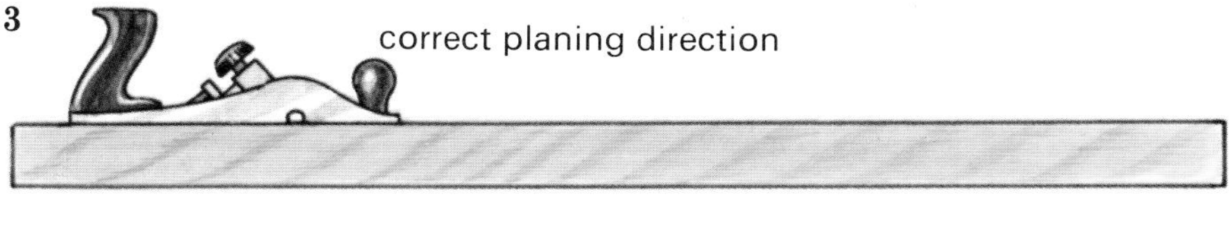

correct planing direction

3

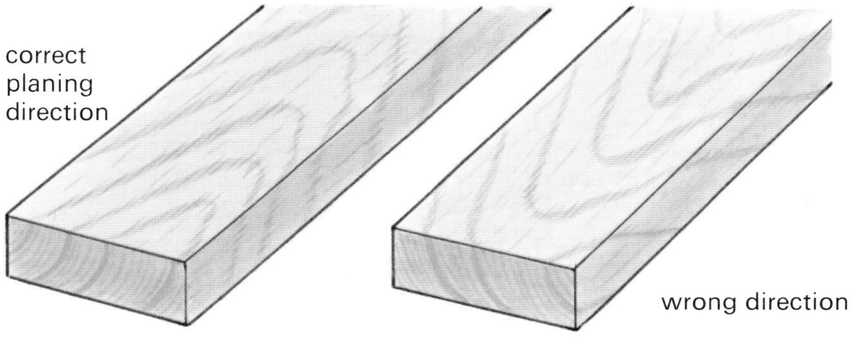

correct planing direction

4

correct planing direction

wrong direction

1. *The parts of a bench plane.*
2. *Two ways of planing end grain in order to avoid breaking and splintering the ends.*
3. *Grain along the edge shows the planing direction.*
4. *Grain on facing surface.*

143

in shape. The flat side is used for flat or convex surfaces, the curved side for concave ones. The teeth are very coarse and set quite widely. They will remove material quickly without clogging. Rasps are usually supplied without handles, and you should fit one before use.

Support the work firmly, preferably at about elbow level. Hold the rasp by its handle. You can use the other handle to hold the tip if necessary for greater accuracy.

Run the tool along the work, using the whole length of the blade of possible. Hold it level with a flat surface, or tilt it as you pass over a curved one. The tool can be used with or across the grain, or on end grain. It will cut quicker across than with the grain, but will tend to tear the surface more. On end grain, use it from both sides and avoid using it across the corners as this will tear them.

Because of the relatively rough surface left by the teeth, you should stop well before you reach the desired profile and finish shaping with another tool, or with glasspaper (see **Finishing**).

Files

Files can be used for finishing and shaping both wood and metal. The blade has a large number of very fine teeth, shaped in different ways to give a fine or coarser cut. The blade is shaped in many different ways— flat, half-round, round or triangular plus many special shapes—to enable it to cope with various tasks. Very fine files (called needle files) can be used for fine shaping and piercing work.

Always fit a file handle before use. Needle files have their own shaped handles. Because of the relatively fine teeth, files tend to clog, especially when they are used on soft materials. You can clean the teeth with a wire brush, or on a special cloth which has wire bristles, called a file card.

Use a file in much the same way as a rasp. It can be used in any direction on wood or metal and will leave quite a smooth surface depending on the cut of the teeth. In general, unless very little material has to be removed, start with the coarsest cut and work through to the finest.

Support the work firmly at about elbow level. Hold the file at an angle to the direction of cut and take smooth strokes forward, applying pressure on the forward stroke only. For a smoother finish on metal, hold each end of the file, lay it across the surface, and draw it straight back towards you. When working over a curved surface, tilt the file as you make the stroke.

Sanding

Sanding is the final shaping process. It is a relatively slow way to remove material—even when the coarsest grades of abrasive are used, but this is an advantage when the work is nearing completion. Because sanding leaves the smoothest finish of all the shaping processes, it is used before the finish is applied. For this reason, details of sanding are included in the **Finishing** section.

Drills

There are several types of drill, and all of them can be used in some part of toy making.

The most useful is a hand drill. This is easier to control than an electric drill for making the majority of small holes. An electric drill is useful, however, for making large holes, and is essential for using a hole saw, which is used when making some types of wheel. You can also use a brace and bit for making large holes and it is easier to control accurately than an electric drill. It does however cost very much more to buy the bits used in a brace than flatbits of comparable size for an electric drill. An Archimedean, or push drill, is quite a useful tool for very small holes.

Use a hand drill by holding it over the work with the back handle, pressing down lightly. Turn the handle smoothly and evenly working clockwise.

The brace should be held with the palm on the back handle to steady it and push down lightly. Rotate the handle in a smooth clockwise sweep.

The electric drill needs only a guiding hand on the handle and a finger on the trigger. Be careful to keep the flex out of the way and avoid wearing loose clothing. Be prepared for the drill to work very quickly.

The Archimedean drill is held steady with a hand on the back

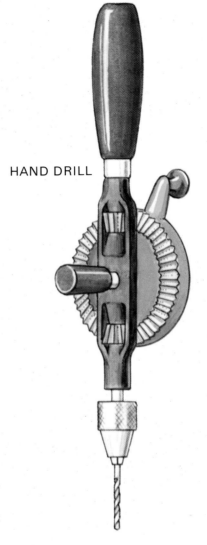

HAND DRILL

handle. Work the collar up and down to spin the drill as you apply pressure.

Though not strictly a drill, the bradawl is a useful tool for making small holes and starting smaller screws. Hold it against the wood with the blade at right angles and apply pressure while twisting it from side to side about a quarter of a turn.

Drill bits

Twist drills are suitable for drilling holes of up to around 6mm ($\frac{1}{4}$in) in wood or metal when used in a hand or electric drill. Buy a set ranging from 1.5mm to 6mm ($\frac{1}{16}$ to $\frac{1}{4}$in) which will cover most jobs. The best and longest lasting types are made from high speed steel (HSS).

For larger holes in wood, use an electric drill fitted with flatbits. Buy only the sizes that you need. Alternatively, use a brace fitted with a bit of the correct size. Bits for a brace are relatively very expensive. They cannot be used in any other type of drill. Flatbits too are only suitable for electric drills.

Hole saws are specialized drills designed to remove a core of the material. They are suitable only for use on thin materials. They consist of a central pilot drill, with, around it, a length of sawblade bent into a circle. The pilot drill serves to start the hole and keep it centred. The saw then works around the surface of the material cutting through it until the centre falls free. Hole saws are preset to a diameter and are quite expensive. Perhaps the most useful type is one which has a range of interchangeable blades to cut circles of several sizes. They are used in toy making for cutting very large holes in plywood, and making wheels.

You will also need a countersink or rose bit, for making countersunk holes for screws.

How to drill
In all types of drilling, accuracy is essential. You should start by fixing the work firmly. Where possible, try to arrange this so that you are drilling vertically. For angled holes, try to clamp the work at the angle, rather than clamping it flat and holding the drill at an angle. Support the work adequately underneath the hole. When a hole is going to pass right through the part, place a piece of scrap wood behind it to take the point of the drill as it breaks through. This is particularly important on thin materials.

Hole saws should be used in much the same way. Use them as slowly as the drill will go and do not force the cut. Stop from time to time if the saw

shows signs of overheating. The saw will make a cleaner cut if you stop before it breaks through. Turn the wood over and insert the pilot drill from the other side. Continue drilling until the two cuts join up.

This double-drilling method can also be used for cleaner cut holes with flatbits and brace bits which pass right through the wood. Watch the underside of the workpiece for the moment that the centre point of the drill breaks through, then remove it and drill through from the other side until the holes join up.

Hammering
Because most of the work is relat-

Opposite: *A hand drill.*
Below: *Ratchet brace and a selection of bits.*

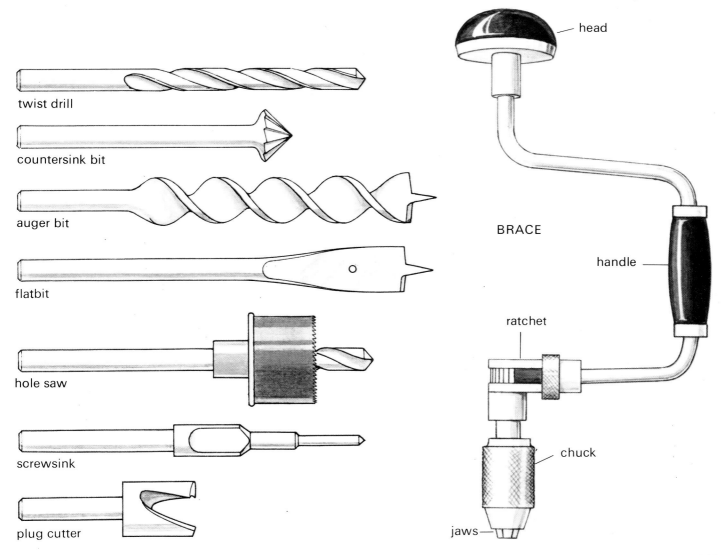

twist drill

countersink bit

auger bit

flatbit

hole saw

screwsink

plug cutter

BRACE

head

handle

ratchet

chuck

jaws

ively light, the basic tool is the smallest, lightest hammer—called a pin hammer. This is light in weight with a small head which has one flat face and which is drawn to a point set at right angles to the handle—called a cross pein.

Use this for most work involving driving pins. Hold it well down the handle and strike the pin squarely and evenly. The cross pein is used for starting pins into the wood. Hold the pin between your finger and thumb and give it a few taps with the hammer until the pin begins to bite. Reverse the hammer and continue pinning with the flat face.

When working with larger nails or into hard timber, you will need a larger hammer. Choose a medium weight Warrington hammer which is also of cross-pein design. Use it the same way, but carefully because of its greater weight (fig. 2).

Avoid striking the work with a hammer. You should continue pinning until the head is almost flush with the surface of the work. Stop hammering at this point and use a punch to push the head right below the surface. The type to use is a nail punch, the end of which is ground concave so it will not slip off the head of the pin. Choose one with a head of about the same diameter as the head of the pin. Strike it evenly with the hammer until the head of the pin has just sunk below the surface. You can then cover the small hole with some filler and sand flush for an invisible nailed joint.

If you do have the misfortune to bend a nail, which usually occurs because it was not struck straight, or because it has hit a hard obstruction, stop at once. Remove the nail with a pair of pincers. Grip the nail between the jaws and lever the handles over to pull out the nail. You should protect the work with an offcut of timber or board under the jaws to prevent them from marking the surface.

To ensure that the work is positioned correctly, drive some or all of the pins through the part to be fixed first. Work on a piece of scrap board and drive them until the point just starts to protrude. Position on the other part so that the points just bite in when it is correctly aligned and drive the nails right home. When it would be very difficult to

hold the part in position while nailing, fix it temporarily with clamps or adhesive tape. You can use light taps from a hammer to drive components together, such as when a rod is to be fitted into a socket which is a little tight. Do not use a hammer when it is likely that it will damage the parts—use a mallet or soft-headed hammer (with rubber or plastic faces) instead. Always use a mallet rather than a hammer for striking a chisel.

Nails

There are many different types of nail, but those most used for toy making are classified as pins. They are described in terms of their length. The larger pins used are called panel pins, the smaller are moulding pins or veneer pins. All have a long thin shank and a small tapering head.

Also used occasionally are round wire nails. These are larger, with a plain round shank and a flat round head. They are classed by length.

Other special purpose nails, where used will be described in detail.

Always discard any misshapen or bent nails as they will almost certainly damage the work. You can minimize the risk of the nail splitting the work by blunting the point slightly with a hammer before driving.

Nail or pin in the positions shown in the diagrams. If nail positions are not shown, space them out evenly. Try to nail through the centre of narrow parts and avoid nailing very close to the edge.

Screws and screwdrivers

Screws of various kinds provide a strong mechanical fixing between two parts. There are different kinds of screws for different kinds of material, but in this book, all the fixings are made into wood, and all screws used are types of woodscrew.

Screws

Most types of screw have three

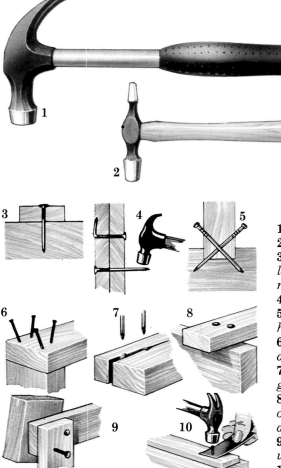

1. *A pin hammer.*
2. *A cross pein hammer.*
3. *Nails should be 3 times length of workpiece. Always nail smaller to large.*
4. *Clench-nailed joints.*
5. *Skew-nailing is best for housing joints.*
6. *Drive nails in at opposing angles for end grain.*
7. *More than one nail along grain line risks splitting.*
8. *Nail small battens overlength and saw off waste to avoid splitting.*
9. *Place a block under the work to avoid "bounce".*
10. *Position small nails with a cardboard holder.*

parts—the thread, which bites into the wood to provide the fixing, the shank, which is an unthreaded part passing through the part to be joined, and the head which is wider than the rest of the screw to draw the parts tightly together.

The head can have various different shapes, according to its use. The ones used in this book are all either countersunk, which is flat on top with angled sides designed to drive in flush with the surface, or domed which is shaped like a half sphere and designed to stand out on the surface. In addition, screws have a slot in the head so that they can be driven with a screwdriver, and are classed according to the type of slot. This can be a plain single slot cut right across the head, or a double slot arranged in a cross. The latter type are called cross-head screws. There are three patterns of cross-head, known as Phillips, Pozidriv and Supadriv. All types are designed for use with different types of screwdriver (see below).

The shank of the screw is the widest part of the screw which goes into the wood and it is this which denotes its size. However, some types of screws are threaded along their whole length.

The different types of screw have different types of thread. Slotted-head screws (the traditional type) taper through their whole length and have a thread with a single helical twist set below a plain shank. Cross-head screws are threaded through their whole length and only taper at the tip. In Pozidriv screws the thread is a single helical twist—Supadriv types have a double helical twist (Twinfast) which makes them faster to drive and provides greater holding power. You may in addition find types which have a combination of these features. The main advantage of the different types for toy making is that the screws which are threaded for their whole length (sometimes also known as chipboard screws) have a much better holding power when they are screwed into the end grain of softwood.

In addition to being classed by their type, screws are classified by their length and thickness. The length is given simply in terms of a metric (mm) or Imperial (in) measurement. The thickness is normally given in terms of a number (No.), called the gauge, which relates to the thickness of the shank and the diameter of the head. The larger the number, the greater the thickness. The sizes most commonly used in this book are No. 8 and No. 6, although others may be encountered.

The final classification of screws is according to the material from which they are made. This is generally of steel (which may be painted or plated to prevent rust), or brass.

Screws are thus classified in terms of all these qualities, e.g. a 25mm (1in) No. 8 (4.2mm) countersunk brass woodscrew.

Screwholes

Although a screwhole might seem quite simple, the relatively complicated shape of a screw means that a screw which is to drive easily and provide a strong fixing needs a carefully drilled hole.

The first point is that the screw should not bite into the part which is being fixed—only into the part it is being fixed to. This means that it needs a hole which is slightly bigger than its thickest part, so that it can pass through without touching. This hole is called the clearance hole, and is determined by the gauge (No.) of the screw.

The screw must bite into the part into which it is fixing, but will not drive in easily unless it has a hole to follow. This hole is called the pilot hole and should be smaller than the thread—to allow it to grip, but large enough to drive easily. The pilot hole size is determined by the gauge of the screw.

Clearance and pilot hole sizes for the screws used in this book are given in the diagrams, but in general a No. 8 (4.2mm) screw needs a 5mm ($\frac{16}{34}$in) clearance hole and a 2mm ($\frac{6}{64}$in) pilot hole. A No. 6 (3.5mm) screw needs a 4mm ($\frac{1}{8}$in) clearance hole and a 1.5mm ($\frac{1}{16}$in) pilot hole.

The total length of the clearance and pilot holes should be the same as the overall length of the screw.

Countersunk heads need a further refinement to the hole. The top should be drilled out with a countersunk bit to allow the head to sink into it and sit flush with the surface.

In very hard wood, pilot holes may need to be drilled slightly larger.

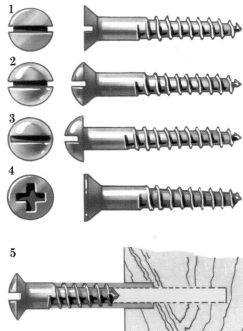

A selection of screws suitable for woodworking.
1. *A flathead screw is flat on top with angled sides. It is designed to lie flush on the work surface.*
2. *A roundhead screw with angled sides lies above the surface.*
3. *A flat-sided roundhead screw.*
4. *A patented Phillips screw.*
5. *Inserting a wood screw. The yellow section shows the first hole, the red the second.*

Special-purpose screws and fittings

Related to screws, the screweye and screwhook are used in several types of application. Instead of a head, the end of the shank is bent round to form a loop, which can be a ring or a hook. They are classified by one measurement alone.

Drive them into a very small pilot hole made with a fine drill or a bradawl. They can be turned with the fingers, with pliers or a screwdriver inserted through the loop.

Some screws are used to form axles for wheels. To ensure that the wheels run smoothly and do not bind against the head or on the chassis, these screws are fitted with washers. The type used are called cup washers. They are designed for use with countersunk heads and have an indentation to fit the countersink. They are classed by the screw gauge.

Driving screws

The correct tool is a screwdriver, but there are several different types and sizes.

Slotted head screws need a screwdriver with a plain blade. It should be almost as wide as the screw head, but no wider, and should be a tight fit in the slot. If it is too loose, it will damage the slot and the screw will be difficult to drive or remove.

Cross-head screws need a cross-head screwdriver. There are types designed for use in Phillips, Pozidriv and Supadriv screws, and the corresponding one is the best to use. You can however use a Phillips type for all three, and Pozidriv and Supadriv are interchangeable. The latter types, however, cannot be used for Phillips. The tip size and angle also vary to suit screw sizes. The correct one to use is one which just fills the recess in the head.

Handles have many different shapes—choose the most comfortable. In general, the bigger the handle, the more driving force you can apply.

Screws will drive more easily into a tight hole if you apply a little wax or soap to the threads. Brass screws are relatively weak and can snap if driven hard. To prevent this, drive a steel screw of the same size and type first, remove it and replace with a brass one.

Where screws have to take a heavy load and need not be removed, the fixing will be firmer if you apply a little woodworking or epoxy adhesive to the threads before driving. This is particularly useful in fixing to end grain and in fixing wheels to a chassis.

If you have the misfortune to snap a screw or damage the head so that it cannot be driven, you should remove it and replace with a sound one.

If it cannot be removed with a screwdriver, grip the head or shank with pliers and use these to twist it free.

Adhesives

Where two parts have to be joined permanently, they should be glued together using an adhesive. In many cases this is supplemented with screws, nails or pins which serve to locate the parts correctly, hold the joint while the adhesive dries and strengthen it when it has set.

PVA woodworking adhesive

This is a general-purpose glue suitable for joining wood to wood or wood to boards. It is available in many container sizes and is applied directly from the bottle. White in colour, it dries clear.

A relatively cheap adhesive, it is the one to use for most general assembly work using wooden parts. It is water-soluble, so you can clean any excess from the work using a damp cloth. You can also thin it with water to make an excellent paste for paper which can be applied with a paint brush.

Apply to one only of the surfaces to be joined. Bring them together and hold with light pressure until set. Do not apply a great deal of pressure as this squeezes adhesive out of the joint. Remove any which does squeeze out using a damp cloth. It sets by evaporation of the water solvent, usually in about half an hour, but reaches full strength over a longer period—a matter of several hours.

The bond produced is very strong and durable, and the adhesive is capable of bridging small gaps between the parts to be joined, but it will not stand up to prolonged exposure to water, so do not use for projects such as model boats.

Waterproof woodworking adhesive

Commonly based on a urea formaldehyde composition, these are the adhesives to use for wood-to-wood joints in projects which will be subjected to immersion or outdoor exposure.

Sold in powder form, mix with water as instructed to form a paste which you should apply to one of the surfaces to be joined. Bring together under light pressure and hold until set. Initial curing takes around an hour but full strength is not reached for a period of hours. It is good at filling small gaps between parts. Clean off any surplus with a damp cloth before it has set.

Safety note

Most adhesives are more or less harmful. Avoid skin contact as far as possible and keep them away from your mouth and eyes. Read the instructions thoroughly before use, and in an emergency seek medical advice. As a matter of course, keep them away from young children.

Finishing

Toys should always be finished thoroughly, so that they have a neat attractive appearance and a smooth clean surface with no roughness or splinters. Good surface preparation is the most important part.

Surface preparation

No surface will take paint or varnish well, or look good when finished, unless it is smooth, clean and dry. The easiest way to achieve this is with thorough sanding and then a final clean.

Sanding is quite a slow way to remove material, so you should aim to cut parts as cleanly as possible before assembly. If you have any holes or gaps left, fill them before sanding. You can use cellulose filler, stopping, plastic wood or a mixture of sawdust and woodworking adhesive for this. Types which have to be mixed should be of the consistency of a stiff paste. Work them into the holes with a filling knife leaving a little standing above the surface. If the part is to be varnished, use a filler which matches the wood in colour.

After filling, if necessary, you can sand the surface. Various types of abrasive paper are used for this. On wood, the most commonly used are glasspapers which are powdered glass bonded to a paper backing. These are available in a range of grades and also by names—fine, medium and coarse. When graded these have numbers—the lowest numbers are the finest. The finest grades are also sometimes called flour papers.

As the names suggest, the finest grades leave the finest finish and remove the least material. A very rough surface will need treatment with coarse paper first, working down through medium to the finest grades. A substantially smooth surface, like that of good-quality plywood, will often need just a very little treatment with the finer grades.

Always use glasspaper with a sanding block which will allow you to apply even pressure over a large area and prevent the paper from digging in. Good quality blocks are made from bonded cork which provides a firm but resilient backing—but you can use a scrap block of softwood. When sanding a concave surface, use a block which is rounded to the same or smaller radius than the curve you are finishing. Offcuts of dowel are ideal for this.

Cut off a piece of paper big enough to fold right round your block. Wrap it round and hold it in place with your fingers or adhesive tape.

Sand with smooth even strokes working along the grain, using no more pressure than is required to allow the paper to bite into the sur-

face and remove a fine dust. On end grain, work from side to side and towards the centre.

A well designed working area is ideal for woodworking. Tool storage is arranged so that you can reach equipment easily.

Offcut toys

Robot

Tools required
Tenon saw; hand or electric drill and bit to correspond to smallest dowel diameter.

Techniques involved
Sawing; drilling; sanding.

Materials
offcuts of wood and dowel
PVA woodworking adhesive
fine glasspaper

Making the robot
Select the pieces of wood that will give the correct proportions. Choose thicker dowel for the legs than for the arms, and a piece of wood for the head which is no more than half the width and thickness of the body.

The arm pivot dowel must be no more than half the thickness of the arms.

Cut the block used for the body to length. To position the arms, drill a hole right through the block near the top. The hole must be slightly larger than the diameter of the arm pivot dowel to allow the arms to swing freely.

Cut the arms to length, slightly longer than the body block. Drill holes through them near the top, the same diameter as the pivot dowel.

Measure the thickness of the body plus both arm dowels and cut the pivot dowel to this size.

Cut the head block to size.

Cut the legs to length.

Smooth all parts with fine glasspaper.

Assemble as illustrated. Pass the pivot dowel through the hole in the body but do not glue. Put a little glue in the holes in the arms and fit them on to the ends of the pivot making sure that they are in alignment.

Glue the legs to the bottom of the body.

Glue the head in place, slightly towards the back of the robot.

You can vary the design to allow the head to turn round. Drill a hole in the head and in the body and use a length for the neck, glued into the body but not the head.

Train

Tools required
Tenon saw; hand or electric drill with bits; screwdriver; paint-brushes; sanding block.

Techniques involved
Sawing; drilling; sanding; painting.

Materials
offcuts of wood and dowel
PVA woodworking adhesive
screweye
screwhook
4 woodscrews at least 25mm (1in) long, No. 8 (4.2mm) or No. 6 (3.6mm)
8 cup washers to fit screws
fine glasspaper
enamel paints
polyurethane lacquer
length of cord

These sturdy little robots are fun to make from remnants left over from carpentry work. They are simple toys to construct, and would make an ideal introductory project to teach your child basic carpentry skills.

Making the engine

Select suitable offcuts of wood and dowel. The base should be about 7.5cm (3in) wide and from 17.5cm to 20cm (7–8in) long. Make it from 12mm ($\frac{1}{2}$in) plywood or soft wood between 16 and 25mm ($\frac{5}{8}$in and 1in) thick. The cab needs a block of 5cm × 5cm (2 × 2in) about 7.5cm (3in) long. The boiler and wheels are made from 3.8cm (1$\frac{1}{2}$in) diameter hardwood dowel, and the chimney from thinner dowel such as 19mm ($\frac{3}{4}$in).

Cut the base to size and smooth all around with glasspaper. Drill pilot holes to suit the screws you are using at two points on each side to mount the wheels.

Cut the cab to size and sand the top corners to a curve as illustrated.

Cut the chimney to length.

Cut a length of dowel for the boiler, about 10cm (4in) less than the length of the base. Flatten one side using glasspaper or a plane if available.

Also from 3.8cm (1$\frac{1}{2}$in) dowel, cut four slices 12mm ($\frac{1}{2}$in) thick to form the wheels. Mark the centres and drill clearance holes for the screws you are using.

Sand and varnish or paint all parts.

Assemble as illustrated. Glue the cab to the base, about 15mm ($\frac{5}{8}$in) from one end. Glue the boiler flat side down in front of the cab. Glue

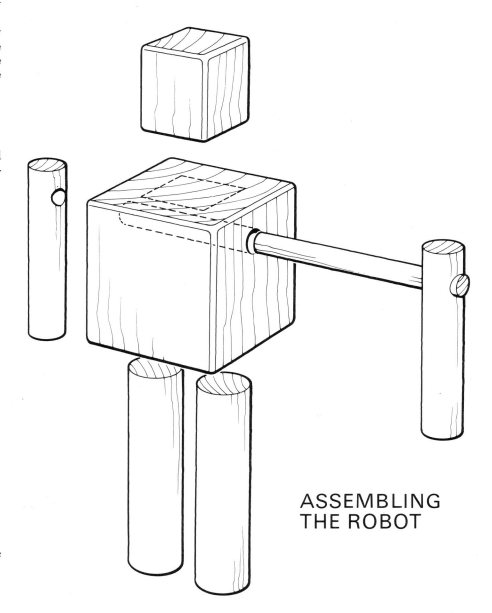

ASSEMBLING THE ROBOT

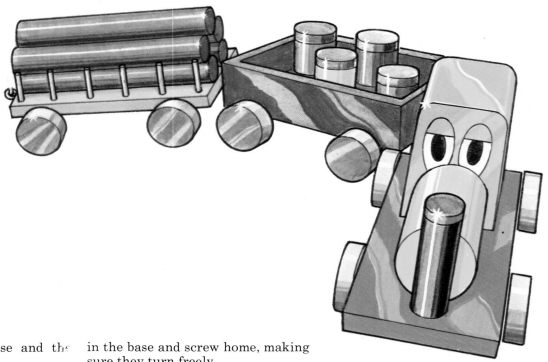

the chimney to the base and the front of the boiler.

Fit a cup washer to each screw and pass through the holes in the wheels. Place another washer over the screw, then insert into the holes in the base and screw home, making sure they turn freely.

Fix a screweye to the front of the base and a screwhook to the rear. Tie on a length of cord for pulling along.

Make a colourful train like this one from scraps of leftover timber.

ASSEMBLING THE TRAIN

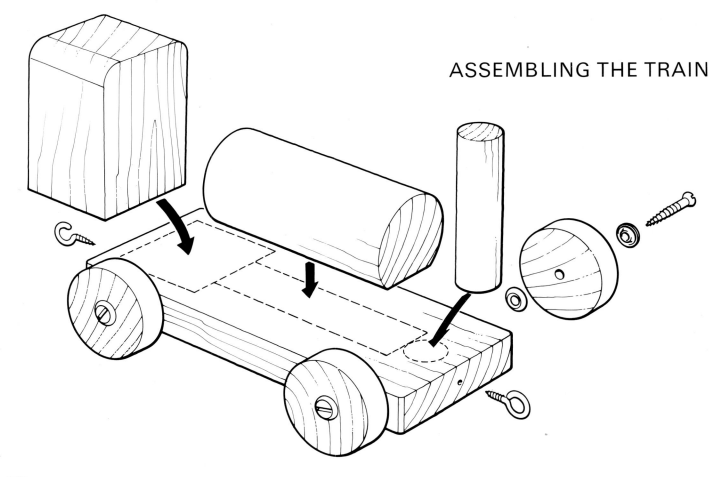

Noughts and crosses

Finished size
30.5cm (12in) square.

Tools required
Try-square; tenon saw; ruler; pencil.

Techniques needed
Marking; cutting; gluing; finishing.

Materials
30.5cm × 30.5cm (12in × 12in) of 12mm (½in) plywood or blockboard

115cm (44in) of 19mm × 19mm (¾in × ¾in) softwood

25cm (10in) of 5cm × 5cm (2in × 2in) softwood

25cm (10in) of 4.5cm (1¾in) diameter dowel
PVA woodworking adhesive
glasspaper
varnish or paint

Making the baseboard

Using a try-square and ruler, mark out a 30.5cm × 30.5cm (12in × 12in) square on a piece of 12mm (½in) plywood or blockboard. Cut this to size using a hand saw, and finish the edges smooth with glasspaper. Sand both surfaces lightly.

Make the board dividers from 19mm (¾in) square softwood. Cut two lengths 30.5cm (12in) long, and six more 9.1cm (3½in) long. Following the drawing (fig. 1) arrange these on the board and glue in place with PVA woodworking adhesive to form nine equal squares.

Sand the exposed ends and edges of the dividers.

Making the noughts

Cut five 5cm (2in) lengths of 4.5cm (1¾in) diameter dowel. To ensure you make a parallel cut, wrap a piece of broad masking tape around the dowel, putting one edge in line with the cutting position. Overlap the ends and keep the edges even. Saw according to the masked edge. Sand the cut ends of each piece of dowel.

Making the crosses

Cut five 5cm (2in) lengths of 5cm × 5cm (2 × 2in) softwood. Mark the cutting lines with a try-square to ensure that the blocks are cut accurately at both ends.

The crosses are formed from these

blocks by cutting away triangular wedges from each side. Mark out the ends of end block as shown in fig. 2. Start by drawing diagonal lines from corner to corner of the block. Then, mark parallel lines on each side of, and 6mm (¼in) away from, the diagonals. Continue the cutting lines over on to the sides.

Clamp each block firmly and make two saw cuts on each face using a tenon saw and following the marked lines. Try to fix the block so that you can make each cut vertically downwards, then turn the block for the next cut.

Finish very carefully using glasspaper to smooth the cut faces and ends of the crosses. A coat of clear varnish will protect the wood.

1
BASEBOARD

2
TRACE PATTERNS FOR CROSSES

Submarines

Finished length:
Small sub, about 12.5cm (5in); large sub, about 30cm (12in).

Tools required
Tenon saw; fretsaw; junior hacksaw; hand or electric drill and bits; craft knife; tinsnips or old scissors; G-clamps; vice; long-nosed pliers; side cutters; pencil; paintbrushes; sanding block.

Techniques involved
Sawing; cutting curves; drilling; sanding; working with tinplate; painting.

Large submarine

Materials
26cm × 4cm ($10\frac{1}{4}$in × $1\frac{5}{8}$in) of 12mm ($\frac{1}{2}$in) exterior WBP plywood
46cm × 14cm (18in × $5\frac{1}{2}$) of 3mm ($\frac{3}{32}$in) plywood
2 15cm (6in) round wire nails

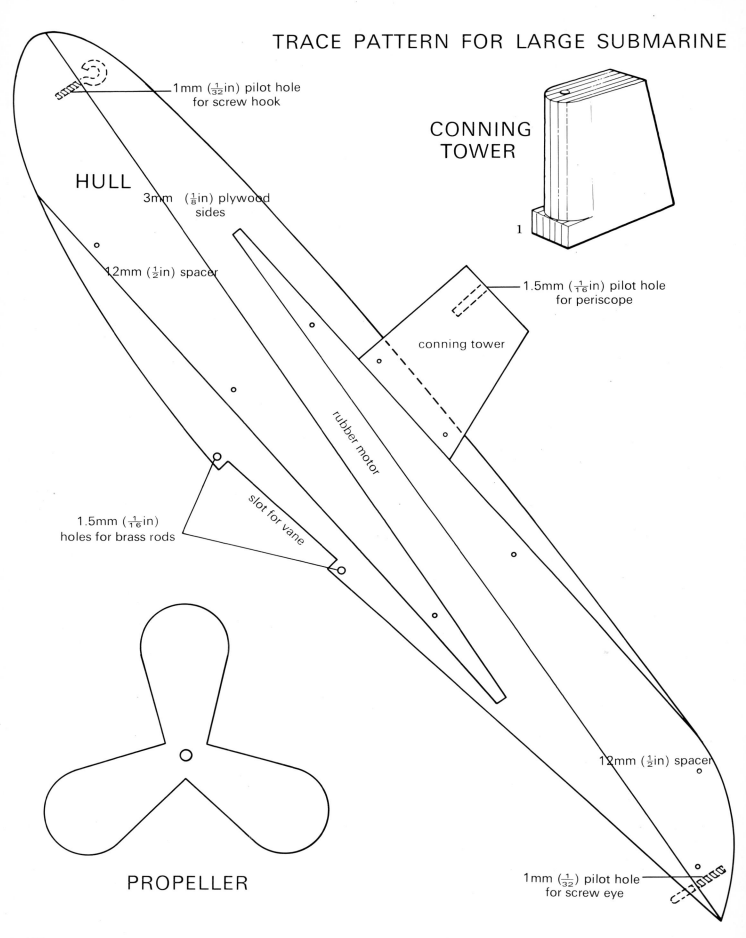

TRACE PATTERN FOR LARGE SUBMARINE

CONNING TOWER

1

HULL

1mm ($\frac{1}{32}$in) pilot hole
for screw hook

3mm ($\frac{1}{8}$in) plywood
sides

12mm ($\frac{1}{2}$in) spacer

1.5mm ($\frac{1}{16}$in) pilot hole
for periscope

conning tower

rubber motor

1.5mm ($\frac{1}{16}$in)
holes for brass rods

slot for vane

12mm ($\frac{1}{2}$in) spacer

1mm ($\frac{1}{32}$) pilot hole
for screw eye

PROPELLER

9cm × 9cm (3½in × 3½in) of tin plate
cut from an old can
large paper clip
2 × 6mm (1¼in) diameter glass beads
20 × 12mm (½in) panel pins
13.5cm (5¼in) × 2mm (5/64in) brass rod
54.5cm (21½in) × 6mm (¼in) rubber
band (from model aircraft shops)
2 × 5cm (2in) rubber bands
plasticine
fine glasspaper
wood primer
rust-resisting primer
enamel paints
waterproof woodworking adhesive
epoxy resin adhesive
paper
card
carbon paper
tracing paper

Warning: Propellers are made of tinplate and should not be handled by small children.

To make the large submarine

Trace the full-scale patterns for the sides, spacers and propeller.

Using carbon paper, transfer the shapes for the sides from the tracing on to 3mm (3/32in) ply wood. Cut out with a fretsaw or coping saw and smooth the edges with glasspaper. Drill 1mm (3/64in) holes in the positions marked on the pattern. Drill 2mm (5/64in) holes for the vane retainers in the positions marked on the plans on either side of the vane slots.

Cut a 11.4cm × 4cm (4½in × 1⅝in) rectangle from 3mm (3/32in) plywood to form the vane. Sand all the edges smooth.

Transfer the tracings of the spacers and conning tower on to 12mm (½in) plywood. Cut out with a coping saw. Drill a 2mm (5/64in) hole 15mm (⅝in) deep into the top of the conning tower in the position shown (fig. 1). Clamp the spacers between the sides in the positions shown and sand the curved portion to the same profile. Shape the front of the conning tower into a smooth curve as shown. Sand all surfaces and edges smooth.

Prime and paint all inside surfaces to prevent them from becoming waterlogged in use. Do not paint the sides of the spacers or the area on the sides to which they are fixed. Allow to dry.

Glue all parts together using waterproof woodworking adhesive, and pin through the pre-drilled holes. Punch the pin heads below the surface.

Fill any blemishes and pin holes with plastic resin filler, then sand, prime and finish with enamel paints, adding decorative details. Use several coats of paint to ensure the finish is waterproof.

Transfer the pattern for the propeller on to a piece of card and cut out the shape. Use this as a template to mark out on tinplate, tracing round with a scriber or a compass point. Cut out the propeller with tinsnips or an old pair of scissors. Drill a 2mm (5/64in) hole through the centre. Bend each blade up at one edge and down at the other as shown in fig. 2.

Straighten a paper clip to make the propeller shaft. Push the end through the centre hole and then bend it round the propeller as shown in fig. 2. Make sure that the propeller cannot move on the shaft. Thread two beads on to the shaft to act as bearings, then bend the end into a hook to take the rubber band motor (fig. 3).

Screw a 6mm (¼in) screweye and a 6mm (¼in) screw hook into the submarine body in the positions shown on the plans. Tie the two ends of the rubber motor together to form a loop. Pass this down the centre of the submarine, hooking one end on to the screw hook. Pass the other end through the eye and hook it on to the end of the propeller shaft. The beads on the shaft are held by the screweye, thus keeping the propeller clear of the submarine.

To make the ballast, cut two 9cm (3½in) lengths from 15cm (6in) round wire nails using a junior hacksaw. Paint with rust-resisting primer and leave to dry.

Cut the 2mm brass rod into two 4cm (1⅝in) lengths for the vane retainers, and one 5.4cm (2⅛in) length for the periscope. Glue the periscope into the hole in the conning tower using epoxy resin adhesive.

Put the ballast in place on the underside of the submarine between the vane slots and fix with plasticine. Fit the vane retainers through the holes on either side of the vane slot. Fit the vane in place

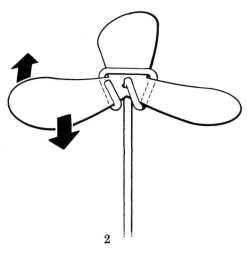

2

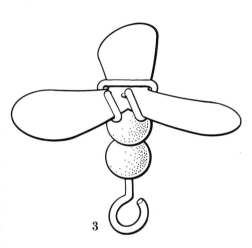

3

1. *Drill hole in conning tower.*
2. *Attaching propeller shaft.*
3. *Attaching beads and making hook on shaft. Also included, trace pattern for propeller.*

in the slot and hold it in place under the ballast with two rubber bands, criss-crossed around the protruding ends of the vane retainers.

Try the submarine in water—its waterline should be where the conning tower joins the hull. Adjust the ballast nails for balance. They slide up and down easily as they are only held in position by the plasticine and the vane. Wind up the rubber motor by turning the propeller. The submarine should move through the water, then submerge.

Small submarine

Materials

12.6cm × 2.5cm (5in × 1in) of 12mm
(½in) plywood
3cm (1¼in) of 6mm (¼in) dowel
3 × 2.5cm (1in) panel pins
50cm (2in) square of tinplate
large paper clip
1 12.5cm (5in) nail
6mm (¼in) screw hook and eye
2 × 6mm (¼in) rubber band
1 × 100m (4in) rubber band
1 or 2 12mm (½in) wooden beads for
heads (optional)
fine glasspaper
enamel paints
rust-resisting primer
epoxy resin adhesive or waterproof
woodworking adhesive
paper and card for pattern and
templates

To make small submarine

Trace shape for hull (fig. 5), transfer
on to 12mm (½in) plywood and cut
out. Carve and shape ends to slight
points as shown in photograph. Drill
a 6mm (¼in) diameter hole 1cm (⅜in)
deep in top of submarine for conning
tower if required.

Drill 1mm (1/32in) pilot holes at
each end of hull for screw hook and
eye. Finally drill a 6mm (¼in) hole,
15mm (⅝in) deep under the bow for
ballast in position shown in fig. 5.

Trace templates for propeller and
vane (figs. 6 and 7) and use them to
cut out the shapes in tin as for large
submarine.

Cut a 2.5cm (1in) piece of 6mm
(¼in) dowel, chamfer end and stick
in to hole in hull for conning tower.
Insert panel pin, bending top, for
periscope. Alternatively, use 12mm
(½in) beads for divers' heads.

Using two panel pins, nail the tin
vane to the underside of the hull
with the flaps to the rear. Fold the
flaps upwards slightly as shown in
the photograph.

Sand and paint hull, conning
tower, divers' heads, and vane.
When paint is dry nail divers' heads
in place. Screw in screw hook under
bow and eye at the stern, in
previously-drilled pilot holes. Cut
off 2.5cm (1in) from the 12.6cm (5in)
nail and paint with rust-proof paint.
When dry nail into place in 6mm
(¼in) hole drilled in bow for ballast.

Bend propeller into shape as for
large submarine. Attach propeller
shaft and heads and make hook at

end as for large submarine.

Fix a 10cm (4in) rubber band to
the propeller hook at one end and to
screw hook at the other. Wind up
rubber motor as before.

ASSEMBLING THE LARGE SUBMARINE

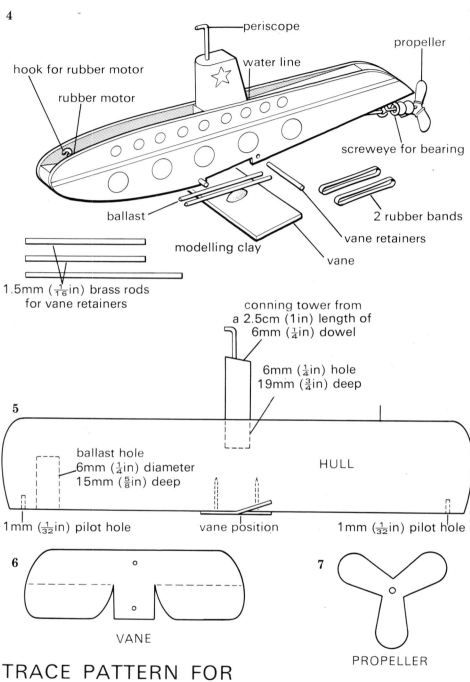

4

periscope

propeller

hook for rubber motor

water line

rubber motor

screweye for bearing

ballast

2 rubber bands

modelling clay

vane retainers

vane

1.5mm (1/16in) brass rods
for vane retainers

conning tower from
a 2.5cm (1in) length of
6mm (¼in) dowel

6mm (¼in) hole
19mm (¾in) deep

5

ballast hole
6mm (¼in) diameter
15mm (⅝in) deep

HULL

1mm (1/32in) pilot hole

vane position

1mm (1/32in) pilot hole

6

VANE

7

PROPELLER

TRACE PATTERN FOR SMALL SUBMARINE

Truck

Finished size
Length: 28cm (11in); width 11.5cm (4½in); height 20.3cm (8in) including wheels.

Tools required
Handsaw, tenon saw, try-square, drill and bits, hammer, punch, screwdriver, hacksaw, sanding block, paintbrush.

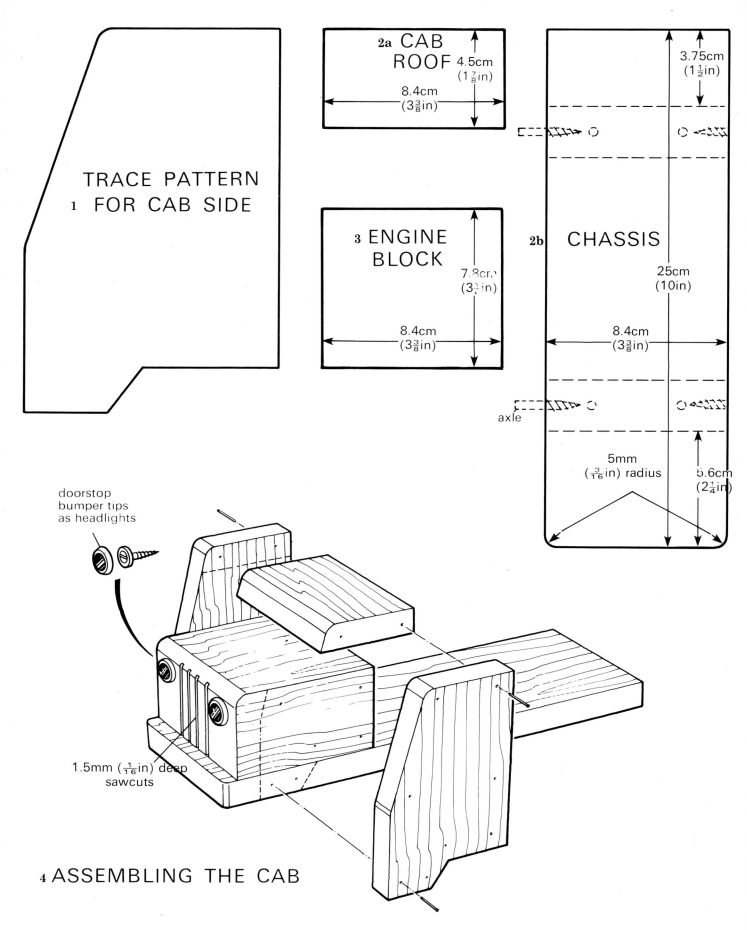

TRACE PATTERN
1 FOR CAB SIDE

2a CAB ROOF
4.5cm (1⅞in)
8.4cm (3⅜in)

3 ENGINE BLOCK
7.8cm (3⅛in)
8.4cm (3⅜in)

2b CHASSIS
3.75cm (1½in)
25cm (10in)
8.4cm (3⅜in)
axle
5mm (3/16in) radius
5.6cm (2¼in)

doorstop bumper tips as headlights

1.5mm (1/16in) deep sawcuts

4 ASSEMBLING THE CAB

Techniques involved

Marking out and measuring; sawing; shaping; screwing and gluing; pinning and gluing; wheels; finishing.

Materials

NB All 16mm ($\frac{5}{8}$in) softwood is planed and should have an approximate finished thickness of 13mm ($\frac{1}{2}$in). All these parts can be made from 12mm ($\frac{1}{2}$in) plywood instead.

140cm (55$\frac{1}{8}$in) of 125 × 16mm (5 × $\frac{5}{8}$in) softwood

17.2cm (6$\frac{3}{4}$in) of 3.2 × 2.5cm (1$\frac{1}{4}$ × 1in) softwood

7.8cm (3$\frac{7}{8}$in) of 10 × 2.5cm (4 × 2in) softwood

8.4cm × 5cm (3$\frac{3}{8}$ × 2in) of 6mm ($\frac{1}{4}$in) plywood

64cm (25$\frac{1}{4}$in) of 5cm × 5cm (2 × 2in) softwood

32cm (12$\frac{5}{8}$in) of 5cm × 2.5cm (2 × 1in) softwood

4 × 5cm (2in) diameter plastic model wheels with hub caps

4 steel washers 5mm ($\frac{3}{16}$in) internal diameter

4 × 38mm (1$\frac{1}{2}$in) No. 8 (4.2mm) countersunk woodscrews

4 × 45mm (1$\frac{3}{4}$in' No. 8 (4.2mm) round headed chipboard screws

2 × 19mm ($\frac{3}{4}$in) No. 8 (4.2mm) round headed chipboard screws

2 × 12mm ($\frac{1}{2}$in) No. 8 (4.2mm) countersunk chipboard screws

PVA woodworking adhesive

19mm ($\frac{3}{4}$in) panel pins

12mm ($\frac{1}{2}$in) panel pins

2 No. 8 (4.2mm) plastic screwhead covers

polyurethane lacquer

silver enamel paint

glasspaper.

As an extra surprise, the top of the box body slips off easily to reveal a nest of polished wooden building blocks inside. The thirteen blocks are fashioned in a variety of shapes and sizes to fit exactly into the back of the truck. There are eight square ones and five long ones in different lengths and widths so that they can make different patterns.

Following the full-size plans in fig. 1, trace off patterns for the chassis, cab sides and cab roof. Transfer them on to 12mm ($\frac{1}{2}$in) softwood or plywood and cut out with a hand saw and tenon saw. Round off the corners where indicated using glasspaper, and sand all the edges

smooth. Drill 4.5mm ($\frac{3}{16}$in) clearance holes for No. 8 (4.2mm) chipboard screws as indicated in the chassis.

Enlarge the pattern in fig. 3 for the engine block. Transfer on to 10cm × 5cm (4 × 2in) softwood and cut out using a tenon saw. Round off the bonnet as shown using glasspaper. Sand the cut ends smooth. Make four 1.5mm ($\frac{1}{16}$in) deep saw-cuts as indicated to form the radiator grille. Drill 12mm deep 1.5mm ($\frac{1}{16}$in) pilot holes for the headlight screws and 16mm deep 1.5mm ($\frac{1}{16}$in) pilot holes for the fixing screws where indicated.

Cut 86mm (3$\frac{3}{8}$in) lengths of 3.2cm × 2.5cm (1$\frac{1}{4}$ × 1in) softwood to form the wheel bearers. Sand the cut ends smooth with glasspaper and drill 1.5mm ($\frac{1}{16}$in) pilot holes 16mm deep at the position indicated. Round or chamfer off the two lower edges. Drill 4.5mm ($\frac{3}{16}$in) clearance holes for No. 8 (4.2mm) fixing screws at the positions indicated.

Take the engine block and one of the wheel bearers. Glue above and below the front end of the chassis using PVA woodworking adhesive. Screw through the holes with 4.5mm (1$\frac{3}{4}$in) round head chipboard screws.

Using PVA woodworking adhesive and 19mm ($\frac{3}{4}$in) panel pins, pin and glue one cab side to the chassis and engine block. Align the back edge of the side with the back of the engine block. Fit the other side of the cab in the same way and pin and glue the cab roof between the tops of the sides. Punch all pin heads below the surface and cover with wood filler. Allow assembly to dry, then sand smooth. Using 12mm No. 8 (4.2mm) countersunk chipboard screws and plastic screwhead cover caps, screw to the front of the engine block to form the headlights.

Making the box

Following the plans in fig. 4, enlarge the patterns for the sides, ends, base and top of the box. Transfer to 12mm softwood or plywood and cut out using a hand saw. Sand all the cut edges smooth and round off the edges of the top as shown. Drill 1.5mm ($\frac{1}{16}$in) pilot holes in the base where indicated. Cut two 8.4cm × 2.4cm (3$\frac{3}{8}$ × 1in) strips of 6mm ($\frac{1}{4}$in) plywood and sand smooth.

Using PVA woodworking adhesive and 19mm ($\frac{3}{4}$in) panel pins, pin

and glue the ends of the box between the sides, taking care to keep the assembly square. Pin and glue the base in position. Punch all pin heads below the surface. Allow to dry, then sand smooth.

Pin and glue the two plywood strips to the underside of the lid using 10mm ($\frac{3}{8}$in) panel pins and PVA woodworking adhesive. Punch the pin heads below the surface, cover with filler and sand smooth

Position the box behind the cab. Fix with PVA woodworking adhesive and two 19mm ($\frac{3}{4}$in) No. 8 (4.2mm) round headed chipboard screws driven through the chassis. Glue the rear wheel bearer in position and fasten with two 4.5cm (1$\frac{3}{4}$in) No. 8 (4.2mm) round headed chipboard screws. Sand all surfaces and edges smooth, then finish the entire truck with at least two coats of polyurethane lacquer.

Fixing the wheels

The wheels are 5cm (2in) diameter truck wheels from model or toy shops. If these are not available, you can use 5cm (2in) diameter wooden wheels cut from 12mm ($\frac{1}{2}$in) plywood using a hole saw. These should be fixed with a domed head screw driven through the centre hole.

Drive 3.8cm (1$\frac{1}{2}$in) No. 8 (4.2mm) woodscrews into the ends of the wheel bearers, leaving the shank projecting. A little adhesive smeared on to the thread will provide a more secure fixing. After fitting the screws, cut off their heads with a hacksaw. Fit a washer to each, then slip on the wheels. Retain them with snap or fixing hub caps.

All the blocks are made from lengths of 5cm × 5cm (2in × 2in) or 5cm × 2.5cm (2in × 1in) softwood. In order for the blocks to fit accurately inside the truck, however, these sizes must be trimmed somewhat. This is best done with a plane, but can be done with a planer-file and sandpaper. You will need timber with a finished size of 4cm × 4cm (1$\frac{9}{16}$ × 1$\frac{9}{16}$in) and 4cm × 2cm (1$\frac{9}{16}$ × $\frac{3}{4}$in). Cut to the lengths shown in fig. 5 and sand all edges and surfaces smooth. Finish each block with at least two coats of polyurethane lacquer and allow to dry. Fit the blocks together as shown inside the box and fit the lid in place. It is retained by the two plywood strips.

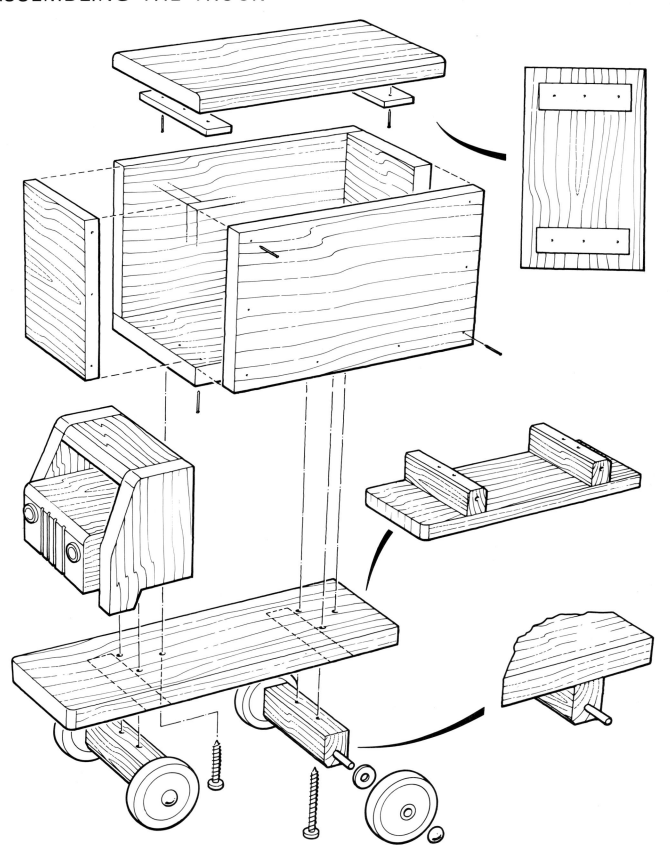

4.

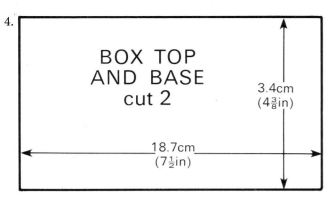

BOX TOP
AND BASE
cut 2

3.4cm
($4\frac{3}{8}$in)

18.7cm
($7\frac{1}{2}$in)

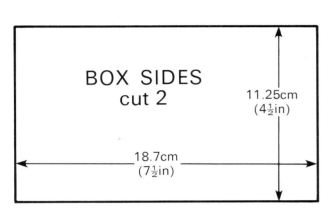

BOX SIDES
cut 2

11.25cm
($4\frac{1}{2}$in)

18.7cm
($7\frac{1}{2}$in)

FRONT
AND BACK
cut 2

8.4cm
($3\frac{3}{8}$in)

11.25cm
($4\frac{1}{2}$in)

5 ASSEMBLING THE BLOCKS

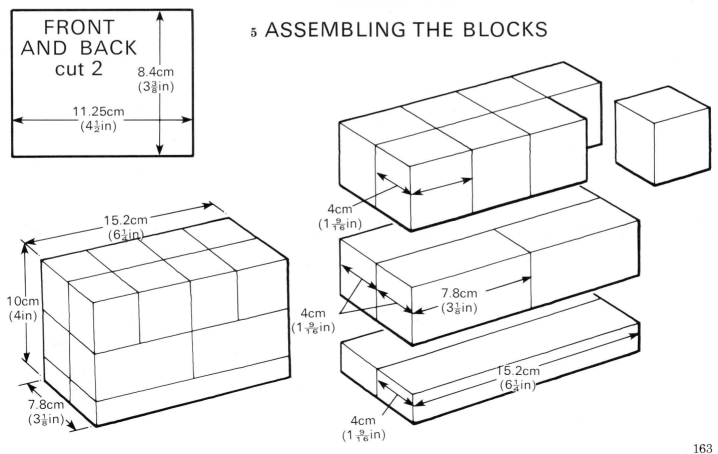

15.2cm
($6\frac{1}{4}$in)

10cm
(4in)

7.8cm
($3\frac{1}{8}$in)

4cm
($1\frac{9}{16}$in)

4cm
($1\frac{9}{16}$in)

7.8cm
($3\frac{1}{8}$in)

15.2cm
($6\frac{1}{4}$in)

4cm
($1\frac{9}{16}$in)

163

Railway engine

Finished length
48cm (19in).

Tools required
Tenon saw; fretsaw; vice; G-clamp; electric drill with 2mm ($\frac{5}{64}$in) and 6mm ($\frac{1}{4}$in) bits, 19mm ($\frac{3}{4}$in) flat bit; countersunk bit; hole saws (6.4cm and 3.2cm) ($2\frac{1}{2}$in and $1\frac{1}{4}$in) diameter; small hammer; crosshead or slotted screwdriver appropriate to screws; pencil; ruler, try-square, paintbrushes; large plastic funnel; scissors; compasses (optional).

Techniques involved
Shaping plywood and dowel; drill-

ing; wheels; painting.

Materials

96cm (37¾in) of 5cm × 2.5cm
(2in × 1in) softwood
71.5cm (28½in) of 10cm × 2.5cm
(4in × 1in) softwood
1m × 10cm (39½in × 4in) of 6mm (¼in)
plywood
61cm (24in) of 6mm (¼in) dowel
12cm (4¾in) of 2.5cm (1in) dowel
7.5cm (3in) of 12mm (½in) dowel
plastic detergent bottle, 26cm
(10¼in) long
1kg (2.2lb) plaster of Paris
16 small plastic electric cable clips
16 No. 1 countersunk screws 15mm
(⅝in) long
12 No. 6 countersunk screws 3.8cm
(1½in) long
4 No. 6 countersunk screws 4.5cm
(1¾in) long
40g (1½oz) box 12mm (½in) panel pins
1 × 6mm (¼in) screweye
12 brass upholstery nails, 10mm (⅞in)
long
2 discarded plastic lids from coffee
tins or similar
contact adhesive
fine glasspaper
enamel paints

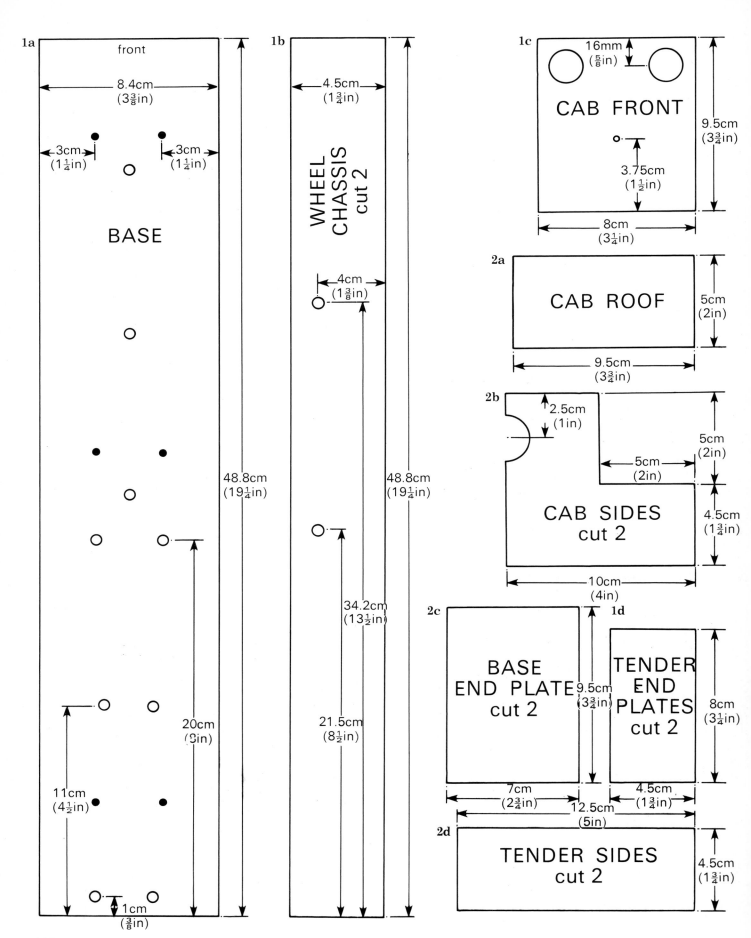

1a front

8.4cm (3⅜in)

3cm (1¼in) · 3cm (1¼in)

BASE

48.8cm (19¼in)

20cm (8in)

11cm (4½in)

1cm (⅜in)

1b

4.5cm (1¾in)

WHEEL CHASSIS cut 2

4cm (1⅜in)

48.8cm (19¼in)

34.2cm (13½in)

21.5cm (8½in)

1c

16mm (⅝in)

CAB FRONT

9.5cm (3¾in)

3.75cm (1½in)

8cm (3¼in)

2a

CAB ROOF

5cm (2in)

9.5cm (3¾in)

2b

2.5cm (1in)

5cm (2in)

5cm (2in)

CAB SIDES cut 2

4.5cm (1¾in)

10cm (4in)

2c

BASE END PLATE cut 2

9.5cm (3¾in)

7cm (2¾in)

1d

TENDER END PLATES cut 2

8cm (3¼in)

4.5cm (1¾in)

12.5cm (5in)

2d

TENDER SIDES cut 2

4.5cm (1¾in)

Construction

Mix plaster of Paris with water to the consistency of thick cream. Remove top from the neck of the detergent bottle and pour in the plaster using a plastic funnel. Pour slowly to avoid a build-up of air bubbles and squeeze the bottle occasionally to make sure that it is

1a,b,c,d. *Measurements for base, cab front, tender end plates and wheel chassis sections.*
2a,b,c,d. *Measurements for plywood parts of engine.*

completely filled. Leave for several hours to allow plaster to set. When the plaster has hardened, mark a line down one side of the bottle. Measure 2cm ($\frac{3}{4}$in) and 13cm ($5\frac{1}{8}$in) down from top and mark these points. Drill 2.5cm (1in) holes, 12mm ($\frac{1}{2}$in) deep at each marked point.

Following measurements in fig. 1 mark out and cut one base, two tender end plates and one cab front from 5cm × 2.5cm (2in × 1in) softwood. Mark and drill six 2mm ($\frac{5}{64}$in) pilot holes (marked A) and countersink on upper side of base. Mark and drill holes B, C and D and counter-

sink on the underside of the base.

Following measurements in fig. 1, mark and cut out two wheel chassis. Mark and drill the two 6mm ($\frac{1}{4}$in) holes in each wheel chassis section. These must be carefully positioned as they carry the axles of the drive wheels.

On cab front mark and drill two 19mm ($\frac{3}{4}$in) holes and one 2mm ($\frac{5}{64}$in) hole as shown.

Plane and sand all softwood parts.

Following measurements in fig. 2 mark out 6mm ($\frac{1}{4}$in) plywood and cut two tender side plates, two base end plates, one cab roof and two cab

ASSEMBLING THE RAILWAY ENGINE

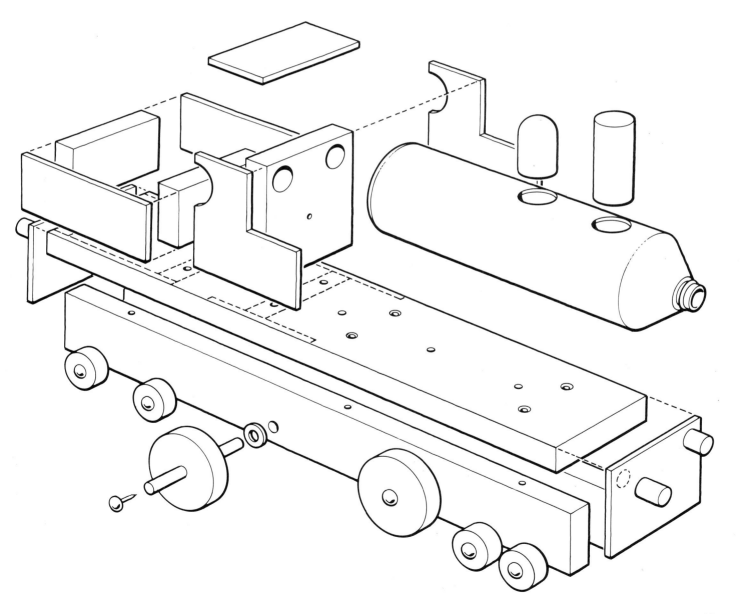

sides. Use a fretsaw to cut the curves of the cab sides. Sand all plywood pieces smooth.

Cut wheels from 12mm ($\frac{1}{2}$in) plywood. Using a hole saw, cut four 6.4cm ($2\frac{1}{2}$in) diameter circles and finish to 5.8cm ($2\frac{1}{4}$in). Cut eight circles to an initial diameter of 3.2cm ($1\frac{1}{4}$in), and finish to 2.9cm ($1\frac{1}{8}$in). Drill 6mm ($\frac{1}{4}$in) centre holes in all wheels (see Techniques section).

Note: If you do not have a hole saw, use a fretsaw for wheels, marking circles with compasses. Drill the 6mm ($\frac{1}{4}$in) centre holes before cutting out wheels. Smooth edges with sandpaper.

From 2.5cm (1in) dowel, cut 7cm ($2\frac{3}{4}$in) length for stack and 5cm (2in) length for dome. Sand top of dome to rounded shape.

Cut four buffers, each 15mm ($\frac{5}{8}$in) long from 12mm ($\frac{1}{2}$in) dowel. Sand and smooth.

Cut six axles, each 8.6cm ($3\frac{3}{8}$in) long from 6mm ($\frac{1}{4}$in) dowel.

Using two 3.8cm ($1\frac{1}{2}$in) No. 6 (3.6mm) countersunk woodscrews and PVA woodworking adhesive, glue and screw the cab front to the base, inserting screws through holes marked C in fig. 1. Attach tender

end plates in the same way, using holes marked D in fig. 1.

Using 3.8cm ($1\frac{1}{2}$in) No. 6 (3.6mm) screws and PVA woodworking adhesive, glue and screw chassis sections to base. Make sure that axle holes in each are aligned, and that the front axle is 14.5cm ($5\frac{3}{4}$in) from the front of the base as shown in fig. 1.

Position boiler on base and hold in place with a 4.5cm ($1\frac{3}{4}$in) long No. 6 screw through the front of cab. Turn assembly over and screw boiler to base using three 4.5cm ($1\frac{3}{4}$in) long No. 6 screws inserted through holes marked B in fig. 1. Make sure that the boiler remains central while the screws are inserted.

Fit cap of detergent bottle onto neck.

Using PVA woodworking adhesive, glue stack and dome into the holes in the boiler.

Using 12mm ($\frac{1}{2}$in) panel pins and PVA adhesive, glue and pin cab sides to base and cab front. Attach tender side plates and roof in the same way.

Before attaching the larger drive wheels, check that the axles revolve freely in the 6mm ($\frac{1}{4}$in) holes drilled

in the chassis sections. If the axles stick, rub down with glasspaper.

Cut twelve plastic washers to fit between the wheels and chassis sections. Cut these from discarded plastic lids.

To attach drive wheels, turn engine upside down and inset two axles into previously drilled holes in chassis. Thread a plastic washer through each end of axle and then coat dowel tips lightly with PVA adhesive. Press the four large drive wheels into position. Tap a brass upholstery nail into the end of each axle, taking care not to split the dowel. You may find it easier to drill a small hole for the nails first.

Glue the smaller wheels to their respective axles before attaching to engine, including plastic washers and finishing with upholstery nails as before.

Fix axles to chassis with electrical cable clips (fig. 3), replacing the nails with 15mm ($\frac{5}{8}$in) long No. 1 screws. Position the front set of wheels 3cm ($1\frac{1}{8}$in) and 7cm ($2\frac{3}{4}$in) from the front of the chassis respectively. Lay each axle in place and fix with cable clips, one on each side of the axle in pairs (fig. 3). Attach the rear set of wheels in the same way, placing them 3.5cm ($1\frac{3}{8}$in) and 10.5cm ($4\frac{1}{8}$in) from the rear of the chassis.

Painting

Sand all parts and paint with the colours of your choice.

Wagons

Various wagons can be constructed for the engine by using shortened versions of the base and chassis, which should be reduced to 12.6cm (5in) in length. The other dimensions remain the same as for the engine. The wheels should be the same size as the smaller engine wheels and attached in the same way using electrical cable clips. The base can either be left as a flat-bed truck, or have sides and a roof added to form carriages and a guard's van. Tanker trucks can be made by screwing small plaster-filled bottles to the base of the truck in the same way as for the boiler engine.

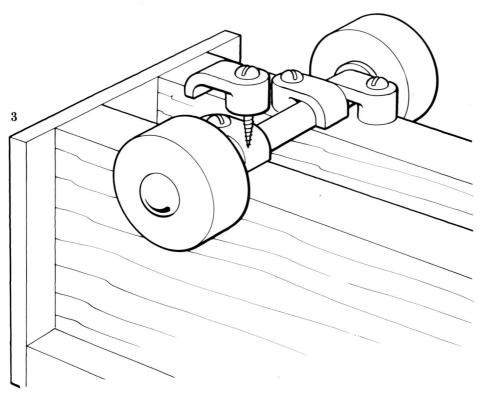

3. *The axles of the smaller wheels, fastened to the chassis with cable clips.*

Toy-box house

Tools required
Jig-saw or panel saw and padsaw;
drill; screwdriver; pin hammer;
glasspaper and block; scissors;
paintbrush

Techniques involved
Sawing; gluing; upholstery;
painting.
Materials
2.44m × 1.22m (8ft × 4ft) standard

sheet of 16mm ($\frac{5}{8}$in) blockboard or
chipboard or offcuts suitable for
cutting panels
2.3m (98in) of 19mm ($\frac{3}{4}$in) triangular
softwood moulding

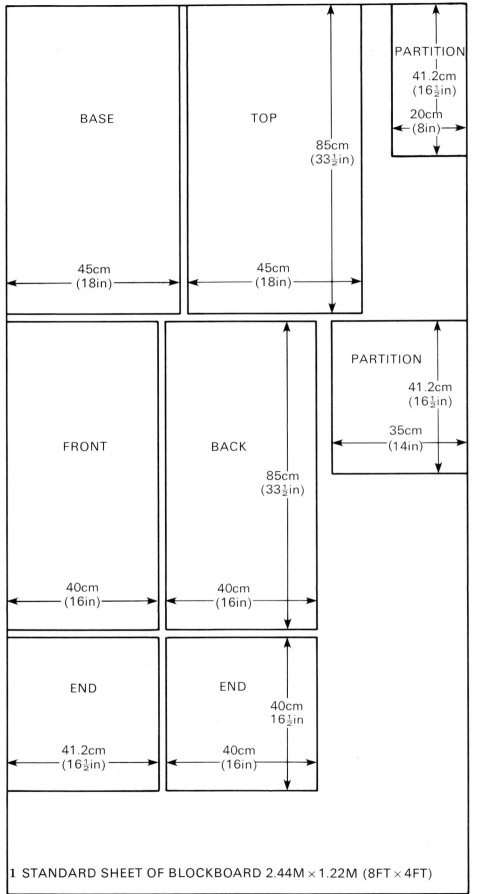

3.2cm × 6mm ($1\frac{1}{4}$in × $\frac{1}{4}$in) hardwood
   dowels
85cm × 45cm ($33\frac{1}{2}$in × 18in) of 5cm
   (2in) high-density plastic foam
105cm × 65cm ($41\frac{1}{2}$ × $25\frac{1}{2}$in) of 12mm
   ($\frac{1}{2}$in) plastic foam
107cm × 67cm (42in × $26\frac{3}{8}$in) natural
   hessian
90cm × 50cm ($35\frac{1}{2}$in × $19\frac{5}{8}$in) natural
   hessian rope
4 rubber buffers
2 heavy-duty single-coated hinges,
   T-hinges or strap hinges as
   available
12mm ($\frac{1}{2}$in) No. 6 (3.6mm)
   countersunk woodscrews
upholstery pins
12mm ($\frac{1}{2}$in) panel pins
PVA woodworking adhesive
wood and primer
enamel paints

Making the box

You can use either 16mm chipboard
or blockboard to make the box.
Blockboard is more durable but
more expensive. Test the assembly
before final fitting by assembling
without gluing.

Mark out all the panels required
on one full standard sheet as shown
in fig. 1, or cut from suitably-sized
offcuts. You will need two panels
85cm × 45cm ($33\frac{1}{2}$in × 18in) for the
base and top, two panels
85cm × 40cm ($33\frac{1}{2}$in × 16in) for the
front and back, and two panels
41.8cm × 40cm ($16\frac{1}{2}$in × 16in) for the
ends. The two internal partitions
are 41.8cm × 37cm ($16\frac{1}{2}$in × $14\frac{1}{2}$in)
and 41.8cm × 20cm ($16\frac{1}{2}$in × 8in). Cut
all the panels using a panel saw or
power jig saw, taking care to keep
the cuts straight.

Following the plans in figs. 3 and
4 mark out the door and window
positions on one end panel and the
front panel. Cut the holes using a
pad saw or power jig saw. Drill
12mm ($\frac{1}{2}$in) holes in the end panels
where indicated.

Using a 6mm dowel ($\frac{1}{4}$in) bit drill
holes in the edges of the front and
back, ends and base at the positions
shown in fig. 2 to take 6mm dowels
for the joints. Mark the hole positions on each joint-face in pairs to
ensure that their positions coincide
precisely. Drill the holes into the
edges of the panels to a depth of 2cm
($\frac{3}{4}$in), and drill the holes into the
faces of the panels 12mm ($\frac{1}{2}$in) deep
as shown in fig. 2.

In the figure:

BASE — 45cm (18in), 85cm ($33\frac{1}{2}$in)

TOP — 45cm (18in), 85cm ($33\frac{1}{2}$in)

PARTITION — 41.2cm ($16\frac{1}{2}$in), 20cm (8in)

FRONT — 40cm (16in)

BACK — 40cm (16in), 85cm ($33\frac{1}{2}$in)

PARTITION — 41.2cm ($16\frac{1}{2}$in), 35cm (14in)

END — 41.2cm ($16\frac{1}{2}$in)

END — 40cm (16in), 40cm $16\frac{1}{2}$in

1 STANDARD SHEET OF BLOCKBOARD 2.44M × 1.22M (8FT × 4FT)

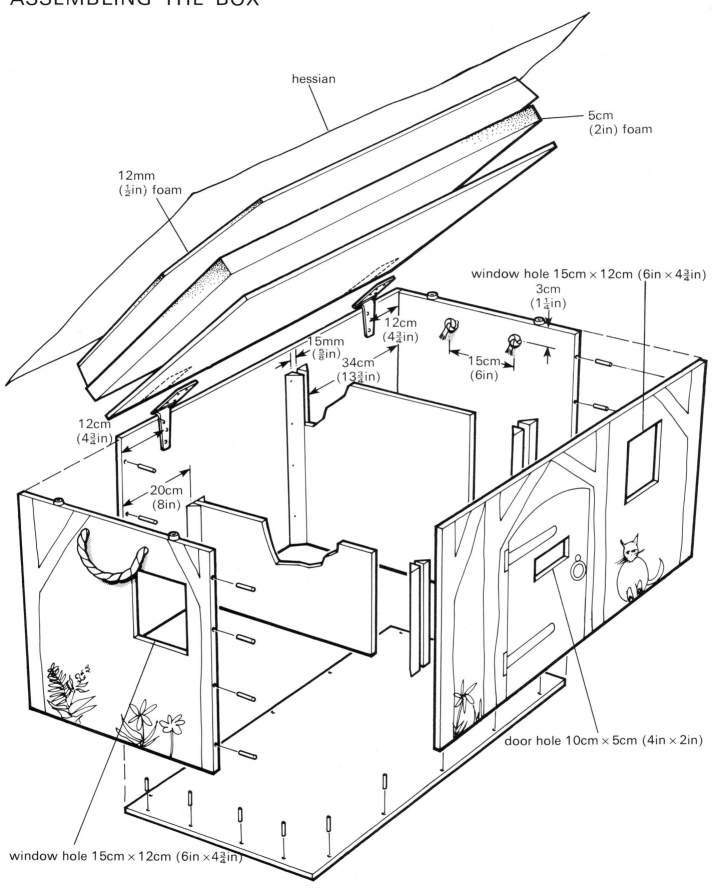

hessian

12mm
($\frac{1}{2}$in) foam

5cm
(2in) foam

window hole 15cm × 12cm (6in × 4$\frac{3}{4}$in)

3cm
(1$\frac{1}{4}$in)

12cm
(4$\frac{3}{4}$in)

15mm
($\frac{5}{8}$in)

34cm
(13$\frac{3}{4}$in)

15cm
(6in)

12cm
(4$\frac{3}{4}$in)

20cm
(8in)

door hole 10cm × 5cm (4in × 2in)

window hole 15cm × 12cm (6in × 4$\frac{3}{4}$in)

Mark the partition positions on the inside of the front and back panels as indicated in fig. 2. Draw two lines separated by 16mm ($\frac{5}{8}$in) at each position. Cut eight 37cm (14$\frac{1}{2}$in) lengths and eight 20cm (8in) lengths of 19mm ($\frac{3}{4}$in) triangular moulding. Pin and glue on either side of the marked lines, leaving a 16mm ($\frac{5}{8}$in) gap between. Check the gap using the edge of an offcut of board.

With a little PVA woodworking adhesive on each, insert 3.2cm × 6mm (1$\frac{1}{4}$in × $\frac{1}{4}$in) dowels into the holes in the edges of both end panels. Push home fully. Apply adhesive to the joint faces on the ends of the front and back panels and apply a drop of adhesive to the end of each projecting dowel. Fit ends, front and back together and apply pressure to each joint. Remove excess adhesive then hold assembly together using a Spanish windlass or sash clamps. Check the assembly is square.

Insert glued 3.2cm × 6mm (1$\frac{1}{4}$in × $\frac{1}{4}$in) dowels into the holes in the base. Apply glue to the joint faces and dowel holes on the edges of the sides, front and back, then fit the base. You can hold it in position with a heavy weight until the glue is dry.

After the glue has dried, fill any gaps with wood filler. Sand all exposed edges and corners smooth.

Fit hinges to the inside of the back as indicated in fig. 2. Note that the hinges are set 12mm ($\frac{1}{2}$in) higher than the edge.

Paint the complete box, inside and out, and both partitions with wood primer. Leave to dry.

Making the lid

The lid panel is upholstered with a padded seat in natural hessian.

Lay the 12mm ($\frac{1}{2}$in) foam on the work surface. Lay the 5cm (2in) foam on top of it in the centre. Mitre

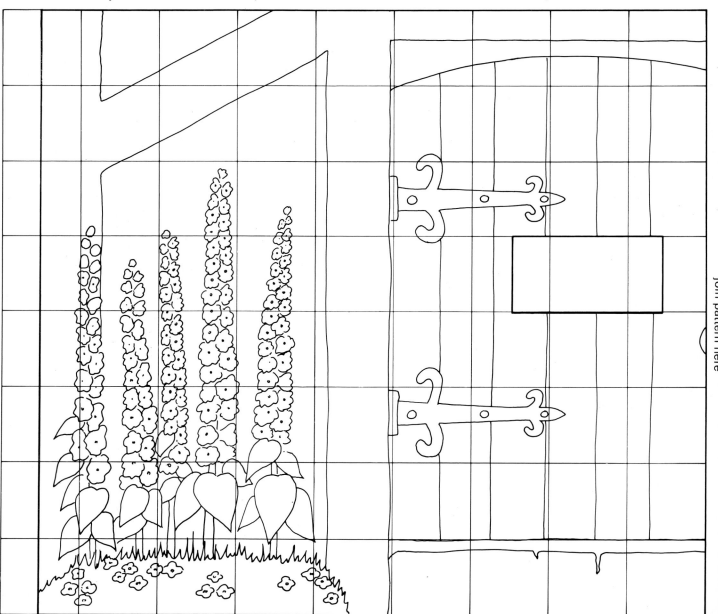

GRAPH PATTERN FOR FRONT DECORATIONS

Each square = 5cm (2in)

join pattern here

all four projecting corners at 45° to the corners of the 5cm (2in) foam. Lay the lid on top of the 5cm (2in) foam and pull the projecting edges of the 12mm ($\frac{1}{2}$in) foam up over it. You can hold the flaps in place temporarily with adhesive tape.

Lay the complete assembly, foam side down, in the centre of the larger piece of hessian. Fold the edges of the hessian over the lid and pull into place tightly, holding them with tacks or staples. Trim excess material at the corners to make a neat finish.

Take the small piece of hessian and turn in 2.5cm (1in) all round.

Lay this over the lid, with the turnings underneath and pin in place with upholstery pins.

Decorating the box

Trace the patterns for the decorations on the end and sides of the box. Transfer these on to the box with carbon paper. Using enamel paints and following the colours in the pictures, add all the details. Paint the walls white first, then add oak beams. Smaller details can be added with fine artist's brushes, but be sure to let each colour dry before adding the next. Allow to dry.

Paint the whole of the inside of

the box and both partitions with any dark-coloured paint. Allow to dry, then slot the partitions in place.

Using fabric paints, add streaks of colour to the lid upholstery to resemble thatch. Allow to dry.

Assembly

Screw four rubber buffers to the top edges of the ends where indicated in fig. 2. These prevent the lid from shutting fully and trapping a child's fingers.

Screw the lid to the hinges and check that it opens freely. Insert two screw eyes in the position shown in the lid and side and join

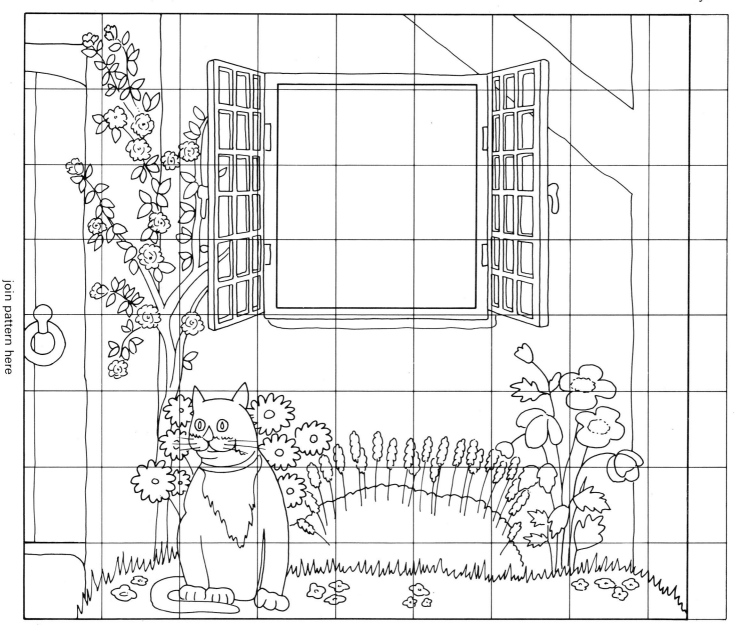

join pattern here

Each square = 5cm (2in)

173

Foam should be squashed down under the hessian

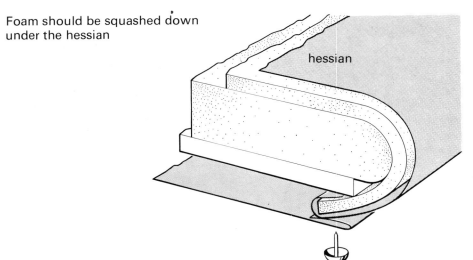

hessian

them with a length of cord to form a lid stay. The lid should be free to open to about 30° from the vertical.

Pass the ends of two 30cm (11¾in) lengths of rope through the holes in each end of the box, and knot securely to form two rope handles.

If you wish, the partitions can be removed. You can cut internal doorways in the larger one. With a little ingenuity, you can even cut out the front door and arrange for it to open on miniature butt hinges.

GRAPH PATTERN FOR END DECORATIONS

Each square = 5cm (2in)

Sailing boat

Finished length
27.5cm (10¾in).
Tools required
Fretsaw with metal cutting blades; hack saw; flat spokeshave; vice; drill with 1.5mm (1/16in), 2mm (5/64in)

and 6mm (¼in) bits; pliers; small hammer; craft knife; scissors; carpenter's square; ruler; pencil; paintbrushes; small bradawl; sanding block.

Techniques involved
Using fretsaw; using spokeshave; using carpenter's square; drilling; painting.
Materials
30cm (12in) of 10cm × 5cm (4in × 2in)

pine or similar softwood without knots

5cm (2in) square of 2mm ($\frac{5}{64}$in) plywood

12cm × 9cm (4$\frac{3}{4}$in × 3$\frac{1}{2}$in) of 2mm ($\frac{5}{64}$in) steel plate, weight 225g (8oz). (Plywood and lead weights can be used as substitutes)

38cm (15in) of 6mm ($\frac{1}{4}$in) dowel

9.5cm (3$\frac{3}{4}$in) of 2mm ($\frac{5}{64}$in) diameter brass tube

brass collar with grub screw, with 2mm ($\frac{5}{64}$in) diameter centre

25cm (10in) square of nylon or cotton fabric

linen thread

parcel string

elastic band

8 × 6mm ($\frac{1}{4}$in) screw eyes

2 small veneer pins

epoxy resin adhesive or metal cement

contact adhesive

fabric adhesive

fine No. 1 and No. 2 glasspaper

coloured enamel paints

polyurethane varnish (optional)

50cm × 20cm (20in × 8in) cardboard

2 30 × 10cm (12in × 4in) sheets of paper

small bolts or lead weights and wood filler as needed for weighting the hull.

Carving the hull

Trace full-size patterns for the top and bottom and profile of the hull following diagrams in figs. 12 and 13.

1. *Marking a centre line.*

2. *Using the carpenter's square to position template lines all around block.*

3. *Overlapping holes are drilled down the centre of the keel slot.*

4. *Transferred pattern for the hull on the other side of block.*

5. *Cutting around the shape of the deck with a coping saw.*

6. *Tape the scrap pieces back in their original position.*

7. *Use a hand saw to remove two wedges from underside of block.*

8. *Remove the excess wood on the hull with a rasp.*

9. *The length of softwood screwed in place to hold the hull in a vice.*

10. *The hull block is clamped securely in a vice and carved into shape.*

11. *Using a template to check the curve of the hull.*

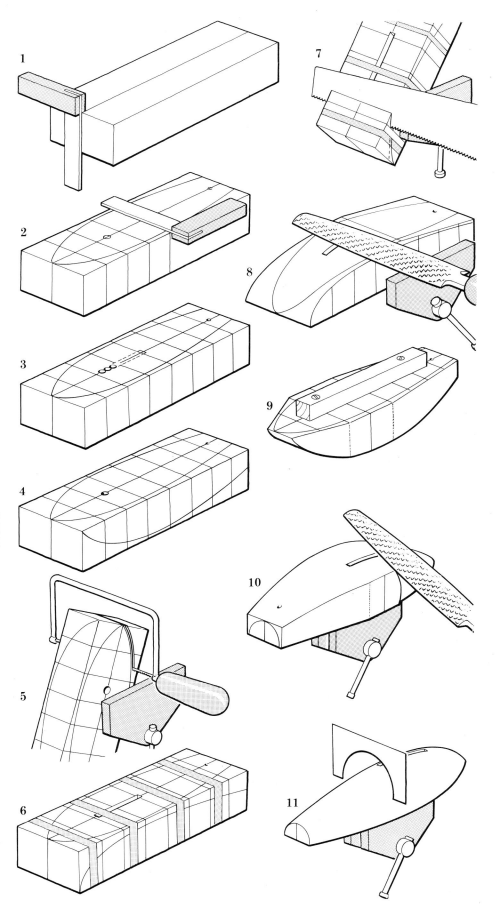

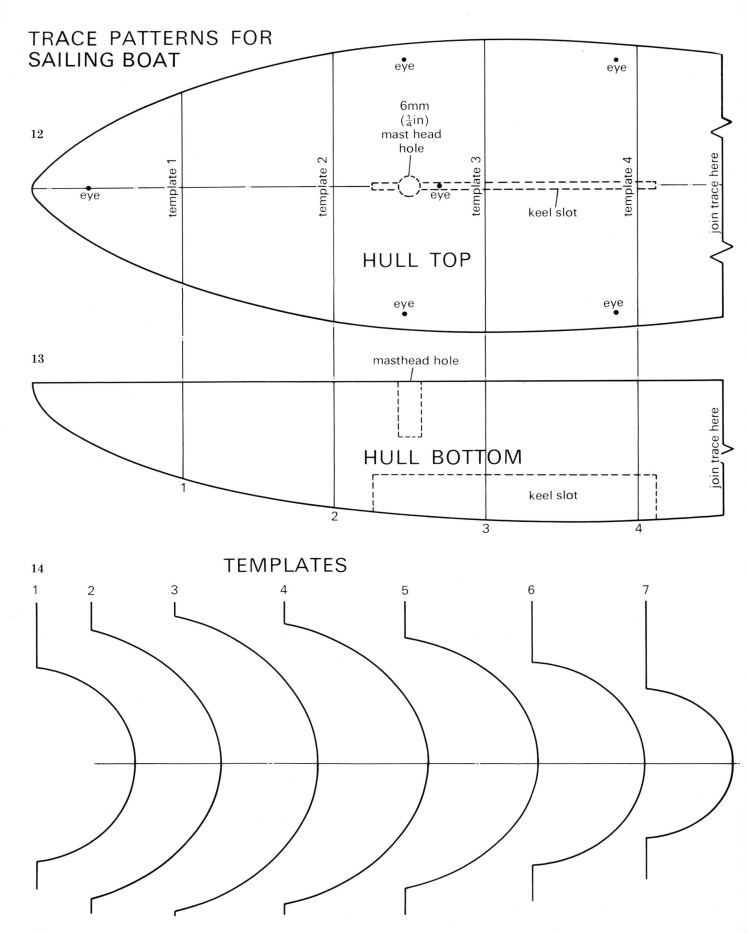

TRACE PATTERNS FOR SAILING BOAT

12

template 1

eye

eye

6mm
($\frac{1}{4}$in)
mast head
hole

template 2

eye

eye

template 3

keel slot

template 4

eye

eye

join trace here

HULL TOP

13

masthead hole

HULL BOTTOM

1

2

3

keel slot

4

join trace here

14

TEMPLATES

1   2   3   4   5   6   7

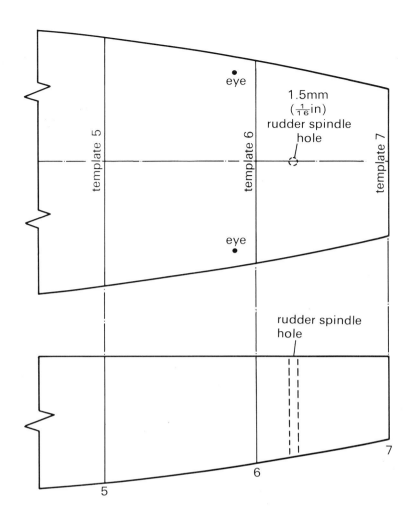

eye

1.5mm
($\frac{1}{16}$in)
rudder spindle
hole

template 5

template 6

template 7

eye

rudder spindle
hole

5

6

7

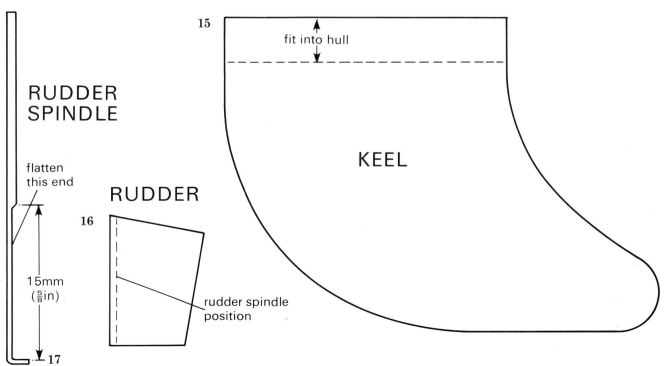

RUDDER
SPINDLE

flatten
this end

15mm
($\frac{5}{8}$in)

17

RUDDER

16

rudder spindle
position

15

fit into hull

KEEL

Mark the centre line along the length of one wide face of your softwood block. Using a carpenter's square and a straight-edge, extend this line down the ends of the block and along the bottom face (fig. 1).

Lay the block down with the intended top side uppermost. Using carbon paper, align your pattern with the marked centre line and transfer to the block the outline of the deck. Also mark the positions of the seven templates and the mast and rudder holes. Use the carpenter's square to continue the template position lines all around the block. Drill a 6mm ($\frac{1}{4}$in) diameter hole 15mm ($\frac{5}{8}$in) deep at the position marked for the mast hole. Drill a 2mm ($\frac{5}{64}$in) hole for the rudder straight through the block, taking care to keep it absolutely square to the surface (fig. 2).

Turn the block upside-down and mark out the outline of the deck on the underside including the position of the keel slot. Make sure that the pattern is aligned with the centre line, and that the template positions correspond. Drill a series of overlapping 2mm ($\frac{5}{64}$in) holes to a depth of 19mm ($\frac{3}{4}$in) down the centre of the keel slot. Use a craft knife to carve out the remainder of the slot (fig. 3).

Turn the block over on its side and transfer the pattern for the hull profile, aligning the deck surface with the top of the block and making sure that all the template positions correspond. Turn the block over and repeat on the other side (fig. 4).

Clamp the block in a vice and cut around the shape of the deck with a coping saw. Take care to cut close to but not over the line, checking the outline on the underside as well from time to time. This is the first of the two basic shapes of the hull. Do not discard the two offcuts, but tape them back in the positions they were cut from. This restores the outline of the profile of the hull (fig. 6).

Turn the block over, and using a handsaw remove two wedges from the underside of the block as shown in fig. 7, working close to but not over the marked line. Using a block plane, rasp, or planer-file remove the bulk of the remaining wood close up to the marked line. Discard the two cut-off side pieces. This completes

the second of the basic shapes of the hull (fig. 8).

Trace full size patterns for the seven templates in fig. 14. Transfer these on to stiff card. With a sharp craft knife, cut out each U-shape, removing the material within the curve. These provide guides to the curvature of the hull at the positions indicated. Mark the curve of template 7 directly on to the stern of your block.

Using two 38mm (1$\frac{1}{2}$in) No. 6 (3.6mm) woodscrews, screw a 20cm (8in) length of 25mm (1in) square softwood down the centre of the deck. Make sure to avoid the mast and rudder holes when positioning your screws. This block will allow you to clamp the hull securely in the vice for carving (fig. 9).

Using the clamping block, fix the hull blank in the vice. You can carve it with a planer-file, a flat spoke-shave, block plane or rasp (fig. 10). In all cases work slowly, to avoid removing too much material and work down the curve from the centre towards the bow and stern. As carving proceeds, check constantly with the templates at each of their marked positions to make sure that you do not cut too deeply at any point (fig. 11). When the templates show that you have nearly reached the correct curve at all positions, stop carving and finish with glasspaper. If you are using a rasp you should stop an appreciable distance before the templates, because of the rough surface that it will leave.

Using a sanding block and working in smooth sweeps, finish the hull until all the templates fit exactly. Start with coarse paper and work down to fine as you near the final shape. This will leave it smooth.

Remove from the vice and unscrew the clamping block. Weigh the completed hull. It should be approximately 168g (6oz). If this is the case, fill the screw holes left by the clamping block screws with wood filler and sand smooth. If the hull is appreciably lighter, you will need to add weight. Drill holes into the top surface to take enough fishing lead shot to make up the difference in weight. Cover the weights with wood filler and sand

Masts, rigging and sails.

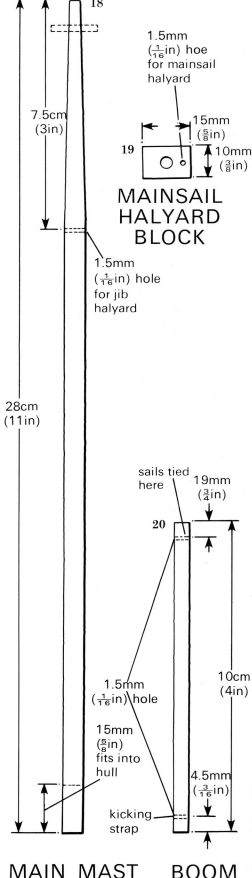

1.5mm ($\frac{1}{16}$in) hoe for mainsail halyard

15mm ($\frac{5}{8}$in)

10mm ($\frac{3}{8}$in)

19

MAINSAIL HALYARD BLOCK

18

7.5cm (3in)

1.5mm ($\frac{1}{16}$in) hole for jib halyard

28cm (11in)

MAIN MAST

sails tied here

19mm ($\frac{3}{4}$in)

20

10cm (4in)

1.5mm ($\frac{1}{16}$in) hole

15mm ($\frac{5}{8}$in) fits into hull

kicking strap

4.5mm ($\frac{3}{16}$in)

BOOM

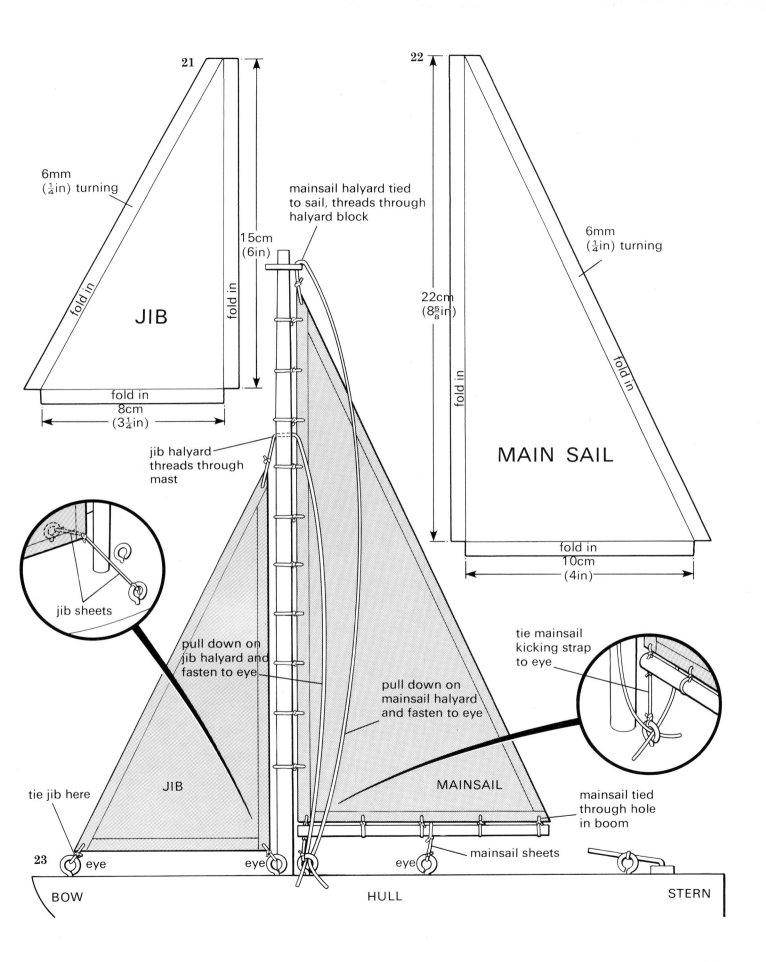

21

6mm
($\frac{1}{4}$in) turning

fold in

JIB

fold in

15cm
(6in)

fold in

8cm
($3\frac{1}{4}$in)

mainsail halyard tied
to sail, threads through
halyard block

22

6mm
($\frac{1}{4}$in) turning

22cm
($8\frac{5}{8}$in)

fold in

fold in

MAIN SAIL

fold in

10cm
(4in)

jib halyard
threads through
mast

jib sheets

pull down on
jib halyard and
fasten to eye

pull down on
mainsail halyard
and fasten to eye

tie mainsail
kicking strap
to eye

JIB

MAINSAIL

tie jib here

mainsail tied
through hole
in boom

23

eye

eye

eye

mainsail sheets

BOW

HULL

STERN

flush. If the hull is too heavy, drill out until it is the correct weight, fill the holes with plastic foam and cover with wood filler as before.

Prime the hull all round and seal with several coats of enamel paint. Alternatively, seal all round with several coats of varnish.

Making the keel

The keel is cut from a piece of 2mm ($\frac{5}{64}$in) mild steel. Substitute plywood if the boat is intended for younger users.

Trace the full size pattern for keel from fig. 15. Glue the pattern to the steel and cut out using a hacksaw (fretsaw for plywood version). Finish with a half round file. The keel is designed to give a weight of 84g (3oz) when cut to size. If your keel is lighter or if you use plywood, you will need to add weights to the keel. You can use large anglers' lead weights (ledger weights) for this. Fix them to the tip of the keel using epoxy adhesive to bring it up to the correct weight. Try to fix an equal number on each side of the keel and in the same position.

Glue the keel into the slot in the hull using epoxy adhesive, with its shape raking back from the bows.

Finish with wood or metal primer as appropriate and then enamel paint.

Making the rudder

Cut out the rudder from 2mm ($\frac{5}{64}$in) plywood, following the dimensions in fig. 16.

Make the rudder spindle from a 10cm (4in) length of 2mm ($\frac{5}{64}$in) brass tube. Flatten 4cm (1$\frac{1}{2}$in) of the end in a vice. Turn up the last 6mm ($\frac{1}{4}$in) of the flattened portion to form a right angle (fig. 17). Position against the leading edge of the rudder with the bent end underneath Fix in place with epoxy adhesive. Sand smooth and finish with enamel paint.

When paint has dried, pass the end of the rudder spindle through the rudder hole in the hull until the rudder is 3mm ($\frac{1}{8}$in) below the hull. Fit the brass locking collar over the top of the shaft and tighten it at deck level to prevent the shaft from slipping through the hole. Bend the end of the shaft over with a pair of pliers until it is parallel to the deck to form a tiller.

Insert screweyes into the deck on either side of the tiller in the positions shown in fig. 12. Stretch an elastic band between these eyes and twist over the tiller to hold it in position for setting the rudder.

Making the mast

Cut a 27cm (10$\frac{5}{8}$in) length of 6mm ($\frac{1}{4}$in) dowel and taper one end as shown in fig. 18 by whittling with a craft knife and finishing with sandpaper. Drill a 1.5mm ($\frac{1}{16}$in) hole through the centre of the mast 7.5cm (3in) down from the tip of this tapered end. Glue the other end of the mast into the pre-drilled hole in the deck using epoxy resin adhesive. Make sure that the hole through the mast faces from bow to stern.

Cut the mainsail halyard block from 2mm ($\frac{5}{64}$in) plywood as shown in fig. 19. Measure the thickness of the tapered mast at a point 6mm ($\frac{1}{4}$in) down from the tip. Drill the large hole in the block to this diameter, and drill a further 1.5mm ($\frac{1}{16}$in) hole as shown. Glue the halyard block on to the mast with epoxy resin adhesive, with the small hole directly towards the stern side of the mast as shown in fig. 12.

Cut out the boom which is a 100mm (4in) length of 6mm ($\frac{1}{4}$in) dowel. Drill 1.5mm ($\frac{1}{16}$in) holes through it at 2cm ($\frac{3}{4}$in) from one end and 5mm ($\frac{3}{16}$in) from the other as shown in fig. 20.

Finish the mast and boom with several thin coats of polyurethane lacquer. You can support the boom on a wire through the holes while drying.

Making the sails and rigging

The sails can be made from any light-weight close-woven nylon or cotton fabric.

Following the measurements in figs. 21 and 22 make two paper patterns for the sails. Pin these on to the sail fabric and mark the shapes on to the fabric. Add 6mm ($\frac{1}{4}$in) turnings all round as shown and cut out the sails.

Fold over the turnings and fix by stitching the hems or gluing with contact or fabric adhesive.

Using a small awl, punch holes 6mm ($\frac{1}{4}$in) from the three corners of each sail.

Insert a screweye into the deck

directly behind the mast and another 15mm ($\frac{5}{8}$in) from the point of the bow as shown in fig. 12.

Cut about 5cm (2in) of twine and tie through the hole in the front corner of the jib. Tie the two ends through the screw eye in the bows, as shown in fig. 23.

Cut about 28cm (11in) of twine and knot to the hole in the top point of the jib. Thread the end of the twine through the hole drilled through the mast. This is the jib halyard. Pull down behind the mast until the jib is taut, then knot through the eye at the foot of the mast.

Use the bradawl to pierce holes 2cm ($\frac{3}{4}$in) apart down the edges of the mainsail as shown in fig. 23. Tie the sail to the mast and boom with short lengths of twine knotted through these holes as shown. Cut the ends of the twine off short and secure the knots with a drop of adhesive. Tie off the twine through the hole in the rear corner of the sail through the hole drilled 2cm ($\frac{3}{4}$in) from the end of the boom.

Tie a 5cm (2in) length of twine to the hole at the front corner of the sail. Pass the end through the screweye at the foot of the mast and tie off so that the boom is 3cm (1$\frac{1}{4}$in) above the deck. This is the mainsail kicking strap.

Cut another 28cm (11in) length of twine for the mainsail halyard. Tie to the hole in the top of the mainsail, then thread through the small hole in the halyard block. Loop over the top and pull down until the tip of the sail almost touches the block. Tie off to the screw eye at the base of the mast.

Insert two screw eyes to secure jib sheets and two screw eyes for mainsail sheets in positions shown in fig. 12.

Cut about 50cm (20in) of string. Thread through corner of jib and knot, leaving equal ends on each side. Thread one end through each of the screw eyes on deck and knot ends of string together. These are the jib sheets which set the sail.

Cut about 40cm (15$\frac{3}{4}$in) of string, loop round centre of boom and tie. Thread each end of the string through its corresponding screw eye on the deck and knot ends of string together. These are the mainsail sheets.

Doll's house

Finished size
The completed house is about 46cm (18in) tall, 30cm (12in) deep, and 54cm (21in) wide.

Tools required
Drill with 6mm ($\frac{1}{4}$in) and 3mm ($\frac{1}{8}$in) bits; fretsaw or tenon saw; hand saw; 6mm ($\frac{1}{4}$in) wide chisel; pencil; mallet and small hammer; screw-

183

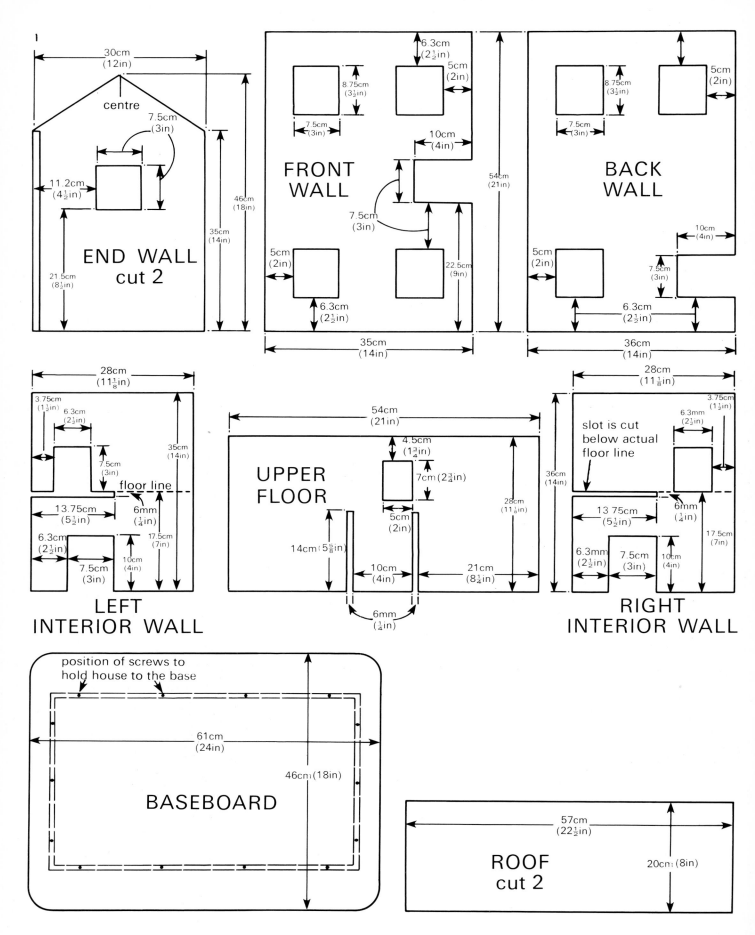

driver; hand plane and coarse wood file; one fine paintbrush and one 5cm (2in) wide paintbrush; tape measure; carpenter's square; sanding block.

Techniques involved
Cutting; sawing; gluing; painting.

Materials
two pieces 6mm × 30cm × 46cm ($\frac{1}{4}$in × 12in × 18in) plywood for end walls

two pieces 6mm ($\frac{1}{4}$in) × 36cm (14in) × 54cm (21in) plywood for front and back walls

two pieces 6mm ($\frac{1}{4}$in) × 20cm (8in) × 57cm (22$\frac{1}{2}$in) plywood for roof sections

two pieces 6mm ($\frac{1}{4}$in) × 28cm (11in) × 36cm (14in) plywood for interior walls

one piece 6mm ($\frac{1}{4}$in) × 28cm (11in) × 54cm (21in) plywood for interior floor

one piece 12mm ($\frac{1}{2}$in) × 46cm (18in) × 61cm (24in) plywood for base

scrap pieces of 6mm ($\frac{1}{4}$in) plywood

sheet clear plastic

2 rolls of 6mm ($\frac{1}{4}$in) wide adhesive tape—one orange, one yellow— available from office suppliers; or cut larger widths to size.

2.5cm × 57cm (1in × 23in) piano hinge for roof hinge

4 × 12mm ($\frac{1}{2}$in) brass hinges and screws

one hook and eye catch

box 12mm ($\frac{1}{2}$in) finishing nails

two pieces corner moulding, 6mm × 36cm ($\frac{1}{4}$in × 14in, cross section looks like a quarter circle)

enamel paints and suitable undercoats

wood filler and primer

scrap of cardboard; plastic tubing

white woodworking PVA adhesive

glasspaper—medium and fine

20 × 6mm ($\frac{1}{4}$in) No. 4 screws

10 × 2.5cm (1in) No. 4 screws

The house is designed so that there is easy access to the rooms. The front slides out so that children can play with the furniture inside, and the roof is hinged to open up the top floor.

Each floor is divided up into three sections consisting of a central hallway and stairway with a room on each side.

Each room can be decorated individually and with imagination as you would your own home, with either bought or homemade furniture. Instructions for furniture made from materials around the home are given on pages 216 to 219.

Making the house
Following the plans in fig. 1, mark out and cut the base from 12mm ($\frac{1}{2}$in) plywood. You can cut the basic rectangle with a hand saw, and cut the rounded corners with a fretsaw or tenon saw. Sand all the cut corners smooth. Mark out the positions of the walls where indicated, and drill 2mm ($\frac{3}{32}$in) clearance holes, countersunk on the underside, for the wall screws.

Following the plans in fig. 1 mark out the basic rectangles for the front and back walls, end walls, interior walls, interior floor and roof sections in 6mm ($\frac{1}{4}$in) plywood. Cut to shape with a hand saw. Mark each piece with the positions of doors, windows and assembling slots, taking care that these are accurately positioned.

Mark the profile of the end gables on the end walls. Cut the gables and slots with the hand saw. You can cut across the ends of the slots with a fretsaw or tenon saw.

Cut the door opening in the same way, cutting the sides with a hand saw, and then across with a fretsaw or tenon saw.

Cut the windows by drilling a starting hole so that you can insert the blade of your fretsaw or tenon saw and cut around the outline.

When you have cut out all the parts, sand all surfaces and edges smooth with glasspaper.

Painting interior
Before assembling the pieces it is advisable to prepare them for painting. Plywood of this thickness has a tendency to split at the edges where it has been sawed, leaving an untidy finish. To avoid this, fill in the splits with wood filler. When the filler is dry, sand the wood down with medium, then fine grade, glasspaper.

To seal the plywood, coat each surface with white primer. At this stage you need only paint the interior of the house. Also paint the base.

1. *Cutting chart for the house.*
Right: *The exterior walls are all ready to be assembled.*
Below: *The finished house with the front wall in position.*

When paint is dry, rub down with fine grade sandpaper before applying an undercoat. Again sand this coat down when dry and finish with a non-toxic enamel paint.

Assembly

The walls can now be assembled and the house attached to the base. Slot the interior walls and floor together and stand them on the base (fig. 2). Next, lay the end walls on the table with the inside surfaces uppermost.

On the left-hand edge of the left end wall, glue a 36cm (14in) strip of corner moulding (see plan). Glue a similar strip to the right-hand edge of the right end wall.

These strips of moulding form the guides that allow the front of the house to slide out.

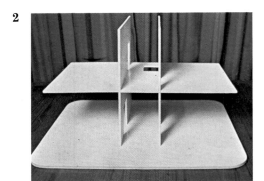

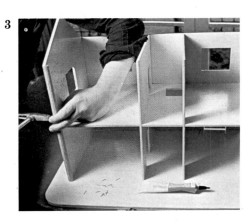

Lay the back wall on the table, inside surface uppermost. Place the interior wall-floor structure onto this, in the position that it is to be attached.

The rectangle cut for the stairway should be nearest the back wall. Use a carpenter's square to check that all the edges are flush.

Draw a line lightly around the interior wall-floor structure where it butts against the back wall. Remove this structure and coat the marked lines with woodworking glue. Coat the edges of the structure, which butt against the back wall, as well.

With the back wall still lying flat, press the two glued edges together and turn the whole structure upright. Tack together with 12mm (½in) finishing nails.

Hold the end walls in place against the interior wall-floor structure and check that the edges are flush. Draw lines around where the interior wall-floor structure butts against the end wall.

Repeat the gluing and nailing as shown in fig. 3 with the other end wall. The front wall should now fit in between the moulding and the inner wall structure.

Doors

The two doors should not be cut from 6mm (¼in) thick plywood. Use scrap or the cut-outs from the doorways if they were not damaged. Cut them the size of the openings but make them 6mm (¼in) shorter at the base. This allows a clearance for a small step to be glued to the baseboard. Paint the doors, then hang them with 12mm (½in) brass hinges.

Attaching house to base

Position the house centrally on the base. Draw around the outer walls, both inside and out, with a pencil. Lift the house off the base and drill holes between the wall lines, as shown in the plan, with the 3mm (⅛in) bit. Countersink the holes from underneath the base. Fasten the house to the base with the 2.5cm

2. The interior walls are slotted together on the base as shown.
3. Attaching the exterior walls with glue and finishing nails.
4. Attaching the piano hinge to the two halves of the roof.

(1in) No. 4 screws.

Having reached this point, it is advisable to paint the outer surfaces of the house and base with primer undercoat and then with an enamel. Remember to paint the edges of the base.

The roof

The front of the roof is designed to fold back, enabling children to reach the furniture on the upper floor. It also allows the front wall to slide out.

Take two pieces of plywood to be used for the roof and chamfer one long edge of each. This is done with a plane and allows the roof to fold upward when you wish to reach inside.

Fill any splits that may have occurred and then sand and paint the inner sides.

Lay the two pieces side by side, beveled edges touching and facing down and screw the piano hinge into position (fig. 4) using the 6mm (¼in) No. 4 screws.

Place the roof section on the end wall supports. The two sections should lie snugly along the pitch of the end walls with the chamfered edge uppermost and the hinge underneath. Make sure the front roof section folds back easily to allow the front section to slide out. Attach the back section of roof to the end walls with finishing nails and finish the roof with enamel.

Making the chimney

Cut four piece of 6mm (¼in) plywood to the dimensions shown in fig. 5a on the plan. Glue together.

Glue a small piece of cardboard onto the top of the chimney. Chimney pots, which can be cut from short lengths of plastic tubing, are attached to the cardboard.

When the chimney is assembled, paint it and glue to the roof 22cm (8½in) along from the left-hand end of the house (fig. 5b). The back of the chimney should be level with the edge of the bevel that you made on the apex of the roof.

Porch, stairway and windows

The final components of the house can now be made and fitted. The porch and stairs are cut from 6mm (¼in) plywood.

Porch

This should be made from three pieces of 6mm ($\frac{1}{4}$in) plywood, 2.5cm (1in) wide. Cut two pieces 11cm (4$\frac{1}{4}$in) long and a third 10cm (4in) long. Smooth with fine grade glasspaper, paint and glue to the area around the front of the door. The two longer pieces should be flush with the edges of the door opening, while the third piece forms the lintel with a slight overlap at each side.

To finish off the doors, screw small screws into them to form handles.

Making the stairs

Cut two pieces of 6mm ($\frac{1}{4}$in) plywood, 21cm (8$\frac{1}{4}$in) long and 2.5cm (1in) wide (fig. 6a).

Measure 1cm ($\frac{3}{8}$in) from the top left-hand corner and bottom right-hand corner of each. Draw a line from this point to the adjacent corner and saw along this line. The steps must be set parallel to this sawn edge.

Cut seven steps from a piece of 6mm ($\frac{1}{4}$in) plywood, 2.5cm × 3.75cm (1in × 1$\frac{1}{2}$in) (fig. 6a).

Fasten to the side pieces with wood glue. Glue the stairway to the inside wall (fig. 6b).

Window glazing

The windows are easily made from clear plastic. The plastic used in packaging is ideal.

Cut the plastic 3mm ($\frac{1}{8}$in) larger than the window. Place the plastic flat on the table and, using the yellow adhesive tape, mark out the window panes. For the frames, use the orange tape. The tape used for the surrounds should overlap the plastic slightly in order to fasten the window to the outside of the wall (fig. 7).

Finally, screw a hook and eye catch to one end of the roof so that it will hold the front flap back when the roof is opened (fig. 8). The front of the house can then be slid into position.

5a. *Making the chimney.*
5b. *Placing the chimney in position.*
6a. *Make the staircase by cutting seven steps and gluing to side pieces.*
6b. *The staircase is moved into position and glued to an inside wall.*
7. *Attach the windows to the outside of the wall.*
8. *Screw a hook and eye catch to one end of the roof.*

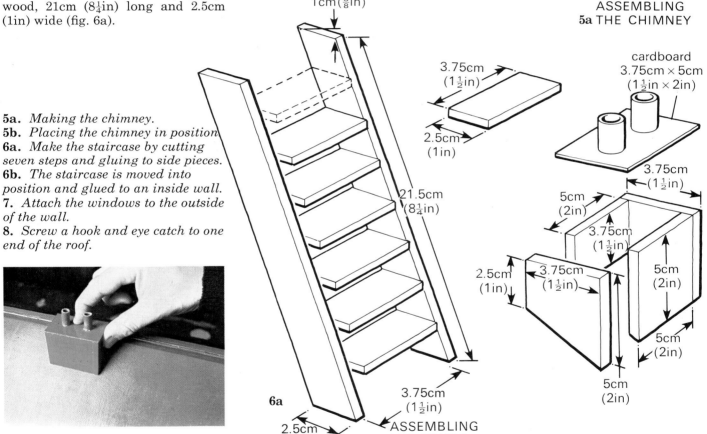

6a ASSEMBLING THE STAIRS

ASSEMBLING
5a THE CHIMNEY

Marquetry chess board

Finished size
36cm (14in) square.

Tools required
Sharp trimming knife; steel rule; set-square.

Techniques involved
Working with veneers.

Materials
36cm (14in) square of 12mm ($\frac{1}{4}$in) thick plywood or chipboard for base

wood veneers, 1.5mm ($\frac{1}{16}$in) thick, as follows

38cm × 30cm (15in × 12in) dark veneer and 38cm × 30cm (15in × 12in) light veneer for squares

38cm × 15cm (15in × 6in) dark veneer and 38cm × 5cm (15in × 2in) light veneer for border

38cm (15in) square of either colour veneer for plain back

for alternative diamond-patterned back, 4 pieces of identical veneer, each 25cm (10in) square

transparent adhesive tape

contact adhesive

fine No. 2 sandpaper

garnet paper, grades 4/0, 7/0 and 9/0 and flour grade glasspaper

polyurethane lacquer

or French polish or 'white' wood polish.

For making cutting board:
60cm × 46cm (24in × 18in) of 6mm
  ($\frac{1}{4}$in) plywood or 12mm ($\frac{1}{2}$in)
chipboard
60cm (24in) strip of 12mm × 6mm
  ($\frac{1}{2}$in × $\frac{1}{4}$in) hardwood
  2 × 6mm ($\frac{1}{4}$in) bolts, 10mm ($\frac{3}{8}$in)
  long, fitted with nuts and
  washers.

Cutting board

Great accuracy is needed for cutting
and assembling the veneers used on
the chessboard. For this the cutting
edge of your knife should be kept
very sharp, so replace the blade as
soon as it is blunt. The veneer strips
can be cut more quickly and accurately by using a straightedge and
a cutting board. The board is made
from 12mm ($\frac{1}{2}$in) thick plywood or
chipboard with a strip of dead
straight 12mm × 6mm ($\frac{1}{2}$ × $\frac{1}{4}$in) hardwood moulding pinned and glued
along one edge to form a guide
face. Details are shown in figs. 2a
and 2b. The bolts for adjustable
stops which should be set to give a
uniform distance between the guide
face and a steel rule placed firmly
against the stops (fig. 1). Make sure
that the slots in which the bolts
slide are set far enough apart to fit
your piece of veneer between them.

To cut veneer strips trim one edge
of the veneer straight and set both
stops to give the required width
between the guide face and the
straightedge. Position the veneer
against the hardwood strip, place
the steel rule over the veneer and
firmly against the stops, and then
cut cleanly against the rule. Do not
try to cut right though the veneer at
one stroke; use several lighter cuts
to avoid splintering or tearing the
veneer.

Making the chessboard
Chequer assembly
Using the cutting board and stops
set to 3.8cm (1$\frac{1}{2}$in). Cut four strips of
dark veneer, each 38cm × 3.8cm
(15in × 1$\frac{1}{2}$in) (fig. 3). These lengths are
trimmed later. Keep them together in

How to use the cutting board:
1. *The bolt is adjustable and can be
set to the required width.*
2a. *The moulding acts as a guide
face. Cut veneer along a steel rule.*
2b. *Cutting the chequered strips.*

the order in which they were cut.
Now cut four strips of light veneer
the same size. Using strips of
adhesive tape, fit the strips of veneer
together in alternate sequence (fig.
4). Note that the strips should be
assembled in the order in which
they were cut and with the grain
running in the same direction.
Check that all strips fit tightly
against one another.

Using steel rule and set-square
trim the assembly at one end at

right angles to the direction of the
veneer strips.

Position the assembly on the
cutting board with the trimmed edge
firmly against the hardwood face, so
that the veneer strips are at right
angles to it.

Carefully cut through the as-
sembly so that a new 3.8cm (1$\frac{1}{2}$in)
wide strip is obtained, comprising
eight squares of alternately light
and dark veneer (fig. 5). Handle
these pieces with care, as the

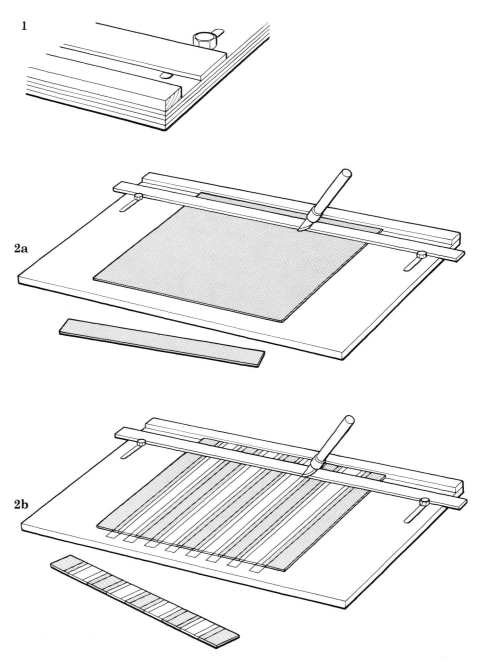

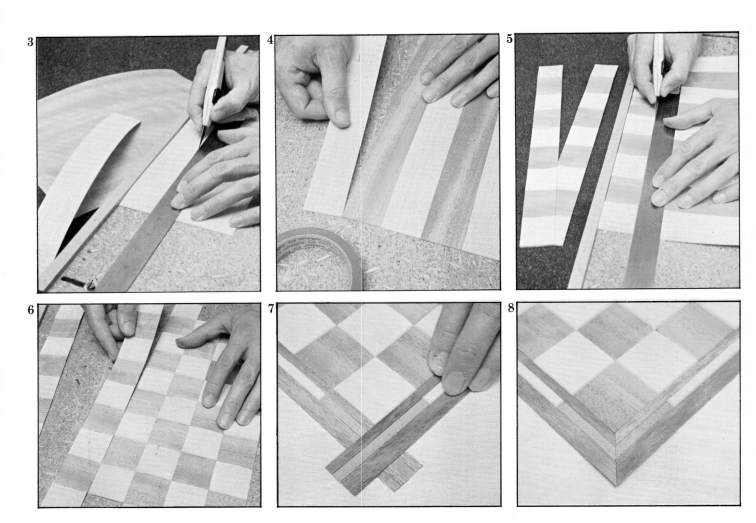

squares of veneer are joined together only by the adhesive tape. In the same way cut seven more 3.8cm (1½in) wide strips of eight squares discard the remaining veneer. Keeping these strips in the same order, lay them out on the cutting board and stagger them to form a chequer pattern (fig. 6).

Using adhesive tape, fix the strips together, again making certain that the joints are tight between adjacent pieces of veneer and checking that the squares meet exactly at the corners. Eight squares of veneer will be left projecting from the assembly. Cut these off and discard. The result should be the familiar chessboard pattern in a perfect square, with each of the small squares meeting its neighbours exactly at the corners.

Back

Begin with the back of the base board (sand the edges smooth if necessary). The back can be covered with a single sheet of veneer, cut

slightly oversize and glued to the back of the base board using contact adhesive.

Trim the edges flush and sand with flour grade glasspaper.

Edges

Cut four strips of veneer, slightly over-size for the edges of the board. Using contact adhesive, stick strips to two opposite edges. Allow to set and sand flush with fine grade glasspaper. Repeat for the remaining edges (fig. 10).

Border

Using the cutting board with the stops reset as appropriate, cut four 38cm × 6mm (15in × ¼in) strips of dark veneer, four 38cm × 12mm (15in × ½in) strips of dark veneer and four 38cm × 6mm (15in × ¼in) strips of light veneer. To highlight the corners 6.3cm (2½in) lengths of 6mm (¼in) wide strips of dark veneer can be inserted as shown in fig. 7.

Tape the border pieces along the edges of the squared veneer as-

3. Begin the chessboard by cutting the light and dark veneers into 3.8cm (1½in) strips each at least 38cm (15in) long. The cutting board enables this task to be carried out quickly and accurately. With the veneer placed against the hardwood strip and the steel rule held firmly against the stops the strips are cut.
4. Taking care to keep the veneers in the order in which they were cut, the strips are taped together with the colors alternated.
5. Strips consisting of eight 3.8cm (1½in) squares are cut.
6. The strips are kept in the same order, but with alternate ones offset to form the chequered pattern.
7. Composite strips form the borders, and these are taped to the trimmed assembly with edges overlapping at the corners.
8. The taped assembly is ready to be fixed to the baseboard.

sembly, overlapping each other at the corners (see fig. 7).

Form mitres at the corner by cutting through the two border strips diagonally (fig. 8, 9, 9a, 9b). The easiest way to do this is with a chisel held vertically over them and pressed down to cut both together. Alternatively, use a knife, but take care not to split the veneers. Remove offcuts of veneer and tape the corners together carefully.

Assembling the chessboard

Make sure that you position the pattern so that the corner square to a player's right is a light square.

Remove all adhesive tape from the side of the chequered assembly that will be stuck to the base board. Take care not to pull the pieces apart or to raise the grain of the wood.

Spread contact adhesive on to base board and then on to back of veneer taking care to cover them fully with a thin overall coat, as any bumps or ridges will show through.

Leave for about 15 minutes or until the glue is touch-dry, then carefully press veneer assembly into position, making sure that no air is trapped underneath.

Make sure that the assembly is exactly square to the board. Take great care as with contact adhesive it is almost impossible to move once it has been wrongly positioned.

Remove all remaining adhesive tape carefuly.

Sanding and polishing

Using increasingly fine grades of garnet paper, rub down the surface of the veneer. Take care neither to round off any corners nor to rub through the surface of the veneer. Continue until the whole surface of the chessboard is absolutely smooth.

You can finish the board all round with polyurethane lacquer, applying at least two thin coats. Alternatively the chessboard can be polished with a clear or "white" wood polish or French polish.

9a. *Making the mitred corners.*
9b. *Finished corner.*
10. *Attaching strips of veneer all around the sides of the baseboard.*

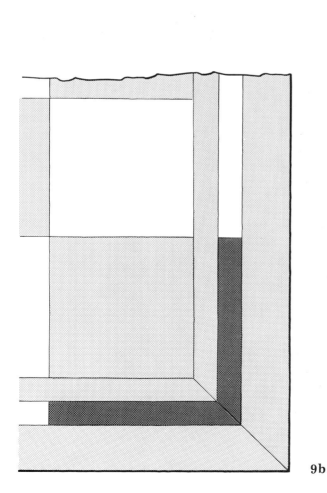

9b

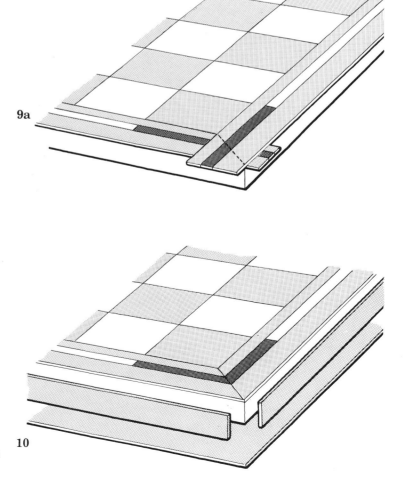

9a

10

Laying hen

Tools required
Pencil; ball-point pen; graph paper; tracing paper; carbon paper; tenon saw; coping saw; fretsaw; craft knife; hand or electric drill and bit; long nosed pliers or tweezers; adhesive tape; rubber band.

Techniques involved
Sawing; cutting out curves; drilling; sanding; gluing; painting.

Materials
26cm × 26cm (10¼in × 10¼in) of 4mm (⅛in) plywood
26cm × 26cm (10¼in × 10¼in) of 9mm (⅜in) plywood

55.8cm × 5.8cm (22in × 2⅜in) of
  1.5mm (1/16in) bending plywood.
  (Grain of outer plies must run
  across the width of the panel)
30.5cm (12in) of 3.2cm × 3.2cm
  (1¼ × 1¼in) softwood. (Note that
  this is a *finished* size)
40cm (16in) of 6mm (¼in) diameter
  hardwood dowel
7.5cm (3in) of 25mm (1in) diameter
  hardwood dowel
5 × 2.5cm (1in) diameter wooden
  balls, for eggs
6mm (¼in) screw hook
2 × 2.5cm (1in) panel pins
3cm (1¼in) panel pin
2 × 12mm (½in) No. 4 (2.7mm)
  countersunk woodscrews
4cm × 6mm (1½ × 1¼in) extension
  spring (medium tension)
PVA woodworking adhesive
fine glasspaper
wax polish
matt enamel paints and varnish

List of parts

Before beginning work, study the
list of parts below. Each part is
numbered as shown in the cutting
plan.

Part No.	Part
1 (2 off)	Inner sides
2 (2 off)	Outer sides
3 (1 off)	Spacer block
4 (1 off)	Spacer block
5 (1 off)	Spacer block
6 (4 off)	Body dowels
7 (1 off)	Outer skin
8 (1 off)	Neck
9 (1 off)	Head
10 (1 off)	Tail
11 (2 off)	Tail sides
12 (2 off)	Legs
13 (1 off)	Feet
14 (1 off)	Trapdoor base
15 (2 off)	Egg tray sides
16 (1 off)	Locking dowel

The moving mechanism inside the
body is quite intricate, and must be
accurately made if the hen is to lay
her eggs properly. So although none
of the individual woodworking
skills needed is particularly ad-
vanced, construction is quite
complicated.

Making the hen

Cut all the parts out first and
assemble them without glue as
instructed to check fit.
  Trace off all the full-size patterns.
With carbon paper and a ball-point

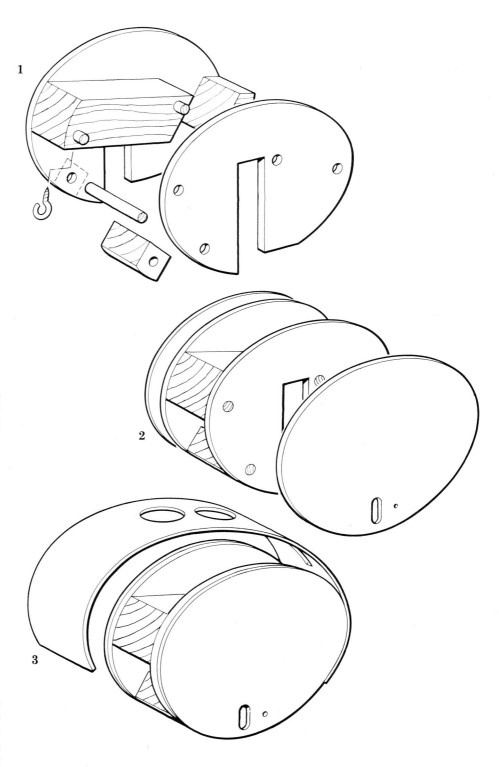

pen, transfer all the pattern parts to
the appropriate timber as indicated
on the digram.
  Cut out the plywood parts with a
fretsaw and tenon saw, using a
tenon saw for the straight cuts. Cut
the slots in 1 by drilling two 6mm
(¼in) holes and joining them with a

fretsaw. Cut the chamfer on the end
of 14 with a tenon saw or plane, and
finish with glasspaper. Drill holes in
all the positions indicated. Cut the
slots in 13 with a fretsaw after
drilling a starter hole. Take care to
keep the corners square. Cut the
holes and the slot in 7 with a fretsaw

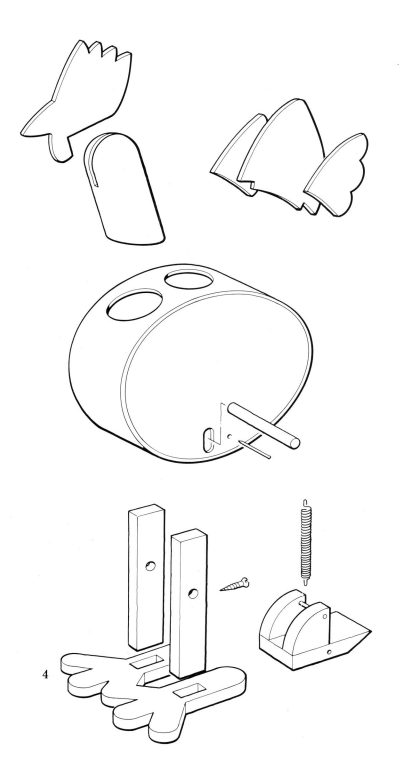

Cut the other end off square and make two cuts with a tenon saw to form the sides of a 4mm ($\frac{1}{8}$in) slot into the end. Remove the waste material with a fretsaw. Use glass-paper to round off this end to form a smooth dome.

Check all the parts for fit. Lay the softwood blocks (3, 4 and 5) on the sides (1) in the positions shown by the dotted lines and check that the drilled holes align. Check that the legs (12) fit into the slots in the feet (13). Make sure also that the legs will slide into the large rectangular slots in sides 1. Check that the trapdoor (14) is at least 2mm ($\frac{1}{16}$in) narrower than blocks 3, 4, 5.

When all these points have been checked and adjusted, assemble as illustrated. Glue the dowels (6) into the holes in the softwood blocks 3, 4, 5, leaving an equal projection of 9mm ($\frac{3}{8}$in) on each side.

Glue the blocks to the sides 1 in the positions shown by the dotted lines, inserting the projecting dowels into the holes (fig. 1). Allow to dry, then sand off any projections.

Glue sides 2 to the outsides of 1 (fig. 2).

Wrap the outer skin (7) around the assembly. Make sure that the holes and slot are the right way round, and that the wrap starts and finishes at the points indicated (fig. 3). Glue and hold in place with rubber bands and adhesive tape until stuck. Sand the edges smooth.

Glue the tail (10) into the slot in the skin and glue sides 11 to it. Insert the neck (8) into the front hole until it touches the block. Glue in place, making sure that the slot faces front and rear. Glue the head into the slot (fig. 4).

Sand the completed body smooth and decorate with enamel paints.

Assemble the legs and egg tray mechanism. Glue the legs (12) into the feet (13). Use an offcut of 3.2cm ($1\frac{1}{4}$in) softwood to ensure that they remain parallel throughout. Glue the sides of the egg tray (15) to the trapdoor base (14) as shown. Pass a 32mm ($1\frac{1}{4}$in) panel pin through the holes in the sides and cut the end off flush. Hook one end of the spring to it.

Sand the completed assemblies. Finish the underside of the trapdoor with enamel paints to match the body. Finish the feet and legs below

after drilling starter holes. Sand all edges smooth, but do not round them off.

Cut out all the softwood parts with a tenon and coping saw. Note that the material used should be exactly 3.2cm ($1\frac{1}{4}$in) thick, so buy oversize and plane down if necessary. Drill the indicated holes in all

these pieces. Screw a 6mm ($\frac{1}{4}$in) screw hook into 3 in the position shown.

Cut the dowels 6 and 16 from 6mm ($\frac{1}{4}$in) diameter dowel using a tenon saw.

Cut the 2.5cm (1in) dowel for the neck (8) to length using a tenon saw to make the angled cut at the end.

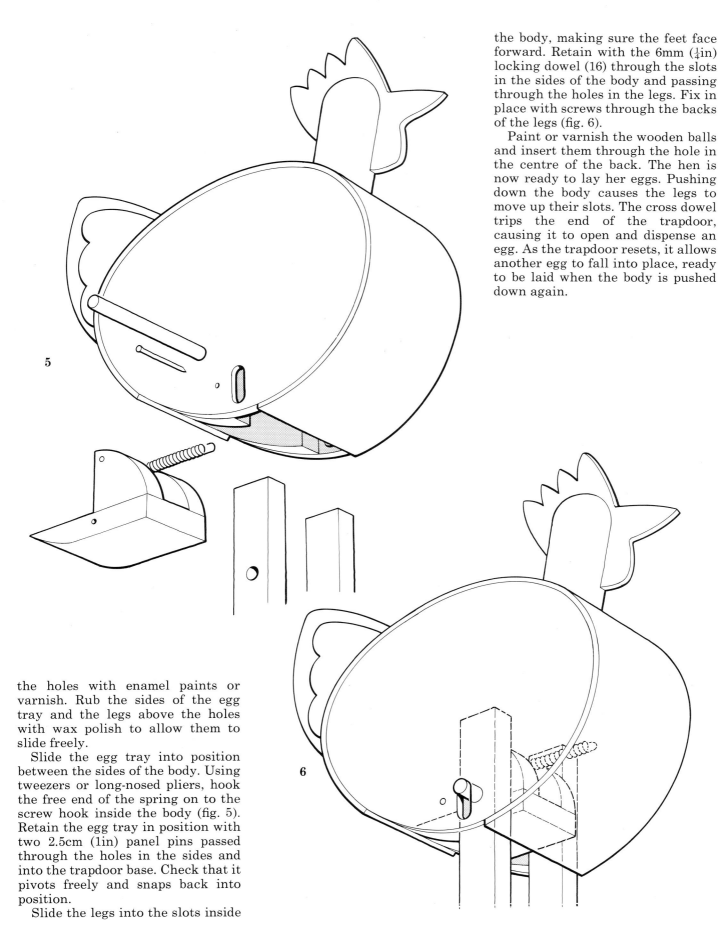

the body, making sure the feet face forward. Retain with the 6mm ($\frac{1}{4}$in) locking dowel (16) through the slots in the sides of the body and passing through the holes in the legs. Fix in place with screws through the backs of the legs (fig. 6).

Paint or varnish the wooden balls and insert them through the hole in the centre of the back. The hen is now ready to lay her eggs. Pushing down the body causes the legs to move up their slots. The cross dowel trips the end of the trapdoor, causing it to open and dispense an egg. As the trapdoor resets, it allows another egg to fall into place, ready to be laid when the body is pushed down again.

5

the holes with enamel paints or varnish. Rub the sides of the egg tray and the legs above the holes with wax polish to allow them to slide freely.

Slide the egg tray into position between the sides of the body. Using tweezers or long-nosed pliers, hook the free end of the spring on to the screw hook inside the body (fig. 5). Retain the egg tray in position with two 2.5cm (1in) panel pins passed through the holes in the sides and into the trapdoor base. Check that it pivots freely and snaps back into position.

Slide the legs into the slots inside

6

TRACE PATTERN FOR HEN

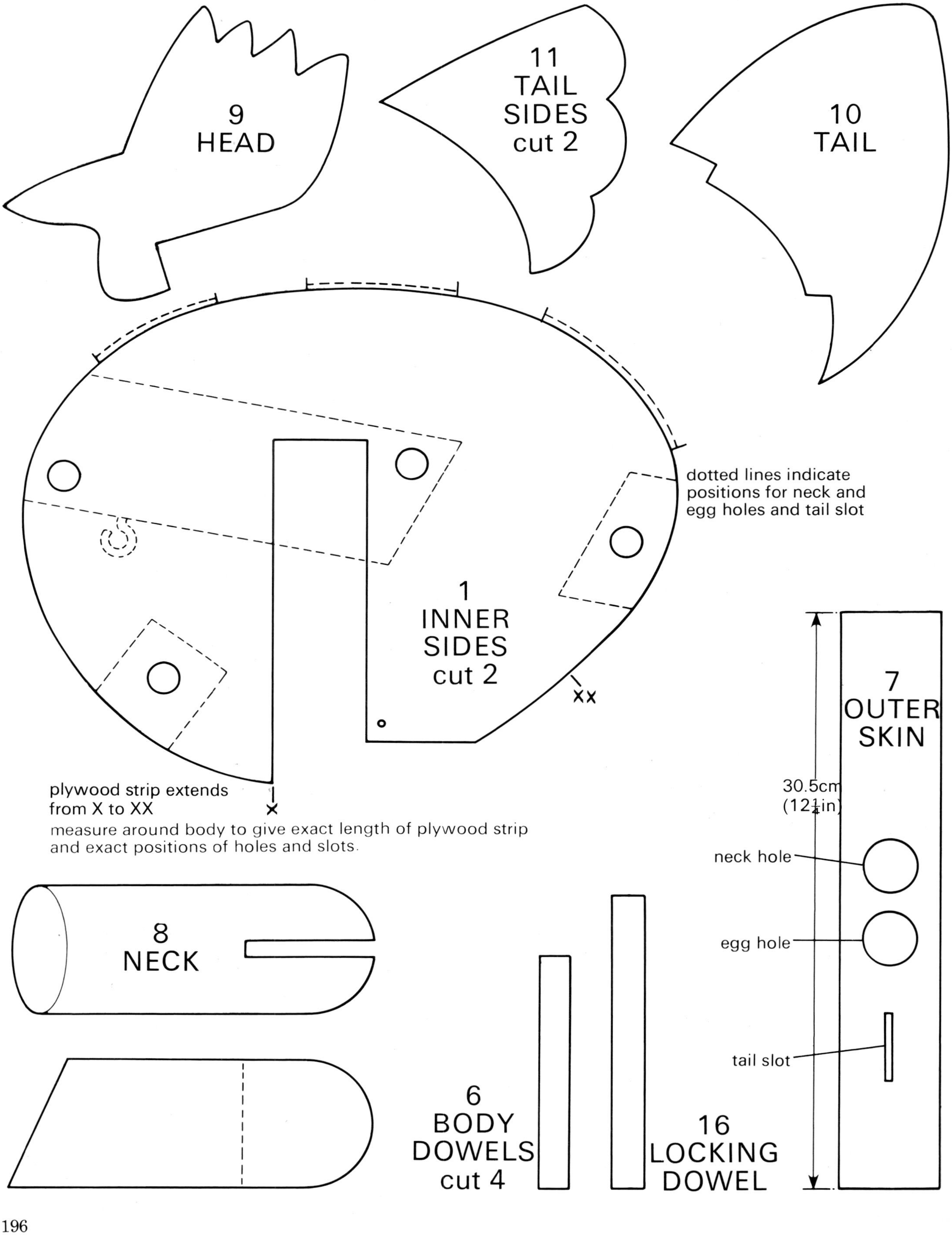

9
HEAD

11
TAIL
SIDES
cut 2

10
TAIL

dotted lines indicate
positions for neck and
egg holes and tail slot

1
INNER
SIDES
cut 2

xx

plywood strip extends
from X to XX
measure around body to give exact length of plywood strip
and exact positions of holes and slots.

8
NECK

6
BODY
DOWELS
cut 4

16
LOCKING
DOWEL

7
OUTER
SKIN

30.5cm
(12¼in)

neck hole

egg hole

tail slot

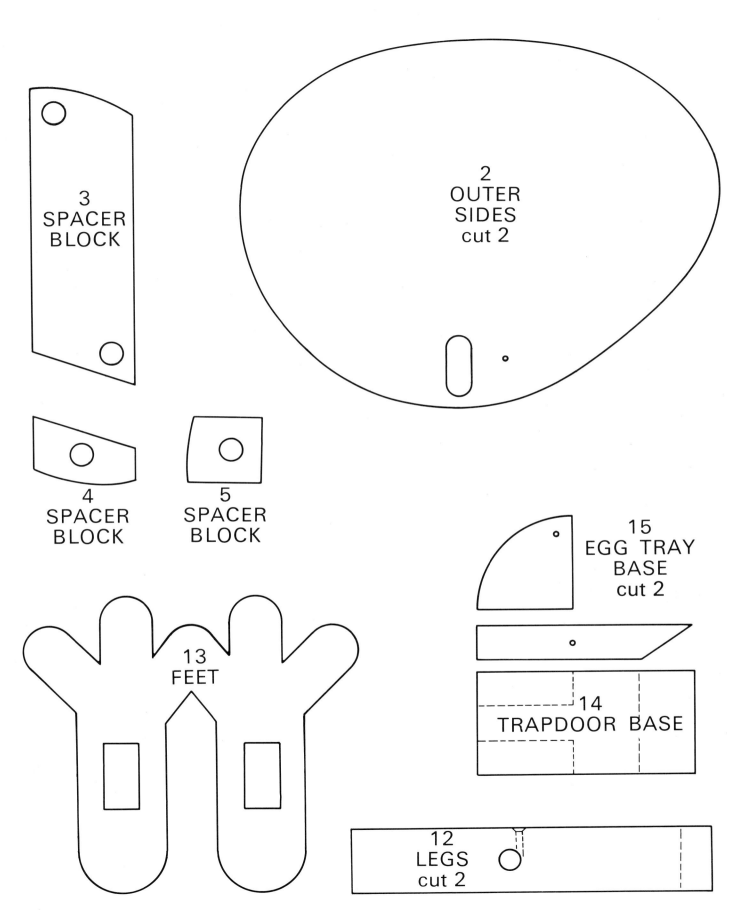

3
SPACER
BLOCK

2
OUTER
SIDES
cut 2

4
SPACER
BLOCK

5
SPACER
BLOCK

15
EGG TRAY
BASE
cut 2

13
FEET

14
TRAPDOOR BASE

12
LEGS
cut 2

MIXED MEDIA TOYS

You'll be truly amazed to see how many amusing and colourful playthings you can make from leftover scrap materials. Papier mâché is cheap and durable, and can be modelled into traditional puppets. Kites are easily constructed from lengths of wood and scraps of paper, and they provide hours of fun and exercise outdoors. We've also included ideas for doll's house furniture made from odds and ends of everyday materials, plus some ingenious toy tidies.

Basic know-how

General techniques

Apart from those toys that are made from papier mâché, the following projects do not require any special expertise. The kites are basically constructed from paper mounted over a frame—either made from light wood such as bamboo, or medium gauge wire. Cutting, folding and gluing the paper onto the frames should be done on a clear surface, with plenty of work space.

Some projects in this section, such as the doll's house furniture and the miniature four-poster bed are excellent ways of using up bits and pieces of household materials in an enjoyable and creative way. The only craft skills needed for these are cutting, gluing and painting—plus a certain amount of imagination and ingenuity.

Three projects in this section are ideas for tidying and storing toys, and are therefore not technically playthings in themselves.

Papier mâché is a modelling material consisting of pieces of paper used with paste or glue and moulded round a shape to make functional and decorative objects. It is a cheap and easy material to use and has the advantage of drying naturally to a hard and durable substance, without having to be baked like clay.

The craft of making objects from papier mâché is an ancient one. Soon after the Chinese discovered how to make paper, about 2000 years ago, they began to experiment with ways of moulding it by tearing it into pieces, mixing it with glue, and shaping it into useful and attractive objects. The interest in this craft declined for hundreds of years until the French revived it in the 18th century. They called it papier mâché, meaning literally "chewed-up paper". They used it to make trays, boxes and even furniture (particularly chairs) which were often inlaid with mother of pearl.

Uses for paper mâché were far more limited then than they are today, since the invention of epoxy resin which makes the papier mâché object much stronger and more durable than traditional water-soluble glues and pastes. Epoxy resin can also be used as a surface finish.

Materials

Most of the materials needed to make papier mâché objects can be found at home.

Paper

The main item is of course paper; old newspapers will probably be your chief source. You can also use paper towels, soft tissues or white tissue paper. It is worth experimenting, too, with other types of paper such as rag paper, which is stronger than ordinary paper because its ingredients include cotton or linen rags as well as wood pulp. Sources of rag paper include used fine stationery, pages from old ledgers and old damaged books, and drawing papers.

You can also use paper to decorate an object built up from several layers of papier mâché, if you wish. Gift wrapping paper, wallpaper, coloured tissue paper and coloured magazine pictures are all suitable. In fact, almost any kind of paper may be used.

Pastes and glues

You will also need some kind of paste or glue for binding the paper together to make papier mâché. The one traditionally used for the purpose is a paste made from flour and water which is stirred over a low heat until enough water has been added to make it smooth and creamy. Wallpaper paste such as Polycell, mixed with water according to the manufacturer's instructions, also makes a strong glue. However, epoxy resin, such as Araldite, is the strongest type of glue to use. It will make papier mâché objects virtually unbreakable, waterproof, flame-proof and dirt-proof. It should always be used for large or complex objects without a base support, since they might otherwise buckle.

Using epoxy resin simply as a surface finish for a smaller piece means that the object will not only be protected as if a varnish were used, but it will also be strengthened as the epoxy penetrates the papier mâché itself.

Moulds

Some sort of mould will also be required to support the papier mâché object while it is being made. It can either be removed after the papier mâché has dried, or integrated into the piece for added strength. The mould can be either a rigid shape (a plastic bottle, tin can, cardboard cylinder, a glass or china dish or bowl, fruit or vegetables, or even a balloon) or it can be flexible (chicken wire, crumpled newspaper, clay or plasticine).

Methods

There are three basic ways of making papier mâché. The most common is to cut or tear the paper into small strips or squares and glue them on to a base or mould. Tearing rather than cutting the paper means that it will have rough edges which will give a smoother surface than straight edges when glued down in layers. Paper may be torn against a ruler to make fairly uniform strips.

Another method, called lamination, consists of gluing together several sheets of paper to make one strong flexible sheet. This can then be shaped over a base or cut into strips before it is applied.

The third method involves breaking down small pieces of paper into a mash or pulp by soaking them in water for several hours. The water is then squeezed out of the paper until it becomes a pulp, and glue is added to make it bind together. Paper mash is often used to add texture and strength to an object moulded from strips of papier mâché but can also be moulded like clay.

There are several commercial mixes available for making "instant" paper mash, for example Letracraft Instant Papier Mâché, to which only water has to be added. These are easy to use and can be bought from art and craft shops.

Opposite: *Objects in papier mâché.*

Papier mâché puppets

Tools required
Basic sewing tools; paints (acrylic or poster) and brushes; polyurethane varnish; wood adhesive; brace with 2cm ($\frac{3}{4}$in) bit and hammer or screw-driver and one 5cm (2in) No. 8 screw; adhesive tape; wooden spoon; scissors; tracing paper and pencil; plastic bucket and bowl; cocktail stick or fork; medium and fine grade glasspaper.

Techniques involved
Making papier mâché; drilling holes; basic sewing; modelling; painting and varnishing.

202

Materials

For the mould

wooden block about 15cm (6in) square and about 2.5cm (1in) thick

dowel 20cm (8in) long and 2cm ($\frac{3}{4}$in) diameter

piece of closely woven scrap fabric at least 12.5cm × 30cm (5in × 12in)

about 230g ($\frac{1}{2}$lb) cat box granules

sheet of newspaper

For modelling heads

newspapers

wallpaper paste with size mixed to packet instructions

For the glove

fabric at least 60cm × 30cm (24in × 12in)

tape, braid or strip of hemmed fabric 7.5cm (3in) long and 6mm–12mm ($\frac{1}{4}$in–$\frac{1}{2}$in) wide

string about 70cm (28in) long to attach head and hands to the glove

For the hands

piece of card about 5cm × 5cm (2in × 2in) or 4 pipe cleaners

newspaper

wallpaper paste solution

The instructions given here are for papier mâché heads which are fairly simple in design but which can be used for a wide range of characters simply by painting on different facial features. By changing the costume (the glove) which is attached to a head, only a few puppet heads need be made in order to represent many different characters. You can also make the hands for glove puppets from papier mâché.

Making both heads and hands of these glove puppets involves two methods of using papier mâché: the strip method and the mash or pulp method (see **Know-how** section). The basic head shapes are made using the strip method, where layer upon layer of paper strips are shaped round the mould. Their features (nose, ears, cheek-bones) are modelled on this basic head shape with paper pulp and secured with more strips of paper to make a smooth surface.

The mould and stand

The mould consists of a cloth bag which is filled with cat box granules (commonly known as "cat litter") and secured to a modelling stand which is a wooden post fixed on to a

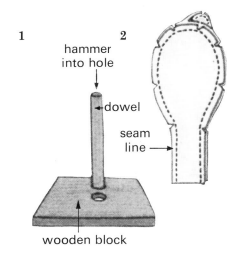

wooden block. The granules absorb the moisture from the papier mâché, helping it to dry easily. The stand makes modelling easier since it provides a steady base on which to shape the papier mâché.

To make the modelling stand

Drill a hole through the centre of the wooden block with the 20mm ($\frac{3}{4}$in) flat bit. Spread glue on one end of the dowel and inside the hole, and hammer the dowel into the hole, to the depth of the wooden block (fig. 1). Alternatively, glue the dowel directly on to the block and screw it in place from underneath with a 5cm (2in) No. 8 screw.

To make the mould

Trace the pattern on this page. Use it to cut three pieces of old sheeting or similar fabric. Leaving 6mm ($\frac{1}{4}$in) seams and following the dotted lines on the pattern, sew the pieces together firmly with strong thread (fig. 2). (It is preferable to machine stitch the pieces.) Leave the neck edge open. Clip curves and turn inside out.

Pack the bag firmly with cat box granules, to about 2cm ($\frac{3}{4}$in) from the neck edge of the bag. Hold the stand upside down and push the dowel into the bag, to a depth of about 7.5cm (3in), or so that the mould does not wobble on its stand.

Wind strong thread round the neck of the bag and the dowel post, just above the filling, and knot securely. Turn the stand and mould upright (fig. 3).

Cover the mould with a single sheet of newspaper, crush it close to the mould and secure with sticky

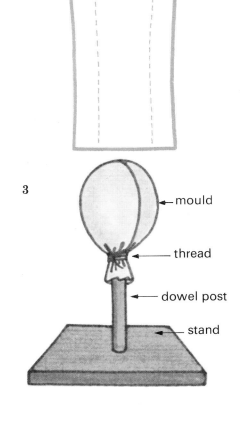

tape at the base of the neck. Tear off any excess paper below the sticky tape. This sheet of newspaper is the base to which the paper strips are stuck, and stops the strips sticking to the mould.

Modelling the head

Tear enough newspaper into small strips to cover the mould with at least eight layers.

Dip the strips, one by one, in the wallpaper paste solution and apply to the mould (for full details of the strip method, see **Know-how** section). Apply at least eight layers of paper strips.

Make up the paper pulp in a bucket according to the instructions given in **Know-how** section, using a little less than 0.25 litre (½pt) of wallpaper paste solution for one puppet head. Squeeze as much water as possible from the soaked paper and add it gradually to the paste, mixing carefully with a wooden spoon. You will know when enough paper has been added to make a firm consistency because, when you squeeze out the excess paste from the pulp, it should bind together as a lump.

Mould the puppet's features on the basic head shape with paper mash (pulp) when the last layer of paper strips is still wet. Mark the positions of the nose, chin, eyes and ears very lightly with a cocktail stick or fork.

Squeeze out a small amount of paper mash and use it to build up the features, smoothing contours with the fingers. Building up cheek-bones and the forehead creates eye sockets. For the face of a child puppet the features should be rounded, not well defined. Try to compact the paper mash very firmly, and to make the surface as smooth as possible.

When the features are formed and while the paper mash is still wet, apply three or four more layers of paper strips to secure the mash to the layers of paper strips beneath it.

Leave the head on the modelling stand to dry for a day or two, until the surface is a uniformly pale grey colour and feels dry to the touch.

Carefully turn the head and stand upside down, untie the thread at the neck and remove the stand. Let the granules fall out of the mould into a basin or bag, so that they can be used again. Pull out the fabric mould and keep it for re-use; it should come away easily.

If the inside of the head is not thoroughly dry, you can put it in an oven at the lowest possible heat and

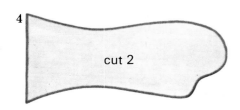

4 cut 2

5 pipe cleaners

paper strips

4. *Trace pattern for the cardboard hands. Cut out two shapes.*
5. *Pipe-cleaners are used to make a hand. Bind together with paper strips.*

with the door open. Check the head frequently and remove it from the oven as soon as it is completely dry. This may take a few hours.

The hands

To make hands, cardboard hand shapes may be covered with paper strips. Pipe-cleaners covered with paper pulp make hands which are capable of holding various props such as a walking stick or baton.

To make a pair of hands using cardboard as a base, trace the pattern for the hands (fig. 4) and draw it twice on to the cardboard. Cut out the shapes.

Stick a pin through each cardboard wrist, so that you can hold the cardboard steady while applying the papier mâché. Tear newspaper into very small strips and, using the strip method already described, apply six layers of strips to both hands and wrists. Leave them to dry away from direct heat; they may curl at the edges if dried in an oven.

To cover pipe-cleaners with paper pulp, making more capable and expressive hands, cut the pipe-cleaners into eight lengths of 5cm (2in) for the fingers and two slightly smaller lengths for the thumbs. Bind four finger lengths and one thumb together with strips of paper and paste round one end, to hold the pipe-cleaners together (fig. 5) before building up the hand shape.

Spread and bend the pipe-cleaners to the desired shape. Cover the main part of the hand with pulp, and the fingers with several layers of paper strips. Finally cover the whole hand with an even, smooth paper strip layer.

Bind the remaining lengths of pipe-cleaner together for the other hand, in the same way as the others, and cover with papier mâché pulp and strips as already described.

Painting and varnishing

Before painting, rub down all surfaces of the head and hands with medium and then fine glasspaper.

Draw the eye shapes on the head and paint them white. Paint the rest of the head and neck flesh colour. While it is still wet, blend in shading and cheek colouring on the face with a dry brush loaded with various shades of pink.

Paint hair with several shades of the same colour for a realistic effect. (If you wish to stick on fur fabric to represent hair there is no need to paint on the hair.)

Paint the hands flesh colour and, if they are made on a cardboard base, paint lines in red on the back and front of each to indicate fingers. Paint fingernails white; these show up well.

Finally, varnish all the painted surfaces with two coats of clear polyurethane varnish.

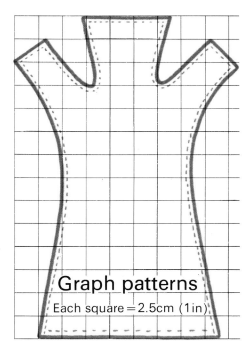

Graph patterns

Each square = 2.5cm (1in)

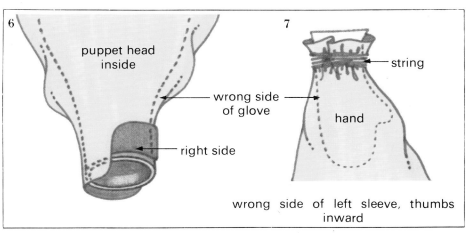

wrong side of left sleeve, thumbs inward

6. *Fitting the neck of the glove over the neck of the head.*
7. *The glove is firmly attached to the hand with string.*

The glove

If you have to adapt the graph pattern given, bear in mind that the usual configuration of the fingers is: index finger in the head, thumb in one arm, second finger in the other arm, and third and fourth fingers folded into the body. Make sure that the thumb and index finger just reach the ends of the arms and that there is plenty of room in the body for the other fingers. Adults can use the pattern if they make it 6mm ($\frac{1}{4}$in) longer all round; for very young children it should be made about 6mm ($\frac{1}{4}$in) smaller all round.

The length of the glove is a matter of choice; this pattern allows for a long glove such as professional puppeteers use, so that the puppet can be moved freely without the puppeteer's arm showing above the stage.

Use strong fabrics such as felt, heavy wool or denim, since these do not have to be lined in order to give a substantial body to the puppet. The fabrics used for the back and front of the glove need not be identical.

Trace, enlarge and cut out the graph pattern and pin it to the fabric.

Cut out two pieces of fabric round the pattern. With right sides together, sew them along the stitching lines shown on the pattern, leaving 6mm ($\frac{1}{4}$in) seams all round. Leave the neck, wrists and bottom of the glove unsewn.

Turn the glove right side out and tack the fabric back 6mm ($\frac{1}{4}$in) inside the neck and wrists of the glove. Turn up and hem the bottom if necessary.

To attach the head to the glove, insert the neck of the head into the neck of the glove. Turn the glove inside out by pushing it up over the head, so that the right side of the neck of the glove faces the neck of the head (fig. 6). Turn up the top 2.5cm (1in) of the neck of the glove so that the cloth is of double thickness and fits tightly round the neck of the head (see fig. 6). Cut a length of string about 50cm (20in) long and wind it round the neck of the head and the neck of the gloves several times and tie securely.

To attach the hands to the sleeves, turn the sleeves inside out and insert each hand into them from the right side of the fabric, up to the wrists, with the thumbs towards the head and palms facing the same way as the face. Fold back about 2cm ($\frac{3}{4}$in) of the fabric from the tacked edge and wind one 10cm (4in) length of string round each sleeve and wrist (fig. 7). Turn glove right side out.

Attaching the glove to the head and hands with string means that it is easy to remove the glove and fit on another for a change of costume.

Wind a strip of tape, braid or hemmed material round the puppet's neck and stitch the ends together.

Additional dress

Additional items of costume such as hats, shawls and aprons can be made from scraps of fabric; pieces of fur can be stuck on to the head to make the hair; and props such as baskets, frying pans and sticks are easy to make from papier mâché. Do not make the props too small for the puppets to grasp and the audience to see.

Doll's head

The doll's head is also made of papier mâché and could be fitted over a stuffed fabric body. Make tiny holes in the papier mâché around the bottom of the neck piece with a bradawl or tiny drill bit and sew head to body with strong thread.

The head (including neck piece) is first modelled in clay, slightly larger than the desired finished size, to allow for papier mâché shrinkage when it dries.

The clay model is then cast in plaster, which is cut in two pieces (from ear to ear). When dry, the two halves of the cast are pulled apart, washed out with clay water and allowed to dry thoroughly.

The inner surfaces of the cast are then greased with margarine or oil, the paper pulp is firmly pressed against them, and the two halves are then pressed together and the pulp allowed to dry. The cast is then removed.

Finally the head is sanded down, painted and varnished in the same way as the puppet heads.

Kite making

Tools required
Scissors; craft knife; pencil; ruler; glue or adhesive tape; Poster paint and brush (optional).
Techniques involved
Cutting sticks; gluing.
Materials
two sticks, one 61cm (24in) the other 91cm (36in) long

large sheet of paper
small ball thin string or strong
   thread
curtain ring to act as towing ring.
scraps of coloured paper or
   streamers for the tail
flying line and reel

Choosing the materials

Surprisingly, there is no need to bother unduly about the weight of a kite unless it is to be flown in very light winds. Choose any paper you like for the cover – heavy papers such as cartridge or wallpaper; medium weights such as decorative wrapping papers, posters or shelf paper; or lightweight papers such as tissue. Crepe is probably the only unsuitable paper because of its tendency to stretch.

The sticks for the frame can be garden canes, balsa or pine battens, dowels or even twigs. Split thicker, heavier sticks lengthwise with a sharp craft knife to make them lighter.

Balance is more important than weight, so shave off any knots or thicker sections. To test for balance, mark the middle of the stick and balance it across the back of the knife blade. If one end dips, shave a little off it.

A cutter kite

Scale the size of this kite up or down as you wish, according to the size required.

The important part is the proportionate length of the sticks; the longer stick should be half as long again as the shorter one.

The frame

First cut two small notches, each about 6mm ($\frac{1}{4}$in) in from each end of both sticks (fig. 1a). Make a mark at the centre of the shorter stick and a mark one-third of the way along the longer one. Lay the sticks across each other at right angles, the marks touching, and bind the join tightly with the thread. Put a dab of glue on the join for extra strength (fig. 1b). Tie a piece of thread to the notched end of each of the sticks in turn, winding it tightly around each notch two or three times (fig. 1c). Tie the ends to complete the frame.

The cover

Lay the frame on the wrong side of

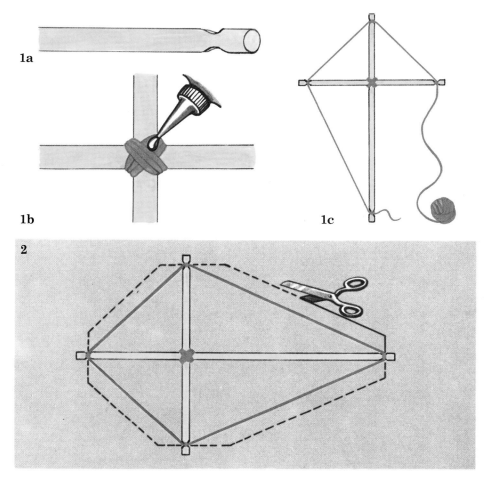

1a. Cut two small notches as shown.
1b. Put a dab of glue on the joined sticks for extra strength.
1c. Tying thread around the frame.
2. Cut around the edges of the paper, fold over and stick down.

the sheet of paper and cut round it, cutting about 2.5cm (1in) outside the string (fig. 2). Trim off the corners of the paper (see fig. 2). Fold the edges of the paper up over the string and stick them down with glue or adhesive tape.

Decoration

Turn the kite face up, with the frame underneath, and decorate the front by painting it or by pasting on paper shapes. Keep the design simple and the colours bold, because details will be lost when the kite is in the sky. A bold motif cut from a poster, or even the poster itself, would make an "instant" decoration.

Bridle

This is the name for the strings which hold the kite at the correct angle to the wind and to which the towing line is attached. The cutter kite has two pieces of string or thread making a double bridle.

Lay the kite on the table, decorated side uppermost. Take a piece of thread long enough to reach

round one short and one long side of the kite with just a little to spare. Tie the ends to the notched ends of the vertical stick where they jut out beyond the cover (fig. 3a).

Tie the second bridle to each end of the horizontal stick. This time the piece of thread should be twice the length of one of the short sides of the kite, with a little to spare (fig. 3b). Loop the curtain ring onto the long bridle (fig. 4) about one-third of the way down it, and then on to the centre of the short bridle.

Test the balance of the kite by holding it above the table by the ring. The two sides should be equidistant from the table and the kite itself should hang at an angle of about 45° to it. If necessary, adjust the angles slightly by slipping the ring along the bridles.

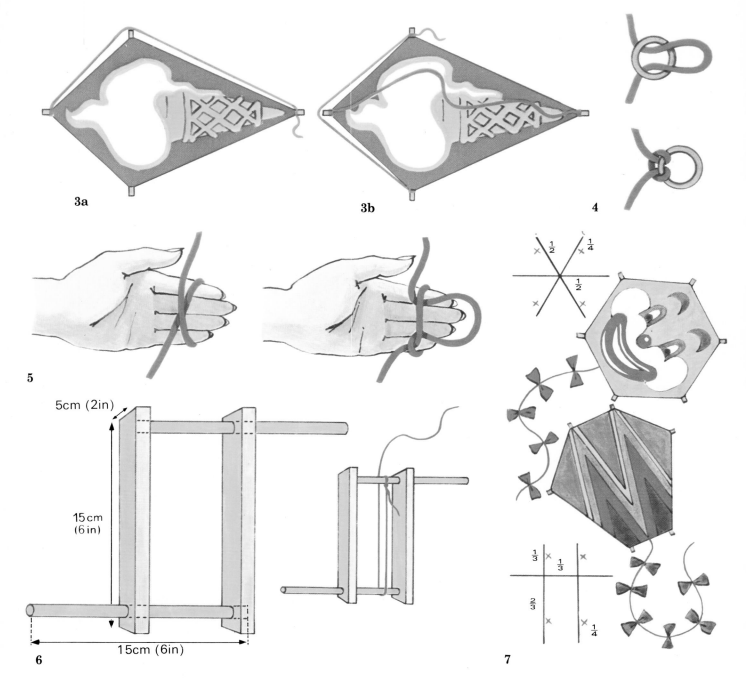

3a

3b

4

5

5cm (2in)

15cm
(6in)

15cm (6in)

6

7

Tail

Some kites will fly well without any kind of tail, but the cutter kite needs one at least three times its own length. Make it from long paper streamers, or make the traditional kind of tail by knotting rectangles of paper onto a length of string.

For a traditional tail, use pieces of paper about 15cm by 6cm (6in by 2½in) and set them about 8cm (3in) apart along the length of string. Attach them by means of a slip knot. To do this, wind the string over your hand to form a loop (fig. 5).

Make a twist in the centre of one of the pieces of paper and then insert it through the loop. Pull the ends of the thread tight. Repeat along the length of the string to form the tail, then tie the tail to the stick at the bottom of the kite.

Flying-line and reel

Before you can fly the kite you need a flying-line and reel which can be bought quite cheaply from toy shops or some sports equipment shops.

To make your own flying-line, use about 60 metres (200ft) of light nylon cord, or fibreglass fishing-line, and wind it onto a length of strong

3a. *Tying the first bridle.*
3b. *Tying the second bridle.*
4. *Attaching the ring to bridle.*
5. *Making a slip knot for the bridle.*
6. *Making a flying line and reel.*
7. *Other kite shapes- X marks bridle position on sticks. Pierce the paper to bring bridle to the right side.*

cardboard tube to act as a reel.

If, on the other hand, you want to make your own reel, you will need two rectangles of plywood, about 15cm by 5cm (6in by 2in), two pieces of dowelling about 15cm (6in) long, a drill and strong glue. Drill two holes in each of the two pieces of plywood, to the same diameter as the dowels, and assemble the reel as shown in fig. 6, gluing each dowel into place.

Tie the end of the line firmly to the reel and wind it on tightly. The other end of the line should be tied to the kite's bridle or towing-ring.

Flying a kite

Do not assume that you need to wait for a really windy day in order to try out your kite. On the contrary, a gentle but steady breeze is all you need, and too much wind can damage a kite. If the tree tops are bending, then the wind is too strong for kite flying. Always take a pair of gloves with you to stop the line cutting into your hands.

Where to fly a kite

Choose a large open space, such as a field or park, and keep well away from trees or telegraph poles. It is not at all necessary to fly a kite from a hill, but if you wish to do so, stand on the windward side about 20 metres (just over 20 yards) from the top so as to take full advantage of the steady upcurrent. If you stand right on the summit the kite will be caught in the turbulence of conflicting air streams and will be difficult to fly.

Launching and landing

Stand with your back to the wind and hold the kite by the towing-ring at arm's length. Have the reel on the ground at your feet. Wait until the wind lifts the kite and then release it, letting the line slip out through your fingers.

If you have a helper, ask him to stand a little way in front of you holding the kite tilted slightly forwards until the wind lifts it out of his hands. Do not let him throw it into the air and do not try to run with it yourself. Neither will help to set it aloft. Make the kite rise by pulling on the line. Grip the line at arm's length and bend your forearm right back at the elbow, still gripping the line. Straighten your arm again slowly, letting the line slip through your fingers as you do so. Continue pulling and letting out the line until the kite is high in the sky.

Land the kite simply by winding in the line. If it is pulling strongly, walk towards it as you wind. If you

have a helper, he can put his hand over the line and walk towards the kite, pulling it down gradually while you wind in the line.

Watch out for any spectators appearing in front of you, as a kite may often crash as it comes in low and could be dangerous.

Repair kit

It is a good idea to take along with you a shoulder bag or satchel to carry a small repair kit made up of a reel of adhesive tape for mending torn paper, several sewing needles that can be taped to broken struts to act as splints, and a pair of scissors for cutting tangles out of the line. Take an extra piece of tail as well.

Correcting faults

There are several common faults, which are easy to correct, thus making all the difference to successful flying. If the kite will not rise, it is probably flying too flat to the wind. Move the towing-ring a little higher. If the tail is hanging down rather than streaming out behind, then shortening the tail may help the kite to rise.

If the kite flutters and dips, it may be flying too close to the wind. Move the towing-ring down a little. Spinning, diving and looping the loop mean the kite needs a longer or heavier tail. This is a common fault. If the kite keeps falling constantly to one side, tape a small weight – a tiny piece of twig, perhaps, or a small fishing weight – to the back of the kite on the opposite side.

Safety note

Believe it or not, kite flying can be dangerous. Be sure to remember these two important points:

Kites can act as lightning conductors, so never fly a kite in stormy weather, or with a wire line, or with a wet line of any description. Kites can be a real hazard to aircraft, so be sure to check for legal restrictions on kite-flying that may exist in your area, particularly near airports.

Oriental kites

Tools required
Poster paints; brush; pencil; scissors; craft knife; razor blade; glue; adhesive tape.
Techniques involved
Cutting sticks; gluing.
Materials
Carp
two large sheets of tissue or other light paper
scraps of coloured paper
medium gauge wire
short length of thread or twine
flying line and reel
Butterfly
3 pieces of bamboo garden cane about 60cm (24in) long
Sheet of strong paper about 60cm (24in) square, or tissue paper for butterfly variations
curtain ring to act as towing ring
twine or strong thread
Bird
bamboo cane
medium weight white paper
newspaper for papier mâché
plasticine

flour and water paste
thread or thin twine

Carp

This fish shape, which is shown in the picture overleaf, is the simplest of all the Japanese kite designs. On the Boys' Festival on 5 May a carp is flown for every male child in the household in the hope that the boy will emulate the character of this fish, which swims upstream, overcoming all difficulties.

The kite is tubular, rather like a windsock, with a hole at each end. Make it any size that you like, provided that the hole at the mouth is larger than the one at the tail so that the wind will inflate the body.

Draw the carp shape freehand on the paper and cut it out, cutting through two thicknesses at once. Glue the pieces together along the top and bottom edges. Fold the seam over and glue down. Paint the carp or, if you have used tissue, decorate it with paper shapes.

Bend the wire into a loop to fit carp's mouth and glue it in place, folding the edges of the paper over it. Tie the ends of the thread or twine to the wire at either side of the carp's mouth. The flying-line can be attached to this loop.

Although very decorative, this kite is not a good flyer and will only rise if there is a very strong upcurrent.

Butterfly

This is a popular design, perhaps because the fluttering of a kite tends to resemble a butterfly.

Fold the paper in half and draw a half butterfly shape on it so that the fold is along the butterfly's spine. Draw the largest shape possible and cut out. Open the paper out flat and paint it with any design you choose.

While the paint is drying, split the cane lengthwise with a knife. You will need firm, rigid pieces for the butterfly's spine and lower wing supports and thin, pliable pieces for the upper wing supports: 30cm (12in) for the spine, two pieces 30 cm (12in) for the lower wings and two pieces 60cm (24in) for the upper wings. Mark the position of the supports on the back of the butterfly, making sure that one side is the exact mirror image of the other for balance. Follow fig. 1.

With the right side of the kite facing you, make tiny holes in the kite and tie a piece of thread through them onto the frame at each of the three points marked X in fig. 1. Tie each thread to the towing-line so that the kite hangs at the correct angle.

This kite, which does not need a tail, will fly even better if it offers a convex surface to the wind. To curve the kite, tie a piece of thread to one upper wing tip, stretch it across behind the kite, and tie it tightly to the opposite wing tip, so that the kite is bowed.

Butterfly variations

When you have made a simple butterfly you may like to go on to a more complex design. The kites in fig. 2 and 3 have rigid spines and

1. *Diagram shows how to position the struts on a butterfly kite.*
2. *Variation on the butterfly shape.*
3. *Double winged butterfly kite.*

pliable wing supports bowed in to shape with thread. Figs. 4 and 5 show the design of the frames, heavy lines representing the canes and dotted lines the threads.

Now enlist the help of a friend. One pair of hands is needed to hold each support in place while the other tapes it in position. Fix the supports in this order: spine, lower supports, lower half of upper supports. Fold the top edge of the paper over the remaining half of the upper supports and tape them (see fig. 1). Tape two thin bamboo antennae to the top of the spine.

Follow the procedure of notching the canes, binding them where they cross, and fitting the cover.

When making the double butterfly (see fig. 5), bow the four wing supports into arcs and bind the sticks where they cross. Add extra thread supports (shown in green) before removing the two longer bow strings (shown in red). Attach a single bridle to the points marked X.

The bird

The body of this bird kite is built on a framework of bamboo slivers rather like the ribs of a rowing boat, and the head is a thin hollow shell of papier mâché.

Begin by splitting a number of pieces of cane to build the body. Construct a framework and bind the pieces where they overlap (fig. 6a). Try to match the two halves perfectly with joins in exactly the same places.

Following fig. 6b, construct the front of the body with a series of curved canes to form the ribs. Spread glue on the curved ribs and cover the sections of the ribbed framework with strips of paper. Use a razor blade to trim the paper where it overlaps to form a butt joint and trim off surplus paper.

Now shape the head in plasticine and cover it with a thin layer of papier mâché. When dry, dig out the plasticine and glue the head to the body.

Make two separate wings and join them together (fig. 7). The wings have bamboo along two sides and a thread (dotted line) to bow the tops to shape. These threads may be removed later if wished. Bind and glue the finished wings on to the back of the body. Cut out a tail shape in paper and reinforce this by gluing on a piece of thin card. Attach it to the bird with loops of thread. Finally, tie a single bridle to the body framework at the neck and three-quarters of the way down its body.

Dragonfly

Make this as for the bird, but build up the tail sections on flat bamboo frameworks. Tie the sections loosely together.

Giant kites

There is no limit to the size and complexity of the kites you can make. A giant kite can be imaginatively built up on a rectangle of thin plywood with a decorative lantern hung in the middle. Fabulous birds and beasts can be perched round the frame; make them all on the same principle as the bird already described and you can let your imagination run riot on the tassels, lanterns and slogans acting as the tail. In spite of this, always remember that the two sides of the kite must balance each other exactly in weight and shape.

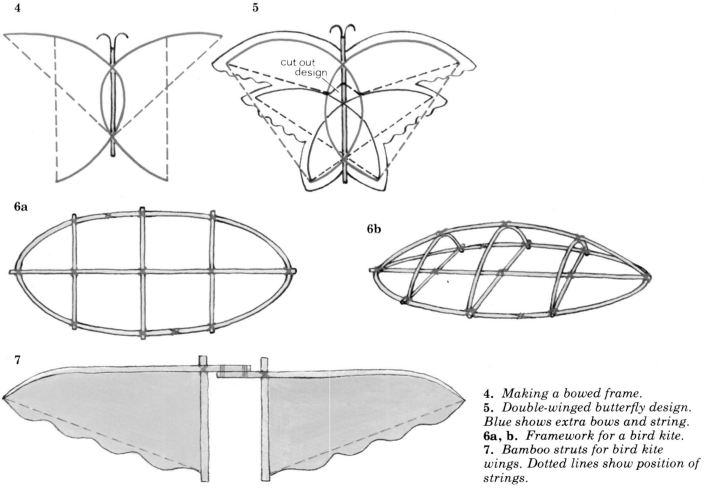

4. *Making a bowed frame.*
5. *Double-winged butterfly design. Blue shows extra bows and string.*
6a, b. *Framework for a bird kite.*
7. *Bamboo struts for bird kite wings. Dotted lines show position of strings.*

Doll's house furniture

Tools required
craft knife; sharp nail scissors;
bradawl; coping saw (optional);
basic sewing tools.
Techniques involved
Basic sewing; simple woodworking.

Materials
matchboxes of various sizes
matchsticks
toothpicks
cardboard
egg boxes

plastic containers and lids, such as
   for yogurt
spools
jar lid
cardboard tube from toilet paper
   roll

scraps of various fabrics: velvet,
  corduroy, or fur fabric for rugs;
  lace for curtains, prints and plain
  colours (closely-woven) for
  upholestery, etc.
buttons
plastic foam
aluminium foil
pencil
plastic straw
pleated fondant cases
magazine picture (small)
thread
moulded plastic container of type
  used to pack model cars
small piece of acetate film
rubber cement
spray paint and poster paints

Children can make some of this
furniture themselves, with a little
parental supervision. You needn't
worry too much about scale, though
you should try to make the pieces
more or less proportional to one
other.

All sorts of materials can be used
for the furniture. Make a collection
of likely objects to keep on hand.
The materials listed above are the
ones you'll need for the complete set
of furnishings shown here, plus
bathroom fittings.

Living room
Armchairs and sofa
Use different-sized matchboxes. For
armchair use the outside of the box
for the base (fig. 1a). Cut away
sections of the box as indicated. Cut
away parts of the inside box as
shown in fig. 1b to make the back of
the chair. Glue the back to the base,
with rounded ends upward, at a
slight angle. When chair is dry,
paint it with poster paints.

For cushions, cut pieces of plastic
foam to fit seat and back.

Coat each piece with glue and
then carefully fold a piece of fabric
around each. Leave to dry and then
glue the cushions into the chairs.

For the legs, make four holes in
the base of the chair and trim four
burned matches to 12mm (½in). Push
the matches into the holes, leaving
the match heads exposed, then paint
the match heads.

Make the sofa in the same way,
using a larger matchbox.

Coffee table
Use a plastic yogurt container for

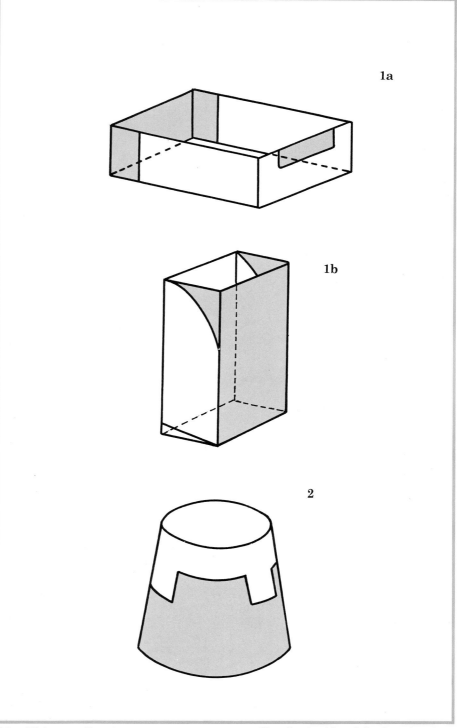

1a

1b

2

this. Using nail scissors, cut away
part of the container indicated in
fig. 2. The bottom of the container is
the top of the table. Paint the table
with spray paint.

Lamps
For the floor lamp use a button and
a plastic straw. Remove the centre
holes of the button by melting the
centre or by cutting with a coping

1a. *Use the inside of the box for the
base of the armchair.*
1b. *Use the outer sleeve for the back
of the armchair.*
2. *Making a simple coffee table.*

saw. Insert the straw into the hole.
Make a shade from the bottom of an
egg box section or from a pleated
fondant case, painted as you like.

For ceiling lamp make shade as

3. *How to make chairs from sections of discarded egg cartons.*
4. *A dresser made from the sleeve of a large matchbox.*

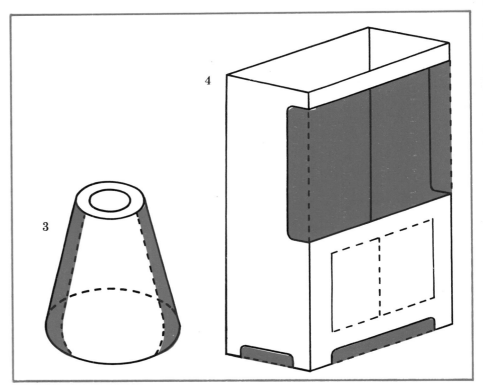

described above; attach it to the ceiling with thread and a dab of glue.

Small cabinet
Cut the inner part of a small matchbox to the required size; paint exterior with poster paint and place against wall.

Rug
Any fabric with pile will do, but if you want an elegant rug, embroider one using needlepoint canvas and tapestry wool. The rug in the living room was made in this way. Or you can simply colour the canvas with felt-tip pens, as was done for the hall rug.

Dining room/Kitchen
Table
If possible, use a very large spool (obtainable from an upholsterer or tailor) for the base. Paint the spool and when it is dry, glue a jar lid to one end. Cover the lid with a circular piece of cloth, glued to the top and sides of the lid.

Chairs
Use a cup section from an egg box for each chair. Cut away most of the sides, as shown in fig. 3. Paint it or leave it the natural colour. Poke four holes in the seat for the legs. Make legs from matchsticks (remove heads first), inserted in holes and fixed with glue. As the chairs are very light, give them a little added weight by making cushions of small coins covered with fabric. Glue the cushions to the seat.

Kitchen cupboard
Cut a large matchbox sleeve cover in half across the width. Cut a top from a piece of cardboard slightly larger than the open end of the matchbox. Cut two doors in the front of the box, leaving the "hinged" sides uncut. Score these sides so they will fold forward easily. Glue the top in place, then paint the entire cupboard with spray paint. Paint and insert matchstick handles in the door fronts.

Stove
Use the remaining half of the matchbox sleeve for the stove. Cut two pieces of cardboard to cover the sides and another for the top—large enough to accommodate the four buttons used for the burners. Cut the oven door as for the cupboard doors. Cut a window in the oven door. Now glue the cardboard sides and top to the box and paint with spray paint. Glue four buttons to the top and a piece of acetate over the wrong side of the oven window.

Sink unit
This is made from another half of a matchbox sleeve cover. Cut three pieces of cardboard as for the stove. Take one cup section from an egg box and cut the top two-thirds away, leaving a shallow cup. Cut a circle at one end of the top cardboard piece to match the upper edge.

In the front of the box, away from the position of the sink, cut a door, as for cupboard. Glue the cardboard top and sides in place and paint the unit.

Glue a piece of foil to the inside of the cup, then glue the cup in the hole.

Dresser
This is made from a whole matchbox sleeve cover. Cut away the sections shown in fig. 4, and cut doors as for cupboard. Cut three pieces of cardboard: two to cover the top and bottom and one to form the bottom shelf, allowing 6mm ($\frac{1}{4}$in) extra along the long edges of each piece. Score and fold the extra 6mm ($\frac{1}{4}$in) to one side. Position and glue these three pieces in the matchbox cover.

Cut shelves to fit within the box and then cut matchstick brackets to the depth of the shelves. Glue a bracket to the ends of each shelf. Glue the shelves in place and paint the dresser. Then glue two small pieces of matchstick on the front as knobs.

Hallway
Coat rack
Insert a pencil into the inside of a plastic spool. Make little holes with a bradawl along the length of the pencil and glue small lengths of matchstick into each hole. Paint the coat rack with spray paint.

Painting or mirror
Use the lid of a small plastic container. Paint the edges and then paste either a magazine picture or a piece of foil in the centre.

Master bedroom
Double bed
Cut a piece of cardboard to the size

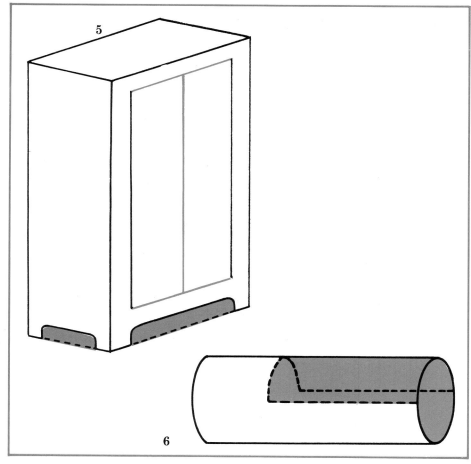

5. *A wardrobe made from the sleeve of a large matchbox.*
6. *An adorable doll cradle can be made from the cardboard tube inside a roll of toilet paper.*

Playpen

For the base use the inside of a large matchbox and a piece of fabric-covered foam for the mattress. For the sides use toothpicks with the sharp ends removed, glued between the mattress and the edge of the box. Or, if it is available, use a small piece of bamboo blind.

Chest of drawers

Glue four small matchboxes one on top of the other. Cover the sides and top with thin cardboard cut to fit. Use matchsticks for handles. Take the inside of another small matchbox and cut away each side so that the corners of the box remain to represent legs. Glue this to the bottom of the drawer unit.

Bathroom

Bathtub

Use the inside of a large matchbox for the exterior of the tub and a moulded plastic wrapper from a model car. Trim the plastic to fit. Paint the outside of the matchbox and leave it to dry. Then glue the plastic wrapper into the box.

Washbasin

Cut off the bottom of one egg box section and glue it to a thin plastic spool. Make a surround for the basin from a square piece of cardboard cut slightly larger than the cup. Cut a hole the size of the cup in the centre of the cardboard and round off two adjacent corners to make the front of the washbasin. Glue the cardboard surround to the cup. Paint basin to match the bathtub.

Toilet

This is made from two cup sections of an egg box, plus a piece of cardboard. For the base cut one cup in half, and for the bowl use the bottom third of another cup. Cut the cardboard to fit the circumference of the bowl, adding a small tab to serve as a hinge. Glue the tab to the back of the bowl and glue the bowl to the bottom of the base piece. Paint toilet to match bath tub and basin.

of bed required. Cut a piece of 2.5cm (1in) deep plastic foam to the same size. Cut a small strip of foam to represent pillows and glue it to the mattress piece. Glue the cardboard to the mattress bottom, and cover the whole bed with a piece of fabric, glued in place.

Dressing table

Cut a plastic lid in half and glue this to a spool. Cut a semicircle of fabric large enough to cover the lid and reach the floor and glue this in place over the lid. Make a mirror from a smaller lid; cut away roughly $\frac{1}{4}$ of the lid and then paint it to coordinate with the skirt. When the paint is dry, glue a circle of foil to the inside of the lid.

Wardrobe

This is made from the outside sleeve cover of a large matchbox. Cut the doors as for the kitchen cupboard, scoring the hinged sides so that they open out easily. Cut away the parts of the box as shown in fig. 5. The top of the wardrobe and the base are cut to size from the inner part of

the box and glued in place. Paint the wardrobe and glue matchstick handles in place.

Chair

Use the lower part of an egg box section for the base and cut another section as shown in the photograph. Glue this to the base and paint with poster paint. Make a foam cushion as for living room chairs.

Children's room

Cradle

Use the cardboard tube from a toilet paper roll. Cut away the areas indicated in fig. 6. Cut two strips of thin cardboard 6mm ($\frac{1}{4}$in) wide and long enough to fit the inner circumference of the tube. Glue these in place just inside each end of the tube, with the outer edges flush. Cut two circles of cardboard the size of the tube openings and glue the circles over the ends, fixing them to the cardboard collars fitted inside. Paint with poster paint.

For the bedding, use a small piece of foam cut to fit within the cradle and covered with fabric.

Four poster bed

Finished height
25.4cm (10in).
Tools required
Scissors; paintbrush; ballpoint pen;

electric iron.
Techniques involved
Basic sewing.

Materials
28 used sewing thread reels
contact adhesive
24.5cm × 18.8cm ($9\frac{1}{2}$in × $7\frac{1}{2}$in) of 6mm

(¼in) thick plywood or piece of
hardboard
4 round wooden beads, 15mm (⅝in)
diameter
enamel paint
2.5cm (1in) thick block of
polyurethane foam,
24.5cm × 18.8cm (9½in × 7½in)
90cm × 52cm (35½in × 20½in) cotton
sheeting
28cm (11in) square of iron-on non-
woven interfacing
112cm (44in) of 15mm (⅝in) wide
cotton frilling
210cm (83in) of 5cm (2in) wide
broderie anglaise
31.5cm × 23cm (12½in × 9in) of
quilted fabric
31.5cm × 23cm (12½in × 9in) of
contrasting backing fabric
185cm (72in) of 6mm (¼in) wide
ribbon; matching thread

The bed

Strip off labels from sewing thread
reels. Using contact adhesive stick
reels on top of each other in four
groups of six. Stick a wooden bead
on top of each column of reels.
Leave adhesive to set.

Paint the four columns of reels
and paint four single reels which
will be feet.

To make the mattress from polyurethane foam, take a spare reel and
draw outline of reel on each corner
of foam. Cut out curves (fig. 1).

To make base of bed, stick the
four single reels at each corner of
plywood or hardboard. Turn over
and stick a column of reels on to
each corner of base (fig. 2). Leave to
set.

Bedding

Cut sheeting into six pieces: two
pieces each measuring 26cm × 22cm
(10¼in × 8¾in) for canopy and base
cover; two pieces, each 42cm × 35cm
(16½in × 13¾in) for sheets; two pieces
each 22cm × 14cm (8¾in × 5½in) for
pillowcases.

6mm (¼in) seam allowances are
included throughout.

Pillow

With raw edges level, tack narrow
frilling all round one piece of
sheeting. Place second piece of
sheeting on top, sandwiching frilling in between. Stitch together
round three sides, leaving the fourth
side open. Turn to right side.

Fill pillow with scraps of foam
and stitch open ends together,
neatening ends of frilling.

Sheets

Stitch narrow hem all round one
piece of sheeting for bottom sheet.
Stitch hem all round top sheet,
adding narrow frilling to finish one
short end.

Base cover and canopy

Stiffen one remaining piece of sheeting with iron-on interfacing. This
piece is for the canopy.

Cut curves on corners of both
pieces to fit round bedposts as for
mattress. Hem curved edges. Tack
hems along straight sides of both
pieces.

Cut broderie anglaise into four
22cm (8¾in) and four 28cm (11in)
pieces. Gather along raw edges of
broderie anglaise until pieces are
the same length as straight sides of
canopy and base cover. With raw
edges level, right sides together,
tack and stitch broderie anglaise to
canopy and base cover (fig. 3). Press
frills downwards.

Cut ribbon into four lengths, each
42cm (16½in). Stitch centre of each

piece of ribbon to centre of cut-out
corner on canopy (fig. 3).

Quilt

Round off corners of quilt and lining
fabrics (fig. 4). With right sides
together, stitch quilt to lining
around three sides as shown. Snip
into seam allowances on curves and
turn to right side. Turn in seam
allowances and stitch remaining
sides.

Assembling the bed

Place base cover on to base, then
put foam mattress on top. Tuck
bottom sheet into mattress. Add top
sheet, quilt and pillows. Tie the
canopy to the top of the bedposts.

1. *Cutting a piece of foam for
the mattress.*
2. *Assembling bed frame.*
3. *Sewing ruffles and ribbons to
canopy.*
4. *Stitching quilt; ends are curved to
fit around bedposts.*

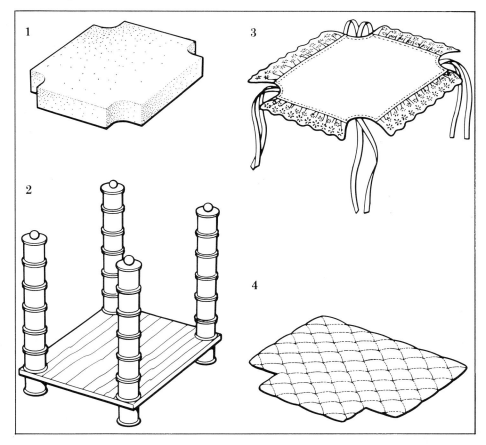

Toy bag

Tools required
Basic sewing tools; sewing machine.
Techniques involved
Basic sewing; machine stitching; machine-sewn appliqué work.
Materials
tracing paper for patterns
dressmaker's carbon paper

150cm × 50cm (59in × 19¾in) of cotton calico fabric
50cm × 20cm (19¾in × 8in) of red heavy-weight poplin or sailcloth

scraps of plain cotton fabric in red,
turquoise, yellow, green and pale
purple
matching and contrasting threads
6cm (2⅞in) of Velcro tape
tissue paper
1 brightly coloured button

Trace off the motifs from the
patterns. A seam allowance of 1.5cm
(⅝in) is included. Using dressmaker's
carbon paper, mark the shapes on
the wrong side of the appropriate
coloured fabrics. Cut out all the
pieces.

Fold the calico fabric in half
widthwise. Press and tack along the
fold line. This will be the base of the
bag. Unfold the calico.

Mark the window frames on the
right side of the turquoise house
piece.

Place the two house pieces together, with turquoise on the right
side and yellow fabric for windows
underneath. Position them on one
half of the calico 5.5cm (2¼in) from
the base fold. Pin and tack (fig. 1).

Put the roof on top of the house so
that the lower edge overlaps the top
of the house. Slip the lower, slanted
edge of the chimney under the edge
of the roof on the left-hand side of
the house. Pin and tack the roof and
chimney in position (fig. 2).

Place the door in the centre of the
base edge of the house. Pin and tack
in place. Mark the position of the
small window on the door. Carefully
tack all round the outer edge of the
house very close to the edge (fig. 3).

Set your sewing machine to satin
stitch on medium width and mini-
mum length of stitch. Place a sheet
of tissue paper under the calico and
the house, and satin stitch along all
the raw edges. (The tissue paper
helps to prevent the material from
puckering as you stitch.)

Begin by stitching the house sides
and base edge and the chimney,
using turquoise thread to match the
house. Stitch round the roof using
red thread and then stitch round the
edge of the door with green thread.
Stitch round the window of the door
with green thread as well. Finally,
stitch round the outlines of the
windows, using dark blue thread to
make the outer frames. You may
find it easier to stitch if you
topstitch the sections in place first
(fig. 4).

Using sharp pointed scissors, carefully cut away the top layer of fabric
from within the window frames,
exposing the yellow fabric which is
underneath. Similarly, cut away the
green fabric and then the turquoise
fabric from inside the window on the
door (fig. 5).

With a contrasting coloured
thread, satin stitch crossed lines in
each of the windows and in the door
window (fig. 6). Using a contrasting
colour, satin stitch a line on the door
to represent the letter box.

Place the smoke clouds in a row,
one above the chimney and the next
two slightly to the right, graduating
in size (fig. 7). Stitch in place as for
the house.

Remove the tissue paper and press
the appliquéd area on the wrong
side.

1. *Place the house pieces together
and tack them onto the calico.*
2. *Pinning and tacking the roof and
chimney into position.*
3. *Tack door into position. Tack
around the outer edges of the house.*
4. *Outline the window, door and
house shapes in satin stitch.*
5. *Clip away the top layer of fabric
in windows to expose yellow fabric.*
6. *Decorate the windows with
crossed lines of satin stitch.*
7. *Position smoke clouds in a row
above chimney and stitch in place.*
8. *Making the side hems of the bag.
Neaten the edges in zigzag stitch.*

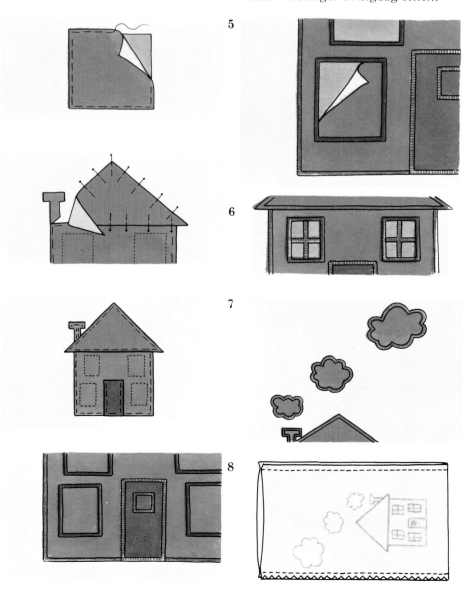

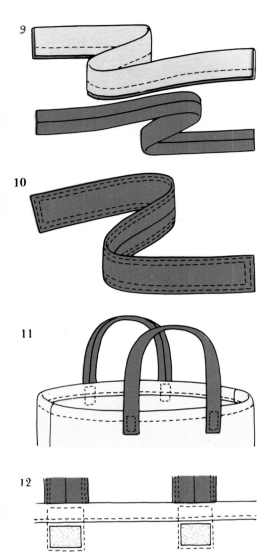

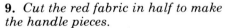

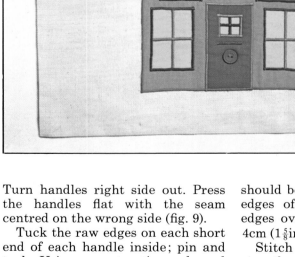

9. *Cut the red fabric in half to make the handle pieces.*
10. *Topstitch around each handle close to the outer edge.*
11. *Position handles, pin and tack. Stitch firmly in place.*
12. *Attaching Velcro tape.*

Sew the button to the middle of the door, underneath the letter box.

Fold the calico in half, right sides facing. Pin, tack and stitch the side seams. Neaten the raw edges of the seams with zigzag stitch (fig. 8).

Fold over a double hem 10mm ($\frac{7}{8}$in) wide all around the top edge. Pin, tack and topstitch round the top edge. Cut the red fabric in half to make two pieces each 50cm × 10cm (19$\frac{3}{4}$in × 4in) for handles.

Fold each handle in half lengthwise; pin, tack and stitch long sides.

Turn handles right side out. Press the handles flat with the seam centred on the wrong side (fig. 9).

Tuck the raw edges on each short end of each handle inside; pin and tack. Using a contrasting coloured thread, topstitch all round each handle close to the outer edge. Topstitch again, about 6mm ($\frac{1}{4}$in) inside the first line of stitching (fig. 10).

Pin and tack the handles to the right side of the top edge of each side of the bag. The outer edges should be 13cm (5$\frac{1}{8}$in) from the side edges of the bag, with the short edges overlapping the top edge for 4cm (1$\frac{5}{8}$in).

Stitch in place at each handle end over the previous stitching lines (fig. 11).

Cut the Velcro tape in half. Pin and tack one half of each piece on the inside of the bag behind the ends.

Pin and tack second halves of fastening behind the opposite handle ends.

Topstitch in place (fig. 12).

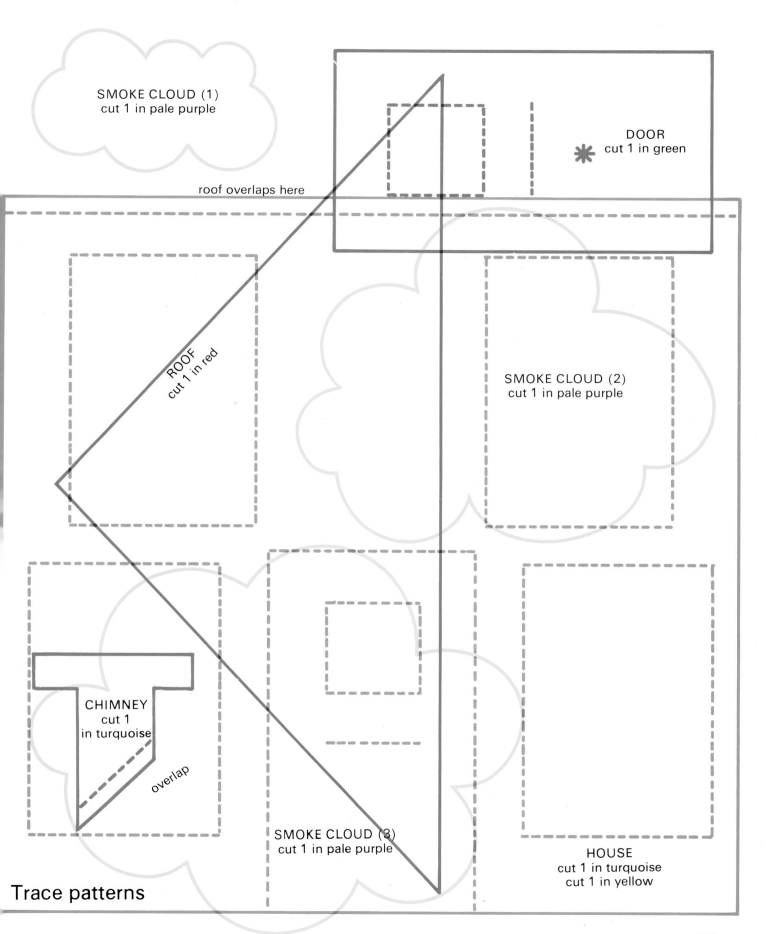

SMOKE CLOUD (1)
cut 1 in pale purple

DOOR
cut 1 in green

roof overlaps here

ROOF
cut 1 in red

SMOKE CLOUD (2)
cut 1 in pale purple

CHIMNEY
cut 1
in turquoise

overlap

SMOKE CLOUD (3)
cut 1 in pale purple

HOUSE
cut 1 in turquoise
cut 1 in yellow

Trace patterns

225

Wall hanging

Finished size
Elephant 90cm × 76cm (36in × 30in) rhino 106cm × 76cm (42in × 30in).

Tools required
Basic sewing tools; sewing machine; hammer; sharp knife or scalpel.

Techniques involved
Basic sewing; machine stitching; drawing patterns.

Materials

For each animal:
squared paper for patterns
115cm × 90cm (45in × 35in) of felt in

main colour of your choice
scraps of felt for the features
matching thread
black embroidery thread
90cm (35in) square of strong cardboard
2 large eyelets (available from

camping shops)
fabric adhesive
For elephant only:
30.5cm (12in) square of felt in
contrasting colour for blanket
squared paper for pattern

To make the elephant

Using squared paper, draw the main
body section to scale. Mark in the
position of each pocket and all
features and lines. Cut out. Trace
the patterns for the eyes and
features and for the blanket top
from the patterns given, and cut out.

Pin the body pattern piece on to
the felt for the body and cut out.
Transfer all markings from the
pattern piece to the fabric.

Cut out the pockets from the
remaining felt measuring as follows:
14.5cm × 5.5cm (5¾in × 2¼in) for the
comb pocket; 15cm × 6.5cm (6in ×
2½in) for pencil holder; 10cm × 2.5cm
(4in × 1in) pencil holder strip;
25.5cm × 23cm (10in × 9in) for one
gusset pocket; 38.5cm × 22.5cm
(15¼in × 8¾in) for second gusset
pocket.

From the scraps of felt cut out the
blanket decoration, the tusk and the
eye. From the contrasting square of
felt cut out the blanket top and the
third gusset pocket 37cm × 16cm
(14½in × 6½in). Finally, cut a strip
28cm × 7cm (11in × 2¾in) for the
fringe of the blanket.

Now pin and stitch the eye and
tusk into the positions marked on
the pattern. Using black embroidery
thread, back stitch around the eye
pieces.

Thread the spool of your sewing
machine with black embroidery
thread, and from the wrong side
machine stitch along the lines for
the legs and ear. Pin and stitch the
comb pocket into place on the
elephant's trunk.

Pin the blanket top into position
and stitch all round the felt as close
as possible to the edge. Press 4.5cm
(1¾in) to the wrong side on each
short edge of the pocket. Sew along
each fold close to the edge.

Pin the pocket into place on the
elephant, overlapping the edge of
the blanket top. Place the side edges
of the pockets to the pocket lines
and stitch down both sides. Fold the
pocket on to the gusset and stitch
along the bottom edge of the gusset.
Fasten off all ends (fig. 1).

Draw a line 4cm (1½in) from the
edge of the blanket fringe and make
cuts in the strip to this line and
1.5cm (½in) apart. Tack the fringe
over the bottom edge of the pocket.
Pin and tack decorations over the
join. Stitch along the centre of the
circles and work another row of
stitching 3mm (⅛in) below the first.

Attach the other two gusset pockets in the same way. Stitch the right-
hand edge of the pencil pocket into
position as indicated on the pattern.
Place a pencil under the strip and
pin the strip to the elephant over the
pencil. Tack beside the pencil (fig.
2). Repeat five times more. Stitch
down each row of tacking and along
the bottom edge of the pocket. Trim
off any excess felt on the left-hand
edge of the pocket. Line up the ends
of the pencil holder strip with the
edges of the pocket. Tack and stitch
into position.

To finish off, press the elephant
with a damp cloth to remove all
creases. Spread adhesive evenly on
the wrong side of the felt and stick
the elephant to the cardboard,
making sure it is completely flat.
Allow to dry. Mark in the positions
of the eyelets so that the pockets
will hang straight. Cut out the holes
and insert the eyelets, using a
hammer. Cut away the excess card
with a sharp knife or scalpel.

To make the rhino

Draw up the pattern pieces and cut
out the main body felt across the
square of fabric, transferring all
markings.

Cut out pockets from the remaining felt as follows: 14.5cm × 5.5cm
(5¾in × 2¼in) for the comb pocket;
18cm × 6.5cm (7in × 2½in) for pencil
holder; 14cm × 2.5cm (5½in × 1in)
strip; 25.5cm × 23cm (10in × 9in) for
first gusset pocket; 38cm × 20.5cm
(15in × 8in) for second gusset
pocket; 23cm × 12.5cm (9in × 5in) for
third gusset pocket.

From the scraps of felt cut out the
spots, eye and ear. Stitch the ear
piece and the eye pieces on to the
head where marked. Sew the spots
to the rhino's back.

Using black embroidery thread on
the spool of the sewing machine,
stitch in the lines for the top of the
head, the neck, mouth and chin from
the wrong side of the fabric. Stitch
the comb pocket into position on the

rhino's back.

Attach three gusset pockets as for
the elephant. Attach the pencil
pocket in the same way, but making
seven loops.

Finish off the rhino as for the
elephant.

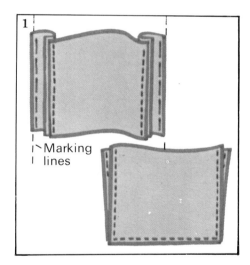

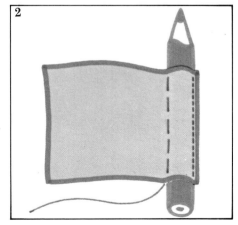

1. *Making a gusset for the pocket.*
2. *Place a pencil under the strip to make slot for pencil holders.*

Trace patterns

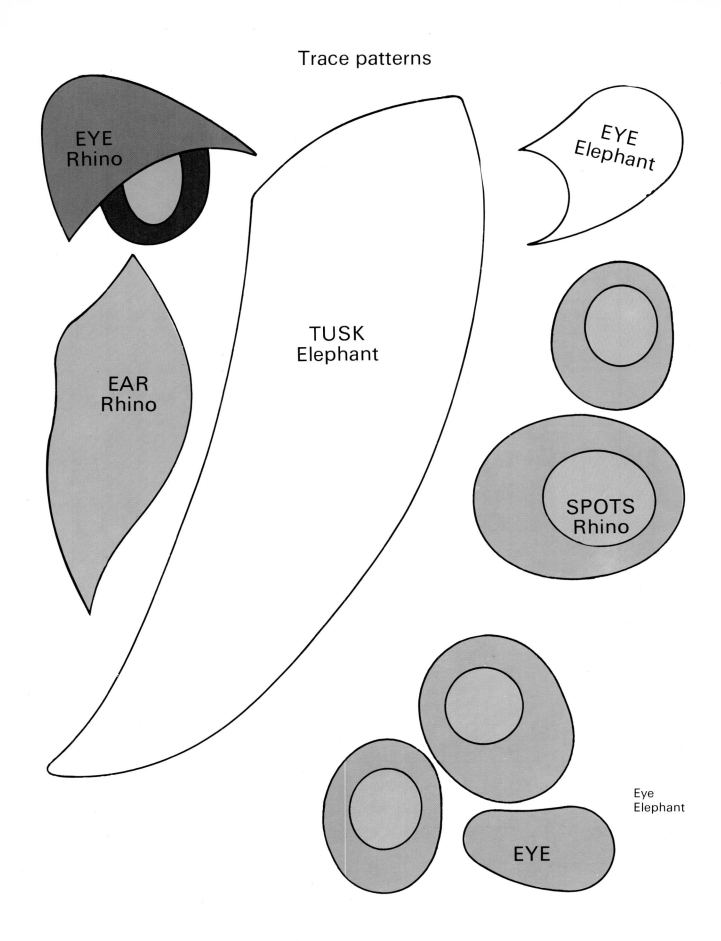

EYE
Rhino

EYE
Elephant

EAR
Rhino

TUSK
Elephant

SPOTS
Rhino

Eye
Elephant

EYE

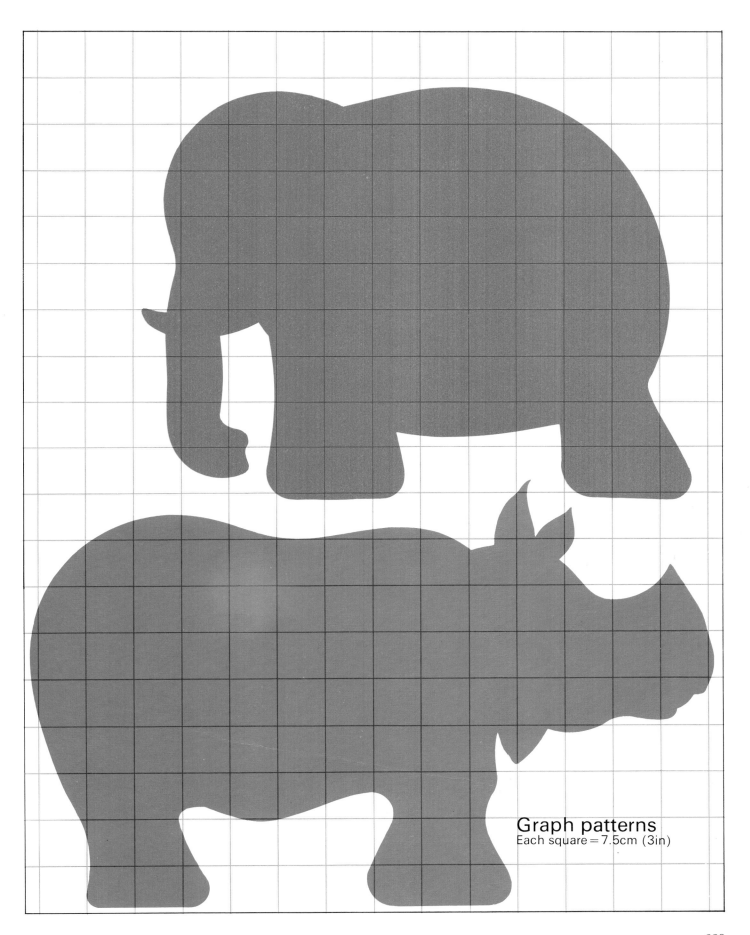

Graph patterns
Each square = 7.5cm (3in)

229

Hanging shelves

Tools required
Basic sewing tools; hand or power drill; drill bit 1cm ($\frac{3}{8}$in) diameter.

Techniques involved
Basic sewing skills
drilling holes.

Materials
2.75m (3yd) heavy duty canvas 90cm (36in) wide
5 pieces of 6mm ($\frac{1}{4}$in) plywood, 45cm × 30cm ($17\frac{3}{4}$in × $11\frac{3}{4}$in)
strong sewing thread to match canvas
heavy machine needle
90cm (1yd) rope 6mm ($\frac{1}{4}$in) thick
4 eyelets 10mm ($\frac{3}{8}$in) diameter
hooks for hanging the shelves

Cut out the canvas pieces as shown in the cutting chart (fig. 1).

Fold the main panel in half across the width and mark the fold line with a tacking stitch to indicate the centre top of the unit.

Join the short ends of the panel, with right sides together, taking 12mm ($\frac{1}{2}$in) turnings. Machine stitch using strong thread and a heavy needle.

Press the turnings open and machine stitch them down to the wrong side of the panel.

Make a narrow hem along the raw edge of the panel. If you have a zigzag machine this can be done with a single line of stitching closely zigzag stitched into place.

Fold the piece for the top pocket in half across the width. Crease lightly.

Open it out and make a narrow hem along one of the longer sides. Turn under a 10mm ($\frac{3}{8}$in) hem on the wrong side along the remaining three sides.

Place the pocket, wrong side down, on the wrong side of the main panel so that the crease line marking the centre of the pocket falls over the tacked line at the top of the panel exactly (fig. 2).

Measure 5cm (2in) diagonally from the corners of the pocket and make tailor's tacks through both layers of canvas. Cut through the tacks and open out the layers. Make eyelet holes in the position of the tacks at each corner in both pieces of canvas (fig. 3).

Replace the pocket, matching the holes. Leaving the side with the narrow hem open, pin and machine stitch the remaining sides of the pocket to the main panel along the

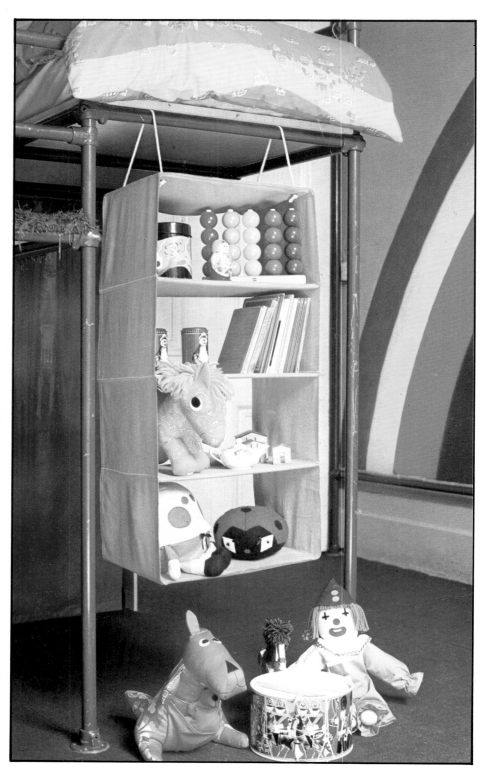

folds of the turnings. Work a second line of machine stitching 6mm (¼in) away from the first line (fig. 4).

Fold the piece for the bottom pocket in half across the width. Crease lightly.

Open it out and make a narrow hem along one of the longer sides. Turn under a 10mm (⅜in) hem on the wrong side along the remaining three sides.

Place the pocket, wrong side down, on the wrong side of the main panel so that the centre crease line falls exactly over the seam line at the bottom of the panel and the hem of the pocket is on the same side as the opening of the top pocket. Machine stitch the pocket to the main panel along the other three sides.

Attaching the shelves
Make narrow hems along the short raw edges of the three remaining pocket pieces. Fold the pockets in half across the width with the right side out and press.

Measure down the required depth of the shelf from the top pocket on each side of the main panel and mark.

Keeping the opening of the pocket to the same side as the others and with turnings up, pin the doubled short sides of the pocket to the main strip along the marks indicated, taking 12mm (½in) turnings. Machine stitch twice (fig. 5).

Attach the other shelves in the same way, ensuring that the distance between them on each side of the main panel is the same.

Strengthening the shelves
To cover the raw edges of the shelves where they are stitched to the main panel, cut six strips. 4cm × 32cm (1½in × 12½in) from the leftover canvas. Turn under a narrow hem on the wrong side of each side of the strips and press.

Place each strip over the raw edges of a seam joining the pockets to the main panel so that the lower edge of the strip is level with the stitch line. Pin in position and machine stitch around all sides. Repeat this procedure with each of the other seams.

Insert the pieces of plywood into the shelves.

Insert the plywood into the pocket

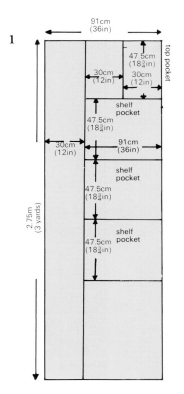

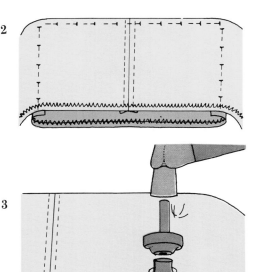

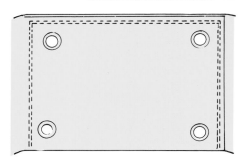

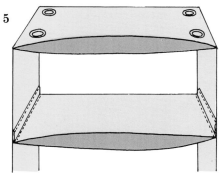

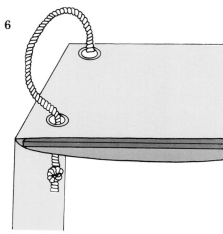

at the top of unit and mark the positions of the eyelet holes in pencil. Take out the wood and drill holes in each position. Replace the wood so that the holes correspond with the eyelets.

Cut the rope in half and tie a double knot at one end of each half. Insert the other end of one of the pieces up through the eyelet hole at the front of the unit and then down through the hole at the back on the same side. Tie a knot underneath. Repeat this with the other piece of rope on the opposite side (fig. 6).

Attach hooks in the required place, adjust the rope to the desired length and hang in position on the hooks, or hang the unit over a horizontal rod as pictured.

1. *The cutting chart.*
2. *Placing pocket onto main panel.*
3. *Making the eyelet holes.*
4. *Secure pocket to the main panel with double line of stitching.*
5. *Attaching shelf pocket to sides of main panel with double stitching.*
6. *Threading rope through eyelets.*

Picture credits

Caroline Arbour: 78, 82
Belinda: 51, 53, 118
Steve Bicknell: 22, 23, 24, 50, 99, 100, 101, 200
Michael Boys: 104, 107
Simon Butcher: 108, 119, 133(l)
Martin Chaffer: 42, 43(br), 48
Roger Charity: 47
Gavin Cochrane: 134(br), 159, 163
Stuart Dalby: 134(bl), 185(tr), 186, 187
Rod Delroy: 130, 133(r)
Alan Duns: 153, 220
Ray Duns: 134(l), 224
Bob Enever: 116, 117
Geoffrey Frosh: 32
Melvin Grey: 28, 41(b), 202, 215
Nelson Hargreaves: 188, 190
100 Idees de Marie Claire: 198(bl), 204 Capurro
Jeany: 183
Paul Kemp: 185(b)
Chris Lewis: 37, 124, 125
Rob Matheson: 57
Dick Miller: 150
Alasdair Ogilvie: 21, 43
Tony Page: 112, 115
Roger Phillips: 25, 26
Spike Powell: 230
John Price: 134(t), 155, 164/5, 176, 192
Peter Pugh-Cook: 91, 198(c), 226
Robin Wools Ltd: 122, 126
Kim Sayer: 70, 86, 90
Bruce Scott: 111
Dennis Stone: 134(bc), 169, 175
Jerry Tubby: 95, 98, 198(t), 198(br), 206, 209, 210, 212/3
Gary Warren: 222
Welcomme Pernelle: 12, 129
Liz Whiting: 74, 77

Artwork credits

Advertising Arts: 137, 160, 162, 163, 171
Rosemary Chanter: 10
Victoria Drew: 203, 205
Paul Emra: 51, 152(b), 154, 167, 170, 172/3, 174, 177, 178/9, 180, 181, 184, 187, 189, 191, 193–197
Terry Evans: 15, 52, 54(l) 56, 71, 72, 79, 82, 83, 87, 90, 223, 224
Bernard Fallon: 138, 141(cr)
Barbara Firth: 28, 38, 96, 97, 98
Lesley Fox: 21, 46, 50
Michael Halton: 156, 157, 158, 166, 168
Malcolm Hatton: 34/5, 63, 64, 68, 69, 217, 218, 219
John Hitchinson: 72/3, 88/9, 109, 225
Terri Lawlor: 59, 61
Trevor Lawrence: 27, 30/1, 49, 75, 146(b)
Brian Mayor: 54/5, 60
Coral Mula: 16, 17, 18, 19, 20, 76, 115, 207, 208, 211, 214
Gwen Simpson: 13(bl)
Joy Simpson: 25
Roy Stringer: 84/5
Tri-Art: 136
Paul Williams: 23, 24, 33(l), 39, 41(tr), 139, 140, 142, 143, 146(t), 149, 152(t)

Glossary

BACKSAW Used for more accurate cutting than can be done with a panel saw. The blade is shorter and has a solid metal back to keep it rigid. Also there are more and finer teeth. The heaviest back saws are called tenon saws. Backsaws for finer work are called dovetail saws.

BACKSTITCH (Embroidery) Bring thread through on stitching line, then take a small backward stitch through fabric. Bring needle through again a litttle in front of first stitch. Then take another stitch, inserting needle at point where first stitch came through.

BENCH HOOK A device for holding work in place while sawing. It is easily made by nailing two scraps of batten to a piece of board and hooking it over edge of workbench.

BLANKET STITCH A simple looped embroidery stitch. When the loops are worked close together, it is known as Buttonhole stitch.

BLOCKBOARDS Group of man-made boards, the most common of which is chipboard.

BRADAWL A chisel-pointed boring tool used for marking screw positions and counterboring for small-size screws.

BRIDLE The name for the strings that hold a kite at the correct angle to the wind, and to which the towing line is attached. The cutter kite has two pieces of string or thread, making a double bridle. See pages 207–208 for working instructions.

BUTTONHOLE STITCH A simple looped embroidery stitch. It is useful for reinforcing both knitted and crocheted buttonholes.

CARPENTER'S SQUARE An instrument for testing the accuracy of square work or for marking right angles. It consists of a thin steel blade about 6in long, set into a wooden stock of similar length and securely fastened at right angles to it.

CASTING OFF (Knitting) Closing off the knitting loops. With the yarn and needles in usual working position, work the first two stitches so that they are transferred to right-hand needle. Use point of left-hand needle to lift first stitch worked over second one and off needle. Work next stitch on left-hand needle and repeat process. See page 16 for full working instructions.

CASTING ON Making the required number of loops onto a knitting needle to supply a foundation for knitted fabric. Subsequent rows are worked into these loops. See page 16 for two-needle method, which gives an especially firm edge. There is also a one-needle method of casting on.

CHAIN STITCH Embroidery stitch worked from right to left, making a chain of loops on the right side of the fabric. The needle returns to the place where it came out, the thread looping under it. When each stitch is held down separately with the working thread, it is called detached chain, or lazy daisy stitch.

CHAMFER To cut or round off in a sloping manner, as the edge of anything square, so as to form a chamfer or bevel.

CHISELS These tools are really a special form of knife, in which the cutting edge is set square to the handle. This concentrates a cutting force on the edge, and makes it possible to reach points that are inaccessible to conventional knives.

CLAMPS Devices to hold the work in place. G-clamps are used to hold two pieces together while they are being joined. Very small modellers' clamps are cheap and convenient for holding small pieces together. When using clamps, always pad the workpiece with scraps of wood to prevent the clamp from marking the work. *See also* **VICE**.

COPING SAW This hand saw cuts curves and shapes in wood. It consists of a frame, in which the blade is held taut, and a handle. The frame curves so that it does not restrict the blade when work is being done away from the edge of a board. Coping saw blades are tensioned by means of a screw in the handle.

COUNTERSINK OR ROSE BITS *see* **DRILL BITS**

CRAFT KNIFE This is similar to a trimming knife, with replaceable blades fitted into a handle. The handle is smaller and lighter, so that it can be controlled between finger and thumb for precise work.

CROSSCUT SAW Used to cut across the grain of hardwoods and softwoods, and for working with the grain on very hard woods. The knife-point shaped teeth give the sharper cuts needed when working across the grain.

CROSS STITCH (Embroidery) For the most even appearance, work cross stitches in two stages: Work the first diagonal all along a row, then work back along the row, adding the second. Stitches should form a perfect square. Whether working this way or one stitch at a time, make sure that top threads of all stitches slant in the same direction.

DOVETAIL SAW *see* **BACK SAW**

DRILL A pointed instrument used for boring holes in wood, metal, etc.

DRILL BITS The boring part of a drill, a whole range is available for use with braces, hand drills and power drills. Each bit is specially shaped to do a specific job, and they are available in a range of sizes. *Twist bits*, often referred to as a twist drill, are for drilling small holes in wood or metal, and can be used in both hand and power drills. A set ranging from 1.5mm ($\frac{1}{16}$) to 12.5mm ($\frac{1}{2}$in) will cover most jobs. *Countersink or rose bits* are used for drilling countersunk holes for flathead screws. *Auger bits* have a clearly defined spiral so that the waste is cleared rapidly from the hole during drilling.

FILES Used for finishing and shaping both wood and metal. File blades have a large number of very fine teeth, variously shaped to give a finer or coarser cut. Very fine files are called needle files and are used for fine shaping and piercing work.

FRENCH KNOT An embroidery stitch made by bringing needle and thread through fabric to right side, winding thread once or twice around needle, and then reinserting needle beside the point where it first emerged and pulling thread through.

FRENCH SEAM A narrow self-enclosed seam sewed on both sides to conceal raw edges of cloth.

FRET SAW Similar to a coping saw but deeper, to allow work with larger boards.

GARTER STITCH Knitting pattern formed by knitting both right-side and wrong-side rows, producing a horizontally ridged effect.

GRAFTING A method of joining two sets of knitting

stitches invisibly without first casting them off. See page 19 for working instructions.

HACKSAWS These saws are used for cutting metal. They have a metal frame and replaceable blades tensioned with a screw and fitted facing away from the handle, the opposite of those of the coping saw. Available in two basic sizes and with a range of blade lengths; for most purposes, the smallest, called a junior hacksaw, is sufficient. They will cut straight lines or mild curves and the smaller blade of the junior type will follow a tighter curve.

HARDWOODS Timber from broad-leaved deciduous trees. Hardwoods are usually more difficult to work than softwoods; they are also heavier and more expensive, but they do last longer. The more commonly available hardwoods include walnut, oak, beech and birch.

HERRINGBONE STITCH This embroidery stitch is worked from left to right, taking a small horizontal stitch in upper layer and then, moving diagonally, a small horizontal stitch in lower layer. See pages 14 and 15.

HOBBY HORSE A horse's head attached to a stick, e.g. a broom handle. For instructions on how to make, see pages 92–94.

HOLE SAW This is a specialized drill designed to remove a core of the material. It is suitable only for use on thin materials. It consists of a drill with, around it, a length of saw blade bent into a circle. The pilot drill serves to start the hole and keep it centred. The saw then works around the surface of the materials, cutting through it until the centre falls free. The hole saw is used in toy-making for cutting very large holes in plywood and for making wheels.

INCREASING AND DECREASING (Knitting/crochet) Adding to or subtracting from the number of stitches in a row of knitting or crochet. For knitting techniques, see pages 18–19.

KERF Groove formed by saw cut.

KNITTING AND PURLING STITCHES see page 17 for working instructions.

KNITTING IN ROUNDS Using a set of four needles, pointed at both ends, to produce a narrow tubular fabric such as for a sock. Three needles are used to hold fabric; the fourth is the working needle.

LAMINATION Here, a method of making papier mâché, by gluing together several sheets of paper to make one, strong, flexible sheet. This can then be shaped over a base or cut into strips before it is applied.

LAZY DAISY STITCH *see* **CHAIN STITCH**

MARQUETRY Work inlaid with *redundant* pieces of variously coloured fine woods. See pages 188–191, for making marquetry chessboard.

NAIL SET OR PUNCH This tool is used for tapping nail heads below the surface of wood. A range of head sizes is available to suit nail sizes.

OILSTONE Used for sharpening the cutting edges of such tools as planes and chisels. Comes in both natural and artificial forms.

OVERCASTING Used on raw fabric edges to prevent fraying, and sometimes to join pieces. Working from either direction, make diagonal, evenly spaced stitches over edge of fabric.

PANEL SAW The most generally useful hand saw, suitable for cuts with or against the grain and having about 10ppi (points, or teeth, per inch, a standard saw specification). The panel saw is used for making long cuts in panel materials or for cutting larger pieces of softwood.

PAPIER MÂCHÉ A modelling material consisting of pieces of paper bound with paste or glue and moulded around a shape to make functional and decorative objects. It is a cheap and easy material to use and has the advantage of drying naturally to a hard and durable substance, without having to be baked like clay. The term literally means "chewed-up paper". The invention of epoxy resin makes today's papier mâché object much stronger and more durable than traditional water-soluble glues and pastes could do.

PIERCING SAW Used for cutting very tight curves in metal. It is similar to a coping saw for wood and takes fine blades.

PIN HAMMER Available in various weights, the pin hammer serves a dual purpose: one side of the head is for driving nails; the other side, shaped to a cross pein, is for removing nails and pins.

PINKING SHEARS Shears with notched blades, used to pevent raw edges of fabric from fraying. Produces a saw-toothed decorative edge.

PLANE This tool is a form of precision knife that pares shavings to produce a smooth surface on wood, or to shape or fit it. The basic plane is available in a wide range of sizes, and there are many special-purpose planes for particular shaping work, including the spoke-shave, which can be used to shape curved surfaces.

PLYWOOD Man-made boards produced by gluing several cross-grained wood sheets together under heat and pressure with the grain of alternate layers at right angles for greater stability. Plywoods are very stiff and stong, although the thinner varieties can often be bent to form curves.

POUPARD DOLL Originally a simple plaything—a wooden ball on a stick wrapped in swaddling clothes—the poupard (French for "baby doll") later became very elaborate. Nineteenth-century poupards were richly dressed and often equipped with music boxes or mechanism for turning their sculpted wax heads.

RAG DOLL Traditionally made from cast-off clothes and odds and ends from the sewing basket.

RASPS These tools are coarser files and normally half-round in shape. The flat side is used for flat or convex surfaces, the curved side for concave ones. The teeth are very coarse and set quite widely. They will remove material quickly without clogging. Rasps are usually supplied without handles, and you should fit one before use.

RUNNING STITCH Weave needle in and out of fabric before pulling it through. Several stitches can be taken on needle at the same time. Running stitches, drawn up, are used for gathering, large running stitches are used for tacking.

SANDPAPER Crushed abrasive bonded to a paper backing. It is available in a range of grades (degree of coarseness). Always use sandpaper with a sanding block. This will allow you to apply even pressure over a large area and prevent the paper from digging in.

SATIN STITCH (Embroidery) Work straight stitches

close together, usually to fix a shape. Stitches should be of even tension and not too long.

SCREW EYE AND SCREW HOOK Related to screws, these are useful in several kinds of application. Instead of a head, the end of the shank is bent around to form a loop, which can be a ring or a hook. They are classified by just one measurement.

SCREWS Screws of various kinds provide a strong mechanical fastening between two parts. Most types of screw have three parts: the thread, which bites into the wood to provide the hole; the shank, which is an unthreaded part passing through the part to be joined; and the head, which is wider than the rest of the screw to stop the screw penetrating further and to draw the parts tightly together. The head may be a so-called flathead or roundhead in shape and has, additionally a slot in it made to take the tip of a screwdriver.

SCRIBER A marking tool, one end of which is ground to a chisel shaped cutting edge for marking timber. The other end is sharpened to a point and can be used for scribing metal.

SINGLE RIB Knitting pattern in which one knit stitch and one purl stitch are alternated across first row; on the next and every even-numbered row, each stitch knitted in the previous row must be purled alternate and each one purled must be knitted. For double rib, alternate two knit stitches and two purl stitches, then reverse.

SLIPSTITCH Used to join two folded edges, or a folded edge to a surface, as in hemming. Working from right to left, take stitch through fabric, and then pass needle through the turned-in edge opposite.

SOFT-HEADED HAMMER A hammer with a rubber or plastic face.

SOFTWOOD Wood from coniferous trees, usually of an evergreen type. The term does not mean that the wood is particularly soft, although it often is. Rather, designates the type of tree from which the boards were cut. Pine is the most common softwood.

SPANISH WINDLASS Used for clamping, this device is made of a loop of cord or strong string wound around the framework to be held together; a lever, such as a screwdriver or scrap of wood is inserted into the loop and twisted around to increase the pressure. As with any clamps, pad the edges of the work with scraps of heavy cardboard to prevent cord from cutting into it.

SPLIT STITCH A form of backstitch rather like chain stitch in appearance and ideal for outlining. See page 14 for working instructions.

SPOKESHAVE A cutting or planing tool consisting of a blade with a handle at either end. So called because it was originally used to shape spokes, it is now used for trimming and smoothing round surfaces.

STEEL RULE Pocket-size adjustable measuring device.

STEM STITCH (Embroidery) Work from left to right, taking regular, slightly slanting stitches along line of the design.

STOCKING STITCH Also known as "plain knitting." Knit and purl rows are worked alternately to produce a smooth fabric on the right side and a ridged texture on wrong side. For reverse stocking stitch, all right-side rows are purled and all wrong-side rows are knitted.

TENON SAW see **BACKSAW**

TACK HAMMER This is the smallest, lightest type of hammer. Its small head has one flat face and is drawn to a point set at right angles to the handle. It may also be a claw type hammer.

TAILOR'S TACKS Used to mark points of a pattern on fabric, especially on delicate or double layers of fabric. Pin pattern to fabric. With thread doubled, make a small stitch through pattern and both layers of fabric. Cut the thread, leaving ends of about 2.5cm (1in). Repeat for all points to be marked. Carefully remove pattern. Separate layers of fabric and cut loops of thread between them. Stitch threads will remain in fabric as markers.

TENSION Standard measure of a knitted fabric expressed in terms of the number of rows and stitches that are worked to produce a given measurement. Since individual variations in the tightness of stitches affect elasticity, and therefore size, tension can be adjusted by changing to a different size needle.

TRIMMING KNIFE This knife usually has a handle shaped to fit the palm of the hand. The blades can be sharpened to prolong their useful life, but are intended to be discarded and replaced when they become blunt. Some types have blades scored with a series of notches so that the point can be snapped off, presenting a new cutting edge. The blade is quite short and stiff, so it can be used for heavy cutting. You can get different blades for various uses, including a hacksaw blade and pad saw blade for light work in metals and wood.

TWIST BITS or **TWIST DRILL** see **DRILL BITS**

VENEERS Very thin sheets of wood, generally hardwood, used to give a decorative finish over cheaper woods. They are not often available except from craft shops or cabinetmakers' suppliers.

VICE A clamping device that is attached to a workbench, for holding an object to be worked on in a fixed position. It consists of a pair of steel-faced jaws moved by a screw or lever. The clamp-on type is the cheapest, and adequate for most purposes.

YARN The word "yarn" once meant only wool yarn, but now a wide range of synthetic yarns, which imitate wool, is also available.

YARN OVER The term for a basic increasing technique in knitting. It has several applications, all of which involve making an extra loop on needle using the working yarn. See page 18 for working instructions.

Index

A

Adhesives, 148
  epoxy resin glue, 200
  PVC woodworking, 148, 151
  safety precautions, 148
  water-resistant, 148
Aeroplanes, crochet, 116–117
Alligator, crochet, 118–119
Animal toys:
  crochet lamb, 124–125
  crochet lion, 122–123
  crochet puppet pets, 131–133
  crochet rabbits, 126–127
  crochet snail and alligator, 118–119
  dog finger puppet, 24, 25
  elephant and rhino wallhanging, 226
  felt dog and cat, 26–27
  glove puppets, 28–31
  hobby horse, 91–94
  knitted rabbit, 107–109
  owl and pussycat, 78–85
  patchwork, 74–77
  teddy bear, 70–73
  wooden laying hen, 192–197
Archimedean, or push drill, 144
Armchairs and sofa, doll's house, 217

B

Baby, finger puppet, 25
  see also Poupard dolls
Back saws, 140, 141
  dovetail, 140
  tenon, 140
Back stitch, 14, 15
  knitting seams, 19
Bag, toy appliquéed, 222–225
Bathroom furniture, doll's house, 219
Bathtub, doll's, 219
Bedding, 221
Bedroom furniture, doll's house, 219
Beds:
  doll's house double, 219
  miniature four-poster, 200, 220–221
Bench hook, 137, 139
Bird kite, 211, 214
Blanket stitch, 14, 15
Blockboard, 139, 189
Box saw, 141
Brace and bit (bit brace), 136, 144
Bradawl, 144, 145, 147
Buttonhole stitch, 14, 15
Butterfly kite, 211, 214
Buttons and buttonholes, 90

C

Cabinet, doll's house, 218
Carp kite, 211
Carpenter's square, 154
Carpenter's workbench, 139
Carpentry tools see Wooden toys
Cat(s):
  crochet puppet, 132
  felt, 26–27
  glove puppet, 29
  owl and pussycat, 78–85
  patchwork, 75–76
Catch stitch, 14, 15
Cellulose filler, 148
Chain stitch, 14, 15

Chairs, doll's house:
  armchairs, 217
  bedroom, 219
  kitchen, 218
Chamfer, 143
Chessboard, marquetry, 188–191
Chest of drawers, doll's house, 219
Chisels, 142, 146
Clamps, 139
  G-, 139
  modeller's, 139
Clown, crochet, 120–121
Coat rack, doll's house, 218
Coffee table, doll's house, 217–218
Compass, 138
Coping saw, 136, 140, 141
Countersink or rose bit, 145
Cradle, doll's, 219
Craft knives, 141
Crochet aeroplanes, 116–117
Crochet clown, 120–121
Crochet Dutch doll, 128–130
Crochet lamb, 124–125
Crochet lion, 122–123
Crochet puppet pets, 131–133
Crochet rabbits, 126–127
Crochet snail and alligator, 118–119
Crochet techniques/stitches, 20
  chains, 20
  double crochet, 20
  half double crochet, 20
  loop stitch, 124–125
  single crochet, 20
  slip stitch, 20
Cross stitch, 14, 15
Cutting board, 189
Cutting out, 10
  felt, 11
  fur fabric, 11

D

Dining room furniture, doll's house, 218
Doctor and nurse, knitted, 112–115
Dog(s):
  crochet puppet, 132
  felt, 26–27
  finger puppet, 24, 25
  patchwork, 75
Dolls:
  crochet Dutch doll, 128–130
  Jenny and Joey, 57–61
  knitted, 104–106
  miniature, 32–36
  patchwork, 77
  poupard, 37–41
  tag, 12, 42–49
  topsy turvy, 51–55
  wool, 62
Doll's clothes/wardrobe, 65–69
  boot, 67
  changing sizes, 65
  duffle coat, 66–67
  knitted doll, 105
  miniature dolls, 33–36
  nightgown, 67
  patterns, 63–64, 68–69
  poupard doll, 40–41
  rag doll, 47–50

  robe, 67
  skirt and blouse, 66
  slip, 65
Doll's house, 183–187
  assembly, 186
  chimney, 186, 187
  painting interior, 185–186
  porch, 186–187
  roof, 186
  stairs, 186, 187
  window glazing, 187
Doll's house furniture, 200, 216–219
  bathroom, 219
  children's room, 219
  dining room/kitchen, 218
  hallway, 218–219
  living room, 217–218
  master bedroom, 219
Dovetail saws, 140
Dowels, 137, 138, 151
Dragonfly kite, 214
Dresser, doll's house, 218
Dressing table, doll's house, 219
Drill bits, 136, 144–145
  auger bit, 145
  countersink or rose bit, 145
  twist drill, 144, 145
Drills, drilling, 136, 144–146
  archimedean, or push, 144
  hand, 136, 144
  hole saws, 144–145, 146
  power, 136, 144
Dutch doll, crochet, 128–130

E

Egg cosies, 22, 25
Elephant wall hanging, 226–229
Embroidery stitches, 14–15
Epoxy resin, 200
Eyes:
  felt, 11
  glass safety, 11
  plastic button, 11

F

Fabric book, 86–90
  cover page, 87
  flowers and snap fasteners, 90
  frog and zipper, 87
  pocket and button, 90
  show and laces, 90
Felt, felt toys:
  cutting and sewing, 11
  dog and cat, 26–27
  egg cosies, 25
  elephant and rhino wallhangings, 226–229
  eyes made from pieces of, 11
  finger puppets, 23–25
File card, 144
Files, 137, 143–144; needle, 144
Fillers, wood, 148
Finger puppets, 22–25
Flat fell seam, 11
Four-poster bed, miniature, 200, 220–221
French knots, 14, 15
French seam, 10–11
Fretsaw, 136, 140–141

Fur fabric:
    cutting and sewing, 11
    traditional teddy bear, 70–73
Furniture:
    doll's house, 216–219
    miniature four-poster bed, 200,
      220–221

G
Garnet paper, 189, 191
G-clamps, 139
Glove puppets *see* Puppets
Grafting, 19
Graph pattern, making, 10

H
Hacksaws, 137, 141
    junior, 141
Hammers, hammering, 145, 146
    pin, 146
    soft-headed, 146
    tack, 146
Hand and embroidery stitches, 14–15
Hand drills, 136, 144
Hand puppets *see* Puppets
Hand saws *see* Saws
Hanging shelves, 230–231
Hen, laying, 192–197
Herringbone (catch) stitch, 14, 15
Hobby horse, 91–94
Hole saws, 144–145, 146
Horse, patchwork, 76–77
Houses:
    doll's house, 183–187
    house-in-the-sky, 101
    jungle house, 101
    play-house, 99–103
    toy-box house, 169–175
    underwater, 101

J
Jenny and Joey dolls, 57–61
Jig, 138–139
Jungle house, 101

K
Kerf, 139
Kitchen/dining room furniture:
    doll's house, 218
    cupboard, 218
    dresser, 218
    sink unit, 218
    stove, 218
    table, 218
Kite-making, 200, 206–209
    bridle, 207–208
    cover, 207
    cutter, 207
    decoration, 207
    flying a kite, 209
    frame, 207
    giant, 214
    Oriental, 210–215
    repair kit, 209
    safety note, 209
    string and reel, 208–209
    tail, 208
Knitted doctor and nurse, 112–115
Knitted doll, 104–106

Knitted pirate, 110–111
Knitted rabbit, 107–109
Knitting stitches, 17–18
    garter, 17
    knitting and purling "tbl", 17
    purling, 17
    reverse stocking, 18
    stocking, 17
Knitting techniques, 16–19
    abbreviations, 16
    casting off, 16, 17
    casting on, 16, 17, 19
    gauge, 16
    grafting, 19
    increasing and decreasing, 18–19
    knitting in rounds, 19
    seams, 19
    yarn over (yo), 18
Knives, 141–142
    craft, 141
    trimming, 136, 141
    using, 141–142

L
Lamb, crochet, 124–125
Lamination, 200
Lamps, doll's house, 218
Layouts, 10
Lazy daisy (detached chain) stitch, 14,
    15
Letter shapes, 21
Lion, crochet, 122–123
Living room furniture, doll's house,
    217–218
Lumber, 137–138
    marking from measurements, 138

M
Mallet, 146
Marquetry chessboard, 188–191
Metals (used in wooden toys), 138
    marking from measurements, 138, 139
    rod and tube, 138
    sheet, 138
    special-purpose saws for cutting, 141
Mirror, doll's house, 218–219
Moore, Colleen, doll's house (Chicago
    Museum), 216

N
Nails, 146–147
    finishing, 146
    round wire, 146
Nail set, 146
Needle set, 146
Noses, 11, 12
Noughts and crosses, 153–154
Nursery furniture, doll's house,
    219

O
Oilstone, 142
Oriental kites, 210–215
    bird, 211, 214
    butterfly, 211, 214
    carp, 211
    dragonfly, 214
    giant, 214
    see also Kites

Overcasting, 14, 15
Owl and pussycat, 78–85

P
Paintbrushes, 137
Painting (in doll's house), 218–219
Papier mâché, 200–201
    "instant" paper mash, 200
    lamination, 200
    moulds, 200, 203
    paper, 200
    pastes and glues, 200
    puppets, 202–205
Patchwork, 12–14
    animals, 74–77
    hand-sewn, 12, 14
    machine-stitched, 12
Patchwork patterns, 13–14
    border of diagonal squares, 13
    "brick wall" rectangles, 13
    "cut and stagger" technique, 13
    diagonal squares, 13
    topstitch squares, 13
Patterns:
    changing size of, 10
    doll's clothes, 63–64
    making graph, 10
Phillips cross-head screws/screwdrivers,
    147, 148
Piercing saw, 140
Pig, crochet puppet, 132–133
Pin hammer, 196
Pine wood, 137
Pinking shears, 10
Pipe-cleaners, 33
    dolls 32–36
Pirate, knitted, 110–111
Planes, 139, 142–143
    block, 143
Plastic wood, 14
Playhouse, 99–103
Playpen, doll's house, 219
Pliers, 136–137, 139
    long-nosed, 139
    self-locking, 139
Plug cutter, 145
Plywood, 137, 138, 139, 189
Pockets, 90
Polishing veneer, 191
Poupard dolls, 37–41
    assembling, 38
    dressing, 40–41
    polystyrene heads, 41
Power band saw, 141
Power drills, 136, 144
Power jig saw, 141
Puppets:
    animal hand, 28–31
    crochet hand puppet pets, 131–133
    finger, 22–25
    papier mâché, 202–205

Q
Quilt, 221

R
Rabbits:
    crochet, 126–127
    crochet puppet, 133

hand puppet, 29–30
knitted, 107–109
Railway engine and tender, 164–168
see also Train
Rasps, 137, 143–144
Rag book, 86–90
Rag dolls, 42–46
faces, 12
wardrobe, 47–50
Rhino wallhanging, 226–229
Rickrack, 119
Robot, wooden, 151
Rug, doll's, 218
Running stitch, 14

S
Safe toys, 11
Sailing boat, 176–182
carving the hull, 180, 182
mast, 182
rudder, 182
sails and rigging, 182
Sanding, 144, 148–149, 191
Sanding block, 148–149
Sandpaper, 137, 139, 148–149
Satin stitch, 14
Sawing, 139–141
blades, 139
cutting metals and plastic, 141
kerf, 139
making curved cuts, 140–141
making slots, 141
making straight cuts, 140
Saws, 136
back, 140, 141
bevel adjustment, 136
box, 141
coping, 136, 140, 141
crosscut, 136
dovetail, 140
fret, 136, 140–141
hacksaws, 137, 141
hand, 140
hole, 144–145, 146
panel, 140
piercing, 140
power band, 141
power jig, 141
tenon, 140
Screwdrivers, 136, 147, 148
cross-head, 148
Screw eye, 147
Screwholes, 147
Screw hook, 147
Screw sink, 145
Screws, 145, 147
classification of, 147
cross-head, 147, 148
flathead, 147
roundhead, 147
slotted-head, 147, 148
special, 147
Scriber, 139
Seams, 10–11
flat fell, 10, 11
French, 10–11
knitting, 19
plain, 10
Sewing tools, 10

Shelves, hanging, 230–231
Shoe and laces, 90
Slipstitch, 14, 15, 20
Snail, crochet, 118–119
Snap fasteners, 90
Softwood, 137–138, 140
Spanish windlass, 139
Split stitch, 14, 15
Spokeshaves, 142, 143
Stab stitch, 14, 15
Steel rule, 136
Stem stitch, 14, 15
Stitches:
crochet, 20
hand and embroidery, 14–15
knitting, 17–19
Stuffing, 11
foam, 11
polyester fibrefill, 11
Submarines, 155–158
large, 156–158
small, 158

T
Tables, doll's house:
coffee, 217–218
dining room/kitchen, 218
dressing, 219
Tack hammer, 146
Tailor's chalk, 10
Teddy bear, traditional, 70–73
Tenon saws, 140
Tepee, 95–98
assembling, 97–98
making cover, 96–97
Toilet, doll's house, 219
Tools, carpentry, 136–137
bradawl, 144
chisels, 142
drills, 136, 144–146
hammers, 145, 146
knives, 141–142
planes, 139, 142–143
rasps, files and wood files, 137, 143–144
saws, 136, 140–141
screwdrivers, 136, 147, 148
spokeshaves, 142, 143
Tools, sewing, 10
Topsy turvy doll, 51–56
Tongues, 12
Toy bag, 222–225
Toy-box house, 169–175
Train, wooden, 151–152
see also Railway engine
Trimming knife, 136, 141
hack saw and pad saw blades, 141
Truck, wooden, 159–163
assembling, 162
attaching wheels, 161
making blocks, 161
making cab, 161
Twist drills, 144, 145

U
Underwater house, 101

V
Veneers, 138
marquetry chessboard made from, 188–191
Vice, 139
clamp-on, 139

W
Wagons, 168
Wall hangings (elephant and rhino), 226–229
Wardrobe, doll's house, 219
Washbasin, doll's house, 219
Whiskers, 11–12
Woods, 137–138
dowels, 137, 138
filling, 148
plywood, 137, 138
sanding, 148
sizes, 138
softwood, 137–138
surface preparation, 148–149
toys made from scraps of, 150–152
veneers, 138, 188–191
Wooden toys, 136–197
adhesives, 148
chisels, 142
cutting special materials, 141
doll's house, 183–187
drills, 144–146
finishing, 148–149
hammering, 146
holding the work, 139
knives, 141–142
laying hen, 192–197
making curved cuts, 140–141
making slots, 141
making straight cuts, 140
marking from measurements, 138–139
marking from patterns, 139
marquetry chessboard, 188–191
metal for, 138
nails, 146–147
noughts and crosses, 153–154
planes, 142–143
railway engine, 164–168
rasps, files and wood files, 143–144
robot, 151
sailing boat, 176–182
sanding, 144
sawing, 139
screws and screwdrivers, 147–148
submarines, 155–158
surface preparation, 148–149
timber and boards, 137–138
tools, 136–137
toy-box house, 169–175
toys from scrap wood, 150–152
trains, 151–152
truck, 159–163
Wool doll, 62
Work bench, 137, 139

Y
Yarns, 16

Z
Zippers, 87